DEVIANCE, CONFLICT, AND CRIMINALITY

DEVIANCE, CONFLICT, AND CRIMINALITY

R. Serge Denisoff
Bowling Green State University

Charles H. McCaghy
Bowling Green State University

Rand McNally & Company
Chicago • New York • San Francisco • London

DEDICATION

To T. B. Bottomore
R.S.D.

To Marshall B. Clinard
C.H.M.

PREFACE

This book is the product of the efforts of two sociologists of diverse interests and backgrounds who have assembled this collection in an attempt to bring together conflict theory with the concepts of deviance and criminality. As the table of contents illustrates, the specific subjects are of a wide variety representing a combination of sociological theory, social problems, political sociology, race relations, and of course, criminology. In part, this variety testifies to the versatility of the conflict perspective. But it is also indicative of the importance of differential political power in understanding events around us, and of the increasing difficulty in distinguishing between the concept of authority and the more traditional concerns of criminologists. The articles included here present a sharp contrast to the usual rhetoric describing deviants in terms of pathology or individual weaknesses. Instead they concern questions of interests and power.

The editors wish to thank several people for their assistance in completing this work. College Editor Larry Malley's help, as always, was invaluable. We found the professionalism of Rand McNally's editorial staff a pleasant experience. The clerical staff in the Department of Sociology at Bowling Green State University has our warmest appreciation for the preparation of this manuscript; we especially acknowledge Lauretta Lahman, Audrey Shaffer, and Phyllis Eaton. Dawn McCaghy is deeply thanked for another great proofreading job. Finally, the senior editor wishes once again to thank his wife for allowing more academic intrusions into home and hearth.

R. SERGE DENISOFF
CHARLES H. MᶜCAGHY

TABLE OF CONTENTS

PART ONE: STRUCTURAL APPROACHES TO DEVIANCE: THEORIES AND ISSUES

Just as "Beauty is in the eye of the beholder," so deviance depends on the viewpoint of the observer. The means by which deviance is defined, observed, and explained are as important as the behavior they define, observe, and explain. The means are the theories, concepts, and methodologies; they constitute the glasses through which social events are scrutinized.

Not all lenses are the same. The predominant approach in the scientific study of deviance and crime is predicated on what Matza (1964:5) calls "hard determinism." This approach focuses on the individual actors who are differentiated on the basis of whether a segment of their behavior is "deviant." Since their behavior is "different," the actors are assumed to be different in the sense that peculiar circumstances must be operating upon them. The goal then is to locate circumstances that are assumed to be determinants of the behavior. Depending on the scientific discipline involved, factors such as biological characteristics, personality variables, and peer group influences have been examined.

The shortcomings of this approach are several.[1] Two are of concern here: First, there is an assumption that behavior is not a matter of choice but is *produced* by factors beyond the actor's control. To use Matza's terminology, hard determinism conceptualizes man as "constrained." This assumption must be regarded as what it is—an assumption and nothing more. Second, the approach fails to recognize that "deviance" and "crime" are labels applied to behavior by those who disapprove of it.

---

[1]For a discussion of hard determinism and its alternatives applied to delinquency research, see Matza (1964:1–32).

Every social group invariably has deviant behavior, but no behaviors are invariably deviant (Turk, 1964:455–56).

The purpose of this collection of writings is to introduce the reader to another sociological perspective, one that rejects the notion of man as constrained. The conflict approach conceptualizes human action as purposive and based on rationality, or at least attempted rationality. Goals and particularly means are seen as lying within the realm of individual choice. In its extreme form the model is that of "instrumental rationalism" which Cohen (1967:79) attributes to Marx:

> He assumed that men have certain goals and that, if circumstances permit, they will use any means available in the pursuit of these. He tended to treat the social actor as a living calculator of tactics and strategies.

The conflict approach also probes the interrelationship between conflict and deviance: *Behavior* that is labelled "deviant" is a manifestation of a conflict situation, yet the *labelling process itself* is also indicative of conflict. In short, "deviance" as it describes either the behavior or the label involves the means by which actors strive for goals within a socio-political context.

This first section will acquaint the reader with the general concepts used throughout the remainder of the book. In the first paper Horton distinguishes between the two types of structural approaches used by sociologists: order and conflict.

"Order theories," argues Horton, "imply consensual and adjustment definitions of social health and pathology, of conformity and deviation." As the French theorist Emile Durkheim (1964:353) originally maintained:

> Though normally the division of labor produces social solidarity, it sometimes happens that it has different and even contrary results. . . . The study of these devious forms will enable us to determine better the conditions in which the normal state exists.

Like the human organism, society is interpreted as possessing many interrelated parts, all of which must function harmoniously if the system is to survive. Unity and cooperation become highly valuable attributes; deviance indicates a malfunction. Advocates of the order approach look for ingredients in society that lead to misunderstandings and are the result of many suborganisms within the social order. In short, deviance leads to social disorganization which is harmful to the system.

Horton describes conflict theories as referring "to what is required to grow and change, rather than to adjust to existing practices and hypothesized requirements for the maintenance of the social system." Within the conflict model there is also an assumption of social order based upon historical evolution. Karl Marx, for example, viewed class struggle as the moving spirit of history. He saw two principal combatants in the struggle: the ruling class and the exploited class. Deviant elements were characterized as hampering the evolutionary process. In several writings, Marx lashed out at what he termed the "dangerous class":

> . . . the social scum (*Lumpenproletariat*), that passively rotting mass thrown off by the lowest layers of old society may, here and there, be swept into the movement by a proletarian revolution; its conditions of life, however, prepare it far more for the part of a bribed tool of reactionary intrigue (Marx and Engels, 1948:20).

Marx's differentiation of the deviant from the revolutionary is an important one as he distinguishes the pathological versus the rational nature of these two roles. Even Michael Bakunin (1964:134), the Russian anarchist who saw deviance as generally the product of a corrupt state, observed that a social revolution forced "to defend itself against incorrigible individuals—not criminal, but dangerous—shall never apply to them any other form of punishment except that of placing them beyond the pale of its guarantees and solidarity, that is, of having them expelled." Both Marx and Bakunin viewed revolutionary activity as rational and normative behavior as opposed to irrational and deviant behavior. This differentiation is further outlined by both Merton and Yinger in the following pages when they contrast aberrant and nonconformist behavior as well as "subculture" and "contraculture." They point out that the deviants engaging in aberrant activity within a subcultural context do not question the social order, whereas in the contraculture nonconformists deny the legitimacy of the dominant social values.

The order and conflict approaches do exhibit some agreement on the basic elements accounting for deviant behavior. Both see the rise of organic society as being based upon complex technology. The complexity of technology requires a high degree of specialization which, in turn, engenders diversity. Diversity, according to Durkheim, is essential for the maintenance of society as each man and institution makes a contribution to it. Complementary differences link men and institutions together in a harmonious order.

In the context of conflict theory, diversity creates inequality because social positions vary according to their relationship and access to wealth, power, and prestige. Due to the scarcity of these valued commodities inequality always exists. The question of inequality has been treated differently by the order and conflict perspectives, however. Davis and Moore (1945) argue that inequality is necessary for the functioning of the technological state: Men must be motivated by rewards to perform the more arduous tasks of preserving the system. Physicians, lawyers, professors, and other highly trained professionals are described as essential to the social order. But these very "functional" professionals are also generators of conflict and social disorganization. Herbert Gans claims:

> Inequality is a major source of social instability and unrest and is even a cause of the rising rates of crime, delinquency and social pathology—alcoholism, drug addiction, and mental illness, for example. . . . Inequality gives rise to feelings of inferiority, which in turn generate inadequacy and self-hate or anger . . . anger results in crime, delinquency, senseless violence—and of course, in political protest as well (Wicker, 1972:39).

While it may lead to inequality, diversity can also be a source of deviance. Sellin's concept of "culture conflict" illustrates this possibility in terms of the crime that results when the norms of migrant groups are not consistent with the legal code of the host nation. In a broader sense, diversity of social, occupational, and ethnic groups can lead to conflicting norms and values.

Inequality and scarcity imply differential distributions of power, status, and wealth that are also linked with the occurrence of deviance. As indicated above, deviance may be explained in terms of the extent to which the "dominant social values" are accepted or rejected by the actors. But the existence of a power differential also means that certain groups are in a more favorable position to define the "dominant social values" since these groups have the wherewithal to impose labels of "deviant" and, particularly, "criminal." This issue will be discussed in detail in Part Two.

In examining Part One, the reader should consider the following propositions:

1. Conflict is a social structural phenomenon.
2. Conflict is the product of disequilibrium in the social structure, either valuative, economic, or political.
3. Conflict results from the scarcity of wealth, status, and power; the diversity of social groups; and the inequality stemming from the differential distribution of wealth, status, and power.
4. Deviance is a manifestation of conflict.

REFERENCES

BAKUNIN, M., "Social and Economic Bases of Anarchism," in I. L. Horowitz, ed., *The Anarchists.* New York: Dell Books, 1964, pp. 120–144.

COHEN, P. S., *Modern Social Theory.* New York: Basic Books Inc., 1968.

Davis, K., and W. Moore, "Some Principles of Stratification." *American Sociological Review,* 10:242–49 (April 1945).

Durkheim, E., *The Division of Labor in Society* (Translated by George Simpson). New York: Free Press (paperback edition), 1964.

Marx, K., and F. Engels, *Manifesto of the Communist Party.* New York: International Publishers, 1948.

Matza, D., *Delinquency and Drift.* New York: John Wiley & Sons, Inc., 1964.

Turk, A. T., "Prospects for Theories of Criminal Behavior," *Journal of Criminal Law, Criminology and Police Science 55:* 454–61 (December 1964).

Wicker, T., "The Rich Get Richer, etc." *New York Times,* June 29, 1972, p. 39.

1. ORDER AND CONFLICT THEORIES
OF SOCIAL PROBLEMS AS COMPETING IDEOLOGIES

JOHN HORTON

A recent best seller, *The One Hundred Dollar Misunderstanding*,[1] should be required reading for every student of social problems and deviant behavior. The novel makes clear what is often dimly understood and rarely applied in sociology—the fundamentally social and symbolic character of existing theories of behavior. In the novel a square, white college boy and a Lolitaesque Negro prostitute recount their shared weekend experience. But what they have shared in action, they do not share in words. Each tells a different story. Their clashing tales express different vocabularies and different experiences. Gover stereotypically dramatizes a now hackneyed theme in the modern theater and novel—the misunderstandings generated by a conflict of viewpoints, a conflict between subjective representations of "objective" reality.

Paradoxically, this familiar literary insight has escaped many social scientists. The escape is most baffling and least legitimate for the sociologists of deviant behavior and social problems. Social values define their phenomena; their social values color their interpretations. Whatever the possibilities of developing empirical theory in the social sciences, only normative theory is appropriate in the sociology of social problems. I would accept Don Martindale's definitions of empirical and normative theory:

> The ultimate materials of empirical theory are facts; the ultimate materials of normative theory are value-imperatives . . . empirical theory is formed out of a system of laws. Normative theory converts facts and laws into requisite means and conditions and is unique in being addressed to a system of objectives desired by the formulator or by those in whose service he stands.[2]

The problem for the sociologist is not that normative theories contain values, but that these values may go unnoticed so that normative theories

---

Reprinted from *The American Journal of Sociology*, 71 (May, 1966), 701–13, by permission of The University of Chicago Press and the author. Copyright 1966, The University of Chicago Press.

[1]Robert Gover, *The One Hundred Dollar Misunderstanding* (New York: Ballantine Books, 1961).
[2]Don Martindale, "Social Disorganization: The Conflict of Normative and Empirical Approaches," in Howard Becker and Alvin Boskoff (eds.), *Modern Sociological Theory* (New York: Dryden Press, 1959), p. 341.

pass for empirical theories. When his own values are unnoticed, the sociologist who studies the situation of the American Negro, for example, is a little like the middle-class white boy in Gover's novel, except that only one story is told, and it is represented as *the* story. The result could be a rather costly misunderstanding: the Negro may not recognize himself in the sociological story; worse, he may not even learn to accept it.

One of the tasks of the sociologist is to recognize his own perspective and to locate this and competing perspectives in time and social structure. In this he can use Weber, Mills, and the sociology of knowledge as guides. Following Weber's work, he might argue that in so far as we are able to theorize about the social world, we must use the vocabularies of explanation actually current in social life.[3] This insight has been expanded by C. W. Mills and applied to theorizing in general and to the character of American theorizing in particular. The key words in Mills's approach to theorizing are "situated actions" and "vocabularies of motive." His position is that theories of social behavior can be understood sociologically as typical symbolic explanations associated with historically situated actions.[4] Thus, Mills argues that the Freudian terminology of motives is that of an upper-bourgeois patriarchal group with a strong sexual and individualistic orientation. Likewise explanations current in American sociology reflect the social experience and social motives of the American sociologist. Mills contends that for a period before 1940, a single vocabulary of explanation was current in the American sociologist's analysis of social problems and that these motives expressed a small town (and essentially rural) bias.[5] He interpreted the contemporary sociological vocabulary as a symbolic expression of a bureaucratic and administrative experience in life and work.[6]

Continuing in the tradition of Weber and Mills, I attempt to do the following: (1) propose a method of classifying current normative theories of deviant behavior and social problems; (2) discuss liberal and sociological approaches to the race question as an example of one of these theories; and (3) point out the implications of the normative character of theory for sociology. My general discussion of competing theories will be an elaboration of several assumptions:

1. All definitions and theories of deviation and social problems are normative. They define and explain behavior from socially situated value positions.

---

[3]For Weber's discussion of explanation in the social sciences see *Max Weber: The Theory of Social and Economic Organization,* trans. A. M. Henderson and Talcott Parsons (Glencoe, Ill.: Free Press, 1947), pp. 87–114.

[4]C. Wright Mills, "Situated Actions and Vocabularies of Motive," *American Sociological Review,* V (December, 1940), 904–13.

[5]C. Wright Mills, "The Professional Ideology of the Social Pathologists," *American Journal of Sociology,* XLIX (September, 1942), 165–80.

[6]C. Wright Mills, *The Sociological Imagination* (New York: Oxford University Press, 1959).

2. Existing normative theories can be classified into a limited number of typical vocabularies of explanation. Contemporary sociological theories of deviation are adaptations of two fundamental models of analysis rooted in nineteenth-century history and social thought. These are *order* and *conflict* models of society. Order models imply an *anomy* theory of societal discontent and an *adjustment* definition of social deviation. Conflict models imply an *alienation* theory of discontent and a *growth* definition of deviation.

3. In general, a liberalized version of order theory pervades the American sociological approach to racial conflict, juvenile delinquency, and other social problems. I use the term "liberal" because the sociological and the politically liberal vocabularies are essentially the same. Both employ an order model of society; both are conservative in their commitment to the existing social order.

4. Alternatives to the liberal order approach exist both within the context of sociological theory and in the contemporary social and political fabric of American society. More radical versions of order models have been used by European sociologists such as Emile Durkheim; radical versions of order models are presently being used in American society by political rightists. The conflict vocabulary has been most clearly identified with Karl Marx and continues today in the social analysis of socialists and communists, while an anarchistic version of conflict theory pervades the politics of the so-called new left.

5. Current vocabularies for the explanation of social problems can be located within the social organization of sociology and the broader society. As a generalization, groups or individuals committed to the maintenance of the social status quo employ order models of society and equate deviation with non-conformity to institutionalized norms. Dissident groups, striving to institutionalize new claims, favor a conflict analysis of society and an alienation theory of their own discontents. For example, this social basis of preference for one model is clear in even the most superficial analysis of stands taken on civil rights demonstrations by civil rights activists and members of the Southern establishment. For Governor Wallace of Alabama, the 1965 Selma-Montgomery march was a negative expression of anomy; for Martin Luther King it was a positive and legitimate response to alienation. King argues that the Southern system is maladaptive to certain human demands; Wallace that the demands of the demonstrators are dysfunctional to the South. However, if one considers their perspectives in relationship to the more powerful Northern establishment, King and not Wallace is the order theorist.

In sociology, order analysis of society is most often expressed by the professional establishment and its organs of publication. Alienation analysis is associated with the "humanitarian" and "political" mavericks outside of, opposed to, or in some way marginal to the established profession of sociology.

ORDER AND CONFLICT THEORIES: ANOMY AND ALIENATION ANALYSIS OF SOCIAL PROBLEMS AS IDEAL TYPES

The terms "alienation" and "anomy" current in the analysis of social problems derive historically from two opposing models of society—order and conflict models.[7] A comparison of the works of Marx and Mills (classical and contemporary conflict models) and Durkheim and Merton or Parsons (classical and contemporary order models) highlights the differences between the two social vocabularies. These competing vocabularies can be abstracted into ideal types of explanation, that is, exaggerated and ideologically consistent models which are only approximated in social reality.

THE ORDER VOCABULARY

Order theories have in common an image of society as a system of action unified at the most general level by shared culture, by agreement on values (or at least on modes) of communication and political organization. System analysis is synonymous with structural-functional analysis. System analysis consists of *statics*—the classification of structural regularities in social relations (dominant role and status clusters, institutions, etc.)—and *dynamics*—the study of the intrasystem processes: strategies of goal definition, socialization, and other functions which maintain system balance. A key concept in the analysis of system problems (social problems, deviation, conflict) is anomy. Social problems both result from and promote anomy. Anomy means system imbalance or social disorganization—a lack of or breakdown in social organization reflected in weakened social control, inadequate institutionalization of goals, inadequate means to achieve system goals, inadequate socialization, etc. At a social psychological level of analysis, anomy results in the failure of individuals to meet the maintenance needs of the social system.

Order theories imply consensual and adjustment definitions of social health and pathology, of conformity and deviation. The standards for defining health are the legitimate values of the social system and its requisites for goal attainment and maintenance. Deviation is the opposite of social conformity and means the failure of individuals to perform their legitimate social roles; deviants are out of adjustment.

---

[7]In contemporary sociology, the concepts of alienation and anomy are often used synonymously. In practice, this usually means that alienation, a key term in conflict analysis, has been translated into a more conservative-order vocabulary; for a discussion of differences between past and present uses of these concepts see John Horton, "The Dehumanization of Anomie and Alienation," *British Journal of Sociology*, XV (December, 1964), 283–300.

A contemporary example of an order approach to society and an adjustment interpretation of health and pathology has been clearly stated in Talcott Parsons' definition of mental health and pathology:

> Health may be defined as the state of optimum *capacity* of an individual for the effective performance of the roles and tasks for which he has been socialized. It is thus defined with reference to the individual's participation in the social system. It is also defined as *relative* to his "status" in the society, i.e., to differentiated type of role and corresponding task structure, e.g., by sex or age, and by level of education which he has attained and the like.[8]

THE CONFLICT VOCABULARY

Conflict theorists are alike in their rejection of the order model of contemporary society. They interpret order analysis as the strategy of a ruling group, a reification of their values and motivations, a rationalization for more effective social control. Society is a natural system for the order analyst; for the conflict theorist it is a continually contested political struggle between groups with opposing goals and world views. As an anarchist, the conflict theorist may oppose any notion of stable order and authority. As a committed Marxist, he may project the notion of order into the future. Order is won, not through the extension of social control, but through the radical reorganization of social life; order follows from the condition of social organization and not from the state of cultural integration.

Conflict analysis is synonymous with historical analysis: the interpretation of intersystem processes bringing about the transformation of social relations. A key concept in the analysis of historical and social change (as new behavior rather than deviant behavior) is alienation—separation, not from the social system as defined by dominant groups, but separation from man's universal nature or a desired state of affairs. Change is the progressive response to alienation; concepts of disorganization and deviation have no real meaning within the conflict vocabulary; they are properly part of the vocabulary of order theory where they have negative connotations as the opposites of the supreme values of order and stability. Within the conflict framework, the question of normality and health is ultimately a practical one resolved in the struggle to overcome alienation.

Conflict theory, nevertheless, implies a particular definition of health, but the values underlying this definition refer to what is required to grow and change, rather than to adjust to existing practices and hypothe-

---

[8]Talcott Parsons, "Definitions of Health and Illness in the Light of American Values and Social Structure," in E. Gartley Jaco (ed.), *Patients, Physicians and Illness* (Glencoe, Ill.: Free Press, 1963), p. 176.

sized requirements for the maintenance of the social system. Health and pathology are defined in terms of postulated requirements for individual or social growth and adaptation. Social problems and social change arise from the exploitive and alienating practices of dominant groups; they are responses to the discrepancy between what is and what is in the process of becoming. Social problems, therefore, reflect, not the administrative problems of the social system, nor the failure of individuals to perform their system roles as in the order explanation, but the adaptive failure of society to meet changing individual needs.

A growth definition of health based on a conflict interpretation of society is implicit in Paul Goodman's appraisal of the causes of delinquency in American society. Unlike Parsons, he does not define pathology as that which does not conform to system values; he argues that delinquency is not the reaction to exclusion from these values, nor is it a problem of faulty socialization. Existing values and practices are absurd standards because they do not provide youth with what they need to grow and mature:

> As was predictable, most of the authorities and all of the public spokesmen explain it (delinquency) by saying there has been a failure of socialization. They say that background conditions have interrupted socialization and must be improved. And, not enough effort has been made to guarantee belonging, there must be better bait or punishment.
>
> But perhaps there has *not* been a failure of communication. Perhaps the social message has been communicated clearly to the young men and is unacceptable.
>
> In this book I shall, therefore, take the opposite tack and ask, "Socialization to what? to what dominant society and available culture?" And if this question is asked, we must at once ask the other question, "Is the harmonious organization to which the young are inadequately socialized, perhaps against human nature, or not worthy of human nature, and *therefore* there is difficulty in growing up?"[9]

The conflict theorist invariably questions the legitimacy of existing practices and values; the order theorist accepts them as the standard of health.

PARADIGM FOR THE ANALYSIS OF CONFLICT AND ORDER APPROACHES TO SOCIAL PROBLEMS

In order more sharply to compare order and conflict models in terms of their implications for explanations of deviation and social problems, essential differences can be summarized along a number of parallel di-

---

[9]Paul Goodman, *Growing Up Absurd* (New York: Random House, 1960), p. 11.

mensions. These dimensions are dichotomized into order and conflict categories. The resulting paradigm can be used as a preliminary guide for the content analysis of contemporary as well as classical studies of social problems.

ORDER PERSPECTIVE	CONFLICT PERSPECTIVE

1. Underlying Social Perspective and Value Positions (Ideal)

a. *Image of man and society*

Society as a natural boundary-maintaining system of action	Society as a contested struggle between groups with opposed aims and perspectives
Transcendent nature of society, an entity *sui generis*, greater than and different from the sum of its parts; lack of transcendence as lack of social control means anomy	Immanent conception of society and the social relationship; men are society; society is the extension of man, the indwelling of man; the transcendence of society is tantamount to the alienation of man from his own social nature
Positive attitude toward the maintenance of social institutions	Positive attitude toward change

b. *Human nature*

Homo duplex, man half egoistic (self-nature), half altruistic (socialized nature), ever in need of restraints for the collective good	*Homo laborans*, existential man, the active creator of himself and society through practical and autonomous social action

or

Tabula rasa, man equated with the socialization process

or

Homo damnatus, the division into morally superior and morally inferior men

c. *Values*

The social good: balance, stability, authority, order, quantitative growth ("moving equilibrium")	Freedom as autonomy, change, action, qualitative growth

2. Modes of "Scientific" Analysis

Natural science model: quest for general and universal laws and repeated patterns gleaned through empirical research	Historical model: quest for understanding (*Verstehen*) through historical analysis of unique and changing events; possible use of ideal type of generalization based on historically specific patterns
Structural-functional analysis	

Multiple causality; theory characterized by high level of abstraction, but empirical studies marked by low level of generalization (separation of theory from application)

Unicausality; high or low level of theoretical generalization; union of theory and practice in social research and social action

Conditions of objectivity: accurate correspondence of concepts to facts; rigid separation of observer and facts observed —passive, receptive theory of knowledge

Utility in terms of observer's interests; objectivity discussed in the context of subjectivity—activistic theory of knowledge

Analysis begins with culture as major determinant of order and structure and proceeds to personality and social organization

Analysis begins with organization of social activities or with growth and maintenance needs of man and proceeds to culture

Dominant concepts: ahistorical; high level of generality; holistic; supra-individual concepts; ultimate referent for concepts —system needs considered universally (i.e., the functional prerequisites of any social system) or relativistically (i.e., present maintenance requirements of a particular social system)

Historical, dynamic; low level of generality and high level of historical specificity; ultimate referent for concepts—human needs considered universally (i.e., man's species nature) or relativistically (demands of particular contenders for power); referent often the future or an unrealized state of affairs

3. Order and Conflict Theories of Social Problems and Deviation

a. *Standards for the definition of health and pathology*

Health equated with existing values of a postulated society (or a dominant group in the society), ideological definition

Health equated with unrealized standards (the aspirations of subordinate but rising groups), utopian definition

b. *Evaluation of deviant behavior*

Pathological to the functioning of the social system

c. *Explanation of deviation or a social problem*

A problem of anomy in adequate control over competing groups in the social system; disequilibrium in the existing society

Possibly progressive to the necessary transformation of existing relationships

A problem of self-alienation, being thwarted in the realization of individual and group goals; a problem of illegitimate social control and exploitation *d. Implied ameliorative action*

Extension of social control (further and more efficient institutionalization of social system values); adjustment of individuals to system needs; working within the system; the administrative solution

Rupture of social control; radical transformation of existing patterns of interaction; revolutionary change of the social system

4. Order and Conflict Theories as Socially Situated Vocabularies

Dominant groups: the establishment and administrators of the establishment

Contemporary representatives: Parsonian and Mertonian approach to social problems as a liberal variant of order models; politically conservative approaches

Subordinate groups aspiring for greater power

C. W. Mills, new left (SNCC, SDS, etc.) approaches and old left (socialistic and communistic)

The order and conflict models as outlined represent polar ideal types which are not consistently found in the inconsistent ideologies of actual social research and political practice. If the models have any utility to social scientists, it will be in making more explicit and systematic the usually implicit value assumptions which underlie their categories of thinking. In this paper as an exercise in the use of conflict-order models, I examine some of the normative assumptions which can be found in the approach of the sociologist and the political liberal to the Negro question. My thinking is intentionally speculative. I am not trying to summarize the vast literature on race relations, but merely showing the existence of an order pattern.

LIBERALS AND SOCIOLOGISTS ON THE AMERICAN NEGRO: A CONTEMPORARY ADAPTATION OF ORDER THEORY

Contemporary liberalism has been popularly associated with a conflict model of society; actually it is a variant of conservative order theory. Within the model, conflict is translated to mean institutionalized (reconciled) conflict or competition for similar goals within the same system.

Conflict as confrontation of opposed groups and values, conflict as a movement toward basic change of goals and social structures is anathema.

The liberal tendency of American sociology and the essentially conservative character of contemporary liberalism are particularly marked in the sociological analysis of the Negro question. In the field of race relations, an order model can be detected in (1) consensual assumptions about man and society: the "over-socialized" man and the plural society; (2) a selective pattern of interpretation which follows from these assumptions: (a) the explanation of the problem as a moral dilemma and its solution as one requiring adjustment through socialization and social control; (b) the explanation of the minority group as a reaction-formation to exclusion from middle-class life; (c) an emphasis on concepts useful in the explanation of order (shared values as opposed to economic and political differences); an emphasis on concepts useful in the explanation of disorder or anomy within an accepted order (status competition rather than class conflict, problems of inadequate means rather than conflicting goals).

THE LIBERAL VIEW OF MAN: EGALITARIAN WITHIN AN ELITIST, CONSENSUAL FRAMEWORK: ALL MEN ARE SOCIALIZABLE TO THE AMERICAN CREED

No one can see an ideological assumption as clearly as a political opponent. Rightist and leftist alike have attacked the liberal concept of man implicit in the analysis of the Negro question: conservatives because it is egalitarian, radicals because it is elitist and equated with a dominant ideology. The rightist believes in natural inequality; the leftist in positive, historical differences between men; the liberal believes in the power of socialization and conversion.

A certain egalitarianism is indeed implied in at least two liberal assertions: (1) Negroes along with other men share a common human nature socializable to the conditions of society; (2) their low position and general inability to compete reflect unequal opportunity and inadequate socialization to whatever is required to succeed within the American system. These assertions are, in a sense, basically opposed to the elitist-conservative argument that the Negro has failed to compete because he is naturally different or has voluntarily failed to take full advantage of existing opportunities.[10]

The conservative, however, exaggerates liberal egalitarianism; it is tempered with elitism. Equality is won by conformity to a dominant set

---

[10]For a conservative argument, see, among many others, Carleton Putnam, *Race and Reason* (Washington, D.C.: Public Affairs Press, 1961).

of values and behavior. Equality means equal opportunity to achieve the same American values; in other words, equality is gained by losing one identity and conforming at some level to another demanded by a dominant group. As a leftist, J. P. Sartre has summarized this liberal view of man, both egalitarian and elitist. What he has termed the "democratic" attitude toward the Jew applies well to the American "liberal" view of the Negro:

> The Democrat, like the scientist, fails to see the particular case; to him the individual is only an ensemble of universal traits. It follows that his defense of the Jew saves the latter as a man and annihilates him as a Jew . . . he fears that the Jew will acquire a consciousness of Jewish collectivity. . . . "There are no Jews," he says, "there is no Jewish question." This means that he wants to separate the Jew from his religion, from his family, from his ethnic community, in order to plunge him into the democratic crucible whence he will emerge naked and alone, an individual and solitary particle like all other particles.[11]

The conservative would preserve a Negro identity by pronouncing the Negro different (inferior), the radical by proclaiming him part of the superior vanguard of the future society; but the liberal would transform him altogether by turning him into another American, another individual competing in an orderly fashion for cars, television sets, and identification with the American Creed. In their attack on the liberal definition of man, the conservative and leftist agree on one thing: the liberal seems to deny basic differences between groups. At least differences are reconcilable within a consensual society.

THE LIBERAL SOCIETY: STRUCTURAL PLURALISM WITHIN A CONSENSUAL FRAMEWORK

Thus, the liberal fate of minorities, including Negroes, is basically containment through socialization to dominant values. Supposedly this occurs in a plural society where some differences are maintained. But liberal pluralism like liberal egalitarianism allows differences only within a consensual framework. This applies both to the liberal ideal and the sociological description: the plural-democratic society *is* the present society.

This consensual pluralism should be carefully distinguished from the conflict variety. J. S. Furnivall has called the once colonially dominated societies of tropical Asia plural in the latter sense:

---

[11]Jean-Paul Sartre, *Anti-Semite and Jew,* trans. George J. Becker (New York: Grove Press, 1962), pp. 56–57.

In Burma, as in Java, probably the first thing that strikes the visitor is the medley of peoples—European, Chinese, Indian, native. It is in the strictest sense a medley, for they mix but do not combine. Each group holds to its own religion, its own culture and language, its own ideas and ways. As individuals they meet, but only in the marketplace, in buying and selling. There is a plural society, with different sections of the community living side by side, but separately, within the same political unit. Even in the economic sphere there is a division along racial lines.[12]

For Furnivall, a plural society has no common will, no common culture. Order rests on political force and economic expediency. For liberals and sociologists, American society has a common social will (the American Creed). Order rests on legitimate authority and consensus. The whole analysis of the Negro question has generally been predicated on this belief that American society, however plural, is united by consensus on certain values. Gunnar Myrdal's influential interpretation of the Negro question has epitomized the social will thesis:

> Americans of all national origins, classes, regions, creeds, and colors, have something in common: a social ethos, a political creed. . . . When the American Creed is once detected the cacophony becomes a melody . . . as principles which ought to rule, the Creed has been made conscious to everyone in American society. . . . America is continuously struggling for its soul. The cultural unity of the nation is sharing of both the consciousness of sin and the devotion to high ideals.[13]

In what sense can a consensual society be plural? It cannot tolerate the existence of separate cultural segments. Robin M. Williams in a recent book on race relations writes: "The United States is a plural society which cannot settle for a mosaic of separate cultural segments, nor for a caste system."[14] Norman Podhoretz, a political liberal who has written often on the Negro question has stated the issue more bluntly. In his review of Ralph Ellison's *Shadow and Act,* a series of essays which poses a threat of conflict pluralism by asserting the positive and different "cultural" characteristics of Negroes, Podhoretz states his consensual realism:

> The vision of a world in which many different groups live together on a footing of legal and social equality, each partaking of a broad general culture and yet maintaining its own distinctive identity: this is one of the noble dreams of the liberal tradition. Yet the hard truth

---

[12]J. S. Furnivall, *Colonial Policy and Practice* (London: Cambridge University Press, 1948), p. 304.
[13]Gunnar Myrdal, *An American Dilemma* (New York: Harper & Bros., 1944), pp. 3–4.
[14]Robin M. Williams, Jr., *Strangers Next Door* (Englewood Cliffs, N.J.: Prentice-Hall, Inc., 1964), p. 386.

is that very little evidence exists to suggest that such a pluralistic order is possible. Most societies throughout history have simply been unable to suffer the presence of distinctive minority groups among them; and the fate of minorities has generally been to disappear, either through being assimilated into the majority, or through being expelled, or through being murdered.[15]

The liberal and the sociologist operating with an order ideology positively fear the conflict type of pluralism. As Sartre rightly observed, the liberal who is himself identified with the establishment, although avowedly the friend of the minority, suspects any sign of militant minority consciousness. He wants the minority to share in American human nature and compete like an individual along with other individuals for the same values.

As Podhoretz has observed, pluralism never really meant the co-existence of quite different groups:

> For the traditional liberal mentality conceives of society as being made up not of competing economic classes and ethnic groups, but rather of competing *individuals* who confront a neutral body of law and a neutral institutional complex.[16]

How then can ethnic groups be discussed within the plural but consensual framework? They must be seen as separate but assimilated (contained) social structures. Among sociologists, Milton Gordon has been most precise about this pluralism as a description of ethnic groups in American society.

> Behavioral assimilation or acculturation has taken place in America to a considerable degree. . . . Structural assimilation, then, has turned out to be the rock on which the ships of Anglo-conformity and the melting pot have foundered. To understand the behavioral assimilation (or acculturation) without massive structural intermingling in primary relationships has been the dominant motif in the American experience of creating and developing a nation out of diverse peoples is to comprehend the most essential sociological fact of that experience. It is against the background of "structural pluralism" that strategies of strengthening inter-group harmony, reducing ethnic discrimination and prejudice, and maintaining the rights of both those who stay within and those who venture beyond their ethnic boundaries must be thoughtfully devised.[17]

---

[15]Norman Podhoretz, "The Melting-Pot Blues," *Washington Post*, October 25, 1964.

[16]Norman Podhoretz, as quoted in "Liberalism and the American Negro—a Round-Table Discussion," with James Baldwin, Nathan Glazer, Sidney Hook, Gunnar Myrdal, and Norman Podhoretz (moderator), *Commentary*, XXXVII (March, 1964), 25–26.

[17]Milton Gordon, "Assimilation in America: Theory and Reality," *Daedalus*, XC (Spring, 1961), 280, 283.

Clearly then the liberal vocabulary of race relations is predicated on consensual assumptions about the nature of man and society. The order explanation of the Negro problem and its solution may be summarized as follows:

1. *An order or consensual model of society.* American society is interpreted as a social system unified at its most general level by acceptance of certain central political, social, and economic values. Thus, the Negro population is said to have been acculturated to a somewhat vaguely defined American tradition; at the most, Negro society is a variant or a reaction to that primary tradition.

2. *Social problems as moral problems of anomy or social disorganization within the American system.* Social problems and deviant behavior arise from an imbalance between goals and means. The problems of the Negro are created by unethical exclusion from equal competition for American goals.

3. *The response to anomy: social amelioration as adjustment and extension of social control.* Liberal solutions imply further institutionalization of the American Creed in the opportunity structure of society and, therefore, the adjustment of the deviant to legitimate social roles.

THE RACE QUESTION AS A MORAL DILEMMA

A familiar expression of liberal-consensualism is Gunnar Myrdal's interpretation of the American race question as a moral dilemma. According to this thesis, racial discrimination and its varied effects on the Negro—the development of plural social structures, high rates of social deviation, etc.—reflect a kind of anomy in the relationship between the American Creed and social structure. Anomy means a moral crisis arising from an incongruity between legitimate and ethical social goals (for example, success and equality of opportunity) and socially available opportunities to achieve these goals. American society is good and ethical, but anomic because the American Creed of equality has not been fully institutionalized; the ethic is widely accepted in theory but not in practice.

Sidney Hook as a political liberal has likewise insisted that American society is essentially ethical and that the Negro problem should be discussed in these ethical terms:

> Of course, no society has historically been organized on the basis of ethical principles, but I don't think we can understand how any society functions without observing the operation of the ethical principles within it. And if we examine the development of American society, we certainly can say that we have made *some* progress, to

be sure, but progress nevertheless—by virtue of the extension of our ethical principles to institutional life. If we want to explain the progress that has been made in the last twenty years by minority groups in this country—not only the Negroes, but other groups as well—I believe we have to take into account the effect of our commitment to democracy, imperfect though it may be.[18]

THE SOLUTION: WORKING WITHIN THE SYSTEM

The liberal solution to the racial question follows from the American-dilemma thesis: the belief in the ethical nature and basic legitimacy of American institutions. Amelioration, therefore, becomes exclusively a question of adjustment within the system; it calls for administrative action: how to attack anomy as the imbalance of goals and means. The administrator accepts the goals of his organization and treats all problems as errors in administration, errors which can be rectified without changing the basic framework of the organization. Karl Mannheim has aptly characterized the bureaucratic and administrative approach to social problems. What he says about the perspective of the Prussian bureaucrat applies only too well to his counterpart in American society.

> The attempt to hide all problems of politics under the cover of administration may be explained by the fact that the sphere of activity of the official exists only within the limits of laws already formulated. Hence the genesis or the development of law falls outside the scope of his activity. As a result of his socially limited horizon, the functionary fails to see that behind every law that has been made there lie the socially fashioned interests and the *Weltanschauungen* of a specific social group. He takes it for granted that the specific order prescribed by the concrete law is equivalent to order in general. He does not understand that every rationalized order is only one of many forms in which socially conflicting irrational forces are reconciled.[19]

The liberal administrator's solution to the Negro question entails the expansion of opportunities for mobility within the society and socialization of the deviant (the Negro and the anti-Negro) to expanding opportunities. Hence, the importance of education and job training; they are prime means to success and higher status. Given the assumption that the American Creed is formally embodied in the political structure, the liberal also looks to legislation as an important and perhaps sole means of reenforcing the Creed by legitimizing changes in the American opportunity structure.

---

[18]Sidney Hook, "Liberalism and the American Negro—a Round-Table Discussion," *Commentary,* XXXVII (March, 1964), p. 31.

[19]Karl Mannheim, *Ideology and Utopia* (New York: Harcourt, Brace & World, 1936), p. 118.

NEGRO LIFE AS A REACTION FORMATION

Another important deduction has followed from the assumption of the political and cultural assimilation of the American Negro: whatever is different or distinct in his life style represents a kind of negative reaction to exclusion from the white society. The Negro is the creation of the white. Like the criminal he is a pathology, a reaction-formation to the problem of inadequate opportunities to achieve and to compete in the American system.

Myrdal states:

> The Negro's entire life and, consequently, also his opinions on the Negro problem are, in the main, to be considered as secondary reactions to more primary pressures from the side of the dominant white majority.[20]

More recently Leonard Broom has echoed the same opinion:

> Negro life was dominated by the need to adjust to white men and to take them into account at every turn. . . . Taken as a whole, the two cultures have more common than distinctive elements. Over the long run, their convergence would seem inevitable. . . . Because Negro life is so much affected by poverty and subservience, it is hard to find distinctive characteristics that can be positively evaluated. In the stereotype, whatever is admirable in Negro life is assumed to have been adopted from the white man, while whatever is reprehensible is assumed to be inherently Negro.[21]

CONFLICT THEORIST LOOKS AT ORDER THEORIST LOOKING AT THE NEGRO

A liberal order model—consensual pluralism, with its corollary approach to the race question as moral dilemma and reaction-formation—colors the sociological analysis of the race question. It is interesting that the fundamental assumption about consensus on the American Creed has rarely been subjected to adequate empirical test.[22] Lacking any convincing evidence for the order thesis, I can only wonder who the sociologist is speaking for. He may be speaking for himself in that his paradigm answers the question of how to solve the Negro problem without changing basic economic and political institutions. He probably speaks least of all for the Negro. The liberal sociologist will have some difficulty describing

---

[20]Gunnar Myrdal as quoted by Ralph Ellison, "An American Dilemma: A Review," in *Shadow and Act* (New York: Random House, 1964), p. 315.

[21]Leonard Broom, *The Transformation of the American Negro* (New York: Harper & Row, 1965), pp. 22–23.

[22]For a recent attempt to test the American dilemma thesis see Frank R. Westie, "The American Dilemma: An Empirical Test," *American Sociological Review*, XXX (August, 1965), 527–38.

the world from the viewpoint of Negro "rioters" in Los Angeles and other cities. In any case, he will not agree with anyone who believes (in fact or in ideology) that the Negro may have a separate and self-determining identity. Such a view suggests conflict and would throw doubt on the fixations of consensus, anomy, and reaction–formation.

Conflict interpretations are minority interpretations by definition. They are rarely expressed either by sociologists or by ethnic minorities. However, a few such interpretations can be mentioned to imply that the end of ideology and, therefore, the agreement on total ideology has not yet arrived.

Ralph Ellison, speaking from a conflict and nationalistic perspective, has made several salient criticisms of the liberal American dilemma thesis. He has argued that Myrdal's long discussion of American values and conclusion of multiple causality have conveniently avoided the inconvenient question of power and control in American society.

> All this, of course, avoids the question of power *and* the question of who manipulates that power. Which to us seems more of a stylistic maneuver than a scientific judgment. . . . Myrdal's stylistic method is admirable. In presenting his findings he uses the American ethos brilliantly to disarm all American social groupings, by appealing to their stake in the American Creed, and to locate the psychological barriers between them. But he also uses it to deny the existence of an American class struggle, and with facile economy it allows him to avoid admitting that actually there exist two American moralities, kept in balance by social science.[23]

Doubting the thesis of consensus, Ellison is also in a position to attack Myrdal's interpretation of the American Negro as a reaction-formation, and assimilation to the superior white society as his only solution.

> But can a people (its faith in an idealized American Creed notwithstanding) live and develop for over three hundred years simply by reacting? Are American Negroes simply the creation of white men, or have they at least helped to create themselves out of what they found around them? Men have made a way of life in caves and upon cliffs, why cannot Negroes have made a life upon the horns of the white men's dilemma?
>
> Myrdal sees Negro culture and personality simply as the product of a "social pathology." Thus he assumes that "it is to the advantage of American Negroes as individuals and as a group to become assimilated into American culture, to acquire the traits held in esteem by the dominant white American." This, he admits, contains the value premise that *"here in America,* American culture is 'highest'

---

[23]Ralph Ellison, *Shadow and Act, op. cit.,* p. 315.

in the pragmatic sense. . . ." Which aside from implying that Negro culture is not also American, assumes that Negroes should desire nothing better than what whites consider highest. But in the "pragmatic" sense lynching and Hollywood, fadism and radio advertising are products of "higher" culture, and the Negro might ask, "Why, if my culture is pathological, must I exchange it for these?" . . . What is needed in our country is not an exchange of pathologies, but a change of the basis of society.[24]

CONCLUSION

The hostile action of Negro masses destroying white property is perhaps a more convincing demonstration of conflict theory than the hopes of Negro intellectuals. But as a sociologist I am not really interested in raising the question of whether a conflict definition of the race question is more correct than the more familiar order model. Each view is correct in a normative and practical sense in so far as it conforms to a viable political and social experience. What indeed is a correct interpretation of the Negro problem or any social problem? The answer has as much to do with consensus as with correspondence to the facts. Normative theories are not necessarily affected by empirical evidence because they seek to change or to maintain the world, not describe it.

Whenever there is genuine conflict between groups and interpretations, correctness clearly becomes a practical matter of power and political persuasion. This seems to be the situation today, and one can expect more heated debate. If conflict continues to increase between whites and Negroes in the United States, the liberal sociologist studying the "Negro problem" had better arm himself with more than his questionnaire. A militant Negro respondent may take him for the social problem, the sociologist as an agent of white society and the scientific purveyor of order and containment policy.

This clash of perspectives would be an illustration of my general argument: explanations of the Negro question or any other social problem invariably involve normative theory, values, ideologies, or whatever one may care to call the subjective categories of our thinking about society. Concepts of deviation and social problems can be discussed only in the context of some social (and therefore contestable) standard of health, conformity, and the good society. Terms like "moral dilemma," "pluralism," "assimilation," "integration" describe motives for desirable action: they are definitions placed on human action, not the action itself independent of social values.

---

[24]*Ibid.*, pp. 316–17.

The error of the sociologist is not that he thinks politically and liberally about his society, but that he is not aware of it. Awareness may help him avoid some of the gross errors of myopia: (1) mistaking his own normative categories for "objective" fact; thus, the liberal sociologist may mistake his belief in the consensual society for actual consensus; (2) projecting a normative theory appropriate to the experience of one group on to another group; this is what Ellison means when he says that the liberal sociologist is not necessarily speaking for the Negro. Indeed, the errors of myopia are perhaps greatest whenever the middle-class sociologist presumes to describe the world and motivation of persons in lower status. Seeing the lower-class Negro within a white liberal vocabulary may be very realistic politics, but it is not very accurate sociology.

Once the sociologist is involved in the study of anything that matters, he has the unavoidable obligation of at least distinguishing his vocabulary from that of the groups he is supposedly observing rather than converting. As a scientist, he must find out what perspectives are being employed, where they are operating in the society, and with what effect. Perhaps this awareness of competing perspectives occurs only in the actual process of conflict and debate. Unfortunately, this is not always the situation within an increasingly professionalized sociology. The more professionalized the field, the more standardized the thinking of sociologists and the greater the danger of internal myopia passing for objectivity. But outside sociology debate is far from closed; conflict and order perspectives are simultaneously active on every controversial social issue. The liberal order model may not long enjoy uncontested supremacy.

2. DEVIANCE AS A TYPE OF SOCIAL CONFLICT

JOHN LOFLAND

As used by sociologists, the concept of deviance and its variants are merely somewhat more abstract versions of common-sense, everyday designations. Such popular designations include "crime," "criminal," "deviate," "pervert," "nut," "kook," "lunatic," "oddball," "weirdo," and the like. The deviance vocabulary represents sociologists' attempt to encompass these more colorful words of the layman. Sociologists and laymen alike bracket together certain acts and categories of persons as deserving a kind of attention that is different from that accorded all other acts and categories of persons. One way, then, to approach a definition of deviance is in terms of the basis upon which sociologists and laymen accomplish this broad bracketing.

PARTIES IN CONFLICT

The basis of this bracketing can best be pursued, not through a search for distinctive features of deviance per se, but rather in terms of general and generic dimensions of social organization and social response. Within such dimensions, the defining of persons and acts as deviant can be seen as a particular instance of generalized ways in which social organization and social definition can differ. At the level of a single and *total society,* such a basis is found in the dynamics of what proportion of a society, how well organized and how powerful, are *fearful* of, and feel *threatened* by, some other portion of the society. Organized social life can be viewed as a game in which actors and collectivities defend themselves against distrusted and suspected others. Suspicion, distrust, fear and threat are central themes in all large-scale and differentiated societies. A political constitution like that of the United States even builds in a division of powers to take account of such feelings and to institutionalize their expression.

The parties playing the game around these basic themes can, of course, differ considerably along a variety of dimensions. Taking first *who is*

From John Lofland, *Deviance and Identity,* © 1969. Reprinted by permission of Prentice-Hall, Inc., Englewood Cliffs, New Jersey.

feared or felt to be threatening, some basic distinctions reside in the *population size* of the feared party, the degree of its *organization* and the amount of its *power* relative to the size, organization and power of those who fear it. Taking only size and degree of organization together, some typically identified feared parties are: (1) individuals or small groups who have a limited degree of organization; (2) relatively small but thoroughly organized groups with leaders; and (3) large, well-organized groups within a total society.

On the other side, that of *who is fearful* or is perceiving a threat, parties may vary along the dimensions of: (1) the proportion of the society which feels threatened (e.g., a small minority, a sizable minority or a majority); (2) how strongly the party feels threatened (ranging from mere amusement to a "basic threat to our way of life"); (3) the extent to which the party is organized; and (4) how much power, relative to the feared party, is possessed by those threatened. The amount of power of who is threatened refers in particular to their ability to bring the resources of the state to bear upon the party felt to be threatening. Those fearful parties who can voice their fears at the public level, who receive at least some public legitimation, and who have the legal structure act in compliance with their wishes (namely, to incarcerate or banish the feared party) are parties with the greatest amount of power.

These variations in size, organization, degree of fear and amount of power among factions of a society provide a basis upon which we can roughly define deviance and see its relation to some other kinds of power games. What is called deviance is but one of a series of generically related situations, some of the more popular forms of which are identified in Chart 2.1.[1] Deviance is the name of the conflict game in which individuals or loosely organized small groups with little power are strongly feared by a well-organized, sizable minority or majority who have a large amount of power.

Under different levels of fear, size, organization and power between parties in conflict, there are corresponding changes in public definitions of the situation. Persons and acts in a small, powerless minority that are at one time regarded as merely deviant may, at another time, be felt to constitute a civil uprising, social movement or civil war. Theft, arson, assault, torture and murder perpetrated by individuals is simply deviance; when perpetrated by a loosely organized minority acting in concert such acts might be imputed to have a political meaning, and, when performed in the context of a civil or revolutionary war—that is, by a well-organized

---

[1] It is testimony to the rich diversity of human life that Chart 2.1 represents only a few of several hundred possible conflict situations. For example, if one combines the three dimensions of party feared (size, organization and power) and the four dimensions of party fearing (size, organization, power and degree of fear), and if each dimension is merely dichotomized (a massive oversimplification), the result is 128 different conflict situations.

minority—they are acts of war or of liberation or legitimate defense. (When undertaken in conflicts between nations, such acts can be among the highest forms of patriotic display. When Audie Murphy killed German soldiers, he was a hero. When Charles Whitman shot Texas civilians, he was a mad killer.)

The imputation of even greatly feared acts and persons as deviant seems to depend less upon particular behavior per se than upon the respective size, degree of power and degree of organization of parties to an issue.

Beyond the excluded conflict situations indicated in Chart 2.1, there are two other items which some investigators have defined as deviant or as a basis for defining deviance. First, acts that are only *mildly* feared, even if so feared by a large and powerful majority in relation to single powerless individuals or small groups, seem more cogently considered simply as *inappropriate* behavior. Social life is replete with occurrences of tardiness, rudeness, impoliteness, overfamiliarity, embarrassments, *faux pas,* etc.[2] These continuing but mild vexations are better analyzed as features of the sociology of everyday life.[3] Second, strong fears of some act or class of actors that emanate from a relatively small and not very powerful minority involves *special pleading* and, at the level of total society, the objects of these fears are not rendered deviant. The Prohibition Party's fear of alcoholic consumption and the people who consume it defines a class of devi-

CHART 2.1   CONFLICT SITUATIONS

	Dimensions of the Character and Relations of Parties in Conflict		
Resulting Popular Definition of the Conflict Situation	Size and Organization of Party Feared	Economic and Political Power of Party Feared Relative to Party Fearing	Degree to Which the Well-organized Opposing Large Minority or Majority Feels Fearful or Threatened
Deviance ("Crime," etc.)	Individual or small, loosely organized groups	Almost none	Very high
Civil Uprising or Disorder	Small loosely organized minority	Relatively low	Very high
Social Movement	Sizable organized minority	Relatively low	Mild
Civil War	Large, well-organized minority	Relatively high or almost equal	Very high
Mainstream Party Politics in the United States	Large, organized minority	About equal	Mild

[2]Definitions of the field like "behavior which violates institutionalized expectations" (Cohen, 1959:462) thus seem much too broad and group together items of too many varieties.

[3]Within perspectives such as presented by Goffman, 1959, 1961 and 1967.

ance for the Prohibitionists, but they are largely bereft of following and social power. Militants of the left and right of both races, who see wisdom in stockpiling firearms to defend against oppressors, apparently have very strong fears of "leftists," "whites," "blacks," or those felt to be ubiquitous Communists in disguise. As long as such groups remain small minorities and lack much power, the objects they define as fearful are merely matters of some slight controversy. Any such group can, of course, come into a position of some power, perhaps to the extent of forcing the game of civil war, or, with sufficient power, of creating a new game of who is defined as deviant about what. Consider, for example, what former Alabama Governor George Wallace and his followers define as deviant:

> Bearded professors on some of our college campuses . . . are sympathizing with the enemy, they are encouraging youths to burn draft cards, and some are saying openly, the Viet Cong should win and furnishin' food, blood and clothes to the enemy.
> If I were President I would hale 'em before a grand jury and prosecute 'em for treason for that is what it is and traitors is what they are . . . never mind the thin line that we haven't declared war (Vestal, 1967).

Given the wide range of groups and perspectives in American civilization, it is probably the case that almost any act or person is strongly feared by *some* social category or organized group. If it is to be possible to isolate a category of deviance rather than simply a multitude of conflicts, it is essential that there be involved at least a powerful minority— even if not a majority—who feel a strong sense of threat and fear. And, as is already evident from the foregoing, the system focus for defining and analyzing deviance is the total society, most typically the nation-state. Items that might be called deviant but that have only a local interest— that can only be of concern within less inclusive or "lower-level" systems such as formal organizations and face-to-face groups—seem best left as topics of analysis within their respective formal areas.[4]

FURTHER SPECIFICATION

The foregoing is a very general guide to types of conflict situations and is lacking in specificity. How, more concretely, may an investigator determine that he is witnessing the deviance game rather than some other kind of conflict? How can one know when he is viewing a constellation of a large and powerful well-organized minority or majority that is highly fearful of lone individuals or small, loosely organized groups with little power? Issues of specificity center, in particular, on the concepts or vari-

---

[4]Cf. Goffman, 1963:140–47, on "in-group deviants." A different conception is presented by Cohen, 1966.

ables of fear and power. What does it mean to say that a party is highly fearful or feels highly threatened or has a great deal of power?

Leaving aside fear and threat arising from relations to extrahuman objects (e.g., other kinds of animals, the supernatural, floods, explosions), the perception that another human is a fearful object centers significantly on the belief that the human impedes or inhibits the pursuit of one's objectives. The threatening party is seen as actually or potentially disrupting or placing in jeopardy one's activities. Disruption and jeopardy are most commonly conceived in terms of possible or actual physical harm or loss of material resources, but I should here like to take a broader view of the matter. The possibilities of physical harm or loss of material resources are not the only ways in which the accomplishment of planned activities can be made problematic. The possibilities of being murdered or robbed are not the only ways in which there can exist serious ambiguity or unpredictability and consequent anxiety about reasonably getting through a day and negotiating a life course generally. Since human plans, under the best of circumstances, are only ambiguously accomplishable, it is reasonable for humans to seek to reduce extraneous sources of ambiguity and unpredictability.

While the more spectacular possible acts, like murder or robbery, are clearcut sources or forms of ambiguity, it is also true that serious ambiguity is an essential feature of other items defined as deviant. Persons defined as mentally ill are precisely so defined because of the havoc of ambiguity they inflict upon the interactional order of the everyday lives of those around them. More than simply violating understandings of face-to-face interaction, they are also unpredictable as to when and in what manner they will commit these violations, and this creates what can be thought of by persons who must associate with them as unreasonable contingencies. In the larger perspective of institutional orders, categories of persons who defy existing conceptions of possible and proper being serve to create ambiguity about that order. Homosexuals of both sexes serve to make ambiguous the institutionalized division between the sexes. Prostitutes make ambiguous the sexual benefits of the familial order.[5]

When the actual or potential disruptive ambiguity is believed to affect the activities most fundamental or central to the pursuit of the initial party's objectives, there is likely to arise a range of demands and practices which are intended to prevent and inhibit such disruption. The demands and practices that ensue will be a function of the size, degree of organiza-

---

[5]When considered in the light of threat, fear, jeopardy and ambiguity, it is not unreasonable to contemplate the possibility that the blind, the physically handicapped and the retarded are deviant. In much the same way that the thief creates extraneous anxiety and ambiguity by his acts, these categories create what can be felt to be extraneous anxiety and ambiguity by their being. Their disabilities block the normal and smooth flow of everyday interaction and special account must be taken of them. Note that the kind of account taken of them is much the same kind as that taken of other rather powerless and unorganized categories; namely, incarceration and other exclusion from civil society. Despite this, in the analysis which follows, they will not be so defined.

tion and, especially, power of the involved parties. Within nation-states, powerful, large and well-organized parties, whose activities are actually or potentially disrupted by small, powerless and unorganized parties, are in a position to demand and perhaps to effect various kinds of exclusions relative to the offensive party. The exclusion may be in the form of banishment or exile (one of the more popular practices, historically), or it may be in the form of ritualized, state-conducted annihilation. In more recent times exclusion by incarceration has become popular, as seen by the growth of such exile institutions as prisons and mental hospitals (as well as homes for the elderly, schools for the blind, sheltered workshops, training schools, etc.).

In modern civil states, one obtains something like a formal measure of power by noting the differential capacity of interest groups to have enacted by the state exclusionary rules and practices which are protective of their activities. The advocates of banishing or annihilating all Blacks or Jews differ from the advocates of incarcerating embezzlers or committing the mentally ill primarily in the degree to which they are able to mobilize the state to enact such rulings. Indeed, in at least one modern state, a group could come to have the power to banish and finally to annihilate Jews, a policy still advocated by some citizens of the United States.

The ideology of democratic societies which asserts that state rulings must have popular support should not obscure the more fundamental fact that large portions of the populace of any society are typically indifferent to and ignorant of any given possible ruling and that any proposed ruling is likely to have one or more groups that vigorously oppose it. Although there is likely to be some degree of support for a given ruling in democratic societies, it should not be assumed that such support is strong or necessarily arises from a majority sense of strong fear. The advent of an exclusionary ruling might only mean that some highly fearful, well-organized and powerful interest group has been able to muster relatively large minority support, perhaps in the midst of widespread apathy or ignorance, and therefore has been successful in having its interests sponsored and protected by the state. The important point is that such a course of events is possible only in relation to people of little power who are not very well organized. If this were not the case, overt political struggles, perhaps even civil war, would ensue. (See, e.g., Becker, 1963:135–46; Dickson, 1968.)

A primary indicator of "this is the type of conflict called deviance," in a total society is, then, the existence of state rulings and corresponding enforcement mechanisms that provide for the possibility of forceably removing actors from civil society, either by banishment, annihilation or incarceration. Again, it is precisely those actors who have little power and who are not organized toward whom such actions can most successfully be undertaken.

Readers who are familiar with sociological definitions of deviance will note that this approach departs somewhat from the more typical emphasis upon deviance as rule breaking or norm violation. It is certainly true that deviance involves the breaking of somebody's rules, but it is also true that the breaking of somebody's rules is not peculiar or unique to the type of conflict called deviance. The types of conflict labeled civil disorder, rebellion, revolutionary and social movements, civil war and even staid American politics also involve one party's feeling that another party is abridging or will abridge proper rules of conduct. "People are in fact always *forcing* their rules on others," as Howard S. Becker has put it (1963:17). The issue, then, is not rule violation per se; rather, it is rule violation *in the context of* relative power, size, degree of organization and sense of fear among parties in conflict. Deviance is rule violation only in the limited sense that it involves violating the rules of relatively large minorities or majorities who are powerful, well organized and highly fearful of individuals or loosely organized or small groups who lack power.

It is in the situation of a very powerful party opposing a very weak one that the powerful party sponsors the *idea* that the weak party is breaking the rules of society. The very concepts of "society" and its "rules" are appropriated by powerful parties and made synonymous with their interests (and, of course, believed in by the naïve, e.g., the undergraduate penchant for the phrases "society says . . . ," "society expects . . . ," "society does . . ."). It is not so easy to sponsor such notions of a solid society in conflicts with organized opponents who possess some power. Hence conflicts with such opponents are conceived in different terms and given different names, as in Chart 2.1.

This point brings us to a further, more general observation. To the degree that sociologists emphasize, *about modern nation-states,* the idea of there being abstract social rules of society, they tend ideologically to align themselves with powerful groups. They sponsor a conception that is congruent with the interests of such groups. The notions of the social rules of the society may have some relevance for smaller, more homogeneous tribal societies and other relatively face-to-face collectivities. But such concepts seem to mislead more than lead in addressing the sprawling, highly diverse, mediated, amorphous and conflictual object that is the technological nation-state (see, further, Douglas, 1969).

CONFLICT OVER THE NAME OF THE CONFLICT

The degree to which rulings are expressions of strong, reasonably widespread beliefs in the threatening character of an act or type of actor is likely to vary quite widely. Almost 100 per cent of a society might feel that premeditated homicide not involving self-defense is highly threatening and that child molesting or the rape of a female by multiple males unknown to her is equally so. But beyond such instances, consensus on strong fear appears to diminish, especially in the area of what are called "crimes without victims," for example, abortion, homosexuality between consenting adults and the use of such drugs as marijuana (Schur, 1965). Indeed, even for items often presumed to be rather strongly disapproved or feared, there seem to be significant portions of the population who do not care much at all about them. A public-opinion poll conducted by the Harris organization asked this question:

> America has many different types of people in it. But we would like to know whether you think each of these different types of people is more helpful or more harmful to American life, or don't they help or harm things much one way or the other? (L. Harris, 1965).

Often-mentioned deviant categories on the list elicited the following distributions:

	More Harmful	More Helpful or Doesn't Matter
American Communist Party members	89%	11%
Homosexuals	70%	30%
Prostitutes	70%	30%

Other categories that some people regard as deviant can be seen (at least in the poll year of 1965) to be not all that widely feared.

	More Harmful	More Helpful or Doesn't Matter
Anti-Vietnam War picketers	68%	32%
Civil rights demonstrators	68%	32%
Student demonstrators at colleges	65%	35%
Young men with beards and long hair	52%	48%
Beatniks	52%	48%
Members of the John Birch Society	48%	52%

Indeed, at least as measured by the Harris Poll, some categories not usually mentioned as deviant turn up, in the popular view, to be almost as widely feared or disapproved as more usual kinds of deviance.

	More Harmful	More Helpful or Doesn't Matter
People who don't believe in God	72%	28%
Women who gossip all the time	65%	35%

Note that on this measure, atheists, agnostics and gossips draw a response distribution rather similar to that drawn by homosexuals and prostitutes. The two sets of categories are perhaps most distinguished by the degree to which powerful organized interests are fearful enough to mobilize themselves for the purpose of making rulings. One set winds up as deviant and the other merely as objects of popular suspicion.

The Harris poll also supplies some material on the point that at least some segment of the population is likely to be fearful of almost anything that can be named. Witness these objects:

	More Harmful	More Helpful or Doesn't Matter
High school students more interested in athletics than studies	45%	55%
College professors active in unpopular causes	58%	42%
Working career women with young children	50%	50%
Women who wear bikini bathing suits	36%	65%
Lawyers who defend notorious criminals	34%	66%
Young people who like rock and roll	10%	90%
Young people who read books most of the time	10%	90%

An act or type of actor over which there is attenuated consensus can come to have a relatively organized set of defenders, despite the fact that some others continue strongly to fear the object and despite the fact that the legal ruling remains in existence and is enforced. This was once the case for workers attempting to organize unions and is the case today relative to the use of marijuana, the obtaining of abortions and engagement in homosexuality. Like workers at the turn of the 20th century, advocates of the use of marijuana and LSD and of homosexuality have organized to promote their interests (H. S. Becker, 1965).

The process of beginning not "to take it" from the political order, the development of organized efforts at change and the creation of a sympathetic segment among the public at large are early steps in the removal of an item from the purview of the deviance game. The revolutionary sect that draws support begins to play at the politics of insurrection and revolutionary upheaval. The advocates of easy abortion who draw support begin to play at the social movement or conventional politics game. Those who refuse to fight in a war and who draw large minority support engage in the vicissitudes of political strife. While that which is deviant accumulates power, those who still fear it and who continue to have the rules and state apparatus in their favor tend to persist in defining the growing opposition as deviant. The question is then posed: At what point is something no longer deviant? It seems most reasonable to confront this question on the same grounds that initially make it problematic for the sociologist. Those grounds are that the participants can themselves be divided and that whether something is deviant or not can be at issue in public discourse. To be true to the character of his materials, the sociologist must reflect ambiguity as well as more or less consensual public definitions. The point here is that there are likely, at any time, to be acts and persons about which it is difficult to make a decision as to their deviance. This ambiguity and conflict over the name of the conflict is an important feature of that act or type of person. By being attentive to such conflict and ambiguity, it becomes possible to follow the dynamics of how items can come to be defined in terms of kinds of conflict other than deviance, or can reach consensual normality (as well as how they can come to be defined as deviant).

In the American sixties, civil disorder among Blacks in urban ghettos has been an outstanding instance of such conflict and ambiguity over the name of the conflict. The pronouncements of some political authorities that rioting and civil disorder "have nothing to do with civil rights" but are simply *crimes* is an attempt to define the conflict as a deviance game. That position is opposed by those who argue that rioting and civil disorders represent at least protopolitical movements which must be defined and dealt with in a political manner. Reviewing the history of articulate protest in the form of riots in England, Allen Silver observes the following:

> Lacking a strong tradition of urban violence in the form of articulate protest [in America], it is all the easier to define ["violence, criminality and riot"] as merely criminal. Such definitions work not only on the respectable but also on the riotous poor. Like American society as a whole, the American poor lack a traditional past: on neither side of the boundaries of class and race do the conditions for "articulate riot" exist in generous measure. "Criminal" acts like looting and violent assault are likely to dominate riotous protest, rather than explicitly political gestures. Similarly, the propertied and respectable are ill-prepared to react in terms other than a confrontation with uncontained and shapeless criminality. Articulate riot, however, requires that both rioters and their target or audience jointly define the meaning of riotous acts. The frequency with which recent riots by Negroes in American cities are interpreted officially as "meaningless" . . . contrasts with the ability of the English elite [in the 19th century] . . . to interpret the meaning of riotous behavior.
>
> Current concern over violence and riot, then, involves a problem of the political language in which these events are described and interpreted (Silver, 1967:22–23).

From the point of view of sociological analysis, whether Black rioting in particular is deviant or not must rest upon an assessment of how powerful interests choose to define it.[6] In the late sixties it is perhaps best said that the matter is still at issue, and that feature is itself a prime topic of sociological interest.

REFERENCES

BECKER, H. S., *Outsiders: Studies in the Sociology of Deviance.* New York: The Free Press of Glencoe, Inc., 1963.

————, "Deviance and Deviates," in D. Boroff, ed., *The State of the Nation.* Englewood Cliffs, N.J.: Prentice-Hall, Inc., 1965, pp. 73–82.

COHEN, A. K., "The Study of Social Disorganization and Deviant Behavior," in R. K. Merton, L. Broom and L. S. Cottrell, eds., *Sociology Today.* New York: Basic Books, Inc., 1959, pp. 461–84.

————, *Deviance and Control.* Englewood Cliffs, N.J.: Prentice-Hall, Inc., 1966.

DICKSON, D. T., "Bureaucracy and Morality: An Organizational Perspective on a Moral Crusade." *Social Problems,* 16:143–56 (1968).

DOUGLAS, J. D., "The General Theoretical Implications of the Sociology of Deviance," in J. C. McKinney and E. A. Tirakian, eds., *Theoretical Sociology: Perspectives and Developments.* New York: Appleton-Century and Appleton-Century-Crofts, 1969.

GOFFMAN, E., *The Presentation of Self in Everyday Life.* New York: Doubleday-Anchor, Inc., 1959.

————, *Encounters: Two Studies in the Sociology of Interaction.* Indianapolis, Ind.: The Bobbs-Merrill Co., Inc., 1961.

————, *Stigma: Notes on the Management of Spoiled Identity.* Englewood Cliffs, N.J.: Prentice-Hall, Inc., 1963.

————, *Interaction Ritual.* New York: Doubleday and Company, Inc., 1967.

GUSFIELD, J. R., "Moral Passage; The Symbolic Process of Public Designations of Deviance." *Social Problems,* 15:175–88 (Fall 1967).

HARRIS, L., "Conformity: The New American Way." *Detroit Free Press,* September 4, 1965.

HOROWITZ, I. L., and M. LIEBOWITZ, "Social Deviance and Political Marginality: Toward a Redefinition of the Relation Between Sociology and Politics." *Social Problems,* 15:280–96 (Winter 1968).

SCHUR, E., *Crimes Without Victims.* Englewood Cliffs, N.J.: Prentice-Hall, Inc. 1965.

SILVER, A., "The Demand for Order in Civil Society: A Review of Some Themes in the History of Urban Crime, Police, and Riot," in D. Bordua,

---

[6]A somewhat similar view is taken by Horowitz and Liebowitz, 1968 (in this volume), although they appear to believe that some items of deviance are really instances of political conflict, that is, to believe that sociologists can decide what is "really political" as opposed to "really deviant." See also Vold, 1958: Chap. 11 (in this volume); and Gusfield, 1967.

ed., *The Police: Six Sociological Essays.* New York: John Wiley and Sons, Inc., 1967, pp. 1–24.

VESTAL, B., "How Wallace Carries Out His 'Spoiler' Campaign." *Ann Arbor News,* June 22, 1967.

VOLD, G. B., *Theoretical Criminology.* New York: Oxford University Press, Inc., 1958.

3. CULTURE CONFLICT, DIFFERENTIAL ASSOCIATION, AND NORMATIVE CONFLICT

DONALD R. CRESSEY

In 1935 the Social Science Research Council appointed Professor Thorsten Sellin and Professor Edwin H. Sutherland to constitute a Subcommittee on Delinquency of the Council's Committee on Personality and Culture. The appointment was based on the view that criminological research and theory is a subsystem or subset within more general anthropological, social psychological, and sociological frameworks. This view had a powerful impact on the criminology of the time, and it has been influential in criminology, especially American criminology, ever since. The Subcommittee on Delinquency decided to explore some of the basic concepts underlying criminological research and to uncover research questions which might, when answered, expand our knowledge of etiological processes. Both tasks were finally undertaken by Professor Sellin, the Chairman of the Subcommittee, and one outcome was his now-famous monograph on culture conflict and crime.[1]

In this monograph, Sellin reaffirmed the notion that the criminal law is a body of norms that are binding on all who live within the political boundaries of a state and are enforced through the coercive power of that state, and he then went on to indicate that the specific character of these legal rules depends upon the character and interests of those groups in the population that influence legislation.[2] He stressed the idea that such groups are not necessarily in the majority, a notion that was becoming popular at the time.[3] His emphasis was on lack of congruence between criminal laws promulgated by a dominant majority or minority and the moral ideas of different social groups subjected to the laws of the state. Because the norms embodied in the criminal law change as the values of the dominant groups change, what is "crime" varies from time to time and place to place.

From *Crime and Culture: Essays in Honor of Thorsten Sellin*, M. E. Wolfgang, editor. Copyright © 1968 by John Wiley & Sons, Inc. By permission of John Wiley & Sons, Inc.

[1]Thorsten Sellin, *Culture Conflict and Crime*, New York: Social Science Research Council Bulletin No. 41, 1938.

[2]*Ibid.*, p. 21.

[3]Sellin cites the following two works: Joseph A. Leighton, *Social Philosophies in Conflict*, New York: Appleton-Century, 1937; Manuel Gamio, *Hacia un Mexico Nuevo*, Mexico City: Author, 1935.

This kind of observation, coupled with observations on the difficulties of identifying the relationships between "culture" and "personality" (an exciting theoretical problem in 1938, as now) led Sellin to formulate the "conduct norms" concept. Conduct norms are rules based on the social attitudes of groups toward the various ways in which a person might act under certain circumstances. When a human acts or reacts, his activity is called "behavior," but when these actions or reactions are governed by rules or norms, they constitute a subtype of this general category and are classed as "conduct." Accordingly, conduct, by definition, can "occur only in situations which are defined by some social group and governed by a rule of some sort."[4]

In his next logical step, Sellin combined two ideas: the notion that the members of a society are not equally committed to the norms contained in the criminal law, and the notion that members of a society are not equally committed to other conduct norms. The result of these variations in degree of commitments, he observed, is conflict:

> Every person is identified with a number of social groups, each meeting some biologically conditioned or socially created need. Each of these groups is normative in the sense that within it there grow up norms of conduct applicable to situations created by that group's specific activities. As a member of a given group, a person is not only supposed to conform to the rules which it shares with other groups, but also to those which are peculiarly its own. A person who as a member of a family group—in turn the transmitting agency for norms which governed the groups from which the parents came—possesses all its norms pertaining to conduct in routine life situations, may also as a member of a play group, a work group, a political group, a religious group, etc., acquire norms which regulate specialized life situations and which sustain, weaken or even contradict the norms earlier incorporated in his personality. The more complex a culture becomes, the more likely it is that the number of normative groups which affect a person will be large, and the greater is the chance that the norms of these groups will fail to agree, no matter how much they may overlap as a result of a common acceptance of certain norms. A conflict of norms is said to exist when more or less divergent rules of conduct govern the specific life situation in which a person may find himself. The conduct norm of one group of which he is a part may permit one response to this situation, the norm of another group may permit perhaps the very opposite reponse.[5]

After making these observations on conflicts of norms, Sellin went on to examine the concept of "culture conflict," pointing out that "in recent years a number of studies have been made on 'culture conflict' and de-

---

[4]*Op. cit.*, p. 28.
[5]*Ibid.*, pp. 29–30.

linquency, studies which assume the existence of legal and nonlegal conduct norms in conflict with each other."[6] He reported that the concept had been used in two senses—sometimes culture conflict was regarded as the result of the migration of conduct norms from one culture to another, sometimes as a by-product of a cultural growth process.[7]

We shall discuss, below, Sellin's refinements of both uses of the term, and then we shall elaborate on the second meaning, which we call "normative conflict." Here, we merely wish to state our belief that, despite Sellin's detailed discussion of the two meanings, the early use of "culture conflict" in two different senses has meant that the impact of the concept on criminological theory and research has not been as great as it might have been had two different terms been used. We believe, in other words, that use of "culture conflict" to refer to *both* kinds of conflicts of norms has meant that the processes associated with immigration and diffusion of norms have been overemphasized, while the processes by which conflicts develop as by-products of increasing societal complexity have been underemphasized.[8] Because American sociologists customarily showed great concern for "the immigrant problem," it was easy to conclude that "culture conflict" was to be used in this context, and it also has been easy to conclude, erroneously, that the concept has lost its usefulness now that assimilation of vast numbers of immigrants is no longer a major social problem.

MIGRATION OF NORMS

Sellin demonstrated that "culture conflict" can arise because of the interpenetration of conduct norms. "Conflicts of cultures are inevitable when the norms of one cultural or subcultural area migrate or come in contact with those of another, and it is interesting to note that most of the specific researches on culture conflict and delinquency have been concerned with this aspect of conflict rather than [with the one stemming from the cultural growth process]."[9] Interpenetration of norms can occur in three different ways.[10]

---

[6]*Ibid.*, p. 57.

[7]*Ibid.*, p. 58.

[8]Three volumes appearing shortly after Sellin's volume was published show the emphasis on migration of norms from one culture complex to another. In 1940, the Gluecks cited three pages of *Juvenile Delinquents Grow Up* (New York: Commonwealth Fund) under "culture conflict" in their index; all three references are to discussions of nativity, birthplace, and religion. Similarly, in the third edition of Gillin's *Criminology and Penology* (New York: Appleton-Century, 1945), Sellin's monograph is cited, but the discussion of "culture conflict" is devoted exclusively to consideration of the idea that alien cultures have been brought into contact with each other through development of easy and rapid means of communication. Consistently, the six references to "culture conflict" in the revised edition of Barnes' and Teeters' *New Horizons in Criminology* (New York: Prentice-Hall, 1945) all refer to immigrant problems.

[9]*Ibid.*, p. 63.

[10]*Ibid.*, pp. 63–67. The following summary is a revision of the discussion appearing in Donald R. Cressey, "Crime and Delinquency," Chapter 14 in Leonard Broom and Philip Selznick, *Sociology: A Text with Adapted Readings*, 3rd ed., New York: Harper and Row, 1963, pp. 549–550.

First, the codes may clash on the border of contiguous culture areas. Behavior which is not defined as crime in one area may be crime in an adjoining area, resulting in serious problems of identifying the legal ways of behaving in border areas. With the growth of communication processes, the borders between such conflicting culture areas has become extremely broad, since knowledge concerning divergent codes no longer arises out of limited direct personal contacts.

Second, in colonization the criminal laws of one group may be extended to the territory of another, with the result that traditional ways of behaving suddenly become illegal. When Soviet law was extended to Siberian tribes, for example, women were forbidden to wear the traditional veils. But those who obeyed the law and laid aside their veils were killed by their relatives for violating the codes of the tribe.

Third, when the members of one cultural group migrate to another culture, they may take with them values which condone ways of behaving that clash with the codes of the receiving culture and are, therefore, illegal. This process is the reverse of the one just mentioned, and it occurs when the migrant group is politically weaker than the group whose territory is invaded. If the Siberians in the above illustration had moved to Russian cities, they would have introduced divergent norms there.

COMPLEX SOCIAL SYSTEMS AND DIFFERENTIAL ASSOCIATION

Sellin also demonstrated that as a modern industrial and mercantile society has arisen, the process of social differentiation has, by itself, produced a conflict of conduct norms, and there has been a vast extension of impersonal control agencies, "designed to enforce rules which increasingly lack the moral force which rules receive only when they grow out of emotionally felt community needs."[11] One by-product of the development of complex civilization, then, is certain life situations "governed by such conflicting norms that no matter what the response of the person in such a situation will be, it will violate the norms of some social group concerned."[12]

It was "culture conflict" of this second kind that Sutherland considered basic to the explanation of crime, and the concept in this sense later became the principle of differential association. Accordingly, the history of the "culture conflict" concept is tightly entwined with the history of the "differential association" concept. In discussing the history of his theory, Sutherland reported that he rather inadvertently stated the fundamentals of differential association before he realized that he had a theory.[13] Sig-

---

[11]*Ibid.*, pp. 59–60.
[12]*Ibid.*, p. 60.
[13]Edwin H. Sutherland, "Development of the Theory," in Albert Cohen, Alfred Lindesmith and Karl Schuessler, eds., *The Sutherland Papers,* Bloomington: Indiana University Press, 1956, pp. 15–16.

nificantly, this statement, made in 1934, included the concept "conflict of cultures."

> The general hypotheses of this book are as follows: First, any person can be trained to adopt and follow any pattern of behavior which he is able to execute. This pattern may cause him to suffer death, physical injury, economic loss, sacrifice of friendship, and any other type of loss or sacrifice, but be followed nevertheless even with joy, provided it is accepted as the thing for him to do. Second, failure to follow a prescribed pattern of behavior is due to the inconsistency and lack of harmony in the influences which direct the individual. *Third, the conflict of cultures is therefore the fundamental principle in the explanation of crime.* Fourth, the more the cultural patterns conflict, the more unpredictable is the behavior of a particular individual. It was possible to predict with almost certainty how a person reared in a Chinese village fifty years ago would behave because there was only one way for him to behave. The attempts to explain the behavior of a particular person in a modern city have been rather unproductive because the influences are in conflict and any particular influence may be extremely evanescent.[14]

It probably also is significant to the history of both the culture-conflict concept and the differential association theory that the 1939 edition of *Principles of Criminology* uses "culture conflict" in a discussion of what crime *is:* "Crime may be considered, in the light of the discussion in the preceding sections, to involve three elements: a value which is appreciated by a group or a part of a group which is politically important; *isolation of or cultural conflict in another part of the group so that its members do not appreciate the value or appreciate it less highly and consequently tend to endanger it;* and a pugnacious resort to coercion decently applied by those who appreciate the value to those who disregard the value."[15] It is possible to derive the theory of differential association from this statement.

In the first formal statement of his theory, Sutherland made seven assertions, in contrast to the nine assertions contained in the revised, and still current, statement. The sixth assertion in the early version went as follows: *"Cultural conflict is the underlying cause of differential association and therefore of systematic criminal behavior."*[16] In elaborating on this assertion, Sutherland pointed out that differential association is possible because society is composed of groups with varied cultures contain-

---

[14]Edwin H. Sutherland, *Principles of Criminology,* Second Edition, Philadelphia: Lippincott, 1934, pp. 51–52.
[15]Edwin H. Sutherland, *Principles of Criminology,* 3rd ed., Philadelphia: Lippincott, 1939, p. 19. Italics added. Only the phrase "or culture conflict in" was added in the 1939 edition. The remainder of the statement appeared on p. 11 of the 1934 edition. It also appeared in Edwin H. Sutherland, *Criminology,* Philadelphia: Lippincott, 1924, p. 21.
[16]Third edition (1939), p. 7.

ing norms supporting conduct which is generally regarded as desirable and also containing norms supporting conduct which is generally regarded as undesirable. "The criminal culture is as real as lawful culture and is much more prevalent than is usually believed." "The more the cultural patterns conflict, the more unpredictable is the behavior of a particular person." The seventh assertion in this early version of the differential association theory was: *Social disorganization is the basic cause of systematic criminal behavior.* In elaborating on this assertion, Sutherland tried, in a brief and fleeting way, to account for "the origin and the persistence of culture conflicts relating to the values expressed in the law and of differential association which is based on the cultural conflicts." He found them in "social disorganization," and then went on to say: "Cultural conflict is a specific aspect of social disorganization and in that sense the two concepts are names for smaller and larger aspects of the same thing."[17] This primitive statement of the theory was summarized as follows: "Systematic criminal behavior is due immediately to differential association in a situation in which cultural conflicts exist, and ultimately to the social disorganization in that situation."[18]

Although these statements seem to take the "by-product of cultural growth" position with reference to culture conflict, Sellin pointed out that Sutherland's early statements really do not argue that culture conflicts arise *solely* within a culture. While such development is theoretically possible, in practice as cultures expand there is an introduction of disharmonious norms from other culture areas or systems.[19] Nevertheless, Sellin argued, a clash between the norms of Negroes and whites in the United States is indigenous in origin, and other clashes of norms in our country could have developed without the influx of national and racial groups who brought with them the legal norms of other cultural or subcultural areas of the world. In time, this idea that "culture conflict" involves more than a clash between the legal norms of immigrant cultures and host cultures became the foundation of the theory of differential association. Sellin pointed out that Shaw's studies of delinquency areas, for example, showed that while the areas were largely inhabited by European immigrants, the fact that the inhabitants were immigrants was of minor importance, compared with the conditions of "disorganization" in the areas.[20] Sellin concluded, "It is likely that in large European cities with homogeneous populations, the same conditions breed high delinquency."[21]

---

[17]*Ibid.*, p. 8.

[18]*Ibid.*, p. 9.

[19]*Op. cit.*, pp. 61–62. Sutherland's uncertainty can be observed in his explicit use of "conflict of cultures" to refer to the migration of norms: "Conflict of cultures has to some extent been studied from the statistical point of view, although these statistics, also, are extremely inadequate as a measure of conflict." He then cites data on cultural marginality, including data on crime rates of immigrants and their sons. Second edition (1934), p. 73; and third edition (1939), pp. 79–80.

[20]Clifford R. Shaw, *Delinquency Areas,* Chicago: University of Chicago Press, 1929.

[21]*Op. cit.*, pp. 62–63.

Despite this conclusion, Sellin placed great emphasis on the migration of legal norms, rather than on the conflict of norms developing as a consequence of the rise of complex social systems. This emphasis may be seen in his view that culture conflict growing out of social differentiation is "secondary":

> If the immigrant's conduct norms are different from those of the American community and if these differences are not due to his economic status, but to his *cultural origin* then we can speak of a conflict of norms drawn from different cultural systems or areas. Such conflicts may be regarded as *primary* culture conflicts. They may in turn aggravate the disorganizing factors in the social environment by forcing an immigrant into lower-paid occupations, bad neighborhoods, etc., which in turn may have etiological importance in abnormal conduct, regardless of the nativity or the cultural origin of those subjected to them. The conflicts of norms which grow out of the process of social differentiation which characterize the evolution of our own culture may be referred to as *secondary* culture conflicts.[22]

As indicated, the social science culture of the 1930's demanded an emphasis on problems of immigration and on the study of the relationship between "personality" and "culture," rather than on problems of social structure and differentiation. Sociologists, psychologists, and psychiatrists were using the term "culture conflict," but in criminology the theoretical controversy about it centered on the problem of whether culture conflict is relevant to crime and delinquency only if it is experienced by individuals as psychological conflict.[23] Sellin settled this controversy by citing the case of a Sicilian father in New Jersey who had killed the seducer of his daughter and who was surprised at his arrest, since he had merely defended his family honor in a traditional Sicilian way. The crime occurred because the acculturation process was so incomplete that there could be no mental conflict at all about the killing. Perhaps it was this controversy and the theoretical efficacy of the case cited that led Sellin to devote most of the last half of his monograph to a discussion of differences between the norms of immigrants and the norms included in American criminal laws.[24]

NORMATIVE CONFLICT

In order to distinguish between the two kinds of "culture conflict," we have found it convenient to use the term "normative conflict" to refer

---

[22]*Ibid.*, pp. 104–105.
[23]Louis Wirth, "Culture Conflict and Misconduct," *Social Forces*, 9:484–492, June, 1931.
[24]*Op. cit.*, p. 68.

to conflicts between legal and other norms that arise through the societal growth process and to restrict the term "cultural conflict" to conflicts arising through the migration of cultural codes. I began using this terminology in 1960, when I found that even my sociologist friends were interpreting "cultural conflict," as used in differential association theory, to mean conflict between American legal norms and the legal norms of immigrant groups.[25] I began calling Sutherland's statement a "principle of normative conflict," and the words "normative conflict" were substituted for the words "culture conflict" in a quotation from Sutherland because colleagues could not understand the quotation in its original form:

> The second concept, differential association, is a statement of [normative] conflict from the point of view of the person who commits the crime. The two kinds of culture impinge on him or he has association with the two kinds of cultures and this is differential association.[26]

Perhaps the most important theoretical problem regarding the epidemiology of crime is one of establishing the relationship between normative conflict on the one hand and high crime rates on the other. This problem was attacked by both Sellin and Sutherland but, as we have seen, the attack was blunted by the popularity of the "migration of norms" meaning of culture conflict. Associated with this theoretical problem is the problem of identifying the processes by which normative conflict develops. This is the problem that Cloward and Ohlin *say* they are going to attack when they ask, "Why do delinquent 'norms' or rules of conduct develop?"[27] However, the book in which they raise this question is devoted principally to examination of the relationship between high rates of gang delinquency and high degrees of normative conflict.[28] The question of how the social structure generates conflicts between legal and illegal norms remains unsettled.

Sorokin, among others, has pointed out that the penal law consists of "law norms" which defined the rights and duties of actors in definite social relationships.[29] Law norms are "universal" rules which ought to be followed by everyone except the very young and the insane. They differ from moral norms, which recommend but do not require certain courses of conduct. Every society has several sets of moral norms which are both

---

[25]Donald R. Cressey, "Epidemiology and Individual Conduct: A Case From Criminology," *Pacific Sociological Review*, 3:47–58, Fall, 1960.

[26]"Development of the Theory," *op. cit.*, pp. 20–21.

[27]Richard A. Cloward and Lloyd E. Ohlin, *Delinquency and Opportunity: A Theory of Delinquent Gangs*, Glencoe: The Free Press, 1960, p. ix.

[28]Donald R. Cressey, "Differential Association and Delinquent Subcultures," paper read at *Det Attende Nordisk Forskningsseminar for Kriminologi*, Helsinki, June, 1966. To appear in the *Proceedings* (in press).

[29]Pitirim A. Sorokin, *Society, Culture and Personality*, New York: Harper, 1947, pp. 69–71.

based on and give support to the ordering of people. These moral norms, thus, make up the dimensions of the social structure. Some common dimensions of social structure of interest to criminologists, for example, are class status, sex status, age status, health status, ethnic status, and family status. The norms surrounding these statuses distinguish persons in terms of rights, privileges, duties, and prestige, which means, simply, that they define expectations for conduct. While the normative expectations of the society as a whole vary with the structural conditions of class, sex, age, ethnicity, etc., the expectations and requirements of the law norms do not allow for this variability.[30] If variations in normative conflict are related to the epidemiology of crime, then crime rates should be high at those points in the system where the laws are incompatible with the moral norms based upon d:fferentiation.

McElrath has suggested that among the characteristics of the legal process that seem relevant to normative conflict are the discrepancies between the moral norms of the lawmakers and the norms of the persons to whom the law norms are to apply; the peculiar characteristics of law norms, as compared to moral norms, in such aspects as specificity, harm, intent, and punishment; the slowness of the process of change in penal law norms (the lagging of law behind morality); and the processes by which judges, juries, prosecutors, and public defenders are selected.[31] For example, if class status is viewed as a set of "positional" moral norms, it becomes obvious that these norms permit differences in power, prestige, and other behavior. Significantly, as Sellin suggested, among the behavior items on which differences are expected is the behavior relevant to establishing law norms. In simple terms, law norms are likely to reflect the more general behavior of the powerful classes. If the moral norms of the powerful classes are incompatible with the moral norms of other classes and, if the norms of the powerful classes become law norms, then variations in crime rates can readily be predicted from a study of the conflicts between the norms of this class and the norms of other classes. Miller has, in a sense, made such predictions on the basis of his studies of the relationships between delinquency and lower class norms.[32]

It should be noted, however, that while the norms of class position allow for implementation in the penal law of the norms of the powerful, the locus of power shifts from time to time. Accordingly, at various times different positional moral norms get incorporated into the law norms. Because the penal law is slow to shed the older norms, normative con-

---

[30]Dennis McElrath, "Normative Conflict and Crime Rates," *Unpublished Manuscript*, January, 1955, p. 8.
[31]*Ibid.*, pp. 4–5.
[32]Walter B. Miller, "Lower Class Culture as a Generating Milieu of Gang Delinquency," *Journal of Social Issues*, 14:5–19, 1958. See also the quotation of Sutherland at note 15, *supra*.

flict comes to reside within the legal structure itself. Sellin made this point by saying, "The criminal norms, i.e. the conduct norms embodied in the criminal law, change as the values of the dominant groups are modified or as the vicissitudes of social growth cause a reconstitution of these groups themselves and shifts in the focus of power."[33]

Further, it probably cannot be rightfully assumed that the content of any set of positional moral norms is itself unitary and harmonious. Even within a socioeconomic class, one norm may recommend something contrary to what is recommended by another. Thus, while individuals may be similar in terms of class position, they differ in terms of other differentiating criteria, such as age, sex, family status, and ethnicity. One is middle class or upper class, but he also is old or young, urban or rural, male or female, sick or well, Negro or white. The moral norms relevant to one of these systems of status differentiation may be inappropriate to the moral norms defining another of the positions.[34] Such conflicts of norms get "resolved" in the legislative process, but such "resolution" does not mean that the ensuing law norms are subscribed to uniformly or universally.

Normative conflict, then, is inherent in social structure. The conflicts of relevance to crime are those in which choices available to a person, because of one or more of his positions in the social structure, are inappropriate to the choices that the law norms demand that he make. Rates of violation of criminal law norms are a function of the system-related norms as well as of the law norms themselves. To take a simple example, it is apparent that young persons do not have the access to the lawmaking process that is available to middle-aged persons. Accordingly, in many respects juvenile crime is an expression of a condition of conflict between the norms of youth and those of adult lawmakers whose norms become the law norms that direct youth to behave in certain ways. However, older persons, who have low crime rates, do not have access to the lawmaking process either, so differential access to the lawmaking process cannot be the only relevant variable.

Yet another problem arises: given incompatible normative expectations at different positions in the social system, why are the criminal law norms, rather than other norms, violated? In any action situation, positional moral norms are subject to broad tolerance limits and, as indicated, they stand as general recommendations regarding desirable but not necessarily compulsory conduct. But law norms are applied universally and, moreover, they *direct* action. In a situation of normative conflict, the tolerance of violations of positional norms may be generalized, even among the lawmakers, to law norms. Williams indicates that this situa-

---

[33]*Op. cit.*, p. 22.
[34]Compare the quotations of Sellin at notes 5 and 12, *supra*.

tion is handled by the following process: "(a) Public affirmation of the norm; (b) covert acceptance of widespread violation or evasion; (c) periodic token or 'ritualistic' punishment and/or punishment of those whose arrears unavoidably become public."[35] By making compulsory that which is ideal and by making specific that which is general, the law imposes demands for common modes of adaptation; this process, by definition, introduces both a condition of normative conflict and a high rate of violation of law norms.

Another source of normative conflict and, consequently, of law violation is mobility. As Sellin showed, mobility sometimes creates a conflict of law norms. But mobility also involves changes in status positions and, hence, in positional moral norms. If one is to conform to either law norms or positional norms, McElrath suggests, he must (1) know what the norms are, (2) identify with them, and (3) receive support and reinforcement from others.[36] Some statuses might not provide for these processes. More important, some statuses might interfere with these processes as they apply to *law* norms. Just as some immigrants experience "cultural conflict," so a young man experiences "normative conflict" as he reaches the age of responsibility, for the legal norms applying to him do not change regularly and systematically as he grows older.

---

[35]Robin M. Williams, *American Society: A Sociological Interpretation,* New York: Knopf, 1951, p. 356.
[36]*Op. cit.,* p. 9.

4. NONCONFORMING AND ABERRANT BEHAVIOR

ROBERT K. MERTON

Deviant behavior on a sizable scale represents quite another kind of social problem. Whereas social disorganization refers to faults in the arrangement and working of social statuses and roles, deviant behavior refers to conduct that departs significantly from the norms set for people in their social statuses. The same behavior may be construed as deviant or conforming, depending upon the social statuses of the people exhibiting the behavior. This fact is simply a corollary of the sociological notion that each social status involves its own set of normative obligations (although many statuses may share some of the same obligations). When a man acts "like a child" or a layman acts "like a physician," he engages in deviant behavior. But as these allusive phrases imply, the same behavior by children and by physicians would of course be in accord with normative expectations. That is why deviant behavior cannot be described in the abstract but must be related to the norms that are socially defined as appropriate and morally binding for people occupying various statuses.

As used by the sociologist, the term "deviant behavior" is thus a technical rather than a moralizing one. But as the term has entered into the vernacular, its morally neutral denotation has become overladen with the connotation of moral censure. The reasons for this are understandable and theoretically interesting. Moralistic responses to deviant behavior have one or another, or both, of two sources, depending upon the distance of people from that behavior. For associates who are in direct social interaction with a person, his sustained deviant behavior is apt to be disruptive. His failure to live up to socially defined expectations makes life difficult or miserable for them. They cannot safely count on him, although in fact they must. Whatever the intent, deviant behavior interferes, at the least, with the measure of predictability required by social relations and thus results in a punishing experience for the associates of the deviating person. They respond in turn by a familiar and important kind of social control. Through spontaneous expression of their injured

From *Contemporary Social Problems* by Robert K. Merton and Robert Nisbet, © 1961, 1966, 1971, by Harcourt, Brace, Jovanovich, Inc. and reprinted with their permission.

feelings or by more deliberate sanctioning behavior, role-partners of the deviating person act in such a way as to bring him back into line with their normative expectations, if only so that they can go about their usual business. This, then, is one source of response to deviant behavior.

Much the same type of response to observed deviant behavior occurs among members of a social system even when they are not *directly* engaged in immediate social relations with the deviating person. In such cases, their hostile responses can be described as disinterested. They themselves have little or nothing to lose by the deviating person's departures from norms; their situation is not damaged by his behavior. Nevertheless, they too respond with hostility. For, having internalized the moral content of the norms that are being violated, they experience the deviant behavior as threatening or repudiating the social validity of norms that they hold to be right and important. Reprisals of various kinds can be described as stemming from moral indignation,[1] a disinterested attack on people who depart from norms of the group, even when the deviation does not interfere with the performance of one's own roles since one is not socially connected with the persons engaging in the deviant act. The pattern of moral indignation has been exemplified in recent times by attacks of American construction workers ("hardhats") on radical students or on those who resemble these students in mere outward appearance.

DEVIANT BEHAVIOR AND SOCIAL RESPONSE

When we say that deviant behavior departs from norms set for given statuses, we do not wish to imply that social responses to such deviation occur uniformly and without respect of person (or to use the sociologist Max Weber's favored phrase, *sine ira et studio*—"without anger or partiality"). On the contrary. Social sanctions are not evenly applied to all those who have violated social rules, with the race, ethnicity, class, sex, and age of violators being only among the more conspicuous bases for differentials.

If it were not already evident to most sociologists, the existence of such differentials in imposing sanctions would alert them to the necessity of having the theory of deviant behavior handle two distinct though related problems: (1) how to account for varying rates of rule-violating behavior in various groups, social strata and other social systems; and (2) how to account for differences in the societal reactions to such behavior, de-

---

[1]The *locus classicus* of the theory of moral indignation is in Svend Ranulf, *Moral Indignation and Middle Class Psychology* (Copenhagen: Levin & Munksgaard, 1938). As Ranulf emphasizes, his work develops the fundamental theory set out by Émile Durkheim. The earlier monograph on the subject by Ranulf can also be profitably consulted in *The Jealousy of the Gods and Criminal Law at Athens: A Contribution to the Sociology of Moral Indignation* (London: Williams & Norgate, 1933).

pending in part on the social characteristics of those exhibiting that behavior and of those judging it.

The theory of anomie-and-opportunity-structure[2] addresses itself primarily to the first of these problems. In brief, it states that varying rates of particular kinds of deviant behavior result from socially patterned discrepancies between culturally induced aspirations and differentials in access to the opportunity structure for moving toward those aspirations by use of legitimate means.

More recently, another orientation to deviant behavior has been evolving, that, variously known as the "labeling theory" or "societal reactions approach," centers on reactions to behavior by the official agents in society. The chief exponents of this theoretical orientation are Edwin Lemert, Howard S. Becker, Kai T. Erikson, John I. Kitsuse and Aaron V. Cicourel.[3] The chief ingredients of this interesting theoretical orientation can be set out in the language of one of its chief exponents:

> Deviance . . . is created by society. I do not mean this in the way it is ordinarily understood, in which the causes of deviance are located in the social situation of the deviant. . . . I mean, rather, that *social groups create deviance by making the rules whose infraction constitutes deviance,* and by applying those rules to particular people and labeling them as outsiders. From this point of view, deviance is *not* a quality of the act the person commits, but rather a consequence of the application by others of rules and sanctions to an "offender." The deviant is one to whom that label has successfully been applied; deviant behavior is behavior that people so label.[4]

This passage puts forward a variety of theoretical claims. The first, which it shares with every other theory of deviance, is blatantly true and

---

[2]Robert K. Merton, "Social Structure and Anomie," *American Sociological Review,* Vol. III (October, 1938), pp. 672–83, further developed in Merton, *Social Theory and Social Structure* (New York: Free Press, 1968), pp. 184–248. For extended discussions, see Marshall B. Clinard, ed., *Anomie and Deviant Behavior* (New York: Free Press, 1964) which includes an annotated inventory by Stephen Cole and Harriet Zuckerman of nearly 200 empirical and theoretical studies of anomie-and-deviant-behavior. During the past five years, almost as many more empirical studies and empirical extensions have critically examined the theory. See Richard Cloward and Lloyd Ohlin, *Delinquency and Opportunity* (New York: Free Press, 1960); Albert K. Cohen, *Deviance and Control* (Englewood Cliffs, N.J.: Prentice-Hall, 1966); Marshall B. Clinard, *Sociology of Deviant Behavior,* 3rd ed. (New York: Holt, 1968), pp. 154–61; David Matza, *Becoming Deviant* (Englewood Cliffs, N.J.: Prentice-Hall, 1969), pp. 57–62, 96–99, who manages to be emphatically opposed to the functional analysis of social patterns by persistently ignoring the focus on *multiple consequences* for different groups and strata in the system. For a theoretical orientation like that adopted here, see William A. Rushing, ed., *Deviant Behavior and Social Process* (Chicago: Rand McNally, 1969), esp. pp. 11–15; Mark Lefton, James K. Skipper, Jr. and C. H. McCaghy, eds., *Approaches to Deviance* (New York: Appleton-Century-Crofts, 1968).

[3]Edwin M. Lemert, *Social Pathology* (New York: McGraw-Hill, 1951) and *Human Deviance, Social Problems and Social Control* (Englewood Cliffs, N.J.: Prentice-Hall, 1967); Howard S. Becker, ed., *The Other Side: Perspectives on Deviance* (New York: Free Press, 1964) which includes the paper by John I. Kitsuse, "Notes on the Sociology of Deviance," pp. 9–21; Howard S. Becker, *Outsiders* (New York: Free Press, 1964); John I. Kitsuse and Aaron V. Cicourel, "A Note on the Use of Official Statistics," *Social Problems,* Vol. II (Fall, 1963), pp. 131–39; Aaron V. Cicourel, *The Social Organization of Juvenile Justice* (New York: Wiley, 1968).

[4]Howard S. Becker, *Outsiders,* pp. 8–9.

trivial: namely, the statement that behavior cannot be considered "deviant" unless there are social norms from which that behavior departs. It seems banal and safe to stipulate: no rule, no rule-violating behavior.

But evidently, much more is intended by the claim that society or social groups "create" deviance; or by the equally strong claim, on the part of Kitsuse and Cicourel, that "rates of deviant behavior *are produced by* the actions taken by persons in the social system which define, classify and record certain behaviors as deviant."[5] This directs our attention away from the question of the social structures and processes which generate differing rates of rule-breaking behavior to the question of how this behavior is identified and responded to by official agencies of social control. In a word, it abandons the sociological question of the sources of rule-violating behavior and proposes to substitute an entirely different sociological question: How is this behavior detected and how is it variously defined by official agencies depending on the status of those engaging in it? As many recent critics of this theoretical position have noted, by merging rule-violating acts and official reaction to them, the labeling school of thought altogether abandons basic questions of a theory of deviant behavior, namely:[6] (1) Why rates of particular acts vary from one population to another; (2) why certain persons engage in these acts while others do not; and (3) why the act is considered deviant in some societies and not in others. In effect, this approach no longer deals with the etiology of behavior that may or may not be tagged as deviant, but confines itself to the alternative question of the processes making for different evaluations of that behavior. This theoretical decision, as Gibbs and others have indicated, results in certain theoretical contradictions. For example, "if deviant behavior is defined in terms of reactions to it, then Becker cannot speak properly of 'secret deviance' [as he emphatically and usefully does]. . . . To be consistent, Becker, Kitsuse, and Erikson would have to insist that behavior which is contrary to a norm is not deviant unless it is discovered and there is a particular kind of reaction to it."[7]

---

[5]John I. Kitsuse and Aaron V. Cicourel, "A Note on the Use of Official Statistics," *Social Problems,* p. 135.

[6]This is drawn from the incisive but sympathetic critique of labeling theory by Jack P. Gibbs, "Conceptions of Deviant Behavior: The Old and the New," *Pacific Sociological Review,* Vol. 9 (Spring, 1966), 9–14. For other pointed yet appreciative criticisms, see Rodolfo Alvarez, "Informal Reactions to Deviance in Simulated Work Organizations," *American Sociological Review,* Vol. 33 (December, 1968), pp. 895–912, esp. pp. 900–02. For an empirical appraisal of the labeling perspective on mental illness, see Walter R. Gove, "Societal Reaction as an Explanation of Mental Illness: An Evaluation," *American Sociological Review,* Vol. 35 (October, 1970), pp. 873–84. In an overview of such criticisms, Schur has rightly suggested that the labeling perspective complements rather than supplants alternative theories of deviant behavior: Edwin M. Schur, "Reactions to Deviance: A Critical Assessment," *American Journal of Sociology,* Vol. 75 (November, 1969), pp. 309–22. In a pointed formulation, Akers indicates that the theory of deviance must deal with *both* the sources and the social definition of deviant acts: Ronald L. Akers, "Problems in the Sociology of Deviance: Social Definitions and Behavior," *Social Forces,* Vol. 46 (June, 1968), pp. 455–65.

[7]Jack P. Gibbs, "Conceptions of Deviant Behavior: The Old and the New," *Pacific Sociological Review,* p. 13.

By distinguishing between deviant behavior and the responses to it, rather than merging them as the labeling perspective would have us do, we can deal with the interaction between them. Thus to put it somewhat parochially, the sociologist does not typically respond to deviant actions as the social system does. The sociologist is trained to distinguish between deviant behavior and the people engaged in such behavior.[8] In contrast, conforming members of social systems tend to identify the *persons* apprehended in deviant conduct as deviant social types (i.e., chronically devoted to rule-breaking behavior): a criminal, a delinquent, an ex-con, a pervert, renegade, or traitor. By doing so, representatives of the social system may help to confirm people in a *career* as deviants through the social process of the self-fulfilling prophecy, as both Becker and Erikson, among others, have noted:

> Treating a person as thought he were generally rather than specifically deviant produces a self-fulfilling prophecy. It sets in motion several mechanisms which conspire to shape the person in the image people have of him. . . . One tends to be cut off, after being identified as deviant, from participation in more conventional groups. . . . When . . . caught, one is treated in accordance with the popular diagnosis of why one is that way, and the treatment itself may likewise produce increasing deviance.[9]

That is the essential process of the self-fulfilling prophecy: Widespread beliefs help to bring about a social environment that so constrains the range of options for the people who are the object of those beliefs that their subsequent behavior can only seem to confirm the beliefs.[10]

Among the labeling theorists, it is primarily Erikson who has recognized all along that they have been writing the prose of structural and functional analysis while trying their hands at labelist prose. For in focusing on the range, intensity, and distribution of societal responses to rule-breaking behavior, they have continued a line of theory stemming from Émile Durkheim's early work on the same problem.[11] And to do so effectively, that theory must, as Gibbs puts it, "identify deviant acts by reference to norms, and treat reaction to deviation as a contingent property."[12] Only so, can one investigate the interaction between rates of

---

[8]For an example in the era of the 1930's, note the observation that the typology of deviant behaviors refers "to role adjustments in specific situations, not to personality *in toto*." Robert K. Merton, "Social Structure and Anomie," *American Sociological Review*, p. 676.

[9]Howard S. Becker, *Outsiders*, p. 34; also Kai T. Erikson, "Notes on the Sociology of Deviance," in Howard S. Becker, ed., *The Other Side: Perspectives on Deviance*, p. 17; Kai T. Erikson, *Wayward Puritans: A Study in the Sociology of Deviance* (New York: Wiley, 1966), p. 17 ff.

[10]On the general process of the self-fulfilling prophecy, see Robert K. Merton, *Social Theory and Social Structure*, Chapter 13.

[11]Emile Durkheim, "Deux lois de l'évolution pénale," *L'Année Sociologique*, Vol. 4 (1899–1900), pp. 65–95.

[12]Jack P. Gibbs, "Conceptions of Deviant Behavior: The Old and the New," *Pacific Sociological Review*, p. 14.

norm-breaking behavior and societal responses to it in a system of feed-back loops which intensify or dampen the rates of both deviant behavior and patterns of response.

NONCONFORMING AND ABERRANT BEHAVIOR

As a first approximation, all substantial departures of behavior from social norms can be caught up in the single concept and associated term, deviant behavior. But first approximations are useful to the degree that they are recognized for what they are: rough discriminations to be pro-gressively replaced by more exacting ones. And so it is with the concept of deviant behavior. Since departures from established norms differ greatly in both character and social consequences, they should not be indiscriminately grouped together.

Two major varieties of deviant behavior can be usefully distinguished on the basis of their structure and their consequences for social systems. The first can be called "nonconforming behavior"; the second, "aberrant behavior." Both types retain the technical conception of deviant be-havior in sociological analysis; the distinction does not smuggle in moral judgments through the back door of connotative language. It only helps us to identify systematic differences in kinds of deviant behavior that are alike only in that they move away from what is prescribed by specifiable social norms.

These types of nonconforming behavior and aberrant behavior differ in several conjoint respects. *First,* the nonconformer announces his dis-sent publicly; unlike the aberrant, he does not try to hide his departures from social norms. The political or religious dissenter insists on making his dissent known to as many as will look or listen; the aberrant criminal seeks to avoid the limelight of public scrutiny. Contrast the pacifist who burns his draft card in public with the draft dodger who tries to escape into obscurity. This patterned attitude toward visibility links up with a *second* basic difference between the two kinds of deviants. The noncon-former challenges the legitimacy of the social norms he rejects or at least challenges their applicability to certain kinds of situations. Organized "sit-in" campaigns designed to attack local norms of racial segregation in restaurants and schools afford a recent example of this aspect of noncon-forming behavior. The aberrant, in contrast, acknowledges the legitimacy of the norms he violates: It is only that he finds it expedient or expressive of his state of mind to violate them. He may try to justify his own be-havior, but he does not argue that theft is right and murder virtuous.

Third and correlatively, the nonconformer aims to change the norms he is denying in practice. He wants to replace what he believes to be morally suspect norms with ones having a sound moral basis. The aberrant, in contrast, tries primarily to escape the sanctioning force of existing norms, without proposing substitutes for them. When subject to social sanction, the nonconformer typically appeals to a higher morality; except as an instrumental device, the aberrant does not; at most he appeals to extenuating circumstances.

Fourth, and possibly as a result of the preceding components of his behavior, the nonconformer is acknowledged, however reluctantly, by conventional members of the social system to depart from prevailing norms for disinterested purposes and not for what he personally can get out of it. Again in contrast, the aberrant is generally assumed to be deviating from the norms in order to serve his own interests. Although the law of the land may not make the formal distinction between the nonconformer and the aberrant in this respect, many members of society do. Whatever the generic concept of deviant behavior might seem to pronounce to the contrary, the two types of social deviants are widely acknowledged as having far different social consequences. Those courageous highwaymen of seventeenth-century England, John Nevinson and his much advertised successor, Dick Turpin, were not of a sociological piece with that courageous nonconformist of their time, Oliver Cromwell. And in the event that one's political or religious sympathies, as well as the detachment made easy by historical distance, serve to make this observation self-evident, one should reexamine those judgements that once made Trotsky and Nehru little more than criminals heading up sizable gangs of followers.

Fifth, and for present purposes finally, the nonconformer, with his appeal to an allegedly higher morality, can in historically propitious circumstances lay claim to legitimacy by drawing upon the ultimate values, rather than the particular norms, of the society. He is trying to make justice a social reality rather than an institutionalized fiction. He is for genuine freedom of speech rather than its everyday pretense. He would rearrange the social structure to provide actual equality of opportunity for all men to develop prized talents and not allow the social simulacra of equality to be mistaken for the real thing. In these ways, his nonconformity can appeal to the moral values that are in some measure being denied in social practice while being reaffirmed in ideological doctrine. The nonconformer can appeal to the tacit recognition by others of discrepancies between the prized values and the social reality.[13] He thus has at least the prospect of obtaining the assent of other, initially less critical and venturesome, members of society whose ambivalence toward the current social structure can be drawn upon for some degree of sup-

---

[13]Talcott Parsons has long ago noted the important point that patterns of social deviation differ significantly according to whether or not they lay claim to legitimation. See *The Social System* (New York: Free Press, 1951), pp. 291–97.

port. Nonconformity is not a private dereliction but a thrust toward a new morality or a promise of restoring a morality held to have been put aside in social practice. In this respect again, the nonconformer is far removed from the other major type of social deviant, the aberrant, who has nothing new to propose and nothing old to restore, but seeks only to satisfy his private interests or to express his private cravings.[14]

Although sociologists continue to lavish more attention on the form of deviant behavior we have described as aberrant, they have begun systematic investigations of what we have described as nonconforming behavior. As a result, the third edition of this book can examine such matters as the rebellious youth culture and collective forms of social protest as well as the principal kinds of aberrant behavior—crime, alcoholism, drug addiction, and so forth. As Francis Bacon put it, "Books must follow sciences, and not sciences, books." As the body of sociological investigation of still other kinds of nonconforming behavior develops, the shape of qualified books on social problems will change even more in this direction.

Future investigations into nonconformity will need to take care that they do not move from an unthinking orthodoxy to an equally unthinking heterodoxy by valuing nonconformity for its own sake. We must remember that what is nonconformity to the norms of one group is often conformity to the norms of another group. There is no merit in escaping the error of taking heterodoxy to be inevitably false or ugly or sinister only to be caught up in the opposite error of thinking heterodoxy to be inevitably true or beautiful or altogether excellent. Put in so many words, this is a commonplace. Yet people alienated from the world about them often do take heterodoxy as a good in itself, whatever its character. And others, perhaps in reaction to the cases, familiar in every age, of true merit being neglected or punished because it is unorthodox, are quick to value heterodoxy or countercyclicalism, all apart from their substance. In every time, apparently shrewd men have recognized that an appropriate kind of seeming heterodoxy appeals greatly even to the more orthodox members of society. As British lecturers to American audiences have evidently known for a long period, and as "radical" American lecturers to civic clubs, literary societies, and businessmen's associations know now: there is no better way to win their audiences' hearts than by attacking part of what they stand for while intimating that they are not beyond redemption.[15]

---

[14]The foregoing account of nonconforming behavior develops somewhat the pattern of behavior identified as "rebellion" in the typology set forth in "Social Structure and Anomie." In that same typology, innovation, ritualism, and retreatism would comprise forms of aberrant behavior. And, as has been indicated in the text, nonconforming and aberrant behavior together compose deviant behavior. See Robert K. Merton, *Social Theory and Social Structure*, p. 194.

[15]This paragraph is based on Robert K. Merton, "Recognition and Excellence: Instructive Ambiguities," in *Recognition of Excellence: Working Papers* (New York: Free Press, 1960), pp. 297–328, especially pp. 321–22.

These and other expressions of specious nonconformity have long been recognized, particularly by some of the most notable nonconformers of their time. It has been said of Marx, for example, that "all his life [he] detested two phenomena with peculiar passion: disorderly life and histrionic display. It seemed to him that Bohemianism and deliberate flouting of conventions was but inverted Philistinism, emphasizing and paying homage to the very same false values by exaggerated protest against them, and exhibiting therefore the same fundamental vulgarity."[16]

---

[16]Isaiah Berlin, *Karl Marx* (London: Oxford University Press, 1960), p. 79.

5. CONTRACULTURE AND SUBCULTURE

J. MILTON YINGER

In recent years there has been widespread and fruitful employment of the concept of subculture in sociological and anthropological research. The term has been used to focus attention not only on the wide diversity of norms to be found in many societies but on the normative aspects of deviant behavior. The ease with which the term has been adopted, with little study of its exact meaning or its values and its difficulties, is indicative of its utility in emphasizing a sociological point of view in research that has been strongly influenced both by individualistic and moralistic interpretations. To describe the normative qualities of an occupation, to contrast the value systems of social classes, or to emphasize the controlling power of the code of a delinquent gang is to underline a sociological aspect of these phenomena that is often disregarded.

In the early days of sociology and anthropology, a key task was to document the enormous variability of culture from society to society and to explore the significance of the overly simplified but useful idea that "the mores can make anything right." In recent years that task has been extended to the study of the enormous variability of culture *within* some societies. It is unfortunate that "subculture," a central concept in this process, has seldom been adequately defined.[1] It has been used as an *ad hoc* concept whenever a writer wished to emphasize the normative aspects of behavior that differed from some general standard. The result

Reprinted from *American Sociological Review*, 25 (October, 1960), 625–35 by permission of The American Sociological Association and the author.

[1]There are a few formal definitions. For example: "The term 'subculture' refers in this paper to 'cultural variants displayed by certain segments of the population.' Subcultures are distinguished not by one or two isolated traits—they constitute relatively cohesive cultural systems. They are worlds within the larger world of our national culture." (Mirra Komarovsky and S. S. Sargent, "Research into Subcultural Influences upon Personality," in S. S. Sargent and M. W. Smith, editors, *Culture and Personality*, New York: The Viking Fund, 1949, p. 143.) These authors then refer to class, race, occupation, residence, and region. After referring to sub-group values and language, Kimball Young and Raymond W. Mack state: "Such shared learned behaviors which are common to a specific group or category are called *subcultures*." (*Sociology and Social Life*, New York: American Book, 1959, p. 49.) They refer then to ethnic, occupational, and regional variations. Blaine Mercer writes: "A society contains numerous subgroups, each with its own characteristic ways of thinking and acting. These cultures within a culture are called *subcultures*." (*The Study of Society*, New York: Harcourt-Brace, 1958, p. 34.) Thereafter he discusses Whyte's *Streetcorner Society*. Although these definitions are helpful, they fail to make several distinctions which are developed below.

has been a blurring of the meaning of the term, confusion with other terms, and a failure frequently to distinguish between two levels of social causation.

THREE USAGES OF SUBCULTURE

Few concepts appear so often in current sociological writing. In the course of twelve months, I have noted over 100 books and articles that make some use, from incidental to elaborate, of the idea of "subculture." The usages vary so widely, however, that the value of the term is severely limited. If chemists had only one word to refer to all colorless liquids and this led them to pay attention to only the two characteristics shared in common, their analysis would be exceedingly primitive. Such an analogy overstates the diversity of ideas covered by "subculture," but the range is very wide. Nevertheless three distinct meanings can be described.

In some anthropological work, subculture refers to certain universal tendencies that seem to occur in all societies. They underlie culture, precede it, and set limits to the range of its variation. Thus Kroeber writes: "Indeed, such more or less recurrent near-regularities of form or process as have to date been formulated for culture are actually sub-cultural in nature. They are limits set to culture by physical or organic factors."[2] In *The Study of Man*, Linton uses subculture to refer to various pan-human phenomena that seem to occur everywhere. Thus good-natured and tyrannical parents may be found in societies that differ widely in their family patterns.[3] This use shades off into other concepts that are similar but not identical: Edward Sapir's "precultural" and Cooley's "human nature" refer to biological and social influences that underlie all cultures.[4] Since subculture is only rarely used today to refer to this series of ideas, I shall exclude them from further consideration, with the suggestion that the use of Sapir's term "precultural" might well clarify our thinking.

Two other usages of subculture represent a much more serious confusion. The term is often used to point to the normative systems of groups smaller than a society, to give emphasis to the ways these groups differ in such things as language, values, religion, diet, and style of life from the larger society of which they are a part. Perhaps the most com-

[2]A. L. Kroeber, "The Concept of Culture in Science," *Journal of General Education*, 3 (April, 1949), p. 187. See also Clyde Kluckhohn's reference to this idea in "Culture and Behavior," in Gardner Lindzey, editor, *Handbook of Social Psychology*, Cambridge: Addison-Wesley, 1954, Vol. 2, p. 954; and A. L. Kroeber in "Problems of Process: Results," in Sol Tax *et al.*, editors, *An Appraisal of Anthropology Today*, Chicago: University of Chicago Press, 1953, p. 119.

[3]Ralph Linton, *The Study of Man*, New York: Appleton-Century, 1936, p. 486. See also his *The Cultural Background of Personality*, New York: Appleton-Century-Crofts, 1945, pp. 148–151. Elsewhere in *The Study of Man*, Linton uses subculture in a different sense, similar to the second usage described below.

[4]Edward Sapir, "Personality," in *Encyclopedia of the Social Sciences*, New York: Macmillan, 1931, Vol. 12, p. 86; Charles H. Cooley, *Human Nature and the Social Order*, revised edition, New York: Scribner, 1922.

mon referent in this usage is an ethnic enclave (French Canadians in Maine) or a region (the subculture of the South),[5] but the distinctive norms of much smaller and more temporary groups (even a particular friendship group) may be described as a subculture. Kluckhohn, for example, refers to "the subculture of anthropologists" and Riesman to "subcultures among the faculty."

This second meaning, which itself contains some ambiguities, as we shall see, must be distinguished from a third meaning associated with it when the reference is to norms that arise specifically from a frustrating situation or from conflict between a group and the larger society. Thus the emergent norms of a delinquent gang or the standards of an adolescent peer group have often been designated "subcultural." In addition to a cultural dimension, this third usage introduces a social-psychological dimension, for there is direct reference to the personality factors involved in the development and maintenance of the norms. Specifically, such personality tendencies as frustration, anxiety, feelings of role ambiguity, and resentment are shown to be involved in the creation of the subculture. The mutual influence of personality and culture is not a distinctive characteristic of this type of subculture, of course, for they are everywhere interactive. Thus:

> Tendencies for parents to respond harshly to their children's aggressive behavior, for instance, if common to the members of a society, are to be referred equally to the culture and to the modal personality of the parents. But the result in the developing child is not a foregone conclusion; present knowledge suggests that under specifiable conditions outcomes as different as rigid politeness or touchy latent hostility may follow. These consequences in turn may lead to cultural elaborations that seem superficially remote from the cultural starting point, yet are dynamically linked with it.[6]

As this quotation suggests, culture and personality are always empirically tied together. Yet the nature of the relation is not the same in all cases. The term subculture, when used in the third way described here,

---

[5]See, e.g., John K. Morland, *Millways of Kent,* Chapel Hill: University of North Carolina Press, 1958; Julian Steward, *The People of Puerto Rico,* Champaign: University of Illinois Press, 1956; Charles Wagley and Marvin Harris, "A Typology of Latin American Subcultures," *American Anthropologist,* 57 (June, 1955), pp. 428–451; Evon Z. Vogt, "American Subcultural *Continua* as Exemplified by the Mormons and Texans," *American Anthropologist,* 57 (December, 1955), pp. 1163–1172; Murray Straus, "Subcultural Variations in Ceylonese Mental Ability: A Study in National Character," *Journal of Social Psychology,* 39 (February, 1954), pp. 129–141; Joel B. Montague and Edgar G. Epps, "Attitudes Toward Social Mobility as Revealed by Samples of Negro and White Boys," *Pacific Sociological Review,* 1 (Fall, 1958), pp. 81–84; Hylan Lewis, *Blackways of Kent,* Chapel Hill: University of North Carolina Press, 1955; Robin M. Williams, Jr., *American Society,* New York: Knopf, 1951, Chapter 10; T. S. Langner, "A Test of Intergroup Prejudice Which Takes Account of Individual and Group Differences in Values," *Journal of Abnormal and Social Psychology,* 48 (October, 1953), pp. 548–554.

[6]Brewster Smith, "Anthropology and Psychology," in John Gillin, editor, *For a Science of Social Man,* New York: Macmillan, 1954, p. 61. See also Talcott Parsons and Edward A. Shils, editors, *Toward A General Theory of Action,* Cambridge: Harvard University Press, 1951, esp. the monograph by the editors; and Ralph Linton's preface to Abram Kardiner, *The Psychological Frontiers of Society,* New York: Columbia University Press, 1945.

raises to a position of prominence one particular kind of dynamic linkage between norms and personality: the creation of a series of inverse or counter values (opposed to those of the surrounding society) in face of serious frustration or conflict. To call attention to the special aspects of this kind of normative system, I suggest the term *contraculture.* Before exploring the relationship between subculture and contraculture, however, the range of meanings given subculture even when it is limited to the second usage requires comment.

SUBCULTURE AND ROLE

The variety of referents for the term subculture is very wide because the normative systems of sub-societies can be differentiated on many grounds. The groups involved may range from a large regional subdivision to a religious sect with only one small congregation. The distinctive norms may involve many aspects of life—religion, language, diet, moral values— or, for example, only a few separate practices among the members of an occupational group. Further distinctions among subcultures might be made on the basis of time (has the subculture persisted through a number of generations?), origin (by migration, absorption by a dominant society, social or physical segregation, occupational specialization, and other sources), and by the mode of relationship to the surrounding culture (from indifference to conflict). Such wide variation in the phenomena covered by a term can be handled by careful specification of the several grounds for sub-classification. Confusion has arisen not so much from the scope of the term subculture as from its use as a substitute for "role." Only with great effort is some degree of clarity being achieved in the use of the role concept and the related terms "position" and "role behavior."[7] Were this development retarded by confusion of role with subculture it would be unfortunate. All societies have differentiating roles, but only heterogeneous societies have subcultures. Role is *that part of* a full culture that is assigned, as the appropriate rights and duties, to those occupying a given position.[8] These rights and duties usually interlock into a system with those of persons who occupy other positions. They are known to and accepted by all those who share the culture. Thus the role of a physician is known, at least in vague outline, by most persons in a society and it is seen as part of the total culture. (This is not to prejudge

---

[7]See, e.g., Neal Gross, Ward S. Mason, and A. W. McEachern, *Explorations in Role Analysis,* New York: Wiley, 1958; F. L. Bates, "Position, Role, and Status: A Reformulation of Concepts," *Social Forces,* 34 (May, 1956), pp. 313–321; Robert K. Merton, "The Role-Set: Problems in Sociological Theory," *British Journal of Sociology,* 8 (June, 1957), pp. 106–120; S. F. Nadel, *The Theory of Social Structure,* Glencoe, Ill.: Free Press, 1957; Theodore R. Sarbin, "Role Theory," in *Handbook of Social Psychology, op. cit.,* Vol. 1, Chapter 6.

[8]It is possible, of course, for a subculture to specify roles within its own system.

the question of role consensus, for there may be many nonrole aspects of being a physician.) But subculture is not tied in this way into the larger cultural complex: it refers to norms that set a group apart from, not those that integrate a group with, the total society. Subcultural norms, as contrasted with role norms, are unknown to, looked down upon, or thought of as separating forces by the other members of a society. There are doubtless subcultural aspects of being a physician—normative influences affecting his behavior that are not part of his role, not culturally designated rights and duties. But the empirical mixture should not obscure the need for this analytic distinction.

Along with confusion with the role concept, subculture carries many of the ambiguities associated with the parent concept of culture. In much social scientific writing it is not at all clear whether culture refers to norms, that is, to expected or valued behavior, or to behavior that is widely followed and therefore normal in a statistical sense only. This dual referent is particularly likely to be found in the work of anthropologists. Perhaps because their concepts are derived largely from the study of relatively more stable and homogeneous societies, they draw less sharply the distinction between the statistically normal and the normative. Sociologists are more apt to find it necessary to explore the tensions between the social order and culture, to be alert to deviations, and they are therefore more likely to define culture abstractly as a shared normative system. Yet much of the commentary on subculture refers to behavior. In my judgment this identification is unwise. Behavior is the result of the convergence of many forces. One should not assume, when the members of a group behave in similar ways, that cultural norms produce this result. Collective behavior theory and personality theory may also help to account for the similarities.

CONTRACULTURE

Failure to distinguish between role and subculture and vagueness in the concept of culture itself are not the only difficulties in the use of the idea of subculture. Perhaps more serious is the tendency to obscure, under this one term, two levels of explanation, one sociological and the other social-psychological, with a resulting failure to understand the causal forces at work. On few topics can one get wider agreement among sociologists than on the dangers of reductionism. If a psychologist attempts to explain social facts by psychological theories, we throw the book (probably Durkheim) at him; we emphasize the "fallacy of misplaced concreteness." In view of the widespread neglect of sociocultural factors in the explanation of behavior, this is a necessary task. It makes vitally important, however, keen awareness by sociologists that they also deal with an abstract model. Perhaps we can reverse Durkheim's dictum to say: Do not try to explain social psychological facts by sociological theories; or, more adequately, do not try to explain *behavior* (a product of the interaction of sociocultural and personality influences) by a sociological theory alone. Yablonsky has recently reminded us that an excessively sociological theory of gangs can result in our seeing a definite group structure and a clear pattern of norms where in fact there is a "near-group," with an imprecise definition of boundaries and limited agreement on norms.[9] Carelessly used, our concepts can obscure the facts we seek to understand.

To see the cultural element in delinquency or in the domination of an individual by his adolescent group, phenomena that on the surface are noncultural or even "anti-cultural," was a long step forward in their explanation. But it is also necessary to see the noncultural aspects of some "norms"—phenomena that on the surface seem thoroughly cultural. Our vocabulary needs to be rich enough to help us to deal with these differences. The tendency to use the same term to refer to phenomena that share *some* elements in common, disregarding important differences, is to be content with phyla names when we need also to designate genus and species.

To sharpen our analysis, I suggest the use of the term contraculture wherever the normative system of a group contains, as a primary element, a theme of conflict with the values of the total society, where personality variables are directly involved in the development and maintenance of the group's values, and wherever its norms can be understood only by reference to the relationships of the group to a surrounding dominant culture.[10] None of these criteria definitely separates contraculture from

---

[9]Lewis Yablonsky, "The Delinquent Gang as a Near-Group," *Social Problems*, 7 (Fall, 1959), pp. 108–117.

[10]By the noun in "contraculture" I seek to call attention to the normative aspects of the phenomena under study and by the qualifying prefix to call attention to the conflict aspects. Similar terms are occasionally found in the literature, but they are either defined only by their use in context or are used differently from the meaning assigned to contraculture in this paper. Harold D. Lasswell uses the term "countermores" to refer to "culture patterns which appeal mainly to the *id* . . ." (*World Politics and Personal Insecurity*, New York: McGraw-Hill, 1935, p. 64). He then designates "revolutionists, prostitutes, prisoners, obscene and subversive talk"—which scarcely suggest a clear analytic category. In *World Revolutionary Propaganda*, New York: Knopf, 1939, Lasswell and Dorothy Blumenstock discuss the use of inverse values as a revolutionary propaganda weapon and comment on the presumed vulnerability of deprived persons to the countermores stressed in this propaganda. In *Power and Society*, New Haven: Yale University Press, 1950, p. 49, Lasswell uses the term somewhat differently: "*Countermores* are culture traits symbolized by the group as deviations from the mores, and yet are expected to occur." A certain amount of bribery, for example, is "normal" "and must be included by the candid observer as part of culture."

At various points, Talcott Parsons more nearly approaches the meaning of the concept contraculture as used here, although more by implication than by direct definition, and without distinguishing it from the concept of subculture. Referring to the ideological aspects of a subculture, he writes: "In such cases of an open break with the value-system and ideology of the wider society we may speak of a 'counter-ideology.' " (*The Social System*, Glencoe, Ill.: Free Press, 1951, p. 355.) And later: "If, however, the culture of the deviant group, like that of the delinquent gang, remains a 'counter-culture' it is difficult to find the bridges by which it can acquire influence over wider circles" (p. 522). It is not clear from these uses how counter-ideology and counter-culture are to be defined;

subculture because each is a continuum. Subsocieties fall along a range with respect to each criterion. The values of most subcultures probably conflict in some measure with the larger culture. In a contraculture, however, the conflict element is central; many of the values, indeed, are specifically contradictions of the values of the dominant culture. Similarly, personality variables are involved in the development and maintenance of all cultures and subcultures, but usually the influence of personality is by way of variations around a theme that is part of the culture. In a contraculture, on the other hand, the theme itself expresses the tendencies of the persons who compose it. Finally, the norms of all subcultures are doubtless affected in some degree by the nature of the relationship with the larger culture. A subculture, as a pure type, however, does not require, for its understanding, intensive analysis of interaction with the larger culture; that is, its norms are not, to any significant degree, a product of that interaction. But a contraculture can be understood only by giving full attention to the interaction of the group which is its bearer with the larger society. It is one thing to say that the subculture of the rural, lower-class Negro encourages slow, inefficient work. It is another thing to say, with Charles S. Johnson, that such a norm represents "pseudo-ignorant malingering," a contracultural way of describing the same phenomenon. Johnson stressed the conflict element, the extent to which the norm was a product of interaction of white and Negro. There is certainly value in emphasizing the subcultural source of some of the values of southern Negroes. Against racist views or individual explanations, the sociologist opposes the subcultural: If they strive less, have different sexual mores, or otherwise vary from standards of the dominant society, it is in part because they have been socialized in accordance with different norms. But this is not enough, for their similar behavior may be interpreted in part as a shared response to a frustrating environment.

Empirically, subcultural and contracultural influences may be mixed, of course. Delinquency and adolescent behavior almost certainly manifest both influences. The need, however, is to develop a clean analytic distinction between the two in order to interpret the wide variations in their mixture.

ADOLESCENT SUBCULTURE AND CONTRACULTURE

The utility of the distinction between contraculture and subculture can be tested by applying it to several research problems where the concept

---

but the important place Parsons gives to the element of ambivalence in his use of the concept subculture suggests that he has in mind something similar to our concept of contraculture in his use of these various terms. (See *ibid.*, p. 286.)

of subculture has been widely used. There is an extensive literature that interprets the behavior of adolescents substantially in these terms.[11] In the words of Havighurst and Taba: "Recent studies of adolescents have emphasized the fact that boys and girls in their teens have a culture of their own with moral standards and with moral pressures behind those standards. This culture has been called the 'adolescent peer culture.'"[12] Or Riesman: "All the morality is the group's. Indeed, even the fact that it is a morality is concealed by the confusing notion that the function of the group is to have fun, to play. . . ."[13] A close reading of the literature on adolescent culture reveals at least four different levels of interpretation, often only partially distinguished:

1. There is a cultural level, in which the roles of adolescent boys and girls are described, or the specialties (in Linton's sense) are designated. There is no reason to introduce concepts other than role or specialty to refer to norms that are generally accepted by elders and youths alike as appropriate to youth.

2. On the subcultural level, there are norms that manifest some separate system of values accepted within the adolescent group. These norms are not part of the role of youth. In part they are unknown to the elders; in part they conflict with standards accepted by the elders. They are learned, not by socialization in the total society, but by interaction within the sub-society of youth. Thus interests, games, speech·patterns, and aesthetic tastes may be communicated among an age-group with little reference to the larger culture.

3. There are currents of fashion or of other collective behavior that sweep through an adolescent group, strongly influencing the behavior of its members.[14] Although it is difficult to distinguish fashion from culture—many empirical phenomena have aspects of both—it is wise to keep them apart conceptually. This is not always done. The terminology of Riesman is closer to that of fashion than of culture, but the net impression of his analysis is that he is thinking of control by the peer group

---

[11]See Talcott Parsons, *Essays in Sociological Theory Pure and Applied*, Glencoe, Ill.: Free Press, 1949, Chapter 5; Howard Becker, *German Youth: Bond or Free*, New York: Oxford, 1946; S. N. Eisenstadt, *From Generation to Generation: Age Groups and the Social Structure*, Glencoe, Ill.: Free Press, 1956; David Riesman *et al.*, *The Lonely Crowd*, New Haven: Yale University Press, 1950; R. J. Havighurst and Hilda Taba, *Adolescent Character and Personality*, New York: Wiley, 1949; Kingsley Davis, "The Sociology of Parent-Youth Conflict," *American Sociological Review*, 5 (August, 1940), pp. 523–534; Ralph Linton, "Age and Sex Categories," *American Sociological Review*, 7 (October, 1942), pp. 589–603; Joseph R. Gusfield, "The Problem of Generations in an Organizational Structure," *Social Forces*, 35 (May, 1957), pp. 323–330. For some contradictory evidence, see W. A. Westley and Frederick Elkin, "The Protective Environment and Adolescent Socialization," *Social Forces*, 35 (March, 1957), pp. 243–249; and Elkin and Westley, "The Myth of Adolescent Culture," *American Sociological Review*, 20 (December, 1955), pp. 680–684.

[12]*Op. cit.*, p. 35.

[13]*Op cit.*, p. 72.

[14]See Harold Finestone, "Cats, Kicks, and Color," *Social Problems*, 5 (July, 1957), pp. 3–13. Here the "cat" among some Negroes is seen as "the personal counterpart of an expressive social movement."

primarily as a cultural phenomenon.[15] And the sentence following the one quoted above from Havighurst and Taba reads: "Boys and girls, desiring the approval of their age mates, follow the fashions of the peer culture in morals, dress, and speech. . . ." If the peer group influence stems from fashion, then strictly speaking it is not culture. The two differ to some degree in their origins, their functions, and their consequences.[16]

4. Many analyses of the control exercised by a youth group over its members employ the *concept* of contraculture, although the terminology and the assumptions are often those of subculture or culture. There is emphasis on the cross-pressures which young people feel: they want to be adults, yet fear to leave the securities of childhood; they experience contradictory adult treatment—a demand for grownup behavior here, the prevention of it there; ambiguity of self-image leads to efforts to prove oneself a full-fledged adult; there is sexual frustration. The peer group may help one to struggle with these cross-pressures, as described by Parsons: "Perhaps the best single point of reference for characterizing the youth culture lies in its contrast with the dominant pattern of the adult male role. By contrast with emphasis on responsibility in this role, the orientation of the youth culture is more or less specifically irresponsible."[17] This irresponsibility cannot be understood simply as another cultural norm, as part of the "role" of youth, although these are Parsons' terms. It must be studied in the context of strain, of role ambiguity. Some sociologists explain this irresponsibility as merely a manifestation of the youth culture, thus obscuring the personality factors also involved. The description and analysis of an adolescent subculture, to be sure, are an important contribution to the sociology of youth. Many adolescents spend a great deal of time in groups that sustain norms different from those of the adult world; and adults often respond to the behavior that follows these norms in an "ethnocentric" way. To rely on a subcultural explanation alone, however, is to disregard the emergent quality of many of the standards and to minimize the fact that they are often in direct conflict with adult standards (which most adolescents themselves will soon accept).

This sharp conflict of values requires explanation. Parsons states the facts clearly: "Negatively, there is a strong tendency to repudiate interests in adult things, and to feel at least a certain recalcitrance to the

---

[15]See Riesman, *op. cit.*, esp. Chapter 3, "A Jury of Their Peers."

[16]The desirability of keeping distinct the analytic concepts of culture and collective behavior, including fashion, cannot be elaborated here. See Herbert Blumer, "Collective Behavior," in A. M. Lee, editor, *Principles of Sociology*, New York: Barnes and Noble, 1951; Ralph H. Turner and Lewis M. Killian, *Collective Behavior*, Englewood Cliffs, N. J.: Prentice-Hall, 1957; Edward Sapir, "Fashion," *Encyclopedia of the Social Sciences*, New York: Macmillan, 1931, Vol. 6, pp. 139–144; Georg Simmel, "Fashion," *American Journal of Sociology*, 62 (May, 1957), pp. 541–558.

[17]Parsons, *op cit. Essays . . .* , p. 92.

pressure of adult expectations and disciplines. . . . Thus the youth culture is not only, as is true of the curricular aspects of formal education, a matter of age status as such but also shows signs of being a product of tensions in the relationship of younger people and adults."[18] At several other points Parsons develops the "reaction" theme and later uses the concept of "reaction-formation."[19] Should these various phenomena be subsumed under the concept of culture? It is one thing for a society to train its youth to certain ways of behaving. It is quite another for a youth group to develop inverse values in an effort to struggle with role ambiguities and strains. The adolescent may experience both as normative sanctions; but that should scarcely lead the social analyst to disregard their differences. I suggest the term contraculture in order to indicate the normative *and* the conflict aspects of this type of situation.

DELINQUENT CONTRACULTURE

The usefulness of separating subcultural and contracultural influences is seen particularly clearly in the analysis of delinquency and of criminality generally. Perhaps in no other field were there more substantial gains in understanding made possible by the introduction of a sociological point of view to supplement and to correct individualistic and moralistic interpretations. There is little need to review the extensive literature, from *Delinquent Gangs* to *Delinquent Boys,* to establish the importance of the normative element in criminal and delinquent behavior. It is a mistake, however, to try to stretch a useful concept into a total theory. A "complex-adequate" analysis[20] may seem less sharp and definitive than one based on one factor, but it is likely to be far more useful. Cohen's excellent work,[21] although labelled as a study of the culture of the gang, does not overlook the psychogenic sources of delinquency. In fact, his explanation of the origins of the subculture (contraculture) and its functions for the lower class male makes clear that the norms of the gang are not learned, accepted, and taught in the same way that we learn what foods to eat, what clothes to wear, what language to speak. The very existence of the gang is a sign, in part, of blocked ambition. Because tensions set in motion by this blockage cannot be resolved by achievement of dominant values, such values are repressed, their importance denied, counter-values affirmed. The gang member is often ambivalent. Thwarted in his desire to achieve higher status by the criteria of the dominant

---

[18]*Ibid.*, pp. 92–93.

[19]See *ibid.*, pp. 101–102, 189–190, 342–345, 355.

[20]See Robin M. Williams, Jr., "Continuity and Change in Sociological Study," *American Sociological Review,* 23 (December, 1958), pp. 619–633.

[21]Albert K. Cohen, *Delinquent Boys,* Glencoe, Ill.: Free Press, 1955.

society, he accepts criteria he can meet; but the reaction-formation in this response is indicated by the content of the delinquent norms—non-utilitarian, malicious, and negativistic, in Cohen's terms. This negative polarity represents the need to repress his own tendencies to accept the dominant cultural standards. This is not to say that the values of the gang cannot be explained partially by cultural analysis, by some extension of the idea that "the mores can make anything right." But I suggest that Cohen's multiple-factor analysis might have been clearer, and less subject to misinterpretation, had he introduced the concept of contraculture alongside the concept of subculture. One reviewer, for example, completely disregards the "negative polarity" theme:

> In an overall summary, cultural delinquency is a phenomenon of culture, society, and sociocultural experience. It is a positive thing: members of the several social classes are socialized, but there is a differential content in the socialization. Delinquency is not a negative thing; it is not a result of the breakdown of society, nor of the failure to curb criminal instincts, nor of the failure of the family, the church, or the school. The same set of concepts, the same social processes, and the same set of logical assumptions account for both delinquency and lawfulness. Since delinquency is of this character, it is unnecessary to invent any pathology to account for it.[22]

This statement neither adequately represents Cohen's thesis nor encourages us to explore a number of important questions: Why do only some of those who are exposed to the delinquent "subculture" learn it?[23] Why do those who follow the subculture often manifest ambivalence and guilt feelings?[24] Why do many of the same patterns of behavior occur in areas and among groups where the presence of the subculture is much less clear (middle-class delinquency)?[25] What is the significance of the fact that the delinquent subculture is not only different from but in part at least a reversal of the values of the dominant culture? The use of a purely subcultural model of analysis discourages or even prevents the raising of these questions and thus precludes adequate answers to them.

Cohen and Short have dealt with several of these issues by suggesting the need for a typology. Specifically for the study of delinquency, they propose five types of subcultures: the parent male (the central pattern described in *Delinquent Boys*), the conflict-oriented, the drug addict, the

---

[22]Frank Hartung, in a review of *Delinquent Boys, American Sociological Review*, 20 (December, 1955), p. 752.

[23]See Solomon Kobrin, "The Conflict of Values in Delinquency Areas," *American Sociological Review*, 16 (October, 1951), pp. 653–661; Alex Inkeles, "Personality and Social Structure," in Robert K. Merton *et al.*, editors, *Sociology Today*, New York: Basic Books, 1959, p. 254.

[24]See Gresham M. Sykes and David Matza, "Techniques of Neutralization: A Theory of Delinquency," *American Sociological Review*, 22 (December, 1957), pp. 664–670.

[25]John I. Kitsuse and David C. Dietrick, "*Delinquent Boys:* A Critique," *American Sociological Review*, 24 (April, 1959), pp. 208–215.

semi-professional theft, and the middle-class subcultures.[26] Although the criteria of classification are not entirely clear, these categories are primarily descriptive. The concept of contraculture might be added to this list as a type of subculture, if the one distinctive criterion used to designate a subculture is the presence in a subsociety of a normative system that separates it from the total society. Such a procedure does not seem, however, to produce an adequate taxonomy. If the shift is made from description to analysis, or from an interest in the content of norms to their etiology, an important difference emerges between subculture and contraculture: the one set of norms derives from standard socialization in a subsociety; the other stems from conflict and frustration in the experience of those who share many of the values of the whole society but are thwarted in their efforts to achieve those values.

It should be stressed once more that these are analytic concepts, no one of which is adequate to handle the empirical variations of delinquent behavior. Failure to recognize the abstract quality of our conceptual tools leads to unnecessary disagreements. When Miller describes the "Lower Class Culture as a Generating Milieu of Gang Delinquency," for example, he points to an important series of influences that derive from the value system of the lower-class community.[27] In his effort to emphasize this aspect of the etiology of delinquency, however, he tends to overlook the kind of evidence reported by Sykes and Matza, Cohen, Finestone, Yablonsky, the McCords, and others concerning collective behavior and personality variables.[28] Surely the evidence is now rich enough for us to state definitively that delinquency is a multi-variable product. The task ahead is not to prove that it stems largely from cultural or subcultural or contracultural influences, but to spell out the conditions under which these and other factors will be found in various empirical mixtures.[29]

---

[26]See Albert Cohen and James Short, "Research in Delinquent Subcultures," *The Journal of Social Issues,* 14, 3 (1958), pp. 20–37.

[27]Walter B. Miller, "Lower Class Culture as a Generating Milieu of Gang Delinquency," *The Journal of Social Issues,* 14, 3 (1958), pp. 5–19.

[28]In addition to the studies of Sykes and Matza, Cohen, Finestone, and Yablonsky cited above, see William McCord and Joan McCord, *Origins of Crime, A New Evaluation of the Cambridge-Somerville Youth Study,* New York: Columbia University Press, 1959.

[29]In a recent manuscript, Sykes and Matza suggest that delinquent behavior can profitably be studied as an exaggerated expression of certain "subterranean values" of the dominant society (the search for excitement, the use of "pull" to get by without too much work, and aggression). This idea deserves careful study. The main research task is to discover the conditions which promote selective and exaggerated attention to these values at the cost of neglect of the more prominent "public" values. It seems likely that this task will lead to the incorporation of the "subterranean values" thesis into the larger complex of theories of delinquency. The thesis raises a question of terminology in connection with the present paper: At what point does exaggerated emphasis on a value become a counter-value by virtue of the exaggeration? *Some* cultural support can be found in a complex society for many patterns of behavior that are not fully valued. A society may accept or even applaud a pattern that is used to a limited degree while condemning its extravagant use. And the meaning of the pattern in the life of the individual when found in culturally approved degree differs from what it is when the pattern becomes a dominant theme. To discover why some subterranean values are raised into a style of life, therefore, requires more than cultural analysis. (See David Matza and Gresham M. Sykes, "Juvenile Delinquency and Subterranean Values," *American Sociological Review* 26 (October 1961), pp. 712–719.

CONTRACULTURE ASPECTS OF CLASS AND OCCUPATION

The same admixture of the concepts of culture, subculture, and contra-culture is found in the extensive literature on occupations and classes. Doubtless all three forces are found in many instances, and the research task is to untangle their various influences. It may stretch the meaning of the term too far to speak of the *position* of the "middle-class member," with its culturally designated role specifications; although in relatively stable societies the usage seems appropriate. In such societies, many of the rights and obligations of various status levels are culturally defined. In more mobile class systems, however, subcultural and contraculture norms became important. Our understanding of the American class system has certainly been deepened in the last twenty years by the descriptions of differences, among classes, in value perspectives, time orientations, levels of aspiration, leisure-time styles, and child rearing practices.[30]

The introduction of the concept of subculture has helped to avoid class derived biasses in the interpretation of the wide variations in these phenomena. In class analysis as in the study of deviations, however, there may be some over-compensation in the effort to eliminate the distortions of a middle-class and often rural perspective.[31] There is evidence to suggest that differences between classes are based less upon different values and norms than the subcultural approach suggests. The "innovations" of lower-class members, to use Merton's term, are not simply subcultural acts defined as innovative by middle-class persons. They are in part responses to a frustrating situation. They are efforts to deal with the disjunction of means and ends. When the disjunction is reduced, the variations in value and behavior are reduced. Thus Rosen found, "surprisingly," that Negroes in the Northeast made higher scores on an "achievement value" test than his description of Negro "culture" led him to expect. This may indicate that the low achievement response is less the result of a subcultural norm than a protest against a difficult situation. If the situation improves, the achievement value changes.[32] Stephenson's dis-

---

[30]Of the many studies in this area, see Charles McArthur, "Personality Differences Between Middle and Upper Classes," *Journal of Abnormal and Social Psychology*, 50 (March, 1955), pp. 247–254; Melvin L. Kohn, "Social Class and Parental Values," *American Journal of Sociology*, 64 (January, 1959), pp. 337–351; A. B. Hollingshead and Fredrick C. Redlich, *Social Class and Mental Illness*, New York: Wiley, 1958; Clyde R. White, "Social Class Differences in the Uses of Leisure," *American Journal of Sociology*, 61 (September, 1955), pp. 145–151; John A. Clausen and Melvin L. Kohn, "The Ecological Approach in Social Psychiatry," *American Journal of Sociology*, 60 (September, 1954), pp. 140–151; A. B. Hollingshead, *Elmtown's Youth*, New York: Wiley, 1949; Louis Schneider and Sverre Lysgaard, "The Deferred Gratification Pattern: A Preliminary Study," *American Sociological Review*, 18 (April, 1953), pp. 142–149; Urie Bronfenbrenner, "Socialization and Social Class Through Time and Space," in Eleanor E. Maccoby *et al.*, editors, *Readings in Social Psychology*, New York: Holt, 1958, pp. 400–425.

[31]C. Wright Mills, "The Professional Ideology of Social Pathologists," *American Journal of Sociology*, 49 (September, 1943), pp. 165–180.

[32]Bernard C. Rosen, "Race, Ethnicity, and the Achievement Syndrome," *American Sociological Review*, 24 (February, 1959), pp. 47–60. It is highly important, in aspiration studies, to compare,

covery that occupational plans of lower-class youth are considerably below those of higher-class youth, but that their aspirations are only slightly lower, bears on this same point. His data suggest that the classes differ not only in norms, but also in opportunity.[33] Differences in behavior, therefore, are only partly a result of subcultural contrasts. The lower educational aspirations of lower-class members are also found to be in part situationally induced, not simply normatively induced. When the situation changes, values and behavior change, as Mulligan found in his study of the response of the sons of blue-collar workers to the educational opportunities of the GI Bill, and as Wilson reports in his investigation of the lower-class boys attending higher-class schools and upper-class boys attending lower-class schools.[34]

In short, our thinking about differences in behavior among social classes will be sharpened if we distinguish among those differences that derive from role influences, those based on subcultural variations, and those that express contracultural responses to deprivation. The proportions will vary from society to society; the research task is to specify the conditions under which various distributions occur. One would expect, to propose one hypothesis, to find more contracultural norms among lower-class members of an open society than in a similar group in a closed society.

The interpretation of differential behavior among the members of various occupational categories can also be strengthened by the distinctions made above. Here the contrast between role and subculture is especially useful. The role of a teacher consists of the rights and duties that *integrate* him into a system of expected and established relationships with others. The teaching subculture, on the other hand, insofar as it exists, *separates* teachers from the cultural world of others. It is either unknown to others or, if known, a source of disagreement and perhaps of conflict with others. There are also contracultural aspects of some occupational styles of life. In interpreting the differences between the values of jazz musicians and "squares," for example, Becker writes: "their rejection of commercialism in music and squares in social life was part of the casting aside of the total American culture by men who could enjoy privileged status but who were unable to achieve a satisfactory personal adjustment within it."[35] Their style of life, in other words, can be understood only by supple-

not absolute levels, but the extent of aspiration above the existing level of individuals or their families. A low absolute target for lower-class members may require a larger *reach* than a higher target for middle-class persons. See Leonard Reissman, "Levels of Aspiration and Social Class," *American Sociological Review,* 18 (June, 1953), pp. 233–242.

[33]Richard M. Stephenson, "Mobility Orientation and Stratification of 1,000 Ninth Graders," *American Sociological Review,* 22 (April, 1957), pp. 204–212.

[34]Raymond A. Mulligan, "Socio-Economic Background and College Enrollment," *American Sociological Review,* 16 (April, 1951), pp. 188–196; Alan B. Wilson, "Residential Segregation of Social Classes and Aspirations of High School Boys," *American Sociological Review,* 24 (December, 1959), pp. 836–845.

[35]Howard S. Becker, "The Professional Dance Musician and His Audience," *American Journal of Sociology,* 57 (September, 1951), pp. 136–144.

menting the cultural and subcultural dimension with the conflict theme. Cameron develops the same point. Although he makes no use of the term subculture, he describes the differentiating norms of the dance-band group, presumably a result of the "esoteric" aspects of their art, the differences in their time schedule, and the like. But he also describes the *contra* aspects of some of the norms, and suggests that they derive from the fact that early recruitment ties the jazz musician to the adolescence problem.[36]

CONCLUSION

Poorly defined terms plague research in many areas, particularly in the specification of relationships between sociological and social psychological levels of analysis. Thus "anomie" is still used to refer both to a social structural fact and to a personality fact, although this confusion is gradually being reduced. "Role" may refer, alternately, to rights and duties prescribed for the occupants of a position or to individual performance of that position. And subculture, I have suggested, is used to designate both the traditional norms of a sub-society and the emergent norms of a group caught in a frustating and conflict-laden situation. This paper indicates that there are differences in the origin, function, and perpetuation of traditional and emergent norms, and suggests that the use of the concept contraculture for the latter might improve sociological analysis.

Hypotheses to guide the study of subculture can most profitably be derived from a general theory of culture. As an illustration, it may be hypothesized that a subculture will appear, in the first instance, as a result of mobility or an extension of communication that brings groups of different cultural background into membership in the same society, followed by physical or social isolation or both that prevents full assimilation.

Hypotheses concerning contracultures, on the other hand, can best be derived from social psychological theory—from the study of collective behavior, the frustration-aggression thesis, or the theory of group formation. One might hypothesize, for example, that under conditions of deprivation and frustration of major values (in a context where the deprivation is obvious because of extensive communication with the dominant group), and where value confusion and weak social controls obtain, contracultural norms will appear. One would expect to find, according to these propositions, many subcultural values among southern rural Negroes. Among first and second generation urban Negroes, however, one would expect an increase in contracultural norms. Both groups are de-

---

[36]W. B. Cameron, "Sociological Notes on the Jam Session," *Social Forces,* 33 (December, 1954), pp. 177–182.

prived, but in the urban situation there is more "value leakage" from the dominant group, more value confusion, and weakened social controls.[37]

The subculture of the sociologist requires sophistication about the full range of human behavior. This desideratum has led to the proposition that the vast diversity of norms believed in and acted upon by the members of a modern society is not a sign of value confusion and breakdown but rather an indication that urban life brings into one system of interaction persons drawn from many cultural worlds. One unanticipated consequence of the sociological subculture may be that we exaggerate the normative insulation and solidarity of these various worlds. An important empirical question concerns the extent and results of their interaction.

---

[37]There are numerous alternative ways in which the protest against deprivation can be expressed. Delinquency and drug addiction often have a contracultural aspect; but somewhat less clearly, political and religious movements among disprivileged groups may also invert the values of the influential but inaccessible dominant group. Thus the concept of contraculture may help us to understand, for example, the Garveyite movement, the Ras Tafari cult, and some aspects of the value schemes of lower-class sects. (See, e.g., Liston Pope, *Millhands and Preachers,* New Haven: Yale University Press, 1942; and George E. Simpson, "The Ras Tafari Movement in Jamaica: A Study of Race and Class Conflict," *Social Forces,* 34 (December, 1955), pp. 167–170.)

PART TWO: CONFLICT AS AN EXPLANATION OF CRIMINALITY

Donald Cressey, in discussing Sellin's conceptualization of "cultural conflict," points out that this notion is timebound. That is, in the 1930s social scientists viewed the immigrant population as a primary source of criminal behavior (see Mills, 1943). In this milieu, conflict was seen as the product of a disparity between the legal norms of a host or contiguous culture and those norms to which a migrating group had been socialized. Native Americans and immigrants had different values. For example, Italian-Americans saw wine as a food staple during Prohibition, while native Protestant "drys" objected that the beverage was the tool of the Devil.

While this interpretation of culture conflict unquestionably represents the major thrust of Sellin's statements, Cressey discusses a neglected but seemingly more useful theme of Sellin; namely, that conflict may also arise as a society becomes more complex or differentiated:

> Culture conflicts are the natural outgrowth of processes of social differentiation, which produce an infinity of social groupings, each with its own definitions of life situations, its own interpretations of social relationships, its own ignorance or misunderstanding of the social values of other groups. The transformation of a culture from a homogeneous and well-integrated type to a heterogeneous and disintegrated type is therefore accompanied by an increase of conflict situations (Sellin, 1938:66).

This is in keeping with the ideas of "order" or "consensus" theorists such as Émile Durkheim who saw technology creating more specialized occupations where individuals exhibited increasingly diverse normative systems. The norms of blue collar workers, for example, and rock and roll singers are not the same. Neither are they totally dissimilar. It is in the realm of disagreement that conflict may arise. Lewis Coser (1956:36) observes:

> It remains true that status groups within the American system often regard each other with invidious or hostile feelings. It is also true that the structure of the systems is maintained partly by these reciprocal antagonisms which preserve graduations of status. Nevertheless, members of the lower strata often emulate the higher, and aspire to membership in higher strata.

However generously one interprets Sellin's position in terms of "normative conflict," it rests on a fundamental assumption that crime results from opposing value systems. As Korn and McCorkle (1959:279–80) point out, Sellin unfortunately fails to distinguish between values as means and as goals. If the goals are different for various groups the occurrence of conflict appears unlikely since there is no competition for limited resources. More logically conflict would emerge when different groups are competing for identical but restricted goals. But even assuming the existence of such competition, the notion of opposing value systems, as suggested by Sellin, is of questionable explanatory usefulness:

> In construing the conflict between the criminal and the noncriminal as lying in the realm of ultimate cultural values, the proponents of the culture-conflict theory may have mistaken a conflict of interests for a conflict of basic principles. The fact that society at large rationalizes its opposition to crime in terms of moral principles tends to foster this confusion. Nevertheless, the widespread existence of white collar crime and other forms of deception and corruption in the general culture serves to weaken the validity of these rationalizations as a true basis of differentiation. In the end, the actual differences between the shrewd business operator and the thief may have less to do with actual differences in procedure and more with differential patterns of social tolerance and indignation—patterns that enable the shrewd manipulator to move through the mine fields of social defense without setting off explosions (Korn and McCorkle, 1959:281).

Two phrases in the above quotation, "conflict of interests" and "differential patterns of social tolerance," foretell the direction that later criminological conflict theorists were to take. The emphasis was to shift toward the political nature of law, and the behavior of the "criminal" was to become of secondary importance to the legislation and enforcement of rules predicated on the influence of interest groups.

The conflict perspective in criminological research has only recently come to the fore. Fourteen years ago George Vold began to explore this area. Later Austin Turk and Richard Quinney adopted a similar approach. Like Sellin, Vold is primarily interested in explaining the *sources of behavior* in violation of existing criminal codes. But consistent with the writings of Quinney and Turk, his interpretation is within a political framework: Criminal behavior stems from the ideological orientations of "minority groups" and from struggles between interest groups to obtain concessions or a power advantage. Vold (1968:37) succinctly restates this theme in a later work:

> Collision and conflict occur when they [groups] become competitive for members or for power and influence. Actions taken in defense of group self-interest to protect place, position, and influence constitute the background for the violent behavior that not infrequently defies lawful authority and tends to become criminal.

Vold also recognizes that the law itself is a political product—legislation and its enforcement occur within the context of a struggle between interest groups seeking to enlist the aid of the state to protect or further their interests. This interpretation serves to shift the focus from the etiology of "criminal behavior" to the question of why behavior, whatever its source or cause, is "criminal." The importance of this distinction is not fully explored by Vold but it is a critical aspect of the writings of Turk and Quinney.

These authors utilize the conflict perspective to reject the order model of society (see Horton's article, chapter 1) and of law. They argue that criminal law is a political artifact stemming from power differentials among interest groups, not from what Hills (1971:3) calls "value consensus":

> Criminal laws reflect those societal values which transcend the immediate, narrow interests of various individuals and groups, expressing the social consciousness of the whole society.

In Chapter 7 Turk claims instead:

> Although some legal norms approximate the social norms of the collectivity, most legal norms will be seen by members of the collectivity as 'legal' only to the extent that the norm of deference to authority has been established.

And Quinney (Chapter 8) writes:

> By formulating criminal law . . . , some segments of society protect and perpetuate their own interests. Criminal definitions exist, therefore, because some segments of society are in conflict with others.

Thus, the contemporary conflict theorists presented here view criminality as an *ascribed status:* It is the result of a *criminalization process* by which individuals become labelled criminal. The purpose of Turk's article is to present in propositional form a theory of criminalization. It hypothesizes the conditions under which conflicts occur and the variables that contribute to the probabilities of criminalization.[1] Quinney's theory of the "social reality of crime" deals with these same issues in a more general manner. But his theory also reintroduces the concept of *behavior* as a part of the criminological conflict approach: Behavior labelled as criminal stems not only from conflicting values and interests but may also emerge as a consequence of the criminalization process itself.

The general propositions suggested by the selections in Part Two are:

1. Conflicts of interest are inherent in society.
2. The formulation and enforcement of criminal law are means by which the more powerful interest groups attempt to neutralize the less powerful.
3. The greater the conflict between interest groups, the more likely the more powerful groups are to rely on a criminalization process to neutralize their opponents.
4. The more extensive the use of the criminalization process the greater the likelihood that criminal behavior patterns will be reinforced.

REFERENCES

Coser, L., *The Functions of Social Conflict.* Glencoe, Ill.: Free Press, 1956.

Hills, S. L., *Crime, Power, and Morality: The Criminal-Law Process in the United States.* Scranton, Pa.: Chandler Publishing Co., 1971.

Korn, R. R., and L. W. McCorkle, *Criminology and Penology.* New York: Holt, Rinehart and Winston, Inc., 1964.

Mills, C. W., The Professional Ideology of Social Pathologists," *American Journal of Sociology* 49: 165–181 (September 1943).

Sellin, T., *Culture Conflict and Crime: A Report of the Subcommittee on Delinquency of the Committee on Personality and Culture.* New York: Social Science Research Council, 1938.

Turk, A. T., *Criminality and Legal Order.* Chicago: Rand McNally and Co., 1969.

Vold, G. B., "Social-Cultural Conflict and Criminality," in Marvin E. Wolfgang, ed., *Crime and Culture: Essays in Honor of Thorsten Sellin.* New York: John Wiley and Sons, Inc., 1968, pp. 33–41.

---

[1] A presentation of this theory in graphic rather than propositional form will be found in Turk (1969).

6. GROUP CONFLICT THEORY AS EXPLANATION OF CRIME

GEORGE VOLD

1. BASIC CONSIDERATIONS IN CONFLICT THEORY[1]

The social-psychological orientation for conflict theory rests on social interaction theories of personality formation and the "social process" conception of collective behavior.[2] Implicit to this view is the assumption that man always is a group-involved being whose life is both part of, and a product of his group associations. Implicit also is the view of society as a congeries of groups held together in a shifting but dynamic equilibrium of opposing group interests and efforts.[3]

This continuity of group interaction, the endless series of moves and counter-moves, of checks and cross checks, is the essential element in the concept of social process. It is this continuous ongoing of interchanging influence, in an immediate and dynamically maintained equilibrium, that gives special significance to the designation "collective behavior," as opposed to the idea of simultaneously behaving individuals.[4] It is this fluid flow of collective action that provides opportuntiy for a continuous possibility of shifting positions, of gaining or losing status, with the consequent need to maintain an alert defense of one's position, and also always with the ever-present and appealing chance of improving on one's status relationship. The end result is a more or less continuous struggle to maintain, or to defend, the place of one's own group in the interaction of

[1] The term *sociology of conflict* relates most directly to the writings of Georg Simmel and other sociologists of the 'formal school.' Conflict is one of the 'forms' of interaction, as distinguished from the 'content' of interaction; that is, the individual episodes of particular encounters which are always different and unique as to time and place, but tend to be alike in having a common 'form.' Hence, 'social conflict,' is said to be a universal form of interaction, while the specific episodes of particular wars or battles have all the peculiarities of definite time and place. Cf. *The Sociology of Georg Simmel,* trans. by and with an Introduction by Kurt H. Wolf, Free Press, Glencoe, Ill., 1950; also the translation from Simmel's *Soziologie* by Albion W. Small under the title, "The Sociology of Conflict," *American Journal of Sociology,* 9:490–501, 1903–4.

[2] Cf. Robert E. Park and Ernest W. Burgess, *Introduction to Science of Sociology,* University of Chicago Press, Chicago, 1924. "Competition," pp. 504–10; "Conflict," pp. 574–9; "Collective Behavior," pp. 865–74.

[3] Cf. Arthur F. Bentley, *The Process of Government,* University of Chicago Press, Chicago, 1908, "Social Pressures," pp. 258–96.

[4] R. E. Park and E. W. Burgess, op. cit., p. 865; also Muzafer Sherif, op. cit. ch. 5, "Properties of Group Situations," pp. 98–121.

groups, always with due attention to the possibility of improving its relative status position. Conflict is viewed, therefore, as one of the principal and essential social processes upon which the continuing ongoing of society depends.[5]

As social interaction processes grind their way through varying kinds of uneasy adjustment to a more or less stable equilibrium of balanced forces in opposition, the resulting condition of relative stability is what is usually called social order or social organization. But it is the adjustment, one to another, of the many groups of varying strengths and of different interests that is the essence of society as a functioning reality.

The normal principle of social organization is that groups are formed out of situations in which members have common interests and common needs that can be best furthered through collective action.[6] In other words, groups arise out of important needs of group members, and groups must serve the needs of the members or they soon wither away and disappear. New groups are therefore continuously being formed as new interests arise, and existing groups weaken ·and disappear when they no longer have a purpose to serve.[7]

Groups come into conflict with one another as the interests and purposes they serve tend to overlap, encroach on one another, and become competitive. In other words, conflicts between groups occur principally when the groups become competitive by attempting to operate in the same general field of interaction. There is never any serious conflict between groups whose operations can be channeled so that they perform satisfactorily without moving in on one another's territory of common interests and common purposes.[8]

The danger that any existing group must protect itself against, when in contact with any other group in the same area of interests and needs, is the ever-present one of being taken over, of being replaced. A group must always be in a position to defend itself in order to maintain its place and position in the world of constantly changing adjustments. The principal goal, therefore, of one group in contact with another, is to keep from being replaced. Where there is no problem of competition and replacement, there is little likelihood of serious intergroup conflict, be it between nations, races, religions, economic systems, labor unions, or any other type of group organization.

Groups become effective action units through the direction and coordination of the activities of their members. For the members, the ex-

---

[5]For a discussion of the relation between the principal social processes and the resulting social order, see R. E. Park and E. W. Burgess, op. cit., pp. 506–10.

[6]Cf. Albion W. Small, *General Sociology*, University of Chicago Press, Chicago, 1905, pp. 495–500.

[7]Cf. Charles H. Cooley, *Social Organization*, Scribner, New York, 1924, "Primary Aspects of Organization," pp. 3–57.

[8]Charles H. Cooley, op cit. "Hostile Feelings Between Classes," pp. 301–09.

perience of participation in group activity and the sharing of troubles and satisfactions operate to make the individual a group-conscious person. It is out of this experience background that group identification and group loyalty become psychological realities. The loyalty of the group member to his group is one of the most profoundly significant facts of social psychology, though there is no assured explanation of *why* the loyalty and identification develop. Both loyalty and identification tend to be emotionally toned attachments not closely related to any rational understanding the individual may have of the place or significance of a particular group in the general scheme of things.[9]

It has long been realized that conflict between groups tends to develop and intensify the loyalty of the group members to their respective groups.[10] This is clearly one of the important elements in developing *esprit de corps* and "group-mindedness" attitudes on the part of individual members. The individual is most loyal to the group for which he has had to fight the hardest, and to which he has had to give the greatest measure of self for the common end of group achievement.[11]

Nothing promotes harmony and self-sacrifice within the group quite as effectively as a serious struggle with another group for survival. Hence, patriotic feeling runs high in war time, and the more desperate the situation (short of collapse and the chaos of defeat and despair) in battle, the higher runs the feeling that nothing is too great a sacrifice for the national good. A group crisis, in which the member must stand up and be counted, is an age-old device for separating the men from the boys. It needs to be remembered that groups have always paid tribute to "service beyond the call of duty." Thus it is that some of our finest ideals of character and manhood are the offshoots of group conflict where the individual has had opportunity to serve the common purpose and not merely to serve his own selfish ends.[12]

The logical outcome of group conflict should be either, on the one hand, conquest and victory for one side with the utter defeat and destruction or subjugation for the other side; or, on the other hand, something less conclusive and decisive, a stalemate of compromise and withdrawal to terminate the conflict with no final settlement of the issues involved. It should be noted that, generally speaking, there is never any compromise with a position of weakness—the weak, as a rule, are quickly overwhelmed, subjugated to and integrated with the victors in some subordinate and inferior capacity. The group that will survive and avoid

[9]Muzafer Sherif, *An Outline of Social Psychology*, Harper, New York, 1948, ch. 13, "Adolescent Attitudes and Identification," pp. 314–38.

[10]Walter Bagehot, *Physics and Politics*, 1869, reprinted by Knopf, New York, 1948, "The Use of Conflict," pp. 44–84.

[11]Muzafer Sherif, op. cit., ch. 7, "The Formation of Group Standards or Norms, pp. 156–82.

[12]Ibid., ch. 12, "Ego-Involvement in Personal and Group Relationships," pp. 282–313; also ch. 16, "Men in Critical Situations," pp. 401–424.

having to go down in defeat is the one strong enough to force some compromise settlement of the issues in conflict. This general pattern has been a commonplace occurrence in the conflicts between national groups and also between political factions within the nation.[13]

2. CRIME AND THE CONFLICT PROCESS

The foregoing brief sketch of some of the elements involved in the conflicts of groups should be sufficient to alert the thoughtful reader to further applications of these general group relationships to more specific situations. For example, politics, as it flourishes in a democracy, is primarily a matter of finding practical compromises between antagonistic groups in the community at large.[14] The prohibitionist wishes to outlaw the manufacture and sale of alcoholic beverages; the distillers and brewers wish unrestricted opportunity to make and sell a product for which there is a genuine economic demand (i.e. "demand" in the sense of not only having a desire for the product but also having the ability to pay for it). The complicated collection of regulations that American communities know so well, including special taxes, special licensing fees and regulations, special inspections, and special rules for closing hours etc., are all part of the compromise settlement in the clash of these incompatible interests in the political organization of society.

As political groups line up against one another, they seek the assistance of the organized state to help them defend their "rights" and protect their interests. Thus the familiar cry "there ought to be a law" (to suppress the undesirable) is understandable as the natural recourse of one side or the other in a conflict situation. Yet for exactly the same reason such action has a necessary logical opposition which resists the proposed legislation. Whichever group interest can marshal the greatest number of votes will determine whether or not there is to be a new law to hamper and curb the interests of some opposition group.[15]

Suppose, for purposes of illustration, that a new law has been enacted by a normal, legal, legislative majority. Those who opposed it and fought it before adoption are understandably not in sympathy with its provisions, and do not take kindly to efforts at law enforcement. In other words, the whole political process of law making, law breaking, and law enforcement becomes a direct reflection of deep-seated and fundamental conflicts between interest groups and their more general struggles for the control of the police power of the state. Those who produce legislative majorities

---

[13]Cf. Park and Burgess, op. cit., p. 575; also Hadley Cantril, *The Psychology of Social Movements*, Wiley, New York, 1941, chs. 8 and 9, "The Nazi Party," pp. 210–70.

[14]Walter Bagehot, op. cit., chs. 3 and 4, "Nation-Making," pp. 85–160.

[15]E. H. Sutherland and Donald R. Cressey, *Principles of Criminology*, 5th ed., Lippincott, New York, 1955, ch. 1, "Criminology and the Criminal Law," pp. 3–22.

win control over the police power and dominate the policies that decide who is likely to be involved in violation of the law.[16]

The struggle between those who support the law and those who violate it existed in the community before there was legislative action; it was the basis for the battle in the legislature; it is then continued through the judicial proceedings of prosecution and trial; and it culminates eventually in the prison treatment of the violators by those who wish to have the law enforced. The principle of compromise from positions of strength operates at every stage of this conflict process. Hence, there is bargaining in the legislature to get the law passed; there is bargaining between prosecution and defense in connection with the trial; between prison officials and inmates; and between parole agent and parolee. This is the background for Sutherland's famous "sociological definition" of crime as a social situation, as a set of relationships rather than as an act of behavior under specific legal definition.[17]

3. CRIME AS MINORITY GROUP BEHAVIOR

Crime and delinquency as group behavior is a familiar topic in criminology that has long been observed and discussed. Shaw and McKay[18] reported that from 80 to 90 percent (depending on the offense) of 5,480 juvenile offenders before the Cook County Juvenile Court in 1928 had committed their offenses with one or more associates. The Gluecks reported that about 70 percent of their 1000 juvenile offenders[19] had had companions in crime; for their reformatory group of 500 older offenders[20] the proportion was nearly 60 percent. From their more recent and more carefully controlled study[21] the Gluecks reported that nearly all delinquents, in contrast to only a very few non-delinquents, preferred to chum with, or pal around with, other delinquents, while more than one-half of the delinquents, as compared with less than 1 percent of the non-delinquents, were members of gangs.

Such statistics, however, report only the formal aspects of the extent to which prosecution has become aware of shared experience and group participation in situations that the criminal law ordinarily prefers to view as individual wrongdoing, and a matter for whch the indivdual should be held responsible. From a more general point of view, however, this prevalence of collective action in crime may reasonably be interpreted as

[16]E. H. Sutherland, "Crime and the Conflict Process," *Journal of Juvenile Research*, 13:38–48, 1929.
[17]Sutherland and Cressey, op. cit., p. 15.
[18]C. R. Shaw and H. D. McKay, "Social Factors in Juvenile Delinquency," *Report on the Causes of Crime*, vol II, no. 13, of the Report of the National Commission on Law Observance and Law Enforcement, Washington, D. C., June 26, 1931, pp. 192–98.
[19]Sheldon and Eleanor Glueck, *One Thousand Juvenile Delinquents*, Harvard University Press, Cambridge, 1934, pp. 100–01.
[20]Sheldon and Eleanor Glueck, *Five Hundred Criminal Careers*, Knopf, New York, 1930, p. 152.
[21]Sheldon and Eleanor Glueck, *Unraveling Juvenile Delinquency*, Commonwealth Fund, New York, 1950, p. 278.

an indication of the banding together for protection and strength of those who in some way are at odds with organized society and with the police forces maintained by that society. The delinquent boys' gang is clearly a "minority group" in the sense that it cannot achieve its objectives through regular channels, making use of, and relying for protection on, the police powers of the state.

The gang, therefore, resorts to direct action with the typical social-psychological reaction of a conflict group (e.g., loyalty to group and leaders, subordination of individual wishes to group ends, adherence to an "approved code" of values and behavior etc.) which has purposes to achieve that are at variance with those set up for it by the elements in control of the official police powers of the state.[22] The juvenile gang, in this sense, is nearly always a "minority group," out of sympathy with and in more or less direct opposition to the rules and regulations of the dominant majority; that is, the established world of adult values and power. The police ordinarily represent the power and values of the adult world, while the gang seeks to operate to get benefits and advantages not permitted it under the adult code. When, in the course of time, members of a gang become adults, many of the gang activities are sometimes continued under the color of a political party name (e.g., as a "Young Republican Club" or a "Fourth Ward Democratic Club" etc.) with political influence now giving it police protection and support, since it now is part of the majority group in control of power.[23]

What happens to members of a minority group with a strong ideological orientation out of sympathy with the established majority pattern is well illustrated by the experience of "conscientious objectors" in time of war.[24] While not a very large proportion of those in prison, the actual numbers nevertheless added up to a considerable total for the United States in World War II. In the war years, 1940–45, there were over 5000 persons who served prison sentences in federal institutions for the "crime" of having convictions which led them to refuse to participate in any way in war activity. This was in addition to the much larger number (over 9000) who registered under the draft as "conscientious objectors" but accepted assignment to non-military service of some kind.[25]

---

[22]Cf. William F. Whyte, *Street Corner Society*, University of Chicago Press, Chicago, 1943; also Solomon Kobrin, "The Conflict of Values in Delinquency Areas," *American Sociological Review*, 16:653–62, October 1951.

[23]These are well-documented facts in the celebrated studies of big city gangs such as Frederick Thrasher, *The Gang*, 2nd ed. rev., University of Chicago Press, Chicago, 1936; Herbert Asbury, *The Gangs of New York*, Knopf, New York, 1928; and his more recent study of Chicago—*Gem of the Prairie*, Knopf, New York, 1940.

[24]A well-documented and reasonably objective account of the prison aspects of this problem for the United States for World War II may be found in Mulford Q. Sibley and Ada Wardlaw, *Conscientious Objectors in Prison, 1940–1945*, The Pacifist Research Bureau, Ithaca, New York, 1945.

[25]See Mabel Elliott, *Crime in Modern Society*, Harper, New York, 1952, pp. 179–97, for a good brief account of the main facts relating to the political criminal and the conscientious objector in the United States in and since World War II.

The full import of the social-psychological fact of minority group orientation, which remains utterly oblivious to and unmoved by continuous contact with an "out-group" majority officially dedicated to changing it, is made abundantly clear in an interesting account of prison experiences by one of the conscientious objectors who served a sentence in the federal institution at Lewisburg, Pennsylvania. *The Diary of a Self-Made Convict* by Alfred Hassler[26] is the story of prison life by a skilled professional writer who, both before and after imprisonment, devoted himself to the task of writing and editorial work for the Fellowship of Reconciliation. His book is intended as an account of the realities of prison life, as lived in a "good" modern prison that practices all the "gimmicks" of contemporary penology. Its intention is not in any way to deal with the problem of the conscientious objector, or with his ideas. Yet the book is completely revealing in its portrayal of the psychological orientation of the author. It is obvious throughout his account of the day to day happenings of prison life that he never had any question in his mind but that his own particular role in becoming a convict was wholly and completely honorable. His title is equally revealing—a "self-made" convict; that is, a convict by his own free choice, a choice of which he obviously was proud.

This is another demonstration of the simple, stubborn fact that minority group members, whose criminal behavior has been consistent with minority group views, are not changed easily by coercive measures applied by the majority group. Every prisoner-of-war stockade in the world testifies to this same general ineffectiveness of majority group pressures on the attitudes and loyalties of minority group members whose "crimes" consist of the fact that they have been overwhelmed in the battle for power. The failure of court conviction, sentence, and prison experience to change Hassler's general self-satisfaction with the rightness of his own course of action is by no means unique with conscientious objectors. It is not only the convinced pacifist who rejects the moral justification for his conviction or who constructs a rationale of his own course of action such that he can remain loyal and faithful to his minority group ideology. Criminals of all kinds who have significant group identification to bolster their morale react in very much the same manner. Well-intentioned efforts at rehabilitation, in these cases, are usually no more effective.

This kind of reaction is one of the logical consequences of the formal organization of political society. This basic relationship between the individual and his group, however, is of genuine significance for criminologi-

---

26Alfred Hassler, *The Diary of a Self-Made Convict,* Foreword by Harry Elmer Barnes, Regnery, Chicago, 1954. The Fellowship of Reconciliation is a Christian pacifist group organized in 1914 in Cambridge, England, and reported to have about 15,000 members in the United States at the present time.

cal theory, and must be given due consideration. Those who reject the majority view and refuse to follow required behavior patterns are inevitably defined as, and treated as, criminals, be they conscientious religious persons, like Hassler, or be they only conscientious devotees of the economic principle of private profit who refuse to accept or follow required practices under a system of government control of consumer prices.[27] Members of such a minority group do not accept the definition of themselves, or of their behavior, as criminal. Looking at their own group of like-thinking associates, they readily persuade themselves that their course of action has been acceptable and, from their point of view, entirely honorable. The more basic problem, therefore, is the conflict of group interests and the struggle for the control of power that is always present in the political organization of any society.

4. THE POLITICAL NATURE OF MUCH CRIMINAL BEHAVIOR

Many kinds of criminal acts must be recognized as representing primarily behavior on the front-line fringes of direct contact between groups struggling for the control of power in the political and cultural organization of society. To surface appearance, the offenses may seem to be the ordinary common-law ones involving persons and property, but on closer examination they often are revealed as the acts of good soldiers fighting for a cause and against the threat of enemy encroachment. The age-old psychological principle of all group centered conflict activity comes to the fore, namely, the end justifies the means, and the end object is the maintenance of the group position.

The fact that the means used may be less than honorable, that they may involve outright criminal behavior is viewed as unfortunate but not therefore to be shirked, if necessary to the accomplishment of group ends. Hence, at the point of contact between groups in conflict all manner of blustering violence, deceit, treachery, and pious disingenuousness become a relatively commonplace part of the struggle. Closer examination of a few type-situations will help make clear some of the ramifications of this aspect of criminal behavior.

1. Numerous crimes result from the direct political reform type of protest movement. Such reform activity often has recourse to violence, the ultimate form of which is rebellion or revolution. A successful revolution makes criminals out of the government officials previously in power, and an unsuccessful revolution makes its leaders into traitors subject to immediate execution. Murder, sabotage, seizure of private property, and

---

[27]Cf. Marshall Clinard, *The Black Market*, Rinehart, New York, 1952. This is a study of and report on the attempt to control consumer prices during war rationing of food and other scarce commodities in the United States during World War II.

many other offenses against the ordinary criminal code are commonplace accompaniments of political rebellion.[28]

But revolutions are by no means the only occasions under which political activity sets the stage for or calls forth a certain amount of criminal activity. Many an election, in many a democratic country, has brought about the direct, physical collision of opposing groups with resulting personal violence and many kinds of personal dishonesty, bribery, perjury, and sometimes outright burglary and theft, all for the sake of winning the election and gaining (or keeping) control of political power.[29] Such conduct will always be deprecated publicly, but its persistence in one form or another in every country in the world where popular elections have significance in the contest for the control of power is further testimony to the important relation between some kinds of crime and the group struggle for the control of power.[30]

2. Many crimes result directly from the clash of interests of company management and labor unions in that form of industrial conflict that we call strikes or lockouts. If management tries to bring in nonstriking employees (strike-breakers), these must cross picket lines and are often forcefully kept out of company property. Each side may use force, and in the resulting fights heads may be broken and property may be destroyed.[31] The company's legal ownership of property usually brings in the police to protect it and prevent its usurpation by non-owners. This has often in the past led to direct physical clashes between police and strikers. In such battles there often have been casualties on both sides, including the killing or maiming of individuals and the destruction of property, both private and public.[32]

Obviously such episodes involve long lists of actual crimes by any ordinary rule of law. Yet there are relatively few instances of successful prosecution of such lawlessness, presumably for the good and sufficient reason that the criminal acts are recognized to be incidental to what is more basically a battle between politically powerful groups whose full power is much more extensive than that exerted on any particular instance of clashing force. The public interest is often ignored, or even brazenly outraged, in these clashes. Public streets and highways, always of direct interest to government and to public convenience, may be closed, or their

---

[28]Hadley Cantril, *The Psychology of Social Movements,* Wiley, New York, 1941, chs. 8 and 9, "The Nazi Party," pp. 210–70.

[29]Cf. Lincoln Steffens, *The Shame of the Cities,* McClure, Phillips, New York, 1904.

[30]Cf. Jack Lait and Lee Mortimer, *New York Confidential,* 1949; *Chicago Confidential,* 1950; *Washington Confidential,* 1951. These three books were published by Crown Publishers, New York.

[31]See, for example, Oscar Lewis, *The Big Four,* Knopf, New York, 1938, pp. 370–84, for the account of the John L. Davie *vs.* Southern Pacific Railroad battle over waterfront rights in the Oakland, California, area.

[32]See Mary Heaton Vorse, *Labor's New Millions,* Modern Age Books, New York, 1938, pp. 118–27, for a short account of the "Chicago Massacre," i.e., the violent encounters between police and workers at the Republic Steel Plant, May 26–30, 1937, that resulted in an eventual death list of 17 killed, and many more seriously wounded.

use made dependent upon an appropriate "permit" from some "strike committee."[33] The general object of any strike or lockout is to bring enough pressure to bear on the other side, through the reaction of an outraged public, so that satisfactory settlement will be reached.

The point of these illustrations is simply that the participants on either side of a labor dispute condone whatever criminal behavior is deemed "necessary" for the maintenance of their side of the struggle. The end justifies the means, and the individual in the struggle does his duty as a good soldier, even if what he has to do is contrary to law and something he would not otherwise do. Thus, as a picket, a labor union member may carry a piece of pipe as a club, swing it on a strikebreaker's head, and be guilty technically of murder or manslaughter, though in reality he has only carried out his duty assignment as a faithful member of his group.

3. Similar in nature but with a different focus for the conflict, numerous crimes result as incidental episodes in the jurisdictional disputes between different labor unions. Such disputes often involve intimidation and personal violence, and sometimes they become entangled with the "rackets" and gang warfare of the criminal underworld. The point to be emphasized is that the violence and criminal behavior of some members of labor unions, in these instances, are part of the general conflict behavior of the group. Any particular individual involved has the psychological advantage of feeling assured of group support. He operates as a soldier in a war— sorry that he has to be nasty and unpleasant, always hoping for an early peace settlement that will be favorable to his union.

4. Numerous kinds of crimes result from the clashes incidental to attempts to change, or to upset the caste system of racial segregation in various parts of the world, notably in the United States and in the Union of South Africa. To the dominant white, the Negro is acceptable and desirable only "in his place," a place of obvious social inferiority. In the economic sphere, he is regarded as a source of cheap labor and not as a skilled professional or as a technician. Regardless of personal qualities or qualifications, to the white majority his place must be one recognizably subordinate to that of the white majority.[34] Again, no one subscribes publicly to violence or to open intimidation as the desirable method of maintaining the status quo, but in practice such lawless action is often supported as "necessary."

---

[33]Cf. Charles Rumford Walker, *American City: A Rank and File History*, New York, Farrar and Rinehart, 1937. Detailed account of the Minneapolis truck strike of 1934 in which a strike committee completely usurped the power of government over streets and highway, so that passage into the city was "on permit" from the committee.

[34]For illustrations of the more recent episodes in this continuing conflict in the United States, often beset with violence and crime, see the issues of *Life* for August and September 1956. Specifically, "Segregation," September 24, 1956, pp. 98–114, and "School Battle Turns to Law," October 1, 1956, pp. 51–2. Illustrated accounts of the violence in Little Rock, Arkansas may be found in *Life* for September 23, September 30, and October 7, 1957.

The type-situation illustrations above have been elaborated in order to emphasize an important kind of criminal behavior, one whereby, technically under the law, individuals are charged with ordinary common-law crimes, yet the specific criminal behavior involved represented for the individual loyal service to a social-political group struggling to maintain, or to improve its position in the struggle for the control of power. Criminological theories based on notions of individual choice and responsibility are not germane to the underlying problem of group conflict involved in this type of situation. Such an individualistic theory, applied to this kind of crime, is like holding the individual soldier in an army at war responsible for the violence he may have inflicted on an enemy in the course of battle. Victorious nations in war sometimes react in this manner in dealing with the top leaders of defeated enemy forces—witness the "war crimes trials" that have dotted the pages of history—but usually the ordinary soldier is guilty primarily of doing his duty as ordered. In the conflict of groups within a society, the analogy with crime and the criminal has genuine psychological significance.

5. IMPLICATIONS AND LIMITATIONS

Criminal behavior that involves the kind of situations discussed in this chapter obviously has far-reaching implications for any kind of general criminological theory. It points to one of the fundamental conditions of life in organized political society. It suggests the probability that there are many situations in which criminality is the normal, natural response of normal, natural human beings struggling in understandably normal and natural situations for the maintenance of the way of life to which they stand committed.

Defectiveness and abnormality hypotheses are clearly inapplicable to the type of situation here discussed. Yet the criminal behavior involved is readily understood and easily explained as the kind of behavior necessary to protect and defend the interests of the individual's group in conflict with other groups. Criminological theory, in this type of situation, becomes a specialized application of the more general theory of a sociology of conflict. The behavior of the individual is viewed as incidental to the course of action required for the group to maintain its place in the struggle with other groups.

On the other hand, it is also clear that group conflict theory is strictly limited to those kinds of situations in which the individual criminal acts flow from the collision of groups whose members are loyally upholding the in-group position. Such theory does not serve to explain many kinds of impulsive, irrational acts of a criminal nature that are quite unrelated to any battle between different interest groups in organized society. Other theories, with different emphases on other factors, need to be considered for such situations.

Like the defectiveness hypothesis, or the hypothesis of individual differences, the group conflict hypothesis should not be stretched too far. Yet there seems to be little doubt but that a considerable amount of crime is intimately related to the course of group conflict situations, and that for these situations the principles of a sociology of conflict become also the solid bases for understanding and explaining this kind of criminal behavior.

7. CONFLICT AND CRIMINALITY

AUSTIN T. TURK

While the term *conflict* has been prominent in the development of criminological theories, a review of the literature indicates that criminologists generally posit relations between conflict and crime without going on to spell out in explicit, tightly reasoned propositions the various ways in which they have conceptualized the terms and their relationship. Even though impressive examples of creative theorizing have been produced, I believe that the unconcern with formal theory-building as such has contributed greatly to persistent confusion about the subject matter and research objectives of criminology, tendencies toward theoretical prospecting before available mines have been worked out, and a proliferation of isolated studies instead of cumulative research programs. Formalization is, of course, no substitute for thinking; it is, however, at least an aid to a clearer statement and more thorough exploration of theoretical alternatives. Consequently, an effort is made to develop, using available theoretical resources as far as possible, highly "systematized" propositions as a basis for research on conflict-crime relations. This paper, more in the nature of a progress report than a formal presentation of polished conclusions, proceeds from (1) a brief summation of the conceptualizations found in previous studies through (2) discussions and suggested resolutions of what appear to be the basic issues in these studies to (3) introduction of a theoretical scheme growing out of consideration of those issues in light of the increasing fund of research in the sociology of law creation and administration.

SUMMARY OF THE LITERATURE ON CRIME AND CONFLICT

Relations between conflict and crime have been conceptualized in four basic ways, although any given discussion can be shown to be in some respects a unique treatment of one or more of the major ideas. The four

Reprinted from *American Sociological Review*, 31 (June 1966), 338–52 by Permission of The American Sociological Association and the author.

Revision of a paper read at the Fifth International Criminological Congress, August, 1965.

conceptual relations are as follows, along with the principal variants of each:

1. Criminal behavior as an indicator of conflict within the person, emphasizing either
   a. failure to resolve tensions generated in the course of interaction between the organism and human figures in its environment,[1] or
   b. tensions generated by the person's inability to satisfy the contradictory expectations of others, or else to mobilize the resources needed to perform a role assigned to him.[2]

2. Criminal behavior as the expression of participation by the offender in a criminogenic subculture, emphasizing either
   a. a basically pathological and largely unsuccessful attempt by persons in similar circumstances and in contact to solve their adjustment problems,[3]
   b. a partly normal and partly pathological effort by persons in similar positions and in contact to adapt to opportunity barriers,[4] or
   c. the trouble-making features of an established sector of the culture, such as a class culture, or of the culture itself.[5]

3. The occurrence of criminal behavior where the offender, because of having been socialized in a different culture, either does not know or does not accept certain legal norms.[6]

4. The violation of laws by essentially normal persons in the course of realistic conflicts of interest, emphasizing either
   a. the activities of those involved in organizations created to satisfy the demand for illicit goods and services, as well as to utilize illegal means to control and profit from legitimate economic activity,[7]
   b. resistance by vested interests to legal restraints, especially where efforts are made to modify institutionalized patterns of legitimate economic activity,[8]

---

[1]Essentially this is the psychoanalytic position. The studies found in K. R. Eissler (ed.), *Searchlights on Delinquency*, New York: International Universities Press, 1949, are representative.

[2]Herbert A. Bloch and Gilbert Geis, *Man, Crime, and Society: The Forms of Criminal Behavior*, New York: Random House, 1962, pp. 125–128.

[3]Lewis Yablonsky, *The Violent Gang*, New York: Macmillan, 1962.

[4]Albert K. Cohen, *Delinquent Boys: The Culture of the Gang*, Glencoe, Illinois: The Free Press, 1955; Richard A. Cloward and Lloyd E. Ohlin, *Delinquency and Opportunity: A Theory of Delinquent Gangs*, Glencoe, Illinois: The Free Press, 1960.

[5]Herbert Bloch and Arthur Niederhoffer, *The Gang: A Study in Adolescent Behavior*, New York: The Philosophical Library, 1958; Walter B. Miller, "Lower Class Culture as a Generating Milieu of Gang Delinquency," *Journal of Social Issues*, 14 (1958), pp. 5–19; Donald R. Taft and Ralph W. England, Jr., *Criminology*, 4th ed., New York: Macmillan, 1964.

[6]Thorsten Sellin, *Culture Conflict and Crime*, New York: Social Science Research Council, 1938; Edwin H. Sutherland, *Principles of Criminology*, 4th ed., New York: J. B. Lippincott, 1947.

[7]For a sampling of the literature see Gus Tyler (ed.), *Organized Crime in America*, Ann Arbor: University of Michigan Press, 1962.

[8]Edwin H. Sutherland, *White Collar Crime*, New York: Dryden, 1949; Marshall B. Clinard, *The Black Market*, New York: Rinehart, 1952; John G. Fuller, *The Gentlemen Conspirators*, New York: Grove Press, 1962.

c. criminal behavior as almost entirely a function of an inequitable and unstable economic structure promoting selfishness and resulting in uncertainty for all and misery for many,[9] or

d. conflict between those who seek to preserve a given authority structure and those who are trying to modify or destroy it.[10]

Thus, one finds some writers emphasizing internal psychological conflicts of which unlawful acts are taken to be symptomatic, others thinking primarily in terms of deviant group formation and/or elements of group cultures in opposition to law-abidingness, still others talking mostly about cross-cultural differences with respect to behavior norms, and a minority concerned with relations between economic and political struggles and the occurrence of criminal behavior. The first two perspectives are associated with an almost exclusive concern with explaining the behavior of deviants who are only incidentally and sometimes officially criminals. The third and especially the fourth evidence more concern with the nature of law and with nonpathological dimensions of intergroup conflict, even though these writers too view crime mainly as problem behavior. Their work suggests at the very least that while crime may be viewed sometimes as an indication that something is wrong with the person or with his social environment as it affects him, it may at other times be more usefully seen as "reasonable" behavior engaged in by individuals, with varying degrees of group support, who more or less consciously disagree with certain laws or patterns of law enforcement perceived as threats to their interests. From the latter viewpoint, that some people act contrary to statutes becomes less a problem than a fact with which analysis begins, and understanding crime becomes less a matter of unraveling social, psychological and biological processes resulting in pathological behavior than a matter of comprehending cultural diversity and patterns of social conflict.

The most critical problem in criminological theory today is to determine whether and how the two orientations—which may be called the "deviance-pathology" and the "social conflict-political"—can be integrated. So far, integrative efforts have been characterized by a lack of careful and consistent distinctions between (a) the stigmatization of deviants, persons who are in some way offensive to others, and criminalization, the processes by which certain persons are officially defined as criminals, violators of legal norms; (b) realistic or normal as opposed to unrealistic or patho-

---

[9]William A. Bonger, *Criminality and Economic Conditions*, Boston: Little, Brown and Co., 1916, is still the best statement from a socialist viewpoint.

[10]The literature on political crime is poor, and there are few developed analyses of the political aspects of crime. Some of the conceptual issues have been usefully discussed by Richard Quinney, "Crime in Political Perspective," *The American Behavioral Scientist*, 8 (December, 1964), pp. 19–22. Perhaps the best study is Otto Kirchheimer, *Political Justice: The Use of Legal Procedure for Political Ends*, Princeton, N.J.: Princeton University Press, 1961. See also Alexander Comfort, *Authority and Delinquency in the Modern State: A Criminological Approach to the Problem of Power*, London: Routledge and Kegan Paul, 1950.

logical behavior and conflict relations; and (c) legal and non-legal norms. The obvious question is, "Can integration be achieved if these distinctions are made?" Apparently not, for both logical and substantive considerations indicate that this is one situation in which compartmentalization promises more than does some sort of forced compromise. The arguments follow, organized around efforts to sharpen each of the distinctions noted above.[11]

STIGMATIZATION AND CRIMINALIZATION

Offensive, dangerous, antisocial, deviant, or pathological behavior has usually been assumed to be the proper focus of criminological research. Contemporary thinking has been devoted primarily to tracing the influences of interpersonal relations, socialization and acculturation, institutional constraints, and other aspects of the social environment upon individual behavior. Though differing in their concern for whether or not the accused are eventually found guilty, most criminologists have, moreover, assumed *for research purposes* that arrest is tantamount to guilt and that arrest and conviction categories are equivalent to homogeneous behavior categories. Variations in legislative, judicial, and enforcement behavior have seldom been treated other than as sources of error in estimating rates of deviance. Granted that the effort to explain and predict offensive behavior is a perfectly legitimate and necessary research enterprise, it does appear, as I have argued elsewhere,[12] that the preoccupation with offensive behavior has resulted in the confusion of two sets of problems: accounting for certain kinds of behavior and accounting for the criminality, the criminal status, of certain people.

The individuals to be found in any crime category defined in law have arrived there after passing through a series of interactions with other people, some of whom have eventually affixed a criminal label to the subjects. Such labels are jurisdiction-specific and subject to numerous kinds of reporting and recording error. A criminal label may also be affixed to persons because of real or fancied attributes and justified by reference to real or fancied behavior. Indeed, a person is evaluated, either favorably or unfavorably, not because he *does* something, or even because he *is* something, but because others react to their perceptions of him as offensive or inoffensive. Some aspect of his behavior or some attribute other than behavior becomes a criterion for either rewarding or sanctioning him.

---

[11]It is evident that some of the thorniest issues in the social and behavioral sciences and in jurisprudence are involved. Nonetheless, the need for precision means that at some point one must settle on a definite set of conceptual tools, recognizing that no one, including the theorist himself, will be entirely satisfied with it.

[12]Austin T. Turk, "Prospects for Theories of Criminal Behavior," *Journal of Criminal Law, Criminology and Police Science,* 55 (1964), pp. 454–461.

If the criterion, perhaps offensive to certain people and inoffensive or even desirable to others,[13] is officially deemed to be grounds for the political authorities to use their power to coerce, the process of evaluation and status assignment is that of *criminalization*. Where the criterion is not officially relevant or where persons without legal authority apply sanctions, the more general concept of *stigmatization* is appropriate.[14]

Since official labelling behavior on the part of legal authorities, rather than the behavior of the individual, is the actual source of his criminality, and since the process can hardly be construed as a disinterested, scientific classification of human behavior,[15] the occupants of a crime category at any given moment can be expected to vary in regard to (a) correspondence between their offensive behavior or attributes and the offense described in the official norm, or statute, under which they have been labelled; and (b) social and psychological characteristics other than those officially viewed as offensive by the creators, interpreters, and enforcers of criminal laws. We do least violence to the data when we view such a category as a category of *status* rather than of *behavior,* i.e., a set of individuals who have been defined, by non-scientists for non-scientific purposes, as members of that particular category, and whose behavior and other attributes vary to a greater or lesser degree from the legal prerequisites for inclusion. In short, criminalization, becoming a criminal, is not synonymous with engaging in "criminal" behavior. Therefore, the problem of relating conflict and crime is one of accounting for the assignment of criminal status, which means that actual offensive behavior is treated, not as the phenomenon to be explained, but instead as one of a number of variables related to the probability of criminalization.

In research on criminal status categories, determination of legal innocence and guilt, whether empirically and/or legally valid or erroneous, would seem to be pertinent for criminologists only because of its effect upon the degree of deprivation associated with criminalization. The official presumption of innocence until guilt has been established is contradicted by the research evidence. *De facto* criminality begins as soon as

---

[13]It is especially noteworthy that persons with the authority and duty to assign criminal status do not necessarily find the legally relevant criteria personally offensive. The attitudes of many law enforcers toward gambling is one example.

[14]Edwin Schur views criminalization as "an extreme form of stigmatization," stressing the greater impact upon the individual in regard to changing his self-image. See his *Crimes Without Victims,* Englewood Cliffs, N. J.: Prentice-Hall, 1965, p. 5. However, it does not necessarily follow that stigmatization is less likely than criminalization to push one toward a deviant career. See Erving Goffman, *Stigma: Notes on the Management of Spoiled Identity,* Englewood Cliffs, N. J.: Prentice-Hall, 1963.

[15]This is inevitably the case, since the aims of legal processing—domination, regulation, or the weakening of an opponent—are fundamentally incompatible with the aims of scientific data processing, which are to facilitate objective analysis and make possible valid interpretation irrespective of implications for the creation, maintenance, modification, or destruction of power structures. John Kitsuse and Aaron Cicourel have, in fact, made the point that official criminal statistics are useful sources of data not on "deviants" and their behavior, but rather on "the organizationally defined processes by which individuals are differentiated as deviant." See "A Note on the Uses of Official Statistics," *Social Problems,* 11 (Fall, 1963), pp. 131–39.

the individual is perceived by legal authorities as a possible or potential offender.[16] The general public, often encouraged by the news media, apparently see little significant difference in most cases between the accused and the convicted insofar as their readiness to condemn and their willingness to punish are concerned.[17] Sizable differences in conviction rates among racial and socioeconomic classes in the United States suggest that criminalization is not solely a function of the legally relevant facts.[18] The experiences of ex-convicts and persons who have been accused but found legally innocent of certain types of offense, indicate that criminal status does not necessarily conform to legal definitions.[19] Similar findings from other countries[20] support the same conclusion: criminalization is not bound within the narrow limits imposed by structures for the administration of justice.

CONFLICT AND BEHAVIOR

Insofar as criminal status is taken to be synonymous with pathological, or maladaptive behavior and noncriminality is equated with normal, or adaptive behavior any differences between the inferred mental and observed

---

[16]"Contacts," some involving detainment for various lengths of time, and recorded arrests are commonly accepted as indicators of legal offensiveness. New York's "stop-and-frisk" statute authorizes action by police officers on the basis of assumptions generally shared by law enforcers about individual characteristics denoting law-violation. "A police officer may stop any person abroad in a public place whom he reasonably suspects is committing, has committed or is about to commit a felony or any of the crimes specified in section five hundred fifty-two of this chapter . . . and if he reasonably suspects that he is in danger of life or limb, he may search such person for a dangerous weapon . . ." ("quoted in Richard H. Kuh, "Reflections on New York's 'Stop-and-Frisk' Law and Its Claimed Unconstitutionality," *Journal of Criminal Law, Criminology and Police Science,* 56 (1965), p. 32.) Such judgments are not necessarily invalid, for police "biases" may be fairly closely associated with objective probabilities. See Robert M. Terry, "Criteria Utilized by the Police in the Screening of Juvenile Offenders," University of Wisconsin, unpublished Master's thesis, 1962.

[17]The public appears ready to believe in the probable guilt of nonwhites, teenagers, and persons with police records, especially in highly publicized cases involving sex and violence. In a recent Indiana case in which a man and his paramour now appear to have planned and carried out the murder of the man's wife, the author found no one among the more than thirty non-academic individuals with whom he informally discussed the case who questioned the husband's original story that two Negro men driving an unmarked car with a flashing red light stopped him on a major highway, robbed the couple, and after forcing him to crawl under the car, shot his wife six times in the head. A local newspaper editorialized on the basis of the original story but has not yet followed up the editorial in terms of the later turn of events.

[18]Edwin H. Sutherland and Donald R. Cressey, *Principles of Criminology,* 6th ed., New York: J. B. Lippincott, 1960, pp. 139 and 190.

[19]In this connection it is significant that arrest on a charge such as violation of a sex offender statute, even though the case may subsequently have been dismissed, is considered by security investigators sufficient to disqualify an individual for certain types of occupations. The working rule appears to be "Where there's smoke, there's fire."

[20]Even in a political structure such as the Republic of South Africa where the discretionary powers of legal authorities are extremely wide and criminality a potentially limitless status category, both police and citizenry appear to generalize beyond existing limits in associating such traits as nonwhite skin color and disagreement with governmental policies with legal offensiveness. The report of the International Commission of Jurists (*South Africa and the Rule of Law,* Geneva, 1960) documents the generous limits to criminalization while there is a constant stream of evidence of varying quality that some police and citizens are unable to keep their actions even within the broad range of legal coercion. Fact papers published by the South African Institute of Race Relations appear to be the least impressionistic and most carefully researched sources of information on specific events. See, for example, "A Précis of the Reports of the Commissions appointed to enquire into the events occurring on March 21, 1960 at Sharpeville and Langa," Johannesburg, 1961, *passim.*

behavior patterns of criminals and of non-criminals tend to be interpreted as though whatever characterizes criminals were intrinsically wrong— despite the fact that most criminologists appear willing in their more reflective moments to grant the relativity of right-wrong standards. The unsurprising result is that any conflict between those who seek to impose legal restraints and those who are resistant is likely to be defined as pathological, and the onus placed on the resisters. The conceptual problem is to find some way to break the pathology-conflict tautology.

General conflict theory[21] suggests that it may be useful to differentiate conflict parties and conflict moves, on the one hand, from persons and behavior on the other. The concept of a conflict party has the advantage of being more neutral in that it enables one to refer to the entities involved in a conflict relation with far fewer and more explicit assumptions about the composition of the entities. A party is simply "a *behavior unit,* that is, some aggregate or organization that is capable of assuming a number of different positions while retaining a common identity or boundary."[22] The only assumptions are that an entity can be defined, that it can move, that it can move to either more or less favorable[23] positions, and that it is "motivated" to move toward the optimum position. The status of a conflict party is defined by the favorableness of its position relative to other positions in the field of possibilities. Since, in the two-party case, moves by the other party either open up or block off possible moves, i.e., are contingencies, a conflict relation is said to exist. The significance of moves lies in the consequences for increasing or decreasing the chances of success, of reaching a position of maximum favorableness and minimum unfavorableness. Given at least two alternatives, one of them strategically "better" than the other, realistic moves are those that increase the probabilities of success; unrealistic moves are those that decrease the probabilities of success. A situation in which unrealistic moves are made by one or both parties may be called unrealistic conflict. Empirical situations are, of course, "more or less," never entirely realistic or unrealistic. Applying these notions to the situation in which the parties are law-enforcing and law-resistant,[24] we can speak of criminal and non-criminal status (unfa-

---

[21]The best introduction to the general theoretical literature on conflict is Kenneth E. Boulding, *Conflict and Defense: A General Theory,* New York: Harper and Brothers, 1962. George Vold (*Theoretical Criminology,* New York: Oxford University Press, 1958) has done most in recent years to direct attention to the possibilities of social conflict theory for criminology, but has not relinquished the idea that there is a class of "impulsive, irrational acts of a criminal nature that are quite unrelated to any battle between different interest groups in organized society," p. 219. This residual category seems to be unnecessary if one avoids equating social conflict with quasi-military encounters between organized groups deliberately engaged in a struggle to assert their respective interests.

[22]Boulding, *op. cit.,* p. 2.

[23]"Favorable" and "unfavorable" refer to increase or decrease in chances of realizing any value, e.g., survival, opportunity, health, liberty, wealth, success, status, security, gratification, and ego-strength.

[24]Specific persons in official law enforcement agencies, as well as persons in purportedly criminal populations and organizations, may be in either the law-enforcing or the law-resistant party in empirical instances.

vorable and favorable positions) acquired in the course of either a relatively realistic or a relatively unrealistic conflict, without prejudging which party contributed how much by its moves to the realism or unrealism of the conflict.

In dealing with persons and behavior, the issue is no longer the relative status of conflict parties or the realism of their moves, but rather the ability or inability of specific individuals in either or both parties to enact some or all prescribed roles. Such inability is indicated, e.g., by extreme novelty in symbols used or in the uses made of symbols, failure to use symbols, excessive or insufficient and/or inappropriate emotional displays—in short, by intolerable breaks in communication.[25] Inability, as evidenced by such indicators, is pathological behavior; behavior will be considered normal where such indicators are absent. Thus, the classification of behavior as pathological or normal is made independent of both the classification of conflict moves as realistic or unrealistic and the statuses which may have been attached to the various parties in a conflict situation.

While the language of conflict parties and moves may avoid hidden assumptions about personalities and behavior, it is legitimate to ask whether use of the one pair of concepts or the other makes any difference empirically—since what we actually observe is behavior and the consequences of behavior. Specifically, one may argue that unrealistic moves are evidenced by pathological behavior and realistic moves by normal behavior, or at least that unrealistic moves are the products of pathological behavior and realistic moves the products of normal behavior. Many discussions of personal and social disorganization have, in fact, assumed these correspondences.[26] However, research along various lines has led to the realization that what is "socially prized" may have undesirable results, and that the deviant may have his functions."[27] Accordingly, the distinction between moves, or consequences, and behavior becomes empirically neces-

---

[25]It is not merely role failure but inferences about the communication breaks associated with such failure that define the actor's behavior in terms of his ability or inability to act differently. Whether or not the role failure and associated breaks in communication persist appears to depend upon the extent to which the deviance is "denied" or "labelled" by others. Thomas J. Scheff, "The Role of the Mentally Ill and the Dynamics of Mental Disorder: A Research Framework," *Sociometry*, 26 (December, 1963), pp. 436–53.

[26]Ernest R. Mowrer, *Disorganization: Personal and Social*, Philadelphia: J. P. Lippincott, 1942, pp. 24–25 and 575–76; Mabel A. Elliott and Francis E. Merrill, *Social Disorganization*, 3rd ed., New York: Harper and Brothers, 1950, pp. 39–49. C. Wright Mills' analysis of "The Professional Ideology of Social Pathologists" (*American Journal of Sociology*, 1942, 49 (September, 1942), pp. 165–80) offers reasons, such as the rural origin and piecemeal reformism of virtually all the authors whose work he considered for the tendency to equate normality with consensus and order and pathology with dissensus and conflict.

[27]The "rediscovery of Durkheim" is proceeding apace. See Robert K. Merton and Robert A. Nisbet, *Contemporary Social Problems*, New York: Harcourt, Brace and World, 1961; Robert A. Dentler and Kai T. Erikson, "The Functions of Deviance in Groups," *Social Problems*, 7 (Fall, 1959), pp. 98–107. Lewis Coser has led the equally relevant "rediscovery of Simmel" with his *The Functions of Social Conflict*, Glencoe, Illinois: The Free Press, 1956. See also his "Social Conflict and the Theory of Social Change," *The British Journal of Sociology*, 8 (September, 1957), 197–207.

sary as well as analytically useful. It turns out that the abilities and inabilities indicated by the terms *normal* and *pathological* may, in each instance, contribute to either the realism or the unrealism of a conflict. It is the *consequences* of behavior that determine the realism or unrealism of moves in a conflict relation, not the *nature* of behavior in a pathological-normal sense.[28]

Two qualifications are in order. The abilities and inabilities of specific persons are more likely to affect the realism of the conflict relation (a) as the numbers of individuals comprising the conflict parties decrease, and (b) where individuals have a disproportionate and perhaps determinative voice in policy decision-making. In the first place, personal pathology looms larger in its effects upon the realism of interpersonal conflict—especially where the individuals are involved less as momentary representatives of collectivities than as "whole persons"—than in its effects upon the realism of conflicts between groups or larger collectivities such as nations. Secondly, the abilities or inabilities of a leader (authority, policy-maker) may tend to increase or decrease the realism of a conflict, depending upon the consequences of leader behavior and upon the existence of effective checks upon the exercise of power. In short, the probability that pathological behavior and unrealistic conflict moves will be coterminous will be maximal when a person is a conflict party, and will decrease with increasing size of a collectivity,[29] while the authority of specific members of a collectivity will have *some* effect (varying with the degree of authority) on the probability of realistic and unrealistic moves by the collectivity. Pathological behavior by authorities may have consequences that raise the probability of unrealistic moves by collectivities, but actual

---

[28]Cf. Coser, 1956, *op. cit.*, pp. 39–65, especially pp. 48–55. There the distinction between "nonrealistic" and "realistic" conflict depends not upon the consequences of moves for decreasing or increasing chances that some value will be realized, but rather upon the motivations of the particular individuals who happen to be involved. Nonrealistic conflict is occasioned by the need for release of aggressive tension in one or more of the interacting persons, while realistic conflict is aimed, at least primarily, at securing some good over the opposition of others. At least two serious weaknesses appear when one tries to apply Coser's distinction to the analysis of conflict relations:

(1) Moves by one or more parties are confused with the whole system of moves by all parties, since the nature of the relations among conflicting parties is apparently determined by the individual motivations behind whatever moves each party may make.

(2) This way of talking about conflict is actually another way of characterizing an individual's behavior. It is a psychological conception, not interactional, and as such can hardly be expected to make sense of inter*person* conflict relations, much less conflict situations where the relevant entities are not individuals but collectivities and social categories such as "authorities" and "subjects." The latter *are* the relevant entities if one is interested in law enforcement and criminality rather than the specifics of an encounter between Officer Jones and John Dillinger. The problem in this case is sociological, or social-structural, instead of psychological, since the relations of interest concern social categories, collectivities, actors, roles, and not human beings.

[29]The "behavior" of collectivities is not an issue. While either persons or collectivities may be conflict parties, and therefore able to move from one position to another, only persons *behave*. Collectivities obviously "behave" only in a shorthand sense that minimizes the variations in the actions of a number of persons and emphasizes the consequences of a combination of numerous individual acts. The point would be trivial by now if it were not for the persistent tendency in the literature of criminology and the sociology of law to concretize and homogenize "the police," "the law," "the government," "the authorities," "the gang," "organized crime," etc.

moves will be the overall consequences of behavior by all participants. Recurrent pathological behavior by high authorities is likely, clearly, to result eventually in unrealistic conflict moves. The central point, nonetheless, still stands: the pathology or normality of behavior is not identical with the unrealism and realism of moves in a conflict situation.

THE LEGALITY OF NORMS

To say that criminalization is status ascription is to say that the behavior of those who define and treat others as criminals is not random but is a response to the others' failure to live up to expectations. Norms, not whims, are being defended, and coercion is occurring not in the course of interpersonal conflict, but rather as members of a collectivity play out the patterns of expectation-violation-coercion that, in large part, characterize the collectivity.[30] Both those who enforce and those who violate norms vary in awareness of the patterns in which they are involved. At the extremes of awareness, a norm may be either (a) a set of cultural objects that define and evaluate a class of attributes or behavior, or (b) an inference from the occurrence of sanctioning, from patterned coercion. In the first case the norm is cultural, since the criteria of offensiveness are announced by the use of symbols; in the second, the norm is social but not cultural, since there is no symbolic representation of what is happening. The distinction at this point is simply between explicit and implicit expectations, the criteria for sanctioning. Sanctioning implies a social norm; if the norm-enforcers are aware of the social norm, i.e., have symbolized it, it is also a cultural norm.

Relations between the cultural and the social are, however, far more complex. Anyone with minimum communication skills can announce a norm. Indeed, the business of announcing norms may itself become a social norm, as in the development of legislatures and courts. Unfortunately, from the perspectives of both those in and those aspiring to be in norm-announcing establishments, to evaluate someone negatively because he does not satisfy explicit criteria of goodness is not equivalent to sanctioning him. Unless the negatively evaluated individual is deprived of something significant to him, including such intangibles as self-esteem and assumptions about personal identity and sanity, he can be quite indifferent

---

[30]While it may be argued that no social relationship can persist without such patterns, however subtle and however far below the thresholds of the participants' awareness, criminology is concerned with "imperatively coordinated" collectivities in which the authority structure is relatively explicit and formalized, i.e., "corporate groups" in Weber's terminology, including "political communities." A. M. Henderson and Talcott Parsons (eds. and trans.), *Max Weber: The Theory of Social and Economic Organization*, Glencoe, Illinois: The Free Press, 1947, pp. 145–46 and 152–53; Edward Shils and Max Rheinstein (eds.), *Max Weber on Law in Economy and Society*, Cambridge, Mass.: Harvard University Press, 1954, pp. 338–48.

to the fact that he is a violator of a cultural norm. Moreover, the greater the cultural difference[31] between the evaluator and the violator, the less likely are psychological sanctions which assume a capacity and readiness to respond to subtle cues to get through to the violator, and therefore sanctioning will have to be more physically coercive in order to enforce the norm. Assuming that those who announce a norm are able to make other people pay attention, there will inevitably be incongruence between the norm as announced and the norm as enforced, since (a) symbolization and the thing symbolized are not identical, (b) no enforcer can be fully aware of and able to control all that conditions his behavior, and (c) only rarely will announcers and enforcers be the same persons. To make the relation between cultural and social norms even more problematic, not only may a cultural norm be an approximation of a social norm, and therefore be supported by the sanctioning associated with the social norm, but a cultural norm may be supported despite the fact that there is no social norm to which the cultural norm corresponds.

Once persons in a collectivity are convinced that some subset of individuals within the collectivity have sufficient power to force others to pay attention to their normative announcements, they may accept announced norms not so much because they understand or "internalize" the norms as because they have learned to defer to the decisions of the powerful subset, i.e., to view that subset as "authorities." The social norm of deference, learned either by direct and unsuccessful conflicts with authorities or through gradual socialization into the authority structure (a derivative of historical or even prehistorical norm conflicts[32]), may then serve to support a wide variety of cultural norms just because they are "authoritative," i.e., "legal."[33]

---

[31]Within political collectivities, differences in cultural norms may be absolute, but cultural differences are far more likely in regard to such variables as priority of norms, appropriate treatment of violators, and the applicability of offensiveness criteria to specific situations (differences in what is meant by "it depends . . .").

[32]H. L. A. Hart (*The Concept of Law*, London: Oxford University Press, 1961), in demonstrating the inadequacies of the doctrine that a legal order consists in habitual obedience to a sovereign, has gone too far toward rejecting all coercive models of legality. In particular, his analysis ignores the clear alternative to person-person ordering and obeying, namely, the social-psychological view that individuals may become conditioned to participation in dominant-subordinate *role* relationships. Moreover, there is a failure to appreciate the need for authority to be periodically asserted if an authority relationship is to continue, even when (and perhaps especially when) authorities and subordinates are in close agreement on behavior norms. Finally, there is an insistence upon a radical difference between "custom" and "law" that seems to rest upon the assumption that because the story of innovation is very old and forgotten in the case of some norms, there was no normative conflict but rather a universal recognition that such fundamental requisites of social life as the prohibition against indiscriminate homicide are indeed "natural" and "right." In contradistinction, it may be argued with equal plausibility that legal norms are no more than relatively new "customs" enforced initially only by exercises of superior force, and later enforced partially by consensus, primarily by conditioned acceptance of the relevant authority structures, and ultimately by force.

[33]The issue of legitimation has generally been seen as a question of the kind or degree of psychological commitment, with the emphasis upon the motives of individuals. The position here is that *acceptance*, on whatever motivational grounds, is legitimation. Cf. Weber, "Acquiescence in an imposed order, in so far as it does not depend upon mere fear or upon considerations of purpose-rationality, presupposes the belief that the power of domination of him or those by whom the order is imposed is in some sense legitimate," Shils and Rheinstein, *op. cit.*, p. 9.

One of the deficiencies of discussions of the nature of "legal norms" in general and of "criminal laws" in particular has been the tendency to treat any officially announced norm (statute) as if each announcement were simply an effort to formulate an actual social norm.[34] Furthermore, there has been a persistent assumption that virtually everyone in a given collectivity except a few individual deviants accepts or takes into account every norm articulated in a law.[35] More realistically, however, an increasing majority of legal norms lack a one-to-one correspondence with any social norm. The announcement of legal norms is more and more likely to be a result of conflicts among different subcollectivities with different norms than an expression of general consensus, and the announcement of legal norms may be more a technique of inter-group conflict than a direct expression of anyone's social norms or even of political compromise.[36]

To summarize, a legal norm is defined here as a cultural norm officially announced by the political authorities in a collectivity. Although some legal norms approximate the social norms of the collectivity, most legal norms will be seen by members of the collectivity as "legal" only to the extent that the norm of deference to authority has been established. The probability of acceptance will vary with the degree to which those in the collectivity but without "authority" have learned to consider normative announcements by certain persons as top priority rules to be taken into account at least as contingencies. Legality is, in empirical cases, dependent upon recognition of the superior *power* of norm-announcers.[37] Where there is no dominant subset, there is no authority; hence the question of legality can be settled only by the emergence of powerful persons able to force recognition of their superior control of resources, especially the means of violence.

PROPOSITIONS FOR A THEORY OF CRIMINALIZATION

By now it is apparent that *criminological* theory—as distinct from *deviant behavior* theory—is viewed as that part of general conflict theory which

[34]Jerome Hall's emphasis on the experiential basis of criminal law illustrates the tendency, although he is obviously well aware of problems arising from disagreements between statutes and norms governing conduct. E.g., *General Principles of Criminal Law*, Indianapolis: Bobbs-Merrill, 1960, pp. 608–21.

[35]As Howard Becker has pointed out in reference to the general concept of deviance, "in addition to recognizing that deviance is created by the responses of people to particular kinds of behavior, by the labeling of that behavior as deviant, we must also keep in mind that the rules created and maintained by such labeling are not universally agreed to. Instead, they are the object of conflict and disagreement, part of the political process of society." *Outsiders: Studies in the Sociology of Deviance*, New York: The Free Press of Glencoe, 1963, p. 18.

[36]In South Africa, for example, it is clear that the population registration and "reference book" laws of today are more understandable as instruments to be used against non-whites than as direct expressions of norms respecting the desirability of identification documents as such. International Commission of Jurists, *op. cit.*, pp. 21–29.

[37]Since a power relation is never entirely one-way, authorities are always faced with the necessity of adjusting to the limits imposed upon their ability or "right" to announce enforceable legal norms. Some of the variables affecting the enforceability of legal norms are the visibility of attributes,

applies to norm conflict within political authority structures, specifically to conflicts defined by authorities in terms of the violation and enforcement of legal norms. Instead of the "criminal behavior" of individual suspects, arrestees, and convicts, the focus is upon the conflict process[38] during which some parties come to be defined as criminal. The theoretical objectives are to account for (1) variations in the probability of criminalization, i.e., in crime rates, and (2) variations in the degree of deprivation associated with criminalization, including both modes of punishment and the point in the legal process at which coercive treatment is officially terminated. The following propositions comprise no more than a rough first approximation of a theory that will hopefully offer not only plausible but precise, systematic, and therefore testable explanations of criminality and punishment.

1. In regard to evaluation of any given attribute, the probability that a cultural difference between authorities and subjects will result in conflict will depend upon the extent to which this difference corresponds to a difference in social norms. In general, the greater the cultural difference, the greater the probability of conflict.

   1.1. Conflict will be most likely when there is high congruence between cultural and social norms for both authorities and subjects, and least likely where there is low congruence for both authorities and subjects.

      1.1.1. When congruence is high for one party and low for the other, conflict will be more probable for the combination of high-authorities and low-subjects, since authorities are less likely to tolerate cultural difference when their cultural norm is strongly supported by a corresponding social norm.

      1.1.2. While social normative conflict is conceivable, i.e., conflict in which the parties have no awareness of why they are fighting, it is unlikely that such a conflict between authorities and subjects can continue for long without one or both parties interpreting the struggle in culture conflict terms. The "real" social-normative reasons for conflict will never exactly coincide with the interpretations given by the parties to the conflict. In fact, there are likely to be various sets of interpretations used, depending mainly upon whether the audience is "public" or "private." Thus, the investigator must not accept at face value any statement by party spokesmen regarding the nature and extent of the normative difference.

---

the relative power of subcollectivities whose norms would be challenged by certain announcements, and the immediate and potential costs of enforcement.

[38]Edwin H. Sutherland saw "crime as part of a process, and that process seems to be essentially a process of conflict." Albert Cohen, Alfred Lindesmith, and Karl Schuessler (eds.), *The Sutherland Papers,* Bloomington: Indiana University Press, 1956, pp. 99–100.

1.2. Authorities will tend to appeal to legal norms, or to announce new ones, in contradistinction to the cultural norms taken to be characteristic of the opposition. The opposition, on the other hand, since they are by definition more or less excluded from law-making positions, will tend to appeal to non-legal, more abstract principles such as justice, natural law, and the right to be left alone.

1.2.1. The less distinct and established the opposition's culture, and the less the sophistication of individuals comprising the opposition party, the more likely—it seems—they are to make essentially negative appeals of the sort described by Sykes and Matza as "techniques of neutralization," implying an effort to justify violation of a norm actually shared with the authorities.[39] The use of such techniques may, however, be due to the lack of verbal skills and the immaturity of the subjects. It is harder to articulate alternative cultural norms and justifications than to offer *ad hoc* excuses for not adhering, in particular instances, to cultural norms formulated by someone else. One extremely important and familiar class of unsophisticated excuses is that of fictional law, in which those who resist legal restraint make an appeal to what they imagine *are* legal norms, or else voice disbelief that some rule is actually "the law."

1.2.2. It may be that the more distinct and established the opposition culture, the greater the probability of conflict, since there is more of a core of potential resistance. However, the variable of "sophistication"—meaning here knowledge of patterns in the behavior of others which is used in attempts to manipulate them—may actually determine whether or not the potential conflict develops. If the level of sophistication of opposition members is generally high, they are likely to be more successful in minimizing the chances of conflict with the authorities without making significant concessions. A solid culture combined with little sophistication is probably most likely to be associated with conflict.

1.3. The greater the extent to which the basis of legitimacy is the social norm of deference rather than norm internalization, the greater will be the probability of conflict, since

1.3.1. The less the importance of normative consensus as the basis of social order, the less likely are subjects to accept the authority structure with reference both to the right of au-

---

[39]Gresham M. Sykes and David Matza, "Techniques of Neutralization: A Theory of Delinquency," *American Sociological Review,* 22 (1957), pp. 664–670.

thorities to announce norms and to the official status of the behavior of enforcers.

2. When the normative conflict has been interpreted by authorities in legal terms, the probability that members of the opposition will be officially dealt with as criminals will depend upon (1) the status of the legal norm in the culture of the authorities, (2) the status of the opposing norm or illegal attribute in the culture of the opposition, (3) the congruence of the legal norm with the cultural and social norms of those specifically charged with enforcement, (4) the relative power of enforcers and resisters, and (5) the realism of moves made by the conflict parties.

2.1. The greater the behavioral significance of the legal norm for authorities, both in regard to congruence of cultural and social norms and in regard to the relative priority of the norm over other norms, the greater the probability that violators will be assigned criminal status.

2.2 The greater the significance of the opposition's norm to them, the greater the likelihood that they will provoke the authorities sufficiently for legal sanctioning to occur. This is, of course, even more likely when the cultural norm of the authorities is also highly significant. Otherwise, the authorities may be reluctant to join the issue, and may prefer either to ignore or to grant a special dispensation to the opposition. The greater the cultural difference, however, the more likely are the authorities to be forced to use their power either to criminalize members of the opposition or, if the opposition is a highly organized, strongly established group, to redefine the position of the opposition in the authority structure, i.e., to come to terms with them, recognizing to some extent their right to be different. Examples would be ethnic enclaves such as Chinatowns with which authorities work out accommodations, whether or not such accommodations are "legal."

2.3. The more offensive the prohibited attribute is to the enforcers, the greater the probability of criminalization of those with the attribute.

2.3.1. If there are various levels of enforcers, i.e., police, prosecutors, judiciary, etc., the more the several levels of enforcers agree that the illegal attribute is offensive, the higher will be the probability of criminalization and the more stages of the legal process the offender will go through.

2.3.2. The more offensive the illegal attribute is to those enforcers with sentencing power, the judiciary, the more severe will be the consequences of criminalization.

2.3.3. When an attribute is highly offensive to first-level enforcers but far less offensive to higher-level enforcers, the offender will be less likely to pass beyond the first stage of the legal process but there will be greater deprivation associated with the first stage. Moreover, there will be a greater proportion of unofficial and illegal cases wherein first-level enforcers coerce norm violators.

2.3.4. When an attribute is highly offensive to higher-level enforcers but far less offensive to first-level enforcers, the offender will, if officially identified at the first (arrest) stage, very likely pass beyond the first stage. Arrest will be associated wtih minimal deprivation and maximal adherence to explicit regulations upon police behavior, but since there is a high probability of charge, conviction, and relatively severe sentence, arrest will imply eventual severe deprivation, given the highly negative evaluation of the attribute by higher-level enforcers.

2.3.5. When an attribute is not offensive to enforcers at any level, arrest rates will be low and offenders will seldom be processed beyond the first stage.

2.3.6. If the attribute is both inoffensive and has low visibility, the law is likely to be a dead letter. Either the law is an approximation of a social norm that no longer exists or a statute adopted for essentially "political" reasons and perhaps not even meant to be enforced.

2.4. In general, the greater the power difference in favor of the authorities, the greater the probability of criminalization of the opposition. However, the relationship seems very likely to be curvilinear if the extremes of the power differential are included in a given set of data.

2.4.1. In the absence of a power differential, the authorities are increasingly likely to perceive the opposition as threatening, the greater and more behaviorally significant the cultural difference. The more threatening the opposition, the more likely are "normal" legal procedures to be officially abrogated in order to fight effectively for survival. Criminalization will be decidedly "political," but at the same time there will be more than ordinary concern for establishing the factual basis of the opposition's "guilt," which will be an almost foregone conclusion. The "facts" may be valid, biased by the fears of the authorities, or fabricated.

2.4.2. When the opposition is virtually powerless, normal legal procedures are likely to be unofficially abrogated in favor of summary and less costly procedures, so that official criminalization rates may well be lower than for more powerful opposition parties. Procedural law is not a gift but a concession. The validity of this proposition depends upon the attribute being found in known proportions at all socioeconomic levels. If the offensive attribute is found almost exclusively at the lowest levels, the criminalization rates will obviously be highest at those levels. Even then, the ratio of official to unofficial enforcement situations will probably be lower for low- than for high-status populations.

2.4.3. The perception of offensiveness will probably be more valid in the "no power difference" case than in the no-contest case, implying a higher frequency of "miscarriages of justice" in the no-contest case, since the potential cost of honest mistakes (e.g., increasing the morale and ferocity of the enemy) is much higher in the former case.

2.5. In general, the more realistic the moves of a conflict party, the more likely the party is to be successful. In the context of normative-legal conflict, success for enforcers is the elimination of resistance; for resisters, success is ending enforcement efforts.

2.5.1. The less realistic the moves of the opposition, the higher the probability of criminalization.

2.5.1.1. Any move that increases the visibility of the offensive attribute is likely to be unrealistic.

2.5.1.2. Any move that increases offensiveness, e.g., by emphasizing the initially offensive attribute, by drawing attention to additional offensive attributes, and by violating a higher-priority norm of the authorities, is likely to be unrealistic.

2.5.1.3. Any move that increases consensus among the various levels of enforcers is likely to be unrealistic.

2.5.1.4. Any move that increases the power difference in favor of the enforcers is likely to be unrealistic. The greater the power difference in favor of the enforcers, the greater the likelihood of unrealistic moves, since powerlessness is associated with ignorance. (Where both parties are fully informed and fully rational, ignorance does not have anything to do with powerlessness. An empirically relevant theory must, however, take into account the complex interaction of ignorance and powerlessness. Ignorance eventually increases powerlessness, while powerlessness, implying lack of access to resources, eventually results in ignorance. Knowledge is a long-run prerequisite of power but not a sufficient condition for the development of a power center; power provides opportunity for the extension of knowledge, but does not imply that the opportunity will be utilized.)

2.5.2. It might seem obvious that the less realistic the moves of the authorities or enforcers, the lower the probability of criminalization. Short-run consequences, however, must be distinguished from long-run consequences of enforcement activity. Measures aimed at victory in a short-run *power* struggle are likely to prove detrimental to the long-run effort to establish or preserve *authority* and induce norm resisters to accept the dominance-subordination relationship as legitimate. In regard to the long-run objective,

2.5.2.1 Any move that shifts the basis of legitimacy from norm internalization toward the deference norm is likely to be unrealistic. The less attention paid to "conversion" of resisters rather than unadorned coercion, the greater the likelihood that the move is unrealistic in the long-run, though a temporary repression of resistance is a likely short-run result, especially when the relative power difference is great.

2.5.2.2. Any move that constitutes a departure from normal legal procedures is likely to weaken the authority structure, and therefore be unrealistic in the long-run. (It may, however, be realistic in the short run through increasing the effectiveness of enforcement activity.) Unofficial departures will have more effect than official departures; less radical departures will have less effect than more abrupt ones.

2.5.2.3. Any move that tends to cause additional attributes of the opposition to become offensive is likely to be unrealistic. While it may be expedient to hate the enemy,[40] generalized hostility will be more likely to increase unrealism. Realistic moves are likely to be associated with specification of what precisely is to be eliminated or changed, not with a vaguely formulated conglomerate of the attributes of the enemy.

2.5.2.4. Similarly, any move by authorities that increases the

---

[40]Georg Simmel, *Conflict,* Glencoe, Illinois: The Free Press, 1955, p. 34.

size, and therefore the power, of the opposition is likely to be unrealistic. Adding attributes, as mentioned above, is likely to increase the size of the offensive population.

2.5.2.5. The less agreement among the various levels of enforcers on the offensiveness of an attribute, the more likely their moves are to be unrealistic, since (a) moves are less likely to reflect the full range of knowledge available to authorities, (b) moves may be made in a context of inter-level rivalry rather than in a context of norm enforcement, and (c) moves will be likely to reflect personal offensiveness norms rather than strictly legal norms.

CONCLUSIONS

The theory as it has been sketched is clearly a long way from a propositional calculus. Moreover, even as "verbal theory" it does not yet come to grips with a number of relevant problems, such as (1) the significance, in terms of effects upon the hypothesized relationships among variables, of the institutionalization of conflict; (2) the upper and lower limits of probabilities of criminalization, i.e., the question, "How large a proportion of the subject population can authorities criminalize, and for how long, before the authority structure either collapses or is transformed?"; (3) specification of the conditions under which certain changes in norms and normative structures will occur, beyond the obvious implication that changes in the values of the variables built into the propositions, especially the power difference, will probably result in *some* changes. Further elaboration of propositions requires additional exploratory and descriptive research. Transformation of the set of propositions into a formal deductive system will be undertaken when the various hypothetical relationships have been thoroughly examined in the light of empirical studies. At present, rigorous formalization would be premature.

8. THEORY: THE SOCIAL REALITY OF CRIME

RICHARD QUINNEY

ASSUMPTIONS: MAN AND SOCIETY IN A THEORY OF CRIME

In studying any social phenomenon we must hold to some general perspective. Two of those used by sociologists, and by most social analysts for that matter, are the *static* and the *dynamic* interpretations of society. Either is equally plausible, though most sociologists take the static viewpoint.[1] This emphasis has relegated forces and events, such as deviance and crime, which do not appear to be conducive to stability and consensus, to the pathologies of society.

My theory of crime, however, is based on the dynamic perspective. The theory is based on these assumptions about man and society: (1) process, (2) conflict, (3) power, and (4) social action.

Process. The dynamic aspect of social relations may be referred to as "social process." Though in analyzing society we use static descriptions, that is, we define the structure and function of social relations, we must be aware that social phenomena fluctuate continually.[2]

We apply this assumption to all social phenomena that have duration and undergo change, that is, all those which interest the sociologist. A social process is a continuous series of actions, taking place in time, and leading to a special kind of result: "a system of social change taking place within a defined situation and exhibiting a particular order of change through the operation of forces present from the first within the situation."[3] Any particular phenomenon, in turn, is viewed as contributing to the dynamics of the total process. As in the "modern systems approach," social phenomena are seen as generating out of an interrelated whole.[4]

From *The Social Reality of Crime,* Richard Quinney, pages 8–25. Copyright © 1970 by Little, Brown and Company (Inc.). Reprinted by permission.

[1]See Robert A. Nisbet, *The Sociological Tradition* (New York: Basic Books, 1966); Reinhard Bendix and Bennett Berger, "Images of Society and Problems of Concept Formation in Sociology," in Llewellyn Gross (ed.), *Symposium on Sociological Theory* (Evanston, Ill.: Row, Peterson, 1959), pp. 92–118.

[2]Howard Becker, *Systematic Sociology on the Basis of the Beziehungslehre and Gebildelehre of Leopold von Weiss* (New York: John Wiley & Sons, 1932).

[3]Robert MacIver, *Social Causation* (New York: Ginn, 1942), p. 130.

[4]Walter Buckley, "A Methodological Note," in Thomas J. Scheff, *Being Mentally Ill* (Chicago: Aldine, 1966), pp. 201–205.

The methodological implication of the process assumption is that any social phenomenon may be viewed as part of a complex network of events, structures, and underlying processes.

Conflict. In any society conflicts between persons, social units, or cultural elements are inevitable, the normal consequences of social life. Conflict is especially prevalent in societies with diverse value systems and normative groups. Experience teaches that we cannot expect to find consensus on all or most values and norms in such societies.

Two models of society contrast sharply: one is regarded as "conflict" and the other, "consensus." With the consensus model we describe social structure as a functionally integrated system held together in equilibrium. In the conflict model, on the other hand, we find that societies and social organizations are shaped by diversity, coercion, and change. The differences between these contending but complementary conceptions of society have been best characterized by Dahrendorf.[5] According to his study, we assume in postulating the consensus (or integrative) model of society that: (1) society is a relatively persistent, stable structure, (2) it is well integrated, (3) every element has a function—it helps maintain the system, and (4) a functioning social structure is based on a consensus on values. For the conflict (or coercion) model of society, on the other hand, we assume that: (1) at every point society is subject to change, (2) it displays at every point dissensus and conflict, (3) every element contributes to change, and (4) it is based on the coercion of some of its members by others. In other words, society is held together by force and constraint and is characterized by ubiquitous conflicts that result in continuous change: "values are ruling rather than common, enforced rather than accepted, at any given point of time."[6]

Although in society as a whole conflict may be general, according to the conflict model, it is still likely that we will find stability and consensus on values among subunits in the society. Groups with their own cultural elements are found in most societies, leading to social differentiation with conflict between the social units; nonetheless integration and stability may appear within specific social groups: "Although the total larger society may be diverse internally and may form only a loosely integrated system, within each subculture there may be high integration of institutions and close conformity of individuals to the patterns sanctioned by their own group."[7]

Conflict need not necessarily disrupt society. Some sociologists have been interested in the *functions* of social conflict, "that is to say, with

---

[5]Ralf Dahrendorf, *Class and Class Conflict in Industrial Society* (Stanford: Stanford University Press, 1959), pp. 161–162.

[6]Ralf Dahrendorf, "Out of Utopia: Toward a Reorientation in Sociological Analysis," *American Journal of Sociology*, 67 (September, 1958), p. 127.

[7]Robin M. Williams, Jr., *American Society*, 2nd ed. (New York: Alfred A. Knopf, 1960), p. 375.

those consequences of social conflict which make for an increase rather than a decrease in the adaptation or adjustment of particular social relationships or groups."[8] It seems that conflict can promote cooperation, establish group boundaries, and unite social factions. Furthermore, it may lead to new patterns that may in the long run be beneficial to the whole society or to parts of it.[9] Any doubts about its functional possibilities have been dispelled by Dahrendorf: "I would suggest . . . that all that is creativity, innovation, and development in the life of the individual, his group, and his society is due, to no small extent, to the operation of conflicts between group and group, individual and individual, emotion and emotion within one individual. This fundamental fact alone seems to me to justify the value judgment that conflict is essentially 'good' and 'desirable.' "[10] Conflict is not always the disruptive agent in a society; at certain times it may be meaningful to see it as a cohesive force.

Power. The conflict conception of society leads us to assume that coherence is assured in any social unit by coercion and constraint. In other words, *power* is the basic characteristic of social organization. "This means that in every social organization some positions are entrusted with a right to exercise control over other positions in order to ensure effective coercion; it means in other words, that there is a differential distribution of power and authority."[11] Thus, conflict and power are inextricably linked in the conception of society presented here. The differential distribution of power produces conflict between competing groups, and conflict, in turn, is rooted in the competition for power. Wherever men live together conflict and a struggle for power will be found.

Power, then, is the ability of persons and groups to determine the conduct of other persons and groups.[12] It is utilized not for its own sake, but is the vehicle for the enforcement of scarce values in society, whether values are material, moral, or otherwise. The use of power affects the distribution of values and values affect the distribution of power. The "authoritative allocation of values" is essential to any society.[13] In any

---

[8]Lewis A. Coser, *The Functions of Social Conflict* (New York: The Free Press, 1956), p. 8.

[9]Lewis A. Coser, "Social Conflict and the Theory of Social Change," *British Journal of Sociology*, 8 (September, 1957), pp. 197–207.

[10]Dahrendorf, *Class and Class Conflict in Industrial Society*, p. 208. The importance of conflict in society is also discussed in, among other works, George Simmel, *Conflict*, trans. Kurt H. Wolff (New York: The Free Press, 1955); Irving Louis Horowitz, "Consensus, Conflict and Cooperation: A Sociological Inventory," *Social Forces*, 41 (December, 1962), pp. 177–88; Raymond W. Mack, "The Components of Social Conflict," *Social Problems*, 12 (Spring, 1965), pp. 388–97.

[11]Dahrendorf, *Class and Class Conflict in Industrial Society*, p. 165.

[12]Max Weber, *From Max Weber: Essays in Sociology*, trans. H. H. Gerth and C. Wright Mills (New York: Oxford University Press, 1946); Hans Gerth and C. Wright Mills, *Character and Social Structure* (New York: Harcourt, Brace, 1953), especially pp. 192–273; C. Wright Mills, *The Power Elite* (New York: Oxford University Press, 1956); George Simmel, *The Sociology of George Simmel*, trans. Kurt H. Wolff (New York: The Free Press, 1950), pp. 181–186; Robert Bierstedt, "An Analysis of Social Power," *American Sociological Review*, 15 (December 1950), pp. 730–38.

[13]David Easton, *The Political System* (New York: Alfred A. Knopf, 1953), p. 137. Similar ideas are found in Harold D. Lasswell, *Politics: Who Gets What, When, How* (New York: McGraw-Hill, 1936); Harold D. Lasswell and Abraham Kaplan, *Power and Society* (New Haven: Yale University Press, 1950).

society, institutional means are used to officially establish and enforce sets of values for the entire population.

Power and the allocation of values are basic in forming *public policy*. Groups with special *interests* become so well organized that they are able to influence the policies that are to affect all persons. These interest groups exert their influence at every level and branch of government in order to have their own values and interests represented in the policy decisions.[14] Any interest group's ability to influence public policy depends on the group's position in the political power structure. Furthermore, access to the formation of public policy is unequally distributed because of the structural arrangements of the political state. "Access is one of the advantages unequally distributed by such arrangements; that is, in consequence of the structural peculiarities of our government some groups have better and more varied opportunities to influence key points of decision than do others."[15] Groups that have the power to gain access to the decision-making process also inevitably control the lives of others.

A major assumption in my conception of society, therefore, is the importance of interest groups in shaping public policy. Public policy is formed so as to represent the interests and values of groups that are in positions of power. Rather than accept the pluralistic conception of the political process, which assumes that all groups make themselves heard in policy decision-making, I am relying upon a conception that assumes an unequal distribution of power in formulating and administering public policy.[16]

---

[14]Among the vast amount of literature on interest groups, see Donald C. Blaisdell, *American Democracy Under Pressure* (New York: Ronald Press, 1957); V. O. Key, Jr., *Politics, Parties, and Pressure Groups* (New York: Thomas Y. Crowell, 1959); Earl Latham, *Group Basis of Politics* (Ithaca, N.Y.: Cornell University Press, 1952); David Truman, *The Governmental Process* (New York: Alfred A. Knopf, 1951); Henry W. Ehrmann (ed.), *Interest Groups on Four Continents* (Pittsburgh: University of Pittsburgh Press, 1958); Henry A. Turner, "How Pressure Groups Operate," *Annals of the American Academy of Political and Social Science*, 319 (September, 1958), pp. 63–72; Richard W. Gable, "Interest Groups as Policy Shapers," *Annals of the American Academy of Political and Social Science,* 319 (September, 1958), pp. 84–93; Murray S. Stedman, "Pressure Group and the American Tradition," *Annals of the American Academy of Political and Social Science*, 319 (September, 1958), pp. 123–219. For documentation on the influence of specific interest groups, see Robert Engler, *The Politics of Oil* (New York: Macmillan, 1961); Oliver Garceau, *The Political Life of the American Medical Association* (Cambridge: Harvard University Press, 1941); Charles M. Hardin, *The Politics of Agriculture: Soil Conservation and the Struggle for Power in Rural America* (New York: The Free Press of Glencoe, 1962); Grant McConnell, *Private Power and American Democracy* (New York: Alfred A. Knopf, 1966); Harry A. Millis and Royal E. Montgomery, *Organized Labor* (New York: McGraw-Hill, 1945); Warner Schilling, Paul Y. Hammond, and Glenn H. Snyder, *Strategy, Politics and Defense* (New York: Columbia University Press, 1962); William R. Willoughby, *The St. Lawrence Waterway: A Study in Politics and Diplomacy* (Madison: University of Wisconsin Press, 1961).

[15]Truman, *The Governmental Process*, p. 322.

[16]Evaluations of the pluralistic and power approaches are found in Peter Bachrach and Morton S. Baratz, "Two Faces of Power," *American Political Science Review*, 61 (December, 1962), pp. 947–52; Thomas I. Cook, "The Political System: The Stubborn Search for a Science of Politics," *Journal of Philosophy*, 51 (February, 1954), pp. 128–37; Charles S. Hyneman, *The Study of Politics* (Urbana: University of Illinois Press, 1959); William C. Mitchell, "Politics as the Allocation of Values: A Critique," *Ethics*, 71 (January, 1961), pp. 79–89; Talcott Parsons, "The Distribution of Power in American Society," *World Politics*, 10 (October, 1957), pp. 123–43; Charles Perrow, "The Sociological Perspective and Political Pluralism," *Social Research*, 31 (Winter, 1964), pp. 411–22.

Social Action. An assumption of man that is consistent with the conflict-power conception of society asserts that man's actions are purposive and meaningful, that man engages in voluntary behavior. This *humanistic* conception of man contrasts with the oversocialized conception of man. Man is, after all, capable of considering alternative actions, of breaking from the established social order.[17] Once he gains an awareness of self, by being a member of society, he is able to choose his actions. The extent to which he does conform depends in large measure upon his own self-control.[18] Nonconformity may also be part of the process of finding self-identity. It is thus *against* something that the self can emerge.[19]

By conceiving of man as able to reason and choose courses of action, we may see him as changing and becoming, rather than merely being.[20] The kind of culture that man develops shapes his ability to be creative. Through his culture he may develop the capacity to have greater freedom of action.[21] Not only is he shaped by his physical, social, and cultural experiences, he is able to select what he is to experience and develop. The belief in realizing unutilized human potential is growing and should be incorporated in a contemporary conception of human behavior.[22]

The *social action* frame of reference that serves as the basis of the humanistic conception of man is drawn from the work of such writers as Weber, Znaniecki, MacIver, Nadel, Parsons, and Becker.[23] It was originally suggested by Max Weber: "Action is social in so far as, by virtue of the subjective meaning attached to it by the acting individual (or individuals), it takes account of the behavior of others and is thereby oriented in its own course."[24] Hence, human behavior is *intentional,* has *meaning* for the actors, is *goal-oriented,* and takes place with an *awareness* of the consequences of behavior.

Because man engages in social action, a *social reality* is created. That is, man in interaction with others constructs a meaningful world of everyday life.

---

[17]For essentially this aspect of man see Peter Berger, *Invitation to Sociology: A Humanistic Perspective* (New York: Doubleday, 1963), chap. 6; Max Mark, "What Image of Man for Political Science?" *Western Political Quarterly,* 15 (December, 1962), pp. 593–604; Dennis Wrong, "The Oversocialized Conception of Man in Modern Sociology," *American Sociological Review,* 26 (April, 1961), pp. 183–93.

[18]Tamotsu Shibutani, *Society and Personality: An Interactionist Approach to Social Psychology* (Englewood Cliffs, N. J.: Prentice-Hall, 1961), especially pp. 60, 91–94, 276–78. Also see S. F. Nadel, "Social Control and Self-Regulation," *Social Forces,* 31 (March, 1953), pp. 265–73.

[19]Erving Goffman, *Asylums* (New York: Doubleday, 1961), pp. 318–20.

[20]Richard A. Schermerhorn, "Man the Unfinished," *Sociological Quarterly,* 4 (Winter, 1963), pp. 5–17; Gordon W. Allport, *Becoming: Basic Considerations for a Psychology of Personality* (New Haven: Yale University Press, 1955).

[21]Herbert J. Muller, *The Uses of the Past* (New York: Oxford University Press, 1952), especially pp. 40–42.

[22]Julian Huxley, *New Bottles for New Wines* (New York: Harper, 1957).

[23]Florian Znaniecki, *Social Actions* (New York: Farrar and Rinehart, 1936); MacIver, *Social Causation;* S. F. Nadel, *Foundations of Social Anthropology* (New York: The Free Press, 1951); Talcott Parsons, *The Structure of Social Action* (New York: The Free Press, 1949); Howard Becker, *Through Values to Social Interpretation* (Durham: Duke University Press, 1950).

[24]Max Weber, *The Theory of Social and Economic Organization,* trans. A. M. Henderson and Talcott Parsons (New York: The Free Press), p. 88.

It is the world of cultural objects and social institutions into which we are all born, within which we have to find our bearings, and with which we have to come to terms. From the outset, we, the actors on the social scene, experience the world we live in as a world both of nature and of culture, not as a private but as an intersubjective one, that is, as a world common to all of us, either actually given or potentially accessible to everyone; and this involves intercommunication and language.[25]

Social reality consists of both the social meanings and the products of the subjective world of persons. Man, accordingly, constructs activities and patterns of actions as he attaches meaning to his everyday existence.[26] Social reality is thus both a *conceptual reality* and a *phenomenal reality*. Having constructed social reality, man finds a world of meanings and events that is real to him as a conscious social being.

THEORY: THE SOCIAL REALITY OF CRIME

The theory contains six propositions and a number of statements within the propositions. With the first proposition I define crime. The next four are the explanatory units. In the final proposition the other five are collected to form a composite describing the social reality of crime. The propositions and their integration into a theory of crime reflect the assumptions about explanation and about man and society outlined above.[27]

PROPOSITION 1 (DEFINITION OF CRIME): *Crime is a definition of human conduct that is created by authorized agents in a politically organized society.*

This is the essential starting point in the theory—a definition of crime—which itself is based on the concept of definition. Crime is a *definition* of behavior that is conferred on some persons by others. Agents of the law (legislators, police, prosecutors, and judges), representing segments of a politically organized society, are responsible for formulating and administering criminal law. Persons and behaviors, therefore, become criminal because of the *formulation* and *application* of criminal definitions. Thus, *crime is created.*

By viewing crime as a definition, we are able to avoid the commonly used "clinical perspective," which leads one to concentrate on the quality

---

[25]Alfred Schutz, *The Problem of Social Reality: Collected Papers I* (The Hague: Martinus Nijhoff, 1962), p. 53.

[26]See Peter L. Berger and Thomas Luckmann, *The Social Construction of Reality* (Garden City, N.Y.: Doubleday, 1966).

[27]For earlier background material, see Richard Quinney, "A Conception of Man and Society for Criminology," *Sociological Quarterly*, 6 (Spring 1965), pp. 119–27; Quinney, "Crime in Political Perspective," *American Behavioral Scientist*, 8 (December 1964), pp. 19–22; Quinney, "Is Criminal Behavior Deviant Behavior?" *British Journal of Criminology*, 5 (April 1965), pp. 132–42.

of the act and to assume that criminal behavior is an individual pathology.[28] Crime is not inherent in behavior, but is a judgment made by some about the actions and characteristics of others.[29] This proposition allows us to focus on the formulation and administration of the criminal law as it touches upon the behaviors that become defined as criminal. Crime is seen as a result of a process which culminates in the defining of persons and behaviors as criminal. It follows, then, that *the greater the number of criminal definitions formulated and applied, the greater the amount of crime.*

PROPOSITION 2 (FORMULATION OF CRIMINAL DEFINITIONS):
Criminal definitions describe behaviors that conflict with the interests of the segments of society that have the power to shape public policy.

Criminal definitions are formulated according to the interests of those *segments* (types of social groupings) of society which have the *power* to translate their interests into *public policy*. The interests—based on desires, values, and norms—which are ultimately incorporated into the criminal law are those which are treasured by the dominant interest groups in the society.[30] In other words, those who have the ability to have their interests represented in public policy regulate the formulation of criminal definitions.

That criminal definitions are formulated is one of the most obvious manifestations of *conflict* in society. By formulating criminal law (including legislative statutes, administrative rulings, and judicial decisions), some segments of society protect and perpetuate their own interests. Criminal definitions exist, therefore, because some segments of society are in conflict with others.[31] By formulating criminal definitions these

---

[28]See Jane R. Mercer, "Social System Perspective and Clinical Perspective: Frames of Reference for Understanding Career Patterns of Persons Labelled as Mentally Retarded," *Social Problems,* 13 (Summer 1966), pp. 18–34.

[29]This perspective in the study of social deviance has been developed in Becker, *Outsiders* (New York: Free Press, 1963); Kai T. Erikson, "Notes on the Sociology of Deviance," *Social Problems,* 9 (Spring 1962), pp. 307–14; John I. Kitsuse, "Societal Reactions to Deviant Behavior: Problems of Theory and Method," *Social Problems,* 9 (Winter 1962), pp. 247–56. Also see Ronald L. Akers, "Problems in the Sociology of Deviance: Social Definitions and Behavior," *Social Forces,* 46 (June 1968), pp. 455–65; David J. Bordua, "Recent Trends: Deviant Behavior and Social Control," *Annals of the American Academy of Political and Social Science,* 369 (January 1967), pp. 149–63; Jack P. Gibbs, "Conceptions of Deviant Behavior: The Old and the New," *Pacific Sociological Review,* 9 Spring 1966), pp. 9–14; Clarence R. Jeffery, "The Structure of American Criminological Thinking," *Journal of Criminal Law, Criminology and Police Science,* 46 (January–February 1956), pp. 658–72; Austin T. Turk, "Prospects for Theories of Criminal Behavior," *Journal of Criminal Law, Criminology and Police Science,* 55 (December 1964), pp. 454–61.

[30]See Richard C. Fuller, "Morals and the Criminal Law," *Journal of Criminal Law, Criminology and Police Science,* 32 (March–April 1942), pp. 624–30; Thorsten Sellin, *Culture Conflict and Crime* (New York: Social Science Research Council, 1938), pp. 21–25; Clarence R. Jeffery, "Crime, Law and Social Structure," *Journal of Criminal Law, Criminology and Police Science,* 47 (November–December 1956), pp. 423–35; John J. Honigmann, "Value Conflict and Legislation," *Social Problems,* 7 (Summer 1959), pp. 34–40; George Rusche and Otto Kirchheimer, *Punishment and Social Structure* (New York: Columbia University Press, 1939); Roscoe Pound, *An Introduction to the Philosophy of Law* (New Haven: Yale University Press, 1922).

[31]I am obviously indebted to the conflict formulation of George B. Vold, *Theoretical Criminology* (New York: Oxford University Press, 1958), especially pp. 203–42. A recent conflict approach to crime is found in Austin T. Turk, "Conflict and Criminality," *American Sociological Review,* 31 (June 1966), pp. 338–52 (both in this volume).

segments are able to control the behavior of persons in other segments. It follows that *the greater the conflict in interests between the segments of a society, the greater the probability that the power segments will formulate criminal definitions.*

The interests of the power segments of society are reflected not only in the content of criminal definitions and the kinds of penal sanctions attached to them, but also in the *legal policies* stipulating how those who come to be denied as "criminal" are to be handled. Hence, procedural rules are created for enforcing and administering the criminal law. Policies are also established on programs for treating and punishing the criminally defined and for controlling and preventing crime. In the initial criminal definitions or the subsequent procedures, and in correctional and penal programs or policies of crime control and prevention, the segments of society that have power and interests to protect are instrumental in regulating the behavior of those who have conflicting interests and less power.[32] Finally, law changes with modifications in the interest structure. When the interests that underlie a criminal law are no longer relevant to groups in power, the law will be reinterpreted or altered to incorporate the dominant interests. Hence, the *probability that criminal definitions will be formulated is increased by such factors as (1) changing social conditions, (2) emerging interests, (3) increasing demands that political, economic, and religious interests be protected, and (4) changing conceptions of the public interest.* The social history of law reflects changes in the interest structure of society.

PROPOSITION 3 (APPLICATION OF CRIMINAL DEFINITIONS): *Criminal definitions are applied by the segments of society that have the power to shape the enforcement and administration of criminal law.*

The powerful interests intervene in all stages in which criminal definitions are created. Since interests cannot be effectively protected by merely formulating criminal law, enforcement and administration of the law are required. The interests of the powerful, therefore, operate in *applying* criminal definitions. Consequently, crime is "political behavior and the criminal becomes in fact a member of a 'minority group' without sufficient public support to dominate the control of the police power of the state."[33]

---

[32]Considerable support for this proposition is found in the following studies: William J. Chambliss, "A Sociological Analysis of the Law of Vagrancy," *Social Problems*, 12 (Summer, 1964), pp. 66–77 (in this volume); Kai T. Erikson, *Wayward Puritans* (New York: John Wiley, 1966); Jerome Hall, *Theft, Law and Society*, 2nd ed. (Indianapolis: Bobbs-Merrill, 1952); Clarence R. Jeffery, "The Development of Crime in Early England," *Journal of Criminal Law, Criminology and Police Science*, 47 (March–April 1957), pp. 647–66; Alfred R. Lindesmith, *The Addict and the Law* (Bloomington: Indiana University Press, 1965); Rusche and Kirchheimer, *Punishment and Social Structure;* Andrew Sinclair, *Era of Excess: A Social History of the Prohibition Movement* (New York: Harper & Row, 1964); Edwin H. Sutherland, "The Sexual Psychopath Law," *Journal of Criminal Law, Criminology and Police Science*, 40 (January–February, 1950), pp. 543–54.

[33]Vold, *Theoretical Criminology*, p. 202. Also see Irving Louis Horowitz and Martin Liebowitz, "Social Deviance and Political Marginality: Toward a Redefinition of the Relation Between Sociology and Politics," *Social Problems*, 15 (Winter 1968), pp. 280–96 (in this volume).

Those whose interests conflict with the interests represented in the law must either change their behavior or possibly find it defined as "criminal."

The probability that criminal definitions will be applied varies according to the extent to which the behaviors of the powerless conflict with the interests of the power segments. Law enforcement efforts and judicial activity are likely to be increased when the interests of the powerful are threatened by the opposition's behavior. Fluctuations and variations in the application of criminal definitions reflect shifts in the relations of the various segments in the power structure of society.

Obviously, the criminal law is not applied directly by the powerful segments. They delegate enforcement and administration of the law to authorized *legal agents,* who, nevertheless, represent their interests. In fact, the security in office of legal agents depends on their ability to represent the society's dominant interests.

Because the interest groups responsible for creating criminal definitions are physically separated from the groups to which the authority to enforce and administer law is delegated, local conditions affect the manner in which criminal definitions are applied.[34] In particular, communities vary in the law enforcement and administration of justice they expect. Application is also affected by the visibility of acts in a community and by its norms about reporting possible offenses. Especially important are the occupational organization and ideology of the legal agents.[35] Thus, *the probability that criminal definitions will be applied is influenced by such community and organizational factors as (1) community expectations of law enforcement and administration, (2) the visibility and public reporting of offenses, and (3) the occupational organization, ideology, and actions of the legal agents to whom the authority to enforce and administer criminal law is delegated.* Such factors determine how the dominant interests of society are implemented in the application of criminal definitions.

---

[34]See Michael Banton, *The Policeman and the Community* (London: Tavistock, 1964); Egon Bittner, "The Police on Skid-Row: A Study of Peace Keeping," *American Sociological Review,* 32 (October 1967), pp. 699–715; John P. Clark, "Isolation of the Police: A Comparison of the British and American Situations," *Journal of Criminal Law, Criminology and Police Science,* 56 (September 1965), pp. 307–19; Nathan Goldman, *The Differential Selection of Juvenile Offenders for Court Appearance* (New York National Council on Crime and Delinquency, 1963); James Q. Wilson, *Varieties of Police Behavior* (Cambridge: Harvard University Press, 1968).

[35]Abraham S. Blumberg, *Criminal Justice* (Chicago: Quadrangle Books, 1967); David J. Bordua and Albert J. Reiss, Jr., "Command, Control and Charisma: Reflections on Police Bureaucracy," *American Journal of Sociology,* 72 (July 1966), pp. 68–76; Aaron V. Cicourel, *The Social Organization of Juvenile Justice* (New York: John Wiley, 1968); Arthur Niederhoffer, *Behind the Shield: The Police in Urban Society* (Garden City, N.Y.: Doubleday, 1967); Jerome H. Skolnick, *Justice Without Trial: Law Enforcement in Democratic Society* (New York: John Wiley, 1966); Arthur L. Stinchcombe, "Institutions of Privacy in the Determination of Police Administrative Practice," *American Journal of Sociology,* 69 (September 1963), pp. 150–60; David Sudnow, "Normal Crimes: Sociological Features of the Penal Code in a Public Defender Office," *Social Problems,* 12 (Winter, 1965), pp. 255–76; William A. Westley, "Violence and the Police," *American Journal of Sociology,* 59 (July 1953), pp. 34–41; Arthur Lewis Wood, *Criminal Lawyer* (New Haven: College & University Press, 1967).

The probability that criminal definitions will be applied in *specific situations* depends on the actions of the legal agents. In the final analysis, a criminal definition is applied according to an *evaluation* by someone charged with the authority to enforce and administer the law. In the course of "criminalization," a criminal label may be affixed to a person because of real or fancied attributes: "Indeed, a person is evaluated, either favorably or unfavorably, not because he *does* something, or even because he *is* something, but because others react to their perceptions of him as offensive or inoffensive."[36] Evaluation by the definers is affected by the way in which the suspect handles the situation, but ultimately their evaluations and subsequent decisions determine the criminality of human acts. Hence, *the more legal agents evaluate behaviors and persons as worthy of criminal definition, the greater the probability that criminal definitions will be applied.*

PROPOSITION 4 (DEVELOPMENT OF BEHAVIOR PATTERNS IN RELATION TO CRIMINAL DEFINITIONS): *Behavior patterns are structured in segmentally organized society in relation to criminal definitions, and within this context persons engage in actions that have relative probabilities of being defined as criminal.*

Although behavior varies, all behaviors are similar in that they represent the *behavior patterns* of segments of society. Therefore, all persons— whether they create criminal definitions or are the objects of criminal definitions—act according to *normative systems* learned in relative social and cultural settings.[37] Since it is not the quality of the behavior but the action taken against the behavior that makes it criminal, that which is defined as criminal in any society is relative to the behavior patterns of the segments of society that formulate and apply criminal definitions. Consequently, *persons in the segments of society whose behavior patterns are not represented in formulating and applying criminal definitions are more likely to act in ways that will be defined as criminal than those in the segments that formulate and apply criminal definitions.*

Once behavior patterns are established with some regularity within the respective segments of society, individuals are provided with a framework for developing *personal action patterns.* These patterns continually develop for each person as he moves from one experience to another. It is

---

[36]Turk, "Conflict and Criminality," p. 340. For research on the evaluation of suspects by policemen, see Irving Piliavin and Scott Briar, "Police Encounters with Juveniles," *American Journal of Sociology*, 70 (September 1964), pp. 206–14.

[37]Assumed within the theory of the social reality of crime is Sutherland's theory of differential association. See Edwin H. Sutherland, *Principles of Criminology*, 4th ed. (Philadelphia: J. B. Lippincott, 1947). An analysis of the differential association theory is found in Melvin L. De Fleur and Richard Quinney, "A Reformulation of Sutherland's Differential Association Theory and a Strategy for Empirical Verification," *Journal of Research in Crime and Delinquency*, 3 (January 1966), pp. 1–22.

the development of these patterns that gives his behavior its own substance in relation to criminal definitions.

Man constructs his own patterns of action in participating with others. It follows, then, that *the probability that a person will develop action patterns that have a high potential of being defined as criminal depends on the relative substance of (1) structured opportunities, (2) learning experiences, (3) interpersonal associations and identifications, and (4) self-conceptions.* Throughout his experiences, each person creates a conception of himself as a social being. Thus prepared, he behaves according to the anticipated consequences of his actions.[38]

During experiences shared by the criminal definers and the criminally defined, personal action patterns develop among the criminally defined because they are so defined. After such persons have had continued experience in being criminally defined, they learn to manipulate the application of criminal definitions.[39]

Furthermore, those who have been defined as criminal begin to conceive of themselves as criminal; as they adjust to the definitions imposed upon them, they learn to play the role of the criminal.[40] Because of others' reactions, therefore, persons may develop personal action patterns that increase the likelihood of their being defined as criminal in the future. That is, *increased experience with criminal definitions increases the probability of developing actions that may be subsequently defined as criminal.*

Thus, both the criminal definers and the criminally defined are involved in reciprocal action patterns. The patterns of both the definers and the defined are shaped by their common, continued, and related experiences. The fate of each is bound to that of the other.

PROPOSITION 5 (CONSTRUCTION OF CRIMINAL CONCEPTIONS): *Conceptions of crime are constructed and diffused in the segments of society by various means of communication.*

The "real world" is a social construction: man with the help of others creates the world in which he lives. Social reality is thus the world a group of people create and believe in as their own. This reality is constructed according to the kind of "knowledge" they develop, the ideas they are exposed to, the manner in which they select information to fit the world they are shaping, and the manner in which they interpret these concep-

---

[38]On the operant nature of criminally defined behavior, see Robert L. Burgess and Ronald L. Akers, "A Differential Association-Reinforcement Theory of Criminal Behavior," *Social Problems*, 14 (Fall 1966), pp. 128–47; C. R. Jeffery, "Criminal Behavior and Learning Theory," *Journal of Criminal Law, Criminology and Police Science*, 56 (September 1965), pp. 294–300.

[39]A discussion of the part the person plays in manipulating the deviant defining situation is found in Judith Lorber, "Deviance as Performance: The Case of Illness," *Social Problems*, 14 (Winter 1967), pp. 302–10.

[40]Edwin M. Lemert, *Human Deviance, Social Problems, and Social Control* (Englewood Cliffs, N.J.: Prentice-Hall, 1964), pp. 40–64; Edwin M. Lemert, *Social Pathology* (New York: McGraw-Hill, 1951), pp. 3–98. A related and earlier discussion is in Frank Tannenbaum, *Crime and the Community* (New York: Columbia University Press, 1938), pp. 3–81.

tions.[41] Man behaves in reference to the *social meanings* he attaches to his experiences.

Among the constructions that develop in a society are those which determine what man regards as crime. Wherever we find the concept of crime, there we will find conceptions about the relevance of crime, the offender's characteristics, and the relation of crime to the social order.[42] These conceptions are constructed by communication. In fact, *the construction of criminal conceptions depends on the portrayal of crime in all personal and mass communications.* By such means, criminal conceptions are constructed and diffused in the segments of a society. The most critical conceptions are those held by the power segments of society. These are the conceptions that are certain of becoming incorporated into the social reality of crime. In general, then, *the more the power segments are concerned about crime, the greater the probability that criminal definitions will be created and that behavior patterns will develop in opposition to criminal definitions.* The formulation and application of criminal definitions and the development of behavior patterns related to criminal definitions are thus joined in full circle by the construction of criminal conceptions.

PROPOSITION 6 (THE SOCIAL REALITY OF CRIME): *The social reality of crime is constructed by the formulation and application of criminal definitions, the development of behavior patterns related to criminal definitions, and the construction of criminal conceptions.*

These five propositions can be collected into a composite. The theory, accordingly, describes and explains phenomena that increase the probability of crime in society, resulting in the social reality of crime.

Since the first proposition is a definition and the sixth is a composite, the body of the theory consists of the four middle propositions. These form a model, as diagrammed in Figure 1.1, which relates the propositions into a theoretical system. Each proposition is related to the others forming a theoretical system of developmental propositions interacting with one another. The phenomena denoted in the propositions and their relationships culminate in what is regarded as the amount and character of crime in a society at any given time, that is, in the social reality of crime.

---

[41]See Berger and Luckmann, *The Social Construction of Reality.* Relevant research on the diffusion of information is discussed in Everett M. Rogers, *Diffusion of Innovations* (New York: The Free Press of Glencoe, 1962).

[42]Research on public conceptions of crime is only beginning. See Alexander L. Clark and Jack P. Gibbs, "Social Control: A Reformulation," *Social Problems,* 12 (Spring 1965), pp. 398–415; Thomas E. Dow, Jr., "The Role of Identification in Conditioning Public Attitude Toward the Offender," *Journal of Criminal Law, Criminology and Police Science,* 58 (March 1967), pp. 75–79; William P. Lentz, "Social Status and Attitudes Toward Delinquency Control," *Journal of Research in Crime and Delinquency,* 3 (July 1966), pp. 147–54; Jennie McIntyre, "Public Attitudes Toward Crime and Law Enforcement," *Annals of the American Academy of Political and Social Science,* 374 (November 1967), pp. 34–46; Anastassios D. Mylonas and Walter C. Reckless, "Prisoners' Attitudes Toward Law and Legal Institutions," *Journal of Criminal Law, Criminology and Police Science,* 54 (December 1963), pp. 479–84; Elizabeth A. Rooney and Don C. Gibbons, "Social Reactions to 'Crimes Without Victims,'" *Social Problems,* 13 (Spring 1966), pp. 400–10.

FIGURE 8.1. Model of the Social Reality of Crime

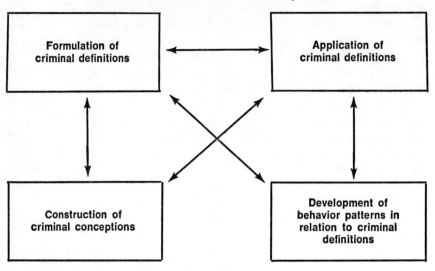

A THEORETICAL PERSPECTIVE FOR STUDYING CRIME

The theory as I have formulated it is inspired by a change currently altering our view of the world. This change, found at all levels of society, has to do with the world that we all construct and, at the same time, pretend to separate ourselves from in assessing our experiences. Sociologists, sensing the problematic nature of existence, have begun to revise their theoretical orientation, as well as their methods and subjects of investigation.

For the study of crime, a revision in thought is directing attention to the process by which criminal definitions are formulated and applied. In the theory of the social reality of crime I have attempted to show how a theory of crime can be consistent with some revisionist assumptions about theoretical explanation and about man and society. The theory is cumulative in that the framework incorporates the diverse findings from criminology.

The synthesis has been brought about by conceiving of crime as a constructive process and by formulating a theory according to a system of propositions. The theory is integrative in that all relevant phenomena contribute to the process of creating criminal definitions, the development of the behaviors of those who are involved in criminal defining situations, and the construction of criminal conceptions. The result is the social reality of crime that is constantly being constructed in society.

PART THREE: THE EMERGENCE OF NONCONFORMITY AND CONFLICT

Lewis Coser (1956:8) defines conflict as "a struggle over values and claims to scarce status, power, and resources in which the aims of the opponents are to neutralize, injure, or eliminate their rivals." He further suggests that conflict can be either *realistic* or *nonrealistic*. Realistic conflict is directed toward a "specific or obtainable result" as opposed to nonrealistic conflict, which "is not oriented toward the attainment of specific results" (Coser, 1956:49).

Coser indicates that conflict is *functional* only under "realistic" conditions of mutually internalized values and norms. Radicals are "nonrealistic." Because they are not "sensitized to clues which would allow them to conclude that a victory has been reached, unable to recognize peace overtures or concessions from the adversary, revolutionary syndicalists are not in a position to take advantage of partial gains" (Coser, 1961:349). Gusfield (1962:23) supports this view in outlining the distinction between contained interest group struggle and deviant political behavior or extremism:

> Extremism is alienated from the institutions of democratic politics.
> It denies the legitimacy of democratic political institutions as devices
> for mediating conflict. Extremist style refuses to accept the possible
> or probable outcomes of a whole or partial defeat. Total victory is
> too important in the hierarchy of values to permit a compromise.

Conflict, as used in the sociological literature, is primarily a process ranging from the mere competition of parties—limited or controlled conflict—to the "zero-sum outcome" of confrontation and revolution. As Neil Smelser (1963:270) argues, struggle can be either *normative* ("realistic") or *valuative* ("nonrealistic"). *Normative* conflict is an "attempt to restore, protect, modify, or create norms in the name of a generalized belief." This form of conflict involves a singular alteration in the social order and is therefore limited and controlled. The alteration can be in the form of a new law, political organization, or party. Normative conflict is based on the assumption that *competing* forces have a common regard for the general values of society.

Political lobbyists, political campaigners, picket lines, pressure groups all engage in this form of conflict. Some criminal activity may be seen as normative since the violator in fact fears competition with segments of legitimate industry, as Professor Schelling indicates in his article in this part on organized crime. Even some forms of collective behavior such as rioting may, in fact, be normative. Lenin terms riots "outbursts of desperation" by those groups unable to articulate their political grievances. Robert Fogelson (1971:16) says of the riots in Negro ghettos that "the rioters demanded that all citizens honor [the American ideology of equality]; *they insisted on changes in practices not principles.*" Another observer, James Geschwender (1968:482) notes that ". . . urban disorders, are, in fact, creative rioting. Creative rioting falls clearly within the evolutionary pattern of the civil rights movement, a social movement which *may or may not eventually become revolutionary.*"

Smelser (1963:313–314) sees *valuative conflict* as transcending the boundaries of the normative as participants may attempt to restore the ideologies of the past; perpetuate those of the present; more frequently, create new values of the future. Valuative or total conflict most frequently involves the elements described by Gusfield as being extremist. Talcott Parsons (1951:355) indicates in a similar view:

> This ideology [counter-ideology] will always include a diagnosis of the basis for the break with the main society and its value system. . . . There will be such beliefs as that "you can't win" in the wider society, that "they're out to get you," and the like. It will also involve an ideology of the relationship system within the deviant collectivity, for instance, as to why leadership and discipline should be accepted.

Political radicals and extremists are the carriers of counter-ideologies. The Black Panther Party, Weathermen, Industrial Workers of the World, and the various Communist movements have questioned the legitimacy of the existent social structure, a fact that places them in a precarious position *vis-a-vis* the legal structure. The determination of which type of conflict emerges—normative or valuative—is made, as Horowitz and Leibowitz suggest, by the reaction of the very body to which the political deviants object. For example, when the courts deem a political demonstration illegal but the marchers persist, the nature of their action has changed from normative to valuative.

Some forms of conflict are not labelled deviant, while others are. Horowitz and Leibowitz note:

> The political climate prescribes both what conflicts will occur between deviants and nondeviants, and the rules by which such conflicts will be resolved. The struggle of groups for legitimation thus constitutes an integral part of deviant behavior.

Deviance is inherent in conflict, as Karl Mannheim (1936:54) originally suggested:

> We are skeptical of the ideas and representations advanced by our opponent. They are regarded as more or less conscious disguises of the real nature of a situation, the true recognition of which would not be in accord with his interests.

As noted in an earlier chapter, every industrial society has both common and diverse norms and beliefs. These are, however, in a constant state of flux. Laws, ideas, fashions all change. Many areas of activity, as all of the papers in this chapter suggest, may fall into the gray areas of public and normative opinion. The arbitration of these definitional questions, as Horowitz and Leibowitz, and Kelly indicate, occurs in the legislative, executive, and judicial arms of government, and is influenced to only a limited extent by public attitudes. As Jack Douglas' analysis suggests, the perceptions of behavior and of those actively engaged in it as deviant may be misleading. Street gangs, political protesters, and carriers of counter-ideologies are all labelled as deviants, yet their relationship to the law and society is poorly defined.

Sagarin's examination of the Gay Liberation Movement provides another example of the competing views of aberrant and nonconformist behavior. Gay Liberationists, however, insist that they are yet another "politically and socially" oppressed nonconformist group. The definition of GLM becomes quite significant in determining the relationship of the homosexual community to the dominant society.

Hobsbawm and Schelling illustrate the distinction between normative and valuative conflict in terms of the original Mafia and contemporary organized crime. The Sicilian Mafia began as a social movement engaged in valuative conflict with foreigners who ruled the island. It denied the legitimacy of their rulers and engaged in total conflict with them. Half a century later, in the United States, organized criminals are engaged in normative conflict. Contemporary organized crime does not advocate the overthrow of the political structure. Rather, it operates with practices consistent with the dominant capitalist ideology, and to a large extent it depends upon the political structure for protection. This differentiation is a product of sociohistorical conditions: the Mafia was once a social movement engaged in fighting "tyranny"; in the United States organized crime has emerged as a clandestine operation engaged in competition within the framework of society.

In examining these articles, the reader should recall the conceptual breakdowns provided by Merton and Yinger in Part One, where nonconformity and contraculture were contrasted in terms of aberrant and criminal subcultures. These designations greatly escalate the conflict that is possible between the power holders and the governed. The application of the criminal label, a common practice in totalitarian states, may render a movement unable to function (Rush and Denisoff, 1971:367–420). Conversely, the ability to escape the politically deviant classification, even if engaged in crime activity, may place the aberrants in an advantageous position, since they are not seen as questioning dominant societal values.

The major propositions to consider in this part are:

1. The causes and consequences of traditional forms of deviant behavior are becoming more political in nature.
2. The degree of conflict is predicated upon the nature of deviance as perceived.
3. Deviant behavior as an economic enterprise in a capitalistic society is a form of normative conflict.

REFERENCES

COSER, L., *The Functions of Social Conflict*. New York: Free Press, 1956.
———, "The Termination of Conflict," *The Journal of Conflict Resolution*, 5:347–53 (December 1961), [pp. 336–44 this volume].
FOGELSON, R. M., *Violence as Protest: A Study of Riots and Ghettos*. Garden City, New York: Doubleday and Company, 1971.
GESCHWENDER, J., "Civil Rights Protest and Riots: A Disappearing Distinction," Social Science Quarterly 49: 474–84 (December 1968).
GUSFIELD, J. R., "Mass Society and Extremist Politics," American Sociological Review 27: 19–27 (February 1962).
MANNHEIM, K., *Ideology and Utopia: An Introduction to the Sociology of Knowledge*. New York: Harcourt, Brace and World, 1936.
PARSONS, T., *The Social System*. New York: Free Press, 1951.
RUSH, G. B., and R. S. DENISOFF, *Social and Political Movements*. New York: Appleton-Century-Crofts, 1971.
SMELSER, N. J., *Theory of Collective Behavior*. New York: Free Press, 1963.

9. SOCIAL DEVIANCE AND POLITICAL MARGINALITY: TOWARD A REDEFINITION OF THE RELATION BETWEEN SOCIOLOGY AND POLITICS

IRVING LOUIS HOROWITZ
and MARTIN LIEBOWITZ

THE WELFARE MODEL OF SOCIAL PROBLEMS

The study of social deviance within American sociology has traditionally been based on a model that consigns delinquent behavior to the instruments of social welfare. This model has sought to liberalize the visible agencies of social control (the police, judiciary, and welfare agents) by converting them from punitive instruments into rehabilitative instruments. This underlying premise that punishment and rehabilitation are the only two possible responses to deviance yields the conventional tendency to evaluate deviant behavior in *therapeutic* rather than *political* terms.[1]

The rehabilitation model seeks a more human redefinition of the moral code as its long-range goal. Its short-range goal is to indicate the superordinate role that agencies of social control adopt in prescribing subordinate status to deviants. Coser has recognized this role conflict in the welfare orientation to poverty when he indicated that "in the very process of being helped and assisted, the poor are assigned to a special career that impairs their identity and becomes a stigma which marks their intercourse with others."[2]

However serviceable this model has been in the past, and notwithstanding its use in resisting encroachments on the civil liberties of accused deviants, the social welfare model does not exhaust present options—either on logical or pragmatic grounds. A relationship among equals is possible only in democratic politics, where conflicts are resolved by power rather than *a priori* considerations of ascribed status. Only in such politics can deviants attain the status of legitimate combatants in social conflict.

Reprinted from *Social Problems* 15 (Winter 1968), 280–96 by permission of The Society for the Study of Social Problems and the authors.

[1]See, for example, Gwynn Nettler, "Ideology and Welfare Policy," *Social Problems*, 6 (Winter 1958–59), pp. 203–12; also see his "A Measure of Alienation," *American Sociological Review*, 22 (April 1957).

[2]Lewis A. Coser, "The Sociology of Poverty," *Social Problems*, 13 (Fall 1965), p. 145.

In the traditional welfare model, deviant behavior is defined as a social problem. This definition implies several important assumptions about the nature of deviance. First, it takes for granted that deviance is a problem about which something should be done. Second, it assumes that deviance is a *public* problem, which means that social agencies have the right to intervene. Finally, deviance is treated as a social problem in contradistinction to a political issue. Thus decisions concerning it are relegated to administrative policy rather than to the political arena. As a result, deviance is handled by experts instead of being debated by the very publics who are supposedly menaced.

These beliefs about the nature of deviance have scant empirical justification. They derive from no intrinsic characteristics of deviance. Rather, they are normative statements about how deviant behavior should be treated. Bernard has shown a singular appreciation of this.

> Values are inherent in the very concept of social problems. The conditions that are viewed as social problems are evaluated by the decision-maker as bad, as requiring change or reform. Something must be done about them. The reason for coming to the conclusion may be humanitarian, utilitarian, or functional. In any case, a system of values is always implicit, and usually quite explicit.[3]

In this framework, identifying the values of the decision-makers is crucial. As Becker indicates, if we take the above seriously, the selection of decision-makers who define deviance as a social problem is a *political* process, not only a value problem.

> The question of what the purpose or goal (function) of a group is, and, consequently, what things will help or hinder the achievement of that purpose, is very often a political question. Factions within the group disagree and maneuver to have their own definition of the group's function accepted. The function of the group or organization, then, is decided in political conflict, not given in the nature of the organization. If this is true, then it is likewise true that the questions of what rules are to be enforced, what behavior regarded as deviant and what people labeled as outsiders must also be regarded as political.[4]

The decision to treat deviance as a social problem is itself a political decision. It represents the political ability of one group of decision-makers to impose its value sentiments upon decisions concerning deviance. The anomaly is that although the political decision has been to treat

---

[3]Jessie Bernard, "Social Problems as Problems of Decision," *Social Problems,* 6 (Winter 1958–59), pp. 212, 215.

[4]Howard S. Becker, *The Outsiders,* New York: Free Press, 1963, p. 7.

deviance as a non-political problem, deviance persists as a political problem. A comprehensive analysis of deviance must include political factors by determining which decision-makers define deviance as a social problem, and indicate why they consider deviance a problem. Lemert was almost alone among the sociologists of the past decade to contend that deviance does not pose an objectively serious problem.

> In studying the problem-defining reactions of a community, it can be shown that public consciousness of "problems" and aggregate moral reactions frequently center around forms of behavior which on closer analysis often prove to be of minor importance in the social system. Conversely, community members not infrequently ignore behavior which is a major disruptive influence on their lives. We are all too familiar with the way in which populations in various cities and states have been aroused to frenzied punitive action against sex offenders. Nevertheless, in these same areas the people as a whole often are indifferent toward crimes committed by businessmen or corporations—crimes which affect far more people and which may be far more serious over a period of time.[5]

A CONFLICT MODEL OF DEVIANCE

Deviance is a conflict between at least two parties: superordinates who make and enforce rules, and subordinates whose behavior violates those rules. Lemert noted the implications of this conflict for understanding the sources of deviance.

> Their common concern is with social control and its consequences for deviance. This is a large turn away from older sociology which tended to rest heavily upon the idea that deviance leads to social control. I have come to believe that the reverse idea, *i.e.*, social control leads to deviance, is equally tenable and the potentially richer premise for studying deviance in modern society.[6]

The conflict model implies alternative formulations of deviance as a problem: the deviant behavior itself, and the actions of rule-makers to prevent such behavior. The political climate prescribes both what conflicts will occur between deviants and non-deviants, and the rules by which such conflicts will be resolved. The struggle of groups for legitimation thus constitutes an integral part of deviant behavior.

Deviance has been studied by employing a consensus welfare model rather than a conflict model because, for the most part, decision-making

---

[5]Edwin M. Lemert, *Social Pathology*, New York: McGraw-Hill, 1951, p. 4.
[6]Edwin M. Lemert, *Human Deviance, Social Problems and Social Control*, Englewood Cliffs, N.J.: Prentice-Hall, 1967, p. 5.

concerning deviance has been one-sided. The superordinate parties who regulate deviance have developed measures of control, while the subordinate parties, the deviants themselves, have not entered the political arena. The conflict, though existent, has remained hidden. As Becker correctly notes, this leads to a nonpolitical treatment of deviance:

> It is a situation in which, while conflict and tension exist in the hierarchy, the conflict has not become openly political. The conflicting segments or ranks are not organized for conflict; no one attempts to alter the shape of the hierarchy. While subordinates may complain about the treatment they receive from those above them, they do not propose to move to a position of equality with them, or to reverse positions in the hierarchy. Thus, no one proposes that addicts should make and enforce laws for policemen, that patients should prescribe for doctors, or that adolescents should give orders to adults. We call this the *apolitical* case.[7]

As the politicization of deviance develops, this apolitical case will become atypical—the hidden conflict will become visible and deviants can be expected to demand changes in the configuration of the social hierarchy.

Although there has been scattered intellectual opposition to asylums in the past, patients have never been organized to eliminate or radically alter mental hospitals; addicts, to legalize drug use; or criminals, to abolish prisons. Synanon, a center formed by addicts to treat drug addiction, is a striking exception to this pattern. Staffed completely by former addicts, it has no professional therapists. Thus, it represents an insistence that deviants themselves are best able to define their own problems and deal with those problems. Ironically, while Synanon challenges both the right and the competency of professional therapists to intervene in the lives of addicts, it has not discarded the value premises of an adjustment therapy. Nonetheless, as Yablonsky indicates, this marks a departure from the conventional welfare model.

> Over the past fifty years, the treatment of social problems has been dropped into the professional lap and has been held onto tightly. The propaganda about the professional's exclusive right to treat social problems has reached its high mark. The professionals, the public, and even patients are firmly convinced that the only "bona fide" treatments and "cures" available come from "legitimate professionals" with the right set of degrees.[8]

Even where deviant social movements have become powerful, they have avoided political participation as special interest groups. For instance,

---

[7]Howard S. Becker, "Whose Side Are We On?" *Social Problems,* 14 (Winter 1967), pp. 240–41.
[8]Lewis Yablonsky, *The Tunnel Back: Synanon,* New York: Macmillan, 1965, p. 368.

Synanon has acted politically only when new zoning codes threatened its very existence. The politicization of deviance is occurring, as groups like homosexuals and drug addicts pioneer the development of organizational responses to harassment. A broad base for the political organization of deviants now exists, and demands for the legitimation of deviant behavior will increasingly be made.

The political questions inherent in a conflict model of deviance focus on the use of social control in society. What behavior is forbidden? How is this behavior controlled? At issue is a conflict between individual freedom and social restraint, with social disorder (anarchy) and authoritarian social control (Leviathan) as the polar expressions. The resolution of this conflict entails a political decision about how much social disorder will be tolerated at the expense of how much social control. This choice cannot be confronted as long as deviance is relegated to the arena of administrative policy-making. For example, public schools are perceived as a repressive institution by many Negro youths, yet there is no political option of refusing to attend or radically altering them. This problem is now being raised by Black Power advocates who demand indigenous control over schools in Negro ghettos despite the city-wide taxation network.

POLITICAL MARGINALITY AND SOCIAL DEVIANCE: AN ABSOLUTE DISTINCTION

Conventional wisdom about deviance is reinforced by the highly formalistic vision of politics held by many social workers and sociological theorists. This view confines politics to the formal juridical aspects of social life, such as the electoral process, and to the maintenance of a party apparatus through procedural norms. In this view, only behavior within the electoral process is defined as political in character, thus excluding from the area of legitimacy acts of social deviance.[9]

In its liberal form—the form most readily adopted by social pathologists —the majoritarian formulation of politics prevails. This is a framework limited to the political strategies available to majorities or to powerful minorities having access to elite groups.[10] The strategies available to disenfranchised minorities are largely ignored and thus the politics of deviance also go unexamined. The behavior of rule makers and law enforcers is treated as a policy decision rather than as a political phenomenon, while

---

[9]See Angus Campbell *et al., The American Voter,* New York: Wiley, 1960; V. O. Key, *Public Opinion and American Democracy,* New York: Alfred Knopf, 1961; Seymour Martin Lipset, *Political Man,* Garden City, N.Y.: Doubleday, 1960; Samuel Lubell, *The Future of American Politics,* New York: Harper, 1952.

[10]C. Wright Mills, "The Professional Ideology of Social Pathologists," *Power, Politics, and People,* Irving Louis Horowitz, editor, New York and London: Oxford U., 1963, pp. 525–52.

a needlessly severe distinction is made between law and politics. Analyses of political reality at the level of electoral results help foster this limited conception of politics. Consequently, the shared inheritance of sociology has placed the study of deviant behavior at one end of the spectrum and the study of political behavior at the other.

Conventional nonpolitical responses on the part of sociology were possible largely because the political world itself had encouraged this kind of crisp differentiation between personal deviance and public dissent. Political deviance is a concept rarely invoked by politicians because the notion of politics itself implies the right of dissent. Lemert points out that this has not always been true for radical political deviants.[11] There is a history of punitive response to political deviants in this country, involving repression of anarchists, communists, socialists, and labor organizers. This has spread at times to a persecution of liberal groups as well. What characterizes the "McCarthy Era" is not the hunt for radicals, but rather a broadening of the definition of radicals to include all sorts of mild dissenters. Only on rare occasions has political deviance been defined as a major social problem requiring severe repression. Thus, with the possible exception of anarchists, communists, and socialists (and sometimes even including these groups in the political spectrum normally defined as legitimate), there is no way of dealing with political life as a deviant area. The nature of American political pluralism itself promotes dissent, at least in the ideal version of the American political system. The onus of responsibility in the castigation of a political victim is upon the victimizer. Rights and guarantees are often marshalled on behalf of a widening of the political dialogue. Indeed, the definition of American democracy has often been in terms of minoritarian supports rather than majoritarian victories.

The area of deviance is not covered by the same set of norms governing minority political life. The source of responsibility for deviant behavior, whether it be drug addiction, homosexuality, alcoholism, or prostitution is not borne by the person making the charges but rather is absorbed by the victims of such charges. The widespread recognition of the juridical shakiness of the deviant's position serves to privatize the deviant and embolden those who press for the legal prosecution of deviance. While the right to dissent politically is guaranteed (within certain limits), the right to dissent socially is almost totally denied those without high social status.

One simple test might be the perceived reactions toward political radicalism in contrast to social deviance. If one is accused of being an anarchist there may actually accrue a certain "halo effect" to the person so charged. Perhaps a charge of naiveté or ignorance might be made against

---

11Edwin M. Lemert, *op. cit.*, pp. 203–209.

the politically marginal man, but not a censorious response demanding nonpolitical behavior.

In the area of deviance, if there is a self-proclamation of drug addiction or alcoholism, the demand for therapeutic or punitive action comes very quickly. If one admits to being a drug addict, there is an attempt to remove the curse from everyday life so that at least the visibility of deviance is diminished.

The line between the social deviant and the political marginal is fading. It is rapidly becoming an obsolete distinction. As this happens, political dissent by deviant means will become subject to the types of repression that have been a traditional response to social deviance. This development compels social scientists to reconsider their definitions of the entire range of social phenomena—from deviance to politics. Wolfgang and Ferracuti have taken an important first step toward an interdisciplinary study of social violence.[12]

For the social sciences, this implies a new connection between social problems and political action. The old division between the two can no longer be sustained. In terms of theory, the new conditions throw into doubt the entire history of political science as an examination of the electoral situation, and of social problems research as a study of personal welfare. If politics is amplified to incorporate all forms of pressure (whether by deviants or orthodox pressure groups) to change the established social order, and if sociology is redefined to include pressure by deviants to redesign the social system so that they can be accepted by the general society on their own terms, then there is a common fusion, a common drive, and a common necessity between sociology and political science, not only on the level of empirical facts, but on the level of scientific interpretation.

Some sociologists have already adapted to this new situation. Cloward's work in organizing welfare recipients is a particularly striking effort, which is an outrageous idea to both the classical Capitalist and Socialist doctrines.[13] This marks the first time that a sociologist has organized welfare recipients. This enlargement of roles demonstrates that changes are occurring in what constitutes political life and social work.

There are several other important directions that applied sociologists might follow: drug addicts might be organized to alter laws concerning drug use; students might be organized to change the character of schools; and mental patients might be organized to change the way they are treated. In each of these cases, change would be initiated from below by

---

[12]Marvin E. Wolfgang and Franco Ferracuti, *The Subculture of Violence,* London and New York: Tavistock, 1967, pp. 1–14.

[13]See Richard A. Cloward and Richard M. Elman, "Advocacy in the Ghetto," *Trans-Action,* 4 (December, 1966), pp. 27–35.

members of subordinate marginal groups. This would be in sharp contrast to the conventional elitist pattern of politics, where decisions are made from above by members of the prevailing majority. This is the primary distinction between the existing political party style and the political outsider style that is currently emerging.

THE POLITICIZED SOCIAL DEVIANT

A serious dilemma for many deviant and marginal groups alike is their failure to perceive any main line organizations (either overtly political or social) as providing the sort of universal legitimation which governed an earlier, more tranquil period in American history. The entire gamut of formal and informal organizations seems arrayed against the kind of deviant particularisms expressed by hippies, hell's angels, or acid heads. Thus, the subgroups, whether of deviant lower-class origins or marginal middle-class origins, begin to align themselves with each other and against the mainstream of American life. A new set of cultural heroes, dance forms, art forms, coalesce to define not just a classical generational revolt for the rage to live, but for a particularistic expression of immediate personal liberation as a prelude to distant public equalitarianism.

The key demonstration effect that such individualistic responses may prove extremely effective, even if they involve small numbers, is the rise of guerrilla insurgency as a military style in the underdeveloped areas. If "colored people" can conduct protracted struggles in Asia and in Africa, why can't the same sort of struggles be conducted from the rooftops of Watts and Newark? Indeed, the expanding internalization of the deviant and marginal groups can best be appreciated in new cultural heroes such as Franz Fanon, Malcolm X, and others connected to the demi-monde of the Black Power movement. The seeds of this were long ago raised in the works of Padmore and DuBois, when they urged precisely such ideological linkages with revolutionary forces elsewhere in the world—particularly in Pan-Africanism. What was absent before was the mechanism for success—and in the guerrilla style, this mechanism, this critical missing ingredient, was finally supplied, and the linkage made complete.

The area of Negro struggles is a particularly fertile source for re-evaluating the relationship between deviance and politics. Originally, there was a clear distinction between vandalism for personal gain and an act of organization for political gain. When the political life of Negroes was circumscribed by the NAACP, it was clear that political life entailed normative behavior within the formal civic culture. Similarly, it was clear that acts of personal deviance fell outside the realm of politics. Indeed, there was little contact between Negro deviants and participants in the civil rights protest.

The rise of civil disobedience as a mass strategy has blurred this distinction. Such obedience entails personal deviance to attain political ends. Regardless of the political goals involved, it is conscious violation of the law. The treatment of civil disobedience in the courts has therefore been marked by ambiguity. It is difficult to predict whether it will be treated as a political act of insurrection or a simple personal violation of the law. Many law enforcement officials see no distinction between civil disobedience and crime, and blame the ideology of law breaking inherent in civil disobedience for rising crime rates and the emergence of race riots.[14]

In turn, these officials may be responding to the large scale denial by Negroes of the traditional police role as keeper of social order. This can perhaps best be gauged not only in the expressed attitudes of political leaders from governors down to sheriffs, but indirectly as well, i.e., by the inability of local gendarmeries to cope with Negro mass rioting. The Watts riots of August 1965, were, in this connection, prototypical of the current breakdown in traditional forms of police legitimacy. In that riot, which lasted four days, witnessed 34 deaths and 1032 injuries, and saw 4000 arrests made, the key fact was the role of the National Guard in quelling the riot. The Los Angeles police were thoroughly unable to cope with a situation once it achieved paramilitary proportions. This lesson has clearly not been lost on Negro ghetto communities elsewhere in the United States.

Confining ourselves to the cluster of race riots which took place in the months of June and July of 1967, we can see how Watts heralded a new stage in the relationship between deviance and politics. In the main riot areas of Chicago, Cleveland, Cincinnati, Buffalo, and Newark (we will disregard for present purposes the satellitic riots which took place in the smaller centers of Plainfield, Louisville, Hartford, Prattville, and Jackson) the following characteristics were prevalent in each community during the riot:

(a) Each city requested and received National Guardsmen to restore social order. Correspondingly, in each city, the police proved ineffectual in coping with the riots once the shield of legitimation was removed.

(b) In each city, there were deaths and serious injuries not only to the rioters but to the established police and invading guardsmen.

(c) In each city, the riots lasted more than one day, the duration of the riots lasting from two to seven days. This indicates the guerrilla-like nature of the struggle.

---

[14] In this connection, see Stanley Lieberson, "The Meaning of Race Riots," *Race,* 7 (1966), pp. 371–78.

(d) In each case, the triggering mechanism for the riot was an alter-cation involving police officials (usually traffic patrolmen) and Negroes accused of reckless driving, driving without a license, or driving under the influence of alcohol.

(e) In each case, the major rioting took place during summer months, when the normal load of Negro male unemployed is swelled by students and teenage former students not yet relocated.

(f) In each city, property damage was extensive, with the sort of sniper tactics and scorched earth policies usually associated with so-called wars of national liberation.

(g) In each case, the major rioting seemed to lack official civil rights organization sponsorship.

The following chart gives some indication of the character and extent to which the conflict model dominates current Negro deviance-marginal-ity. The parallel with what Eckstein has termed "internal violence,"[15] and what is more customarily referred to as guerrilla warfare,[16] is clear. What this amounts to is a military rather than a civil definition of the situation in racial ghettoes. The essential deterrent was raw fire power rather than the legitimated authority of the police uniform. Under such circumstances, the established welfare distinction between juvenile delinquency and guerrilla warfare means very little.

The rapidly rising crime rates indicate a further ambiguity in the tradi-tional formulation of social deviance. It is of decreasing *sociological* im-portance whether "crime" is perceived as an act of politics or deviance. The consequences are the same in either case: cities are becoming in-creasingly unsafe for whites, and white-owned businesses are suffering mounting losses. Whether it is political insurgency or traditional crime,

TABLE 9.1. MAJOR NEGRO RIOTS IN URBAN GHETTOS

Date	Place	Killed	Injured	Arrested	National Guard*	Riot Duration (days)	Property Damage (thousands)
8/65	Watts (LA)	35	1000+	4000+	14,000	5	$50,000+
7/66	Cleveland	4	55	275	nd	5	4,000+
6/67	Buffalo	—	68	182	500	4	100+
6/67	Cincinnati	1	50	300	1,100	2	2,000
7/67	Chicago	2	100+	500+	4,200	4	nd
7/67	Newark	24	1150	1600+	3,375	6	15,000+
7/67	Detroit	36	1500+	2665+	13,000**	5	500,000+

*National Guard figures exclude City Police.
**Includes 8,000 National Guard and 5,000 Federal Troops.
Source: Compiled from *New York Times Index*.

[15]See Harry Eckstein, *Internal War*, New York: Free Press, 1964; and for a more specific account, Harold Black and Marvin J. Labes, "Guerrilla Warfare: An Analogy to Police-Criminal Interaction," *American Journal of Orthopsychiatry*, 37 (July 1967), pp. 666–70.
[16]See Irving Louis Horowitz, "The Military Elite," in *Elites of Latin America*, Seymour Martin Lipset and Aldo Solari, editors, New York and London: Oxford U., 1967.

the consequences remain the same—a disruption in the legitimation system of American society.

THE DEVIANT POLITICAL MARGINAL

At the opposite pole—namely minoritarian politics—a similar set of ambiguities plague those in search of precise boundary lines. An example is the behavioral pattern of the Left wing. Among the radical youth of the thirties certain characteristics clearly emerged: a relatively straitlaced "Puritan" ethos concerning sexual mores; a clear priority of politics over personal life—what might be called the ascetic purification of self—and a concern for a relatively well defined ideology, combined with encouragement for all to participate in the life of the working classes. The radical Left of an earlier generation shared with the dominant cultural milieu a distinct, even an intense, disaffiliation from deviant patterns. Indeed, the Old Left pointed to social deviance as illustrative of the moral degeneration of bourgeois society. The need for social revolution came about precisely because the existing social order was considered incapable of controlling social deviance. Thus, the demands of the traditional Left were not very different from establishment demands with respect to social deviance.

This contrasts markedly with the position of the New Left on conventional indicators of deviance. First, they exhibit substantial positive affect toward an extreme and libertarian ethos replacing Puritanism. Second, there is an identification with deviant forms stemming from a continued affiliation with the "beatnik" movement of the fifties. There has been a considerable absorption of the Beat Generation of the fifties into the Activist Generation of the sixties. The ideology of the New Left, insofar as it has clear guidelines, is based on freedom from repression. It has both political and social components: freedom for the Negro from the effects of racial discrimination; freedom for the student from the constraints of university regulations; freedom for the young generation from the demands of their elders; and freedom for politically powerless groups from the growing authority of the centralized State. In this sense, Freud feeds the ideology of the New Left at least as much as Marx defined the ideology of the Old Left.

The traditional notion of a noble affiliation of radical youth with the working class has already dissolved in favor of a highly positive response to deviant and marginal groups in American society. There is a relative unconcern for the traditional class formations engaged in the struggle for upward mobility. If there is a hero, it is the alienated man who understands what is wrong and seeks escape. Often, escape takes the form of social deviance, which is considered no worse than the forms of behavior which are traditionally defined as normative. The traditional hero has been supplanted by the anti-hero who wins and attains heroic proportions by not getting involved in the political process. This anti-hero is defined by what he is against as much as by what he is for; he is for a world of his own, free from outside constraints, in which he is free to experiment and experience.

What this means operationally is that the line between Left-wing political behavior and personal deviance has been largely obliterated. Nowhere has this been more obvious than in the student protest movement, where it is impossible to separate the deviant student subculture from the substantive demands of the student revolt. Spence accurately describes the significance of this student movement at the University of California at Berkeley.

> This was the first successful student strike at a major university in the United States. But more important, this was the first significant white-collar rebellion of our time. These sons and daughters of the middle class demonstrated and walked picket lines, not behind the moral banner of the oppressed Negro, but on the basis of their own grievances against a system that had deprived them of their rights of responsibility and self-expression.[17]

The student rebellion underlies a major thesis herein proposed, since it led not to organized political responses of a conventional variety, but rather to a celebration of deviance itself as the ultimate response to orthodox politics. Stopping "the operation of the machine," which for Mario Savio "becomes so odious, makes you so sick at heart that you can't take part; can't even tactically take part," led to only one conclusion: "the machine must be prevented from running at all."[18] It is interesting that victory was not defined as taking over the operations of the machine, not in the classical capture of organized political power, but rather in non-participation and in non-acceptance. Savio himself, as if in conscious defiance of Michel's "iron law," simply refused to participate in any leadership functions in the Berkeley post-rebellion period. The definition of victory then is in the ability of marginal groups to disrupt the operations of political power either in its direct parliamentary form or in surrogate forms.

Among young members of the New Left, draft evasion has become an important form of deviance. The number of people who adopt the tradi-

---

[17]Larry D. Spence, "Berkeley: What It Demonstrates," *Revolution at Berkeley,* Michael V. Miller and Susan Gilmore, editors, New York: Dell, 1965, p. 217.
[18]Jack Newfield, *A Prophetic Minority,* New York: New American Library, 1966, p. 27; on this general theme, see Irving Louis Horowitz, "Radicalism and Contemporary American Society," *Liberation,* 10 (May 1965), pp. 15–18.

tional political path by refusing to serve and going to jail as political prisoners is small compared to the number who adopt the deviant path, using mental illness, homosexuality, or drug addiction (whether these be real or feigned) to avoid serving. In effect, they are taking advantage of the prevailing established norms toward deviants. However, this path is made much more accessible with the merger of Leftist politics and social deviance, since only politics can transform private desires into public principles.

An important social characteristic of the New Left is its self-definition as a "swinging" group, or conversely, not being "square." This new definition of Leftism is also a central definition of the deviant subculture. So it is that Berkeley and Watts became the symbols of the twin arms of radical politics: the university campus and the Negro ghetto. Even in terms of social psychological definitions of friends and foes the line between the political Left and social deviance is now largely transcended. Thus, there is a deep distrust of formal politics and of the people who operate within the bureaucratic channels of the political apparatus. This definition of friends and foes is obvious at Berkeley, where many students feel that they cannot trust anyone over 30.

The Right-wing movement in America also illustrates this perspective. The Old Right was characterized by extreme antipathy for any kind of promiscuous behavior or overtly immoral behavior. The American Right viewed with alarm attacks upon law-enforcement officials. The Old Right perceived itself conventionally as a paragon of law enforcement. This is the core around which the Right wing has traditionally been established. But a phenomenon such as the Minutemen reveals a spinoff from law-abiding to direct approaches to politics. The Minutemen, for example, are encouraged to acquire possession of fully automatic weapons, even though many such weapons are forbidden to individuals by law. They are urged to join the National Rifle Association to become eligible for rifles and handguns at cost as well as free ammunition. The Minutemen *Handbook* contains lessons on such subjects as "Booby Traps," "Anti-Vehicular Mines," and "Incendiary Weapons Composition." The self-made saboteur is encouraged to improvise lethal weapons. Espionage and infiltration of established political groupings are also encouraged. A subunit is called the Minutemen Intelligence Organization, in possession of a fairly sophisticated organization, not unlike those of paramilitary units.[19]

Breakaway segments of the New Right, like their opposite numbers in the New Left, are concerned with redefining the relationship of the person to the legal code in very loose terms. The appeals to youth are in terms of training in weaponry rather than in law. When confronted by the law, the

---

[19]See William W. Turner, "The Minutemen: The Spirit of '66," *Ramparts*, 5 (January 1967), pp. 69–76.

Minutemen dissolved their public leadership and created a new under-ground leadership. This phenomenon could be an extreme situation in American life precisely because so many armed forces veterans may be attracted to such a combination of politics and deviance. A situation has arisen in which the use of weapons for personal enjoyment, such as in hunting, has been fused—particularly in the releases of the American Rifleman's Association—with the uses of weapons for protection against criminals, and assistance to police authorities. Political conflict may be-come marked by opposing marginal political groups confronting each other in armed conflict, with the legitimated State agencies of power the enemy of both.

THE POLITICS OF DEVIANT VIOLENCE

In a previous section we drew attention to the growing Latinization of Negro riots and student revolts in the present period. This was done in terms of rough macroscopic data. Here we wish to underscore this point by taking closer note of the workings of the new style of subculture in America. The largest Negro gang in Chicago, the Blackstone Rangers, is a clear example of the breakdown in the distinction between crime and marginal politics, as well as the course which the politics of marginality is likely to follow. The Rangers act as an autonomous group, in conflict with both local residents and police. The strategies employed in this conflict indicate the style of the new politics. They entered into negotia-tions with the Chicago police, and reached a satisfactory settlement: they agreed to surrender their weapons and stop fighting other gangs if the police would drop certain charges against their leaders and disarm a rival gang.

Negotiation of this sort is a major strategy of international politics, al-though it has seldom been used to resolve conflicts involving marginal domestic groups. The negotiation process itself entails the recognition that marginal groups represent legitimate political interests. So far, the art of negotiation has not been adequately developed for dealing with such situations, just as it has not been adequately developed for dealing with unconventional international conflicts.

The problem posed by marginal groups like the Rangers is not yet viewed as a political problem to be solved by political strategies. When police violated the negotiated settlement, the Blackstone Rangers planned to file suit in the Federal Courts to prohibit a pattern of harassment. It is novel for such deviant groups to engage in political conflict with legitimate agencies like the police. But it does indicate a step beyond the "good bad boy" approach of social welfare.

There is a growing impulse to develop political means of resolving conflicts that involve marginal groups, as an alternative to the military means that have thus far prevailed. The Woodlawn Organization, composed of local residents, received a federal grant of $927,341 to work with gangs like the Rangers and the Disciples. The Chicago police raided the first meeting between the gang leaders and leaders of the Woodlawn Organization, demonstrating a conflict between advocates of a political solution and proponents of what amounts to a military solution to the gang problem.[20] In the absence of acceptable political solutions, it is probable that increasing reliance upon domestic military solutions will be sought—just as the failure of political solutions internationally often leads to pressure for quick military solutions.

This trend toward marginal politics reflects a rejection of conventional political styles that have proven unsuited to the needs of marginal groups. In the past, the powerless had recourse to two choices for political action: legitimate means, to which they do not have sufficient access, and by which they invariably lose; or accessible but ineffective illegitimate means that bring little structural change. Marginal minorities are now searching for the development of political means that are both accessible and effective. It is probable that these new styles will be illegitimate rather than legitimate, and that the distinction between social deviance and political insurgency will be further reduced.

Race riots differ from both orthodox politics and personal delinquency. They offer some important insights into these new styles. Race riots have an ideological core, while many other forms of collective behavior do not. They are avowedly political, organized, and purposeful. Typically, deviant acts like theft, assault, and homicide have none of these attributes. For these reasons, race riots may be closer to organized unconventional warfare than they are to conventional crime. Once perceived in this way, they constitute a powerful if latent political weapon.

At present, in most American cities a relatively small police force can effectively control the populace. But this is true only as long as police are accorded legitimacy. When conflicts are defined totally in terms of power and force rather than authority and legitimacy, as during race riots, they cannot effectively maintain control. For this reason, riots constitute a major departure from established patterns of interaction between police and deviants. Deviants are not organized to battle police, and they have no ideology which labels police as enemies to be attacked and destroyed. Police have legitimacy as long as deviants avoid rather than attack them. However, police traditionally mount an organized collective effort against deviants, who typically respond only as unorganized individuals. The

[20]Rowland Evans and Robert Novak, "The Negro Gangs," *Herald Tribune, International Edition,* July 5, 1967.

existing conflict is a one-sided war. The emergence of a bi-lateral conflict situation promises to be a major development in the link between politics and deviance. Race riots are the first indication of this change.[21]

This conflict can take several alternative forms: on a *minimax* scale there could be de-escalation to the English system, in which both Negro militants (or deviants in general) and police would not carry arms; at the other end, there could be escalation to race riots, which are sporadic and constitute a relatively unorganized set of events. Beyond sporadic racial strife lies the possibility of sustained conventional war. This is most closely approximated in American history by the Indian Wars and the Civil War. Presently, unconventional warfare is coming into focus. The latter two possibilities indicate how social deviance could spill over into insurrectionary politics, given both the peculiar racial division which exists in American society and the consistent exclusion of marginal groups from political and social legitimacy.

This marginal style of politics is being adopted by groups of all "extreme" ideological persuasions. Marginals of both the Left and Right fear the growing power of the centralized government, which they feel will be used to repress them, and are opposed to the consolidation of power by the majority. This commonality is demonstrated by the high amount of social interaction that occurs, in places like Greenwich Village and Berkeley, between politically opposed deviant groups. Even such political opposites as the Hell's Angels and opponents of the Vietnam War shared a common social network in California. Their political enmity was matched by their similar enjoyment of deviant social patterns.[22]

The clearest example of this movement toward violence, and one easily overlooked, is the reappearance of assassination as a political style, coupled with the inability to know whether Left, Right, or Deviant is spearheading this style. It is almost impossible to say whether the assassination of John F. Kennedy or Malcolm X was a deviant act or a political act. No group took responsibility for the assassinations as overt political acts, and the assassins did not link the deaths to ideological demands. Without taking into account the breakdown in the distinction between politics and deviance, the meaningfulness of both sociology and political science is seriously compromised.

MARGINAL SECTORS AND DEVIANT VALUES

Applied social science must take account of this new view of marginality in American life. If any group has emerged as the human carrier of the

---

[21]See Ed Cray, *The Big Blue Line: Police Power vs. Human Rights,* New York: Coward-McCann, 1967, p. 121.

[22]See Hunter S. Thompson, *Hell's Angels: The Strange and Terrible Saga of the Outlaw Motorcycle Gangs,* New York: Random House, 1966, pp. 231–57.

breakdown between political and private deviance, it has been the *lumpenproletariat,* or the non-working class. This group has replaced the established working and middle classes as the deciding political force in America. Lang and Lang point out,[23] in their discussion of collective dynamics, that this is precisely the condition which breeds collective deviance.

> Ordinarily the cleavages within a society are between clearly constituted social strata or between parties whose special interests seek recognition within a broader framework of order. But when the cleavages occur between constituted authority and those who do not accept it, or between those who feel unable to share in them, one can refer to the condition as one of widespread and general alienation.

The army of marginally employed comprises a significant segment of *both* politically radical and socially deviant cultures. If the bureaucracy grew disproportionately to all other classes in Western Europe, the disproportionate rise of the marginally employed characterizes contemporary America. This group, rather than disappearing or, as Marx would have it, becoming a social scum to be wiped out by revolutionaries, grows ever larger. At a practical level, there is now a new and powerful intermediary class that performs vital roles in the authoritarian political system, while at the same time it sets the style for a new libertarian morality.

The boundaries of American politics reflect the growing affluence which typifies the American social structure. However, a significant minority of disaffected marginals exists in the midst of this affluence. It is becoming increasingly clear that these marginals threaten to destroy the fruits of general affluence, and indeed threaten to disrupt the entire system. Increasing crime rates are merely the first indication of this situation. Race riots are a more serious indicator of the inability of the political system to maintain an equilibrium despite the general affluence.

The overlap of deviance and marginality is well captured in a current book on the Hell's Angels. The Hell's Angels—with the Swastika, German helmet, and Iron Cross as their main symbols—differ but slightly from the pseudo-Maoist organizations of the Left. Without wishing to equate Maoists with either Minutemen or Hell's Angels, it is clear that each of these groups is marginal and deviant with respect to established political norms. Further, it is difficult to give conventional definitions to those holding a gun in one hand and a flower in the other.

> The Angels have given up hope that the world is going to change
> for them. They assume, on good evidence, that the people who run

---

[23]Kurt Lang and Gladys Engel Lang, *Collective Dynamics,* New York: Thomas Y. Crowell, 1961, p. 18.

the social machinery have little use for outlaw motorcyclists, and they are reconciled to being losers. But instead of losing quietly, one by one, they have banded together with a mindless kind of loyalty and moved outside the framework, for good or ill. They may not have the answer; but at least they are still on their feet. It is safe to say that no Hell's Angel has ever heard of Joe Hill or would know a Wobbly from a bushmaster, but there is something very similar about their attitudes. The Industrial Workers of the World had serious blueprints for society, while the Hell's Angels mean only to defy the social machinery. There is no talk among the Angels of building a better world, yet their reactions in the world they live in are rooted in the same kind of anarchic, para-legal sense of conviction that brought the armed wrath of the Establishment down on the Wobblies. There is the same kind of suicidal loyalty, the same kind of in-group rituals and nicknames, and above all, the same feeling of constant warfare with an unjust world.[24]

The policy response to this dilemma has been the Welfare State: an attempt to "cool out" the marginal underclass and minimize the potential danger it poses. It is an attempt to avoid the consequences of large-scale marginality without making any social structural changes. Schatzman and Strauss contend that this welfare style deals with the problem by avoiding its political implications.

America pours its wealth into vast numbers of opportunity programs to achieve its goals and names almost any conceivable group, event, or thing a social problem if it can be seen as threatening the achievement of these goals. Hence its concern for the culturally deprived, the under-achievers, the school dropouts, the job displaced, the aged, the ill, the retarded, and mentally disturbed. This concern goes beyond that of the nineteenth century humanitarians who involved themselves with the underprivileged outgroups on moral grounds. Now all these aggregates are seen as special groups whose conditions are intolerable to society, if not actually threatening, in light of today's social and economic requirements.[25]

This attempt to depoliticize a highly political problem has proved inadequate. The welfare solution has not erased the consequences of having a growing number of disaffected people in the midst of general affluence. Indeed, the very existence of affluence on so wide a scale creates demands that parallel those made by the "poor nations" on the "rich nations." Because of this, a political attempt to solve the problem is bound to emerge.

---

[24]Hunter S. Thompson, *op. cit.*, pp. 265–66.
[25]Leonard Schatzman and Anselm Strauss, "A Sociology of Psychiatry," *Social Problems,* 14 (Summer 1966), p. 12.

If this attempt is not initiated from above within the legitimate political or electoral apparatus, it will be generated from below and probably take illegitimate paramilitary forms.

The implicit exchange system which formerly existed between the very poor and the very rich in American society was simple: "don't bother us and we won't bother you." In exchange for the poor not disturbing the rich, the wealthy provided just enough money for the poor to live at Ricardian subsistence levels. This exchange has been the basis of American social work, and continues to define the boundaries of the welfare system. The rich have only vaguely appreciated the magnitude of the poor's potential power, and their ability to disrupt the entire system. For their part, the poor only vaguely appreciate the power at the disposal of the rich, which accounts for the suicidal characteristics of many race riots.

This interchange system is now being threatened. The poor are gradually developing an appreciation of their own power, while at the same time they have a greater appreciation of the power held by the rich. For their part, the rich are becoming more aware of the power available to the poor, as seen in the generalized fear created by rising crime rates and race riots. In short, there is a greater polarization of conflict between the two classes.

The primary political problem of deviance can be framed as a Hobbesian dilemma. Hobbes sought the creation of the State as a solution to the problem of social disorder, in which individuals war with each other in pursuit of their individual interests. The dilemma is that the creation of the State creates a problem of social control. The solution to the problem of chaos or the *Anarch* is the *Leviathan*. But the *Leviathan* is the *totalitarian* State. Indeed, totalitarianism is the perfect solution to the problem of disorder. The dilemma for those who consider social problems obstacles to be overcome is that any true overcoming of social problems implies a perfect social system. And this entails several goals: first, the total institutionalization of all people; second, the thoroughgoing equilibrium between the parts of a system with respect to their functioning and the functioning of other sectors; third, the elimination of social change as either a fact or value. Thus, the resolution of social problems from the point of view of the social system would signify the totalitarian resolution of social life.

The political problem posed by deviance is how to avoid social disorder while at the same time avoiding the problem of total social control. It is a dilemma precisely because of the impossibility of solving both problems simultaneously. Political decisions about deviance must reflect judgments about the relative dangers of these two problems, and must constitute a weighing process based on ethical no less than empirical considerations.

Connections between deviance and politics take place most often when a society does not satisfactorily manage its affairs. For better or worse, a well ordered society is one that can impose a distinction between responses to deviance and responses to marginality. Antecedents for the linkage of deviance and marginality exist in two "conflict societies." In the eighteen nineties in Russia, the Narodnik movement was directly linked to the movement toward personal liberation. In Germany of the nineteen twenties, the "underground" movement, aptly summed up by the Brecht theater, Nihilism, and amoralism, gave rise to both the Nazi and Bolshevik political tendencies. The merger of the Beat Generation and the current Radical Student movements reveals this same pattern of connecting political revolution with demands for personal liberation.

These examples indicate how the fusion between deviant behavior and political processes is a prelude to radical change. If the fusion of politics and deviance is the herald of revolution, or at least indicates a high degree of disassociation and disorganization within the society, then radical changes in the structure of American social and political life are imminent.

What takes place in personal life has major political ramifications in contemporary society. American life has been resilient enough to forestall a crisis in treating marginality until now. This is a testimonial to the flexibility of the American system of political legitimation. But it might well be that the extent of deviance in the past was not sufficient to cause more than a ripple in the political system.[26] In the emerging system, with automation and cybernetics creating greater dislocation and marginal employment, personal deviance may generate a distinct transformation in normal political functions; it marks the point at which the political system cannot cope with deviant expressions of discontent.

A political description of this condition begins with the inability of American society to resolve political problems that are important to *marginal* people. Almost one-third of the potential voting population does not vote, and is therefore without even the most minimal political representation.[27] The fact that these disenfranchised people have important problems in common that cannot be managed within existing arrangements creates a volatile situation.

Political styles evolve that are not presently labeled as political behavior, much as race riots are not now generally considered political behavior. These new styles are characterized first, by a rejection of the legitimacy of the existing political system (the challenge to the rules by which the game is now played); second, by a rejection of compromise as a political

---

[26]Rex Hopper, "Cybernation, Marginality, and Revolution," *The New Sociology*, Irving Louis Horowitz, editor, New York and London: Oxford U., 1964, pp. 313–30.

[27]See E. E. Schattschneider, *The Semi-Sovereign People*, New York: Holt, Rinehart, and Winston, 1960, pp. 97–114.

style; and third, by a willingness to oppose established authority with illicit power in order to change not merely the rules but the game itself. Ends will attain a primacy over means, whereas a concern with the legitimacy of means has traditionally characterized American politics. Direct expressions of power might assume a more important role than legitimate authority in resolving important conflicts.

Political legitimacy is itself subject to change in order to meet the demands of a society in which social deviants and political marginals have become more, rather than less, important in determining the structure of American society.

10. COOPERATIVE SUBCULTURES, DEVIANT SUBCULTURES, AND REBELLIOUS SUBCULTURES

JACK D. DOUGLAS

What is striking about any social situation that is examined in detail is how complex all the circumstances are, and while one risks losing an overall configuration in the patent effort to sort out the details, the effort to find meaning—in sociology as in language—has to begin with the simplest description of what happened. This is especially true in the case of Columbia, for if one looks at the background—the years, say, from 1966 to 1968—the events which exploded in April and May are, at first glance, largely inexplicable. It is easy, of course, since history is always written after the fact, to give some apparently plausible account of "the causes" and "the determining factors," and these tend to give an air of inevitability to the sequences. But as I have studied this history, and reflected on my own participation in it, I find the "outbreak," "uprising," "revolution"—none of these words is adequate—extremely puzzling.[1]

As one should really expect of an open group with ambiguous or problematic categories and criteria of membership, a group which everyone eventually leaves, and which is largely dominated by and intertwined with the supragroup of the adult world, the social world of American youth is very pluralistic and fragmented. Aside from the generally shared youth subculture, which, as we have seen, consists primarily of the self-identification with "youth," a vague disidentification (or separation) from adults, and, to a much lesser extent, certain esthetic and personal styles, American youth have been fragmented and pluralistic. There have been a great number of different subcultures with different orientations toward adult society. In a very general way these many different subcultures can be profitably described and analyzed for our purposes in terms of their general orientations toward what *they* see as adult society. From this

---

Reprinted from *Youth in Turmoil: America's Changing Youth Cultures and Student Protest Movements* by Jack D. Douglas, a monograph sponsored by the Center for Studies of Crime and Delinquency, National Institute of Mental Health. Washington, D.C.: Government Printing Office, 1970, 32–60.

[1]Daniel Bell, "Columbia and New Left," chapter 5 in *Confrontation*, Daniel Bell and Irving Kristol, eds., New York: Basic Books, Inc., 1969, pp. 67–68.

standpoint these subcultures are, roughly, either *Cooperative-Cultures, Independent-Cultures,* or *Contra-Cultures.* That is, either they cooperate with what they see as the distinct adult society, or they act without regard to adult society, or they act against adult society. Obviously, any particular youth subculture tends to be a combination of such orientations, especially because youth subcultures in general tend to be somewhat ambivalent toward the adult world. But many of the larger ones that have considerable influence have a reasonably consistent emphasis on one orientation.

COOPERATIVE-CULTURES: STRAIGHT YOUTH

Most youth subcultures are either directly or indirectly cooperative with adult society. While these groups are specifically socially defined as being for the young, they are generally sponsored and even administered by adults. These Boy Scout and Girl Scout groups, Y.M.C.A. and Y.W.C.A. groups, moral rearmament groups, athletic associations, chess clubs, business opportunity groups, church youth groups, and so on, receive very little headline publicity, but they continue, though to a decreasing degree, to be massive youth groups. Taking together all groups with a dominant cooperative attitude toward the adult world, they make up by far the majority of American youth. They receive little attention because today as always they are simply continuing to do the day-to-day work of teaching youth the values and motives of the adult work world. These groups have this as a specific goal—learning the values of manhood, etc. They make use of the various motives assumed to be possessed by youth (play, sports, interest in new places, etc.), but which have actually been taught at an earlier age and can now be turned to other ends, to motivate them to learn adult tasks. While it is possible that the youth in this situation might feel some form of what Max Scheler called "ressentiment," a form of highly repressed resentment that leads to a strong support of the repressing force, there is simply no evidence for this sort of thing. Probably only very prolonged, intimate participant observation could reveal such phenomena and, as we have seen, there are no such studies as yet. At the present time, all arguments that such adolescents or any other segment of youth necessarily experience frustration from the demands for "conformity" of adult society must simply remain in opposition to what appears to be obvious: these youth, who are probably a majority of American youth and certainly constitute a vast majority of youth organized into groups, appear to very willingly cooperate with their adult teachers in progressively making themselves into adults. They see themselves, and adults see them as well, as adults-in-the-becoming, as future adults very much like past adults, very much like their own parents. Though he and others who share his views have almost always failed to see how rapidly the generalized youth culture has developed and how very rapidly many more youth, especially college students, have become "alienated" in recent years, Samuel Lubell is certainly right in the conclusion from his research that most youth, even students, remain "straight" today:

> One of the more disquieting aspects of the much advertised "generation gap" is our apparent inability to analyze, diagnose, and understand it.
> Few phenomena have received more publicity and even study during the last four years than the new "youth generation." Still, all this attention has brought little public understanding.
> The dominant impression left by the term "generation gap" is that of a unified younger generation that is breaking drastically from both its elders and society in almost every conceivable way. Actually, though, my interviewing over the last four years on how young people differ in their thinking from their parents suggests that (1) much more continuity than gap exists between the two generations; (2) parents have not been rendered obsolete but continue to exert an almost ineradicable influence on their children.[2]

For every "teeny-bopper," "hippie," or "student rebel" who captures the attention of the mass media, there are many others who constitute what Matza calls the "scrupulous youth"—the Boy Scouts, church youth groups, and so on; for every surfer or member of any other leisure subculture, there are many others who work at junior achievement businesses, study to become apprentices, work for grades, and so on. Certainly even these "straight" youth are more "tuned in" to such groups than adults because of their shared identity as youth and they often have a "secret envy," or gain vicarious gratification from identifying with them, especially since so many adults have chosen to identify the offbeat as the spokesmen of youth. But any such identification with the offbeat youth is far too slight to warrant considering the great majority of youth to be part of that particular subculture.

CONTRA-CULTURES: DEVIANTS, DROPOUTS, AND REBELS

There are probably some youth groups that simply have little or no specific orientation toward the adult world. Perhaps some leisure groups are *Independent Cultures* of this sort, simply dedicated to fishing, rowing, or whatnot, without much consideration of how this might be related to the adult world. There seem, however, to be relatively few of these. In our society youth seems to be largely defined only in relation to adult-

---

[2]Samuel Lubell, "That 'Generation Gap'," Chapter 4 in Bell and Kristol, *op. cit.*, p. 58.

hood, to what he will become in the future, whereas the adult stands whole without any necessary reference to what he once was. In addition, youth—the future—is generally considered to be too important to be left alone by adults. While youth are by no means *forced* to conform, as many social scientists believe, or forced to rebel, as others believe, they are largely forced to take either a predominantly cooperative or predominantly antagonistic orientation toward the adult world.

Those that take a predominantly antagonistic orientation are *contracultures*. The youth subcultures that have attracted the widest attention, especially in recent years, are those that in some way are oriented against —or, at least, *away* from—the adult world as they see it. There seem to be three distinct and important orientations of this type, which differ in qualitative factors as well as in degrees. These are the *deviant subcultures*, the *leisure subcultures* and the *rebellious subcultures*. While each general category covers a wide variety of rapidly changing groups, there seem to be three roughly distinct modes of intertwined elements that warrant distinctive categories and analyses.

Deviant Subcultures. The deviant subcultures have been far more widely studied and analyzed by social scientists than either of the other two. Construing the term "deviant" in the narrow sense normally used by sociologists in discussing youth, I refer by this term to those groups who share in a general "troublemaking," "tough" orientation. While they sometimes engage in criminal activities, the greatest amount of their time, effort, and creativity goes into noncriminal activity, much of which has the purpose of aggrandizing their self-esteem and group prestige.[3]

As Thrasher long ago argued in his study of 1313 gangs in Chicago, ganging has been a normal aspect of lower class, urban youth in American society.[4] These gangs begin early, certainly by the age of four or five, become increasingly distinct and differentiated as the members grow into their teens, normally engage to some degree in various forms of "tough" and "troublemaking" behavior that frequently brings them into conflict with the police, and begin to disintegrate as the members move into their twenties, get jobs and marry. While sociologists in the last few decades have been almost exclusively concerned with delinquent gangs, most of these gangs are only peripherally or intermittently involved in delinquent behavior. Most of them are much more like the Nortons described in Whyte's classic work on Street Corner Society,[5] except that the Nortons remained unemployed and unmarried well into their later twenties because of the depression and were involved in the earlier ethnic machine politics of America's great cities.

---

[3] D. Matza, *Delinquency and Drift*, New York: Wiley, 1964.
[4] F. M. Thrasher, *The Gang*, Chicago: University of Chicago Press, 1928.
[5] W. F. Whyte, *Street Corner Society*, Chicago: University of Chicago Press, 1937.

There are a great number of different studies of these gangs and many very different theoretical explanations of them by sociologists, ranging from the ecological theories of the Chicago school[6] up to the present-day, modified subculture[7] and situational theories. In spite of their many dif ferences, almost all of these studies and analyses have agreed that these lower class, urban gangs are deeply concerned with "toughness," which they see as indicative of "manliness," and engage at times in activity that gets them into "trouble" with the police.[8] It has also been generally agreed that these are the basic factors that distinguish these youth groups from middle-class youth groups. The disagreements have come more in the interpretation of the facts.

As David Bordua has argued, since Thrasher's study of Chicago gangs emphasized the ("positive") excitement and fun of gang activity, including the delinquency, sociologists have come increasingly to view the toughness and troublemaking of lower-class gangs as ("negative") reactions against their status positions. This is especially true of such recent subculture theories of delinquency as that of Albert Cohen,[9] who argues that this delinquency is totally negativistic and is the result of their ambivalent rejection of (or rebellion against) the middle-class standards enforced on them in school. These theorists who see delinquency as a form of rebellion against middle-class society are in general agreement with those officials and members of the public who argue commonsensically that delinquency is a form of rebellion that constitutes an attack on the "moral foundations" of our society and threatens "anarchy and the dissolution of society." These analysts have generally believed that there is a direct relationship, either of similarity in origins or causality, between the "rising tide of criminality among the young" and the growing "youth rebellion." In fact, many see the students as "hooligans" who are just like "hoods." (Ten years ago there was as much public and official concern over delinquency as there is today over student rebels. There is still concern over delinquency, but, in spite of the rapidly rising official rates of delinquency, the students have banished the "hoods" from the mass media. Perhaps each has served the same function of focusing adult fears and resentments of youth and of justifying—to adults—the continued exercise of power over youth—as youth.)

These various theories of common sense and social science that see lower class, urban gangs and delinquency as a form of rebellion against the

---

[6]On the ecological theories, see especially Clifford R. Shaw, and Henry D. McKay, *Juvenile Delinquency and Urban Areas,* Chicago: University of Chicago Press, 1942.

[7]A. K. Cohen, *Delinquent Boys,* Illinois: Free Press, 1955.

[8]W. Miller's ideas about false concerns agree with this description, but he invokes homosexual fears to explain such phenomena. He has simply overlooked the obvious importance of physical strength in the work of these people. See W. Miller, "Lower Class Culture as a Generating Milieu of Gang Delinquency," *Journal of Social Issues,* 1958, Vol. 14, No. 3, pp. 5–19.

[9]Cohen, *op. cit.*

adult, conventional society have failed to consider a number of crucial points that invalidate the whole theory:

1. They have generally failed to consider the importance of the urban situation of these adolescents. As Yablonsky and the few others with direct contact with these boys have reported,[10] the boys themselves consider their toughness and violence to be "defensive," a direct response to the threat of other groups, and they often compare their actions with those of nations. (In many cases they have used names that show such identifications.) To most sociologists this has seemed irrelevant or rhetorical justification; after all, even if this were true for a few, wouldn't this defensive explanation itself demand that for each defensive group there be at least one offensive group, so that at least half these gangs would be "sociopathic" aggressors? I think the answer to this can be an unqualified no. These gangs have normally existed in urban situations where there was very great ethnic heterogeneity which involves differences in values, motives, beliefs, language, and behavior. The external control agencies such as the police have, for many reasons, been quite incapable of preventing much of the violence in such areas, so the boys have no such higher forces to whom they can appeal. Now *it is precisely these complex, heterogeneous situations in which one finds resort to violence by nations and individuals: at least in part, violence is a last resort, a continuance of conflict by other means, when differences cause conflicts which cannot be resolved by argument and negotiation.* (Where youth boards and the police have helped to bring about negotiations between warring gangs, the boys have generally responded very favorably.) Moreover, and very importantly, in such a situation it is not at all true that there must be an aggressor group for each defensive group: in this amorphous, conflict-filled situation a very few aggressive groups can victimize all the others, very much in the way a Nazi Germany could effectively assault all the other nations of Europe. In addition, in a complex situation like this, and one in which there are not formal channels of negotiation, it is always likely that one group will interpret some of the actions of some of its neighbors as attacks. Once this pattern is established, as it was in America's cities over a hundred years ago, it tends to be perpetuated both because the gangs tend to perpetuate themselves by training new members (i.e., gangs become their own reason for being, comparable to a nation's "raison d'être") and because distrust and suspicion tends to perpetuate itself—and each of these tends to feed the other. Finally, it seems reasonably apparent that gangs have become less organized, less frequent, and less violent in American cities as the ethnic groups have slowly become more alike ("assimilated") and more accommodated to

---

[10]Lewis Yablonsky, *The Violent Gang*, New York: Macmillan, 1962.

each other. There is almost no comparison in terms of violence between what we have today and what Thrasher found earlier in this century and late in the nineteenth century.

2. Sociologists and other analysts, especially those who feel threatened by gang violence in the lower class, have generally failed to see that delinquents and gang boys are generally emphasizing certain values and feelings in their violent behavior held and accepted by the other class groups as well. All groups in our society highly prize manliness, strength, and courage, though it is certainly possible that these boys, coming more often from southern European peasant groups, would emphasize these and male dominance more than do the older, northern European groups in this country. All of the evidence clearly indicates that these boys see their actions as a way of proving courage and manliness. To the middle classes and sociologists this has always seemed overemphasized ("counter-action") and absurd, since they seem to violate the rules on appropriate means of expressing or proving such things. What they fail to see is that, living in a very different situation, these boys *must* find different means of expressing even the same values, feelings, and beliefs.[11] Middle-class boys can find their tests of strength and courage in the Boy Scouts and organized sports, and some of the lower class boys do so as well; but for most of them these simply do not seem realistic paths. Besides, the apparent aggression of other gangs must be met either by counterviolence or by submission. In general, there seems to be a great deal of agreement on *abstract* values of the different groups in American society, but there are a great number of these abstract values in our pluralistic society (courage, strength, sacrifice, wealth, beauty, truth, sexiness, virtue, purity, work, leisure, simplicity, savoir-faire, standing up for one's rights, keeping one's cool, etc.). Even more importantly, different groups find themselves in different situations in which different values are more relevant and in which some values can be more plausibly realized than others. The members of these groups in different situations find that they can more plausibly *construct certain specific, concrete value-positions* with their implied status and prestige meanings than they can other value-positions. Consequently, even given the same abstract values and the same striving for self-esteem and social status or prestige, the different situations will lead individuals (even the same individuals over time) to emphasize different values in constructing their concrete, situated meanings from the same general realm of abstract meanings. Middle classes degrade lower classes as poor and dangerous; upper classes degrade middle classes as petty and self-righteous; lower classes degrade upper classes as lazy, selfish, and effeminate. What is of crucial importance, and

---

[11]J. Douglas, *The Social Meanings of Suicide.* Princeton, New Jersey: Princeton University Press, 1967.

what positivistic sociologists who have assumed the social world to be homogeneous and unidimensional have failed to see, is that each of these value-positions or constructions of situated meanings is potentially equally plausible, depending on the situation from which one views it.

3. One of the strongest forms of evidence supporting this situational interpretation is the fact that almost all of the members of these youth gangs leave the gangs soon after meeting the most basic criteria of adulthood for males in our society, that is, a steady job and marriage. It is only when the members do not get jobs and, largely as a consequence of that, do not get married that the gangs and the tough, troublemaking behavior continues. This was true of the quasi-adult gangs found among ethnic groups in the nineteenth and early twentieth centuries, true during the depression (as is seen in the Nortons gang), and seems true of Negroes today, among whom streetcorner gangs sometimes extend well beyond the twenties.[12]

4. It is also very clear that the vast majority of instances of serious troublemaking by the members of such youth cultures do not involve any attack on the adult world in general. They rarely cause trouble, especially in the form of violent attack, for the adults in their neighborhoods. If the grocer chases them away from his store, they hate him, not the generalized, abstract adult world. Certainly most of their serious trouble, and a very great deal of their petty trouble as well, comes from their relations with the police. From early childhood they struggle with the police over the right to "hang out" on the streets and sidewalks in their neighborhoods.[13] (Thrasher was probably right in seeing this as a basic force leading to the integration of play gangs into troublemaking gangs.) As teenagers, they are seen by the police as more dangerous than middle-class youth doing the same thing, so they deal far more punitively with these lower class groups, arresting them in situations in which they "talk to" the middle class youth.[14] Even stealing is directed very largely at specific, outsider "marks,"[15] so that there is not some generalized attack against the adult world or the world of law and order. Even convicts from this group believe in the justice of the "system" and often "idealize" it, while attacking the law enforcement individuals as corrupters of the "system."[16] There is, then a great deal of evidence that the trouble with the law that the members of these youth groups have is not due to any "rebelliousness" against the adult world, such as a great number of sociologists

---

[12]E. Liebow, *Talley's Corner,* Boston: Little, Brown, and Company, 1967.
[13]C. Werthmann, "Police Action and Gang Delinquency," in D. Bordua, ed., *The Police,* New York: Wiley, 1966.
[14]A. Cicourel, *The Social Organization of Juvenile Justice,* New York: Wiley, 1968.
[15]H. Schwendinger and J. Schwendinger, "Delinquent Stereotypes of Probable Victims," in M. W. Klein, ed., *Juvenile Gangs in Context,* Englewood Cliffs, New Jersey: Prentice-Hall, 1967, pp. 91–105.
[16]Prisoners in isolation in maximum security prisons have been found especially prone to such idealization.

have assumed.[17] As I have argued in much greater detail elsewhere,[18] their relative troubles are caused in good part by the policies the law enforcement agencies have toward them because they are lower class, urban, and ethnic, not simply because they are more deviant.

In general, then, these deviant youth subcultures are very *situational.* They are closely associated with the situation of the urban lower class groups, especially the ethnic groups, and there is no reason to believe that their behavior is a form of "rebellion" against the adult world. There is, in addition, every reason to believe that the often proclaimed dangers to the "foundations of our society" from the supposed increases in this form of behavior are simply the result of a misunderstanding of official statistics on delinquency and crime. It now seems reasonably clear that there are anywhere from three to ten times as many serious crimes in this society as are actually reported in the official statistics.[19] This does not at all mean that there has been any change. My impression from historical sources, and certainly from works such as Thrasher's, is that the actual rate of crimes, especially violent crimes, is probably far less today and decreasing most of the time, though there may be perturbations. But with the vast majority of serious crimes always going unreported, it is extremely easy for better reporting of crime in the official statistics to produce increases in crime rates of 300 percent to 1000 percent. (In Philadelphia and New York City, revisions of crime reporting have doubled the official rates in one year or less.)

There is some definite indication that these deviant youth cultures are not only not rebellious but are also on the decline. New waves of immigration could reverse this, but even that would probably not give such subcultures a rebellious orientation.

While it seems highly doubtful that the public schools have been important in causing delinquent subcultures, as Cohen and others have argued, it does seem likely that these subcultures have helped to isolate the boys from the demands of education. If the marked decline in gang violence should prove indicative of a decline in the strength of the gangs, just at the time when lower class groups have become so greatly aware of the financial value and the availability of higher education, the effect could be an increasing effectiveness of education with this segment of American youth.

On the other hand, an increasing percentage of such deviant youth are Negroes, simply because the older ethnic groups have left the core areas.

---

[17]Matza has, on the contrary, followed the usual assumption that delinquency is a form of rebellion ("Position and Behavior Patterns of Youth," *op. cit.,* p. 207).

[18]J. Douglas, "Deviance and Order in a Pluralistic Society," in *Sociological Theory,* E. Tiryakin and J. McKinney, eds., New York: Appleton-Century-Crofts, 1970.

[19]See *The President's Crime Commission Report,* Washington, D.C.: Government Printing Office, 1966.

The politicizing and radicalizing of the urban Negroes have clearly affected significant minorities among the high school and junior high students. This could give an increasingly rebellious orientation to their gang activities, which could further alienate them from education and the job market, and, thereby, help to feed them into continuing rebellious subcultures even at the adult level. All previous gangs have shown a strong tendency to simply leave education, work, and politics alone and then to disintegrate as the boys entered the job market, which meant that the gangs had little lasting effect on them. However, a radicalizing of Negro gangs could be taking place that would make the gangs more oriented toward rebellion against the adult world, at least insofar as the adult world is seen as the world of middle-class values, work, and the power of officials such as the police. There is, in fact, some clear evidence that this is taking place.

In Chicago the Blackstone Rangers, which is a combination of young and adult members, was definitely caught up in the politicization process resulting partly from the community action work of certain government agencies. They seem to have gone from being a reasonably typical youth gang concerned with various forms of protective work, aggressive attacks, and similar activities that brought them into great conflict with the police to being a rebellious youth group with far more organization than is typical of youth gangs. Though they do seem to most people to have become politicized as a result of their direct involvements in OEO programs, Senate investigations, and systematic police harassment, the Blackstone Rangers seem to represent an in-between youth culture that could move in the direction of far more political action. As James Alan McPherson has concluded in the best study yet made of this gang:

> The Rangers do not appear to be militant either, at least not in the contemporary sense of the word. They have refused to make a coalition with the Black Panthers. They do not seem to have any political philosophy. If anything, they believe only in themselves and in their motto: "Stone Run It!" But they are waiting too. Whether it is for more federal funds or for their presence and power to be recognized by the black community through their influence over ghetto youth, they are waiting. And their energy is at work.[20]

The Black Panthers are a far more obvious example of a politically oriented, rebellious Black youth culture. While using many of the tactics of youth gangs and apparently sharing many of the common hatreds of such gangs, and, possibly doing some of their recruiting from such gangs, they have developed a political program that constitutes a direct chal-

---

[20]James Alan McPherson, "The Blackstone Rangers," *The Atlantic,* Vol. 223, No. 5, May 1966.

lenge to the official power of the police. The Black Panthers more than any other group have also forged certain alliances, however shifting, with some of the student protest groups, especially the Black ones; and they are apparently seeking to build a coalition of radical groups to increase the power of all such groups.

These groups, largely as a result of activities of members of the adult world, and even to some extent, though quite inadvertently, by government policies, have increasingly become the link between the traditionally patterned delinquent subculture of lower class youth and certain groups involved in some of the student protest movements. The Black Panthers have had many close contacts with various student groups and in some cases have become informal spokesmen of student protest. This has been especially clear in California, where some of the leaders of the Panthers have been treated as visiting celebrities by large student groups and where the Panthers have had many direct and indirect influences on the Black student protest groups.

> The center of political interest for a great many Californians these past weeks was not so much the national elections as the tumult provoked when some University of California students invited Black Panther "Minister of Information" Eldridge Cleaver to lecture at Berkeley. The uproar over that has been followed by fresh confrontations between students and police at San Francisco State College after the ouster of Black Panther "Minister of Education" George M. Murray, an English instructor. Murray had advised students to "get guns" if their demands were not speedily met. The trustees of the college system, ignoring normal procedures, fired him without formal investigation or hearings. This set off a wave of demonstrations: electric typewriters were tossed out of windows. Police were summoned; the campus was shut down on November 14 and only last week reopened by the trustees.
>
> Once thought of as not much more than a handful of petty desperadoes in black spectacles, berets and leather jackets, more poseurs than effective militants, the Black Panthers have been thrust by such incidents into a position of influence among black power nationalists. They are especially prominent in the San Francisco Bay communities, from which they sprung a bare two years ago. The founders were college dropouts, some of them having been schooled also in state prisons or county jails. . . .
>
> All this hubbub has enormously enhanced the attractiveness of Black Panthers as public speakers. Murray and Bobby Seale are all over the state, arguing their impatience for an equal share in the benefits of American society. Asked by one student why they persisted with dirty words, Seale said, "Because the filthiest word I know is 'kill' and this is what other men have done to the Negro for years." Cleaver is kept hopping from state colleges to the lunch-

eon circuit, from Stanford to Harvard to Jesuit schools. Indeed, the Cleaver exhortation to revolution, pocked with explicit barn-yard terms, has become something of a fad. Cleaver has made it into several of the major magazines. Forty thousand copies of his book have been sold. When Cleaver drew a ticket for speeding, the re-action of the arresting highway patrolman was immediately noted ("He was a gentleman"). When Cleaver missed a date in court (because he was lecturing at Harvard), the judge gently admon-ished him to keep an engagement calendar now that he is such a busy man. Even candidate Spiro T. Agnew used Cleaver (his ap-pearance on campus "makes my blood boil") as an issue.[21]

While such groups are not yet large, they add a new dimension to the protest movements, for they have the physical courage, the knowledge of weapons, and the desire to use them which student protest groups have not had. There can be little doubt that some of the more extreme mem-bers of the student protest movements would like to use them as a source of power for achieving their own ends, including armed rebellion, espe-cially in the form of urban guerrillas. On the other hand, it is clear that thus far these Black *political youth gangs* have successfully resisted be-coming the "Storm Troopers" for the white radicals. But the whole situa-tion is very fluid and it is quite uncertain as to the direction these political youth gangs will take in the years ahead. We can only be reasonably cer-tain that they will continue to exist and to be important, especially since they are actively recruiting and training ever younger members, so that they are to some degree succeeding in politicizing the traditional delin-quent gangs even at the junior high school level. This politicization of the junior high and high school gangs is also taking place in part be-cause other adult groups, including parent and teacher groups seeking support for the school decentralization plans, have actively recruited their political help. If these combined moves continue with the success they have had thus far, there is little reason to doubt that the traditional pat-tern of apolitical delinquent gangs will be replaced by a pattern of po-litically oriented, rebellious gangs involved in both traditional patterns of crime and newer patterns of political pressure and violence, which will likely be centered in the urban schools. Indeed, there is some reason to suspect that the political rhetoric and goals of the radical adult groups are already coming to serve many gang youths as rhetorical justifications for their traditional patterns of crime as well as their newer forms of political action.

Rebellious Subcultures. Rebellious subcultures of youth are distin-guished from the more political and radical protest movements of youth

---

[21]Mary Ellen Leary, "The Uproar Over Cleaver," *The New Republic*, November 30, 1968, pp. 21–24.

by their basically unradical, nonactivist (nonviolent) focus. The rebellious subcultures reject much of American life, as they define it (the "square world"), and do attempt to create their own alternative way of life; but they do both without becoming very political about it, without doing much to convince others, to organize support, to defeat their "enemies." Most of this rebellion is, in fact, low key, quiet, sometimes even secret. Much of it is indistinguishable from what we have early dealt with as the growing generalized youth subculture. Very importantly, much of this rebellion is the result of the patterned encounter of "idealistic youth" with the "cynical, hypocritical adult world." There are some very important reasons why each generation of American youth finds itself "idealistically" in conflict with the "lack of values" or the "hypocrisy" of adult American groups.

A I have previously argued, American society is a morally pluralistic society made up of a great number of different ethnic groups, economic groups, educational groups, religious groups, and so on. In spite of this great moral pluralism, the members of American society have been able to work together very effectively in many spheres of activity, except for one revolution, one extremely bloody Civil War, and many rebellions and riots of lesser dimensions over the first two hundred years of the Nation's existence. This moral pluralism of American society poses the constant threat of open conflict. The way in which American society seems to have coped reasonably well with the problem is through a strong insistence on adherence to the procedural rules of public activity (i.e., majority rule, etc.), the development of certain overarching but largely amoral goal commitments (i.e., health, wealth, security, and personal freedom), and the all-important division between public morality and private morality. It is this separation of one's private moral feelings from one's public moral statements and actions that seems especially important in helping to produce the rebellious youth who become the core of the rebellious youth cultures.

Public morality in a pluralistic society does two things which are well understood common-sensically. It prevents our being continually involved in moral argument, prevents fights and so on. The importance of this is most easily seen in the case of moral entrepreneurs who try to enforce their morality (or public morality) on others, especially on their private actions. Such people are seen as surly, cranky, moralistic, prudish, mean, nasty, and brutish.

These are people who don't understand or cannot adopt the pluralistic nature of our (situated) moral meanings. These are people who do not share those commitments and understandings that make successful *accommodation* possible in a pluralistic society. *If members of a pluralistic society are going to "work" successfully together, they must be able to accommodate themselves to conflicting commitments* and they probably must be able to withdraw to their own enclaves to express themselves freely to the like-minded. This latter condition (or "expressive function") of knowing and expressing the "true self" (one's self-image) is achieved in our society through a strong emphasis on *privacy*—private clubs, sanctity of the home and the anonymity of the massive cities. Of far greater importance, *accommodation* is achieved largely through the development of specific commitments to moral meanings and understandings. It is very striking that some of our only highly-shared moral commitments should be specifically in that area—public behavior—of our lives in which we come into contact with many thousands of strangers from every conceivable "walk of life"; that these commitments should be strongest and most widely shared among the executive middle class groups who are specifically the people who must *manage the moralities* of strangers to achieve work goals; and that these groups specifically socialize their children to live by these morals for the expressed purpose of "getting along with people." As Melville Dalton has so clearly seen, in a pluralistic society acting in accord with such *accommodative morals* as courtesy, tolerance, minding one's own business, keeping your nose clean, decency, playing it cool, keeping your cool, not being too assertive, etc., are of utmost importance in achieving social status in our society. One of the common culture shocks in our society comes when adolescents raised in the private, homogeneous morality of the home first encounter the accommodative morality of the puralistic world of work and political action. They see it as cynical (which it is), hypocritical (which it has to be), and damnable (which it is only to those who aren't committed to accommodative morals).[22]

In most cases these morally committed youth remain quite rebellious toward the "cynical" and "hypocritical" adult society throughout their formal education. American higher education has nurtured and fostered such views, since large percentages of the faculty have been "alienated intellectuals" in open conflict with the accommodative morality of the business world. It is no surprise, then, that we should get more "idealistically" inspired youth rebellion as we get more youth more involved in higher education.

But there are many different forms of more specific subcultures that are in more open rebellion against the "square world," the "over-30 world," and "the adult world," the world of "Dadism and Momism." Many of the larger rebellious subcultures involve the least amount of rebellion and the coolest forms of rebellion. Probably the most important of these are what we can rightly call *leisure subcultures*. These subcul-

---

[22]Douglas, "Deviance and Order in a Pluralistic Society," *op. cit.*

tures are built primarily around a simultaneous rejection of work and the whole work ethic and work-a-day world built around work and the glorification of some leisure activity as the being and end of life—often called *The Life,* as we find among the surfers.

If it were not for the negative connotations of the term, the leisure subcultures of American youth could best be described as *leisure cults.* While most American adults and youth are members of some form of leisure subculture (e.g., golfing), many of the leisure subcultures of youth are distinguished by the great intensity of members' commitments, the degree of public expressiveness with which they communicate this involvement, and the tendency of their members to build a way of life around the leisure activity that is in opposition to ordinary adult ways of life, especially the work-a-day, organized, nonspontaneous life.

There seem to be two general orientations toward leisure in these youth subcultures. The earlier orientation, which until recent years was almost the only orientation, consists in simply being devoted to certain forms of "fun" or "play" activity, especially to certain entertainment styles, and acting out this devotion. This acting-out has often been the basis for creating *entertainment subcultures.* The second orientation, which has been growing rapidly in recent years, consists in viewing leisure as antithetical to work (i.e., "free time") and, sometimes, as conducive to more fulfillment of one's (creative) self than the hated "square world." It is this latter development, in which the leisure subcultures merge with more rebellious subcultures, that concerns us most here.

These leisure-dominated, rebellious subcultures are of many kinds, but have rarely been studied or even noted by social scientists. No one has yet done a better job of studying and describing them than Tom Wolfe:

> After World War II, a number of sets of young men in California began to drop out of the rationalized job system and create their own status-spheres. In every case they made a point of devising new fashions, *role* clothes, to symbolize their new life styles. These were the beats, the motorcycle gangs, the car kids, and, more recently, the rock 'n' roll kids, the surfers, and, of course, the hippies. The hell with the jobs they had or might ever get. They wanted roles, as Rebels, Swingers, Artists, Poets, Mystics, Tigers of the Internal Combustion Engine, Monks of the Sea, anything that would be dramatic, exciting, not powerful or useful or efficient but . . . yes! a little bit *divine,* right out of the old godhead of the hero.
>
> They have all been able to pull it off, set up their own styles of life and keep them going and make them highly visible, because of the extraordinary amount of money floating around. It is not that any of these groups is ever rich. It is just that there is so much money floating around that they can get their hands on enough of it to express themselves, and devote time to expressing themselves,

to a degree nobody in the netherworld position could ever do before.[23]

The *entertainment subcultures,* which are often derided by adults as "crazes," have been prevalent for several decades. The "bobby-soxer craze" of the 1940's was possibly the most intense and widespread, though the earlier "flapper craze," the "Elvis Presley" craze, and the "Rock craze" and various dance crazes probably rivaled it in popularity. Aside from the physiological exuberance of youth, and the obvious overtones of burgeoning sexual feelings, some of these *entertainment subcultures* have had much of the appearance of mass movements.

In the last decade some of the most popular *entertainment movements* have been increasingly mixed with the ideologies and styles of the fully developed leisure subcultures, those which involve an attack on the work-a-day, middle-class, organizational way of life. For example, certainly one of the most widespread entertainment movements of any period has been the Beatles movement. Their entertainment has increasingly become *entertainment with a message,* a message that is critical of society, without being rebellious. Their style is more one of poking fun at, and, more recently, ridiculing the adult world than of seeking to overthrow it.

But some of the other entertainment youth movements have become more directly tied up with the leisure subcultures and some with the rebellious subcultures. The linkages between much of the youth music, poster art, and some drama and the hippie subcultures is especially clear. In recent years there has been a growing relation between the Rock movement in youthful music and various other forms of "entertainment" and the hippie subculture(s). This has been so much the case that it is probably not an exaggeration to speak of the rise of the Hip Culture among the young. We have already examined the growing importance of this Hip Culture, especially as represented by Rock music, in the generalized youth culture; but it is important here to see the importance of the bridge between the hippie subculture and the generalized youth movement for youthful rebellion by analyzing the rebellious nature of the hippie subculture. It is certainly not true (or even worth thinking about) that the hippies are "seducing" a whole generation of American youth. Rather, increasing numbers and subcultures of the youth have found that the hippie subculture expresses certain of their own feelings, and it is this that has made them respond so favorably to the entertainment forms involving the hippie world-view that the professionals and merchants have created and sold. In this way they have helped to produce the burgeoning Hip Culture. (There are very complex relations between pop artists and

---

[23]Tom Wolfe, "The Pump House Gang," in *The Pump House Gang,* New York: Farrar, Straus and Giroux, 1968, pp. 20–39.

mass audiences in our complex society in which so many groups and situational factors intervene between the creators and the consumers of the esthetic "product." But there has long been a very direct relation between the desires of the youthful audience and the products of the Rock artists and other artists involved in the Hip Culture. These art forms have been dominated by small producers, and the "products" sell in a highly competitive market with rapidly changing tastes and, hence, sales rates. For example, in 1941 the nearly monopolistic powers of the American Society of Composers, Authors, and Publishers were broken by court rulings, and since then the popular music field has been extremely decentralized, competitive, and changeable. The producers and distributors, some of whom today are young "rich hippies," move toward what will pay, which is what the audience is "ready for" or already wants.[24] They cannot dictate the messages, even if they wanted to do so. Even many of the famous Hip performers, including the Beatles and such folk singers as Joan Baez, have seemed for years to be running to keep up with the increasingly Hip orientation of their audiences, rather than pushing the audience in their direction. However, it seems very likely that the media do serve to spread the "message" of the Hip Culture to a much larger audience than would be possible without the marketing structure, advertising, publicity effect, and so on.)

The hippies, and their immediate antecedents, the Beats, were in good part direct descendants of the ancient Bohemian subcultures of various kinds that have existed in Western cultures for centuries and can already be found referred to in Benvenuto Cellini's *Autobiography*. It would no doubt be possible to trace the direct lines of descent in terms of ideas and persons from the romantic Bohemian subcultures of early nineteenth century France[25] up to such present day groups as the hippies. While various schools of artists, who are very often intermingled with members of the Bohemian subcultures, have adopted both favorable and unfavorable orientations toward involvement in the work ethic and the rationalistic, bourgeois society,[26] the *Bohemian culture, including the hippie culture today, are characterized by a basic rejection of this work-a-day world and an idealization of the opposite values of leisure, feeling, idealism, and so on.* Their attacks on formal education, industrial society, Christian purity, and the rationalistic discipline of scientific thought have been unrelenting; and, while we certainly have no reliable quantitative information on such things, there is no reason to believe that the (hard core) members of these leisure subcultures today are larger in proportion to the general

---

[24]Mooney, *op. cit.*
[25]Matza, *op. cit.*
[26]R. Silvers, "The Modern Artist's Construction of Associability," in *Deviance and Responsibility*, J. D. Douglas and R. Scott, eds., New York: Basic Books, 1970.

population (indeed, they may be smaller today) or attract more general sympathy and public interest today than they did in the nineteenth century. Just as many hard-working, straight bourgeoisie today adopt hippie beads or smoking habits, so did bankers' wives read the romantic novels in the nineteenth century, and there were undoubtedly weekend Bohemians comparable to our weekend hippies. It is probably precisely because these leisure cultures have been so different from our everyday lives that they have always generated so much interest. As members of our society generally see such things, they are generally an "escape," not a program for the future. (This relation between our general culture and the hippie world-view is very much in line with the relation we earlier suggested exists between the Hip Culture of the young and the generalized youth culture.)

In recent years, however, these leisure cultures have begun to change, to become more oriented toward questions of "realistic" possibilities. They have begun to adopt more of the ideologies common to the rebellious subcultures, though without becoming activated by ideologies.

The hippies, being the dominant Bohemian subculture today, have been in the forefront of this development. Having inherited the Bohemian mantle in a period when industry was being automated and bureaucracy computerized at a rapid rate, the hippies and their audiences have suddenly realized that the traditional Bohemian antiwork ethic might be a realistic choice for those still committed to conventional ideas of material well-being and status. Perhaps because of this, they and their interpreters have strongly emphasized the leisure aspects of their world view and the consequent attack on current industrial-technological-organizational society. Perhaps this is also why they have been treated as presages of our common future by so many people.

As is probably true of most social movements with a minimal or zero degree of organization, the origins and actual nature of those who consider themselves to be "hippies" are very unclear. The hippies have so often been used as symbolic weapons by so many different groups, both Left and Right, that there is a great buzzing confusion about their messages. Very importantly, it is quite impossible today to weed out those messages they set out to communicate and those which they came to adopt as a result of their interaction with the rest of our society. But this does not matter too much. After all, we are interested both in the messages intended and in the messages as interpreted by the rest of society, especially by the youth who have responded favorably to them.

It has generally been agreed that the hippies are fundamentally a dropout subculture, a subculture that first and foremost rejects American society, a subculture whose members' primary response is one of rejection and withdrawal, even flight to the deserts and mountains to escape prying eyes. Though overdoing their uniqueness, Lewis Yablonsky has truthfully represented this aspect of the hippie movement:

> The hippie movement's posture of *total rejection* places it in a unique position as an American social movement. Most small and even powerful social movements in America have been geared to modify only part of the social structure. The Townsend Plan movement, for example, was essentially related to a greater distribution of the wealth to older people. The civil-rights movement essentially has had the objective of acquiring equal civil rights for all people regardless of race or creed. Even the most militant "black power" advocates live their daily lives American style. The new left and other campus political activist groups had and have limited political goals. The labor movement sought a particular kind of arrangement and relationship to management. *Unlike these efforts at partial changes in the society, the hippie phenomenon, although fetal and relatively powerless, emerges as the first American social movement that totally rejects the American social system.*[27]

Because the work ethic has formed such a basic part of the cultures of all Western societies for centuries, the hippie rejection has been primarily focused on a rejection of the whole complex of values and ideas associated with work, the work-a-day world view. But this has merely been the focal point of a generalized rejection. Sex has obviously served the same functions of demonstrating rejection insofar as young people can reject the whole society by insisting on violating all the ordinary rules concerning sex. Again, drugs can be used even more strikingly to show this *total* rejection by showing that even the basic form of thought—"rationality"— is rejected, is purposefully destroyed by the ecstasy of drugs (though "ecstasy" is not normally the actual experience of the drug user). Sex and drugs more than anything else constitute an ancient symbolization of the Dionysian rejection of the humdrum world in which emotions are controlled for "practical" purposes. (The Bacchus cult used sex and alcohol— the divine grape; but the hippies cannot use alcohol because it is so intimately tied in with the social practices of the business culture and has so many ordinary status meanings.) "Dropping out" and "turning on" have been the two basic messages of the hippies, at least in the beginning.

This dominant sense of rejection made the hippies very much like the "alienated" college youth Keniston studied in the 1950's. Their emphasis on not-doing, on not-working, not-controlling, not-being-rational, not-being-part-of distinguished them very strongly from the more actively political youth who make up the youth protest movements:

---

[27]Lewis Yablonsky, *The Hippie Trip*, New York: Pegasus, 1968, p. 320.

. . . after having worked for several years with a group of under-graduates who *are* intensely repudiative of American culture, I am inclined to see most student protest not as a manifestation of aliena-tion (as I have used the term), but rather of commitment to the very values that alienated students repect. . . . The activist seems determined to implement and live out his parents' values, whereas the alienated student is determined to repudiate them and find alter-native values.[28]

At this early stage probably the only positive side to the hippie world-view was that of being free—"doing free" or "doing your own thing." The rest of society was totally rejected because it was constraining, enslaving, dominated by a drive for power, which necessarily means that some or most are going to be less free, less powerful, whereas the positive goal one sought was freedom, doing what one wanted when and how he wanted—joy. In a *Berkeley Barb* article on the Haight-Ashbury way of life we can see both this description of the hippie life and the growing tone of justi-fication (at least in material written to be published, hence read by out-siders—a reason why so many "real hippies" will not write anything or say anything to social researchers for publication):

From around September of 1966 until around April of 1967, before all the national publicity and the coming of the tourists, in the free community part of the Haight-Ashbury, there were very few power, control, manipulation, and coercion games. When people do free they do free.

Millions of free events on individual and large novas scale have been enacted in the last year. These free actions have generated energies of free joy to tens of millions of people in the United States and the world. Tens of thousands of people have lived here during the last year, free from power games and almost totally free from violence.

Until April we lived on the street for over a year, and we saw only one fight and heard of only five others (not counting incidents of police brutality). If you're wondering what this riff is about, the point is that it is totally believable that men can live in an almost totally free environment without power games or violent performances.[29]

In the same way, the use of drugs became something more than simply a way to joy, a free doing-one's-own-thing, that was sometimes sex, some-times Indian chants, and sometimes anything else—or nothing. As the pressures from outside became greater, as "social controls" of many forms,

---

[28]Kenneth Keniston, *Young Radicals,* New York: Harcourt, Brace and World, Inc., 1968, p. 341.
[29]Anonymous, "Mutant's Commune," pp. 30–50, in *Notes From the New Underground,* Jesse Kornbluth, ed., New York: The Viking Press, 1968, p. 43.

especially the informal ones of rousting and firing and showing contempt, were increasingly applied, the use of drugs, sex, and most other patterns of hippie activities were increasingly presented as superior to the ordinary American way of life, as a proof of the superiority of the hippie vision. This is very clear in the mystical rationale of drug use developed over the years by Timothy Leary, especially after his struggles with Harvard and the police. Leary's glorification of the drug-induced mystical experience came after his struggles, and probably largely as a result of them. There is, of course, a strong support for "real" mysticism and for religious experience in general—the "experience of inner, true, real Being—the Discovery of God"—in Western cultures, and Leary simply tapped this ancient cultural tradition to show in a culturally plausible fashion (to some) that his was a superior path to the "worldly" ways of most Americans, the citizens of Mammon (how many Americans publicly believe in being "materialistic"?), even though he denied the existence of such cultural support. Indeed, he argued that drug experience showed (even "scientifically") that this "materialistic game" was not even "real"; it was all illusory compared to what the mystical experience induced by drugs (the "new game") revealed; and this new experience revealed the superiority of a whole new way-of-life, a way of freedom and equality:

> Unfortunately the West has no concepts for thinking and talking about this basic dialogue. There is no ritual for mystical experience, for the mindless vision. What should provoke intense and cheerful competition too often evokes suspicion, anger, impatience. What can be holy and intensely educational in the action of CE drugs on the cortex finds no ritual for application. This is to me one of the greatest challenges of our times.
>
> The nongame visionary experiences are, I submit, the key to behavior change. Drug-induced *satori* [Enlightenment]. In three hours under the right circumstances the cortex can be cleared. The games that frustate and torment can be seen in the cosmic dimension. But the West has no ritual, no game to handle the CE drug experience. In the absence of relevant rituals we can only impose our familiar games. The politics of the nervous system. The mind controlling the brain. Physicians seek to impose their game of control and prescription. The Bohemians naturally strive to impose their games of back-alley secrecy. The police, the third member of the happy, symbiotic drug-triangle naturally move in to control and prosecute.
>
> Clearly we need new rituals, new goals, new rules, new concepts to apply and use these precious substances for man's welfare. To give the brain back to the species.[30]

---

[30]Timothy Leary, "How to Change Behavior," pp. 498–512, in *Interpersonal Dynamics,* Warren G. Bennis *et al.,* eds., Homewood, Illinois: The Dorsey Press, 1964, pp. 506–07.

Not very surprisingly, this whole justification of drug use by the argument that it induces a better self and better way of life was later picked up and repeated point for point by hippie propagandists:

> In a communiqué distributed on Haight Street this spring by a group of Diggers, the statement is printed: "Enlightenment," described in many tongues and in many ways, teaches, among other truths, that truly to feel the unity of all men that is love requires the giving up of the illusion of game-playing abstractions. A perfection of inner self, sometimes attainable through LSD-25 or other psychedelics, reveals the failure of all political games . . . the failure to *let it go.* Do you want to *show* people a groovy way of life, or do you want to *tell them how to live* and back it up with bottles, bricks, boards and even bullets?[31]

Once a social movement is created, once it has distinctive features, it can be made use of by other members of society for their own purposes, in precisely the same way that personal styles of hair and dress can be used by new groups, independently of their originally intended meanings. In the case of the hippies, all kinds of people who wanted to attack American society, for whatever reason, began to expropriate the symbols of the hippie way-of-life. Those symbols came to be seen as powerful in American society today, as generators of publicity, of fear, hatred, and of many other things. "Flower power," the antithesis of the hippie message in the beginning, became a reality and social protesters sought to turn "flower power" to their own ends. As Ralph Gleason has argued:

> The increasing attraction of the long-haired Haight-Ashbury hippies is in the obvious fact that what they do generate is power. You may call them flower children, call them The Love Generation, call them mindless LSD idiots, call them anything you please— they are the most powerful single social movement in the country amongst Caucasians. They generate psychic force; they accomplish things and they have created a community that is effectively functioning, surviving the guerrilla attacks made upon it by the Establishment, and within the ordinary society. And, as the hard reality of white politics is revealed to youth—the Free Speech Movement never had a chance and its leaders are in jail this minute, not for revolting against the stodgy University of California administration, but for trespassing, i.e., threatening property—more and more of them are simply turning away from the traditional forms of dissent because they find dissent meaningless.[32]

Being a power in the land, a powerful symbol of rebellion, the hippie social movement was increasingly reinterpreted by more politically ori-

---

[31]Ralph J. Gleason, "The Power of Non-Politics or the Death of the Square Left," pp. 214–23, in Kornbluth, *op. cit.*, pp. 216–17.
[32]*Ibid.*, p. 215.

ented, more activist individuals and groups to suit their radical political purposes. Ralph Gleason's own "description" of the hippie movement is a good example of this social redefinition, this politicizing of the movement and its symbols:

> "Turn on, tune in and drop out" is widely read as meaning drop out completely from society, which is what the beatniks did. This is not at all what is going on with the hippies. They are doing something else, much more constructive and much more meaningful and infinitely creative. They are, in effect, the first creative social movement in decades among white people in the U.S.
>
> The hippies are dropping out of the Madison Avenue, LBJ society in which a Hubert Humphrey can publicly put his arm around Lester Maddox and say there's room for him in the Democratic Party. They are dropping out of a society which condones napalm (and from the radical intellectual society which condones it in one country and condemns it in another).
>
> But they are not just dropping out into Limbo or Nirvana. They are building a new set of values, a new structure, a new society, if you will, horizontal to the old but in it. . . .
>
> Now the point of that is that the rock groups and the Diggers represent communal, low-pressure-on-the-individual organization in which the whole of the Haight-Ashbury hippie world operates, as opposed to plastic uptight America.
>
> Communes, handcrafts, survival in the wilderness, farming, and other similar activities are a part and parcel of the movement. Maybe the Luddites did have a bad press, as E. J. Hobsbawm has suggested, and we may have to go back to them or even before, to take up the thread of history and straighten things out.
>
> But the fact of the matter is that these people are trying by demonstration, to show the world *how to live now*.[33]

Once this redefinition had begun, the individuals who recruited themselves under the hippie banner—for the hippie movement is certainly a do-your-own-categorizing-thing—became far more complicated, more mixed. There were an increasing number with political goals—they were *political hippies*. The recruitment, then, had the same effect as the polarizing attacks of the officials and public: each drove the movement into a more rebellious position, at least insofar as the social definition of what constituted the movement was concerned. Those who still were primarily concerned with the rejection of American society and the freedom to do their own thing moved out—they "split"—to live in the hippie communes that now dot the countryside, the mountains, the forests, and the deserts of America. Others floated in various directions at different times. Some

---

[33]*Ibid.*, pp. 215–16.

moved resolutely to create and use "flower power"—but by any means other than the sowing of flowers.

One of the most apparent effects of hippie cultural elements was in the college drug scene. Drugs, especially marihuana and, much less frequently, LSD, had become symbols of rebellion for American college youth, probably in good part for independent reasons but also in significant part because of the vast publicity concerning the relations between drug use and the hippie rebellion. The hippie ideas, especially their rationales for using drugs and their commitment to attacks on American "square" society, became standard parts of this vastly larger and more diffuse subculture of college drug users.

"Marihuana users" and users of other drugs in college range all the way from the "straight" sorority girl who secretly tries it "just once," or the occasional "recreational user," to the hard-core "head." But there are many thousands of students, especially in the "elite schools" like Berkeley, who systematically smoke pot or use other drugs as part of a generalized subculture of rebellion. For them, smoking pot has become symbolic of this rebellion, of this rejection of the work-a-day, square world; and as a symbol of that rebellious subculture, it becomes a way of taking part in the secret communion of believers, a sharing in the new freedom, and a demonstration of one's belonging in that amorphous, otherwise invisible group of rebels. James Carey, in his excellent study of *The College Drug Scene*, has argued that marihuana and LSD users have in fact almost always started in good part *because* they were dissatisfied with society in general:

> The beginning for everyone seems to be some critical awareness of the way things are in society. A sense of disillusionment is strong. As a 24-year-old reformed head and laboratory technician put it: "I guess it takes a dissatisfaction with—first you have to be dissatisfied with what you see around you in society. Because if you're satisfied with other people and yourself, and just whatever you see when you walk down the street or look out the window, then you'll probably never take it, because, because, if you're satisfied with it, then you accept all the norms. One of the norms is that you don't smoke pot. And, eventually somebody is going to come along and offer you some. And eventually if enough people offer it to you, you are going to take some."[34]

But the rebellious youth cultures, especially the hippie rebellion and the drug rebellion, have also flowed into more radical, more political forms of protest. The Yippies are the most extreme group of politicized, radicalized hippie-types. They make use of the hippie styles, the hippie strategies of personal encounters, the hippie expressions, the hippie ideas,

---

[34]James T. Carey, *The College Drug Scene*, Englewood Cliffs, New Jersey: Prentice-Hall, Inc., 1968, pp. 48–49.

and the hippie category in slightly revised form. But they use all of these as part of a radical, confrontationist movement with the general goal of "revolutionizing" American society, though what that "revolutionizing" might be is hard to say and among the Yippies the rebellious subcultures mingled with and overlapped the radical protest subcultures; youth who used confrontationist tactics were generally willing to take part in violent encounters, at the very least as the *dramatized victims,* in order to achieve their quasi-political goals of "revolutionizing" American society. But in some ways the Yippies also represent the outer fringes of the youth rebellions, a real "freak-out," a nongroup seeking to dramatize the necessary absurdity of the whole "social game." In some ways "revolution" to them means simply dramatizing this necessary absurdity and then watching the pieces fall apart as the players come to see through that drama that it is all only a game that is ultimately absurd. The Yippies are political-psychedelics *acting out* the message of drugs. As Abbie Hoffman has said in a "chapter" entitled "Revolution: The Highest Trip of Them All":

> Revolution for the hell of it? Why not? It's all a bunch of phony words anyway. Once one has experienced LSD, existential revolution, fought the intellectual game-playing of the individual in society, of one's identity, one realizes that action is the only reality, not only reality but morality as well. One learns reality is a subjective experience. It exists in my head. I am the Revolution.[35]

THE SIGNIFICANCE OF THE REBELLIOUS YOUTH SUBCULTURES

The Yippies, while important in themselves for certain reasons, were indicative of a far more important aspect of the youth subcultures, movements, and organizations: they show very clearly how *fluid* all such social categorizations of youth are, how vague the membership criteria and self-identifications are, how changing they are, how overlapping, how problematic are the meanings of the various symbols used in any given situation, and how any given subculture and organization flows into so many others. It is not even possible to say with *any* certainty whether any given group or subculture or movement is "revolutionary." In fact, it is often not possible to even be sure of the goals and the situational desires of any given (vaguely defined) group. This is, of course, true of any political movement or group, since the goals, values, desires, and so on, of the group are socially meaningful in many ways and become politically meaningful in vastly complex ways, helping to determine who will support or attack the group. Such goals, values, etc., become subject to *political*

---

[35]Abbie Hoffman, *Revolution For the Hell Of It,* New York: The Dial Press, Inc., 1968, p. 9.

definition by many different groups for the purposes they have at hand in the immediate situation, so that different groups are purposefully manipulating the meanings of these things and, hence, the meanings of the group and its significances for our society as a whole. This, for example, is perfectly clear in the immensely complex (and lurid) official reports concerning the goals of the Yippies at the Chicago Democratic National Convention, as reported by Jerome Skolnick in *The Politics of Protest:*

> The variety of intelligence received by law enforcement officials is indicated by this listing of Yippie threats published in the mass media: "There were reports of proposals to dynamite natural gas lines; to dump hallucinating drugs into the city's water system; to print forged credentials so that demonstrators could slip into the convention hall; to stage a mass stall-in of old jalopies on the expressways and thereby disrupt traffic; to take over gas stations, flood sewers with gasoline, then burn the city; to fornicate in the parks and on Lake Michigan's beaches; to release greased pigs throughout Chicago, at the Federal Building and at the Amphitheater; to slash tires along the city's freeways and tie up traffic in all directions; to scatter razor sharp three-inch nails along the city's highways; to place underground agents in hotels, restaurants, and kitchens where food was prepared for delegates, and drug food and drink; to paint cars like independent taxicabs and forcibly take delegates to Wisconsin or some other place far from the convention; to engage Yippie girls as 'hookers' to attract delegates and dose the drinks with LSD; to bombard the Amphitheater with mortars from several miles away; to jam communication lines from mobile units; to disrupt the operations of airport control towers, hotel elevators and railway switching yards; to gather 250 'hyper-potent' hippie males into a special battalion to seduce the wives, daughters and girlfriends of convention delegates; to assemble 100,000 people to burn draft cards with the fires spelling out: 'Beat Army'; to turn on fire hydrants, set off false fire and police alarms, and string wire between trees in Grant Park and Lincoln Park to trip up three-wheeled vehicles of the Chicago police; to dress Yippies like Viet Cong and walk the streets shaking hands or passing out rice; to infiltrate the right wing with short haired Yippies and at the right moment exclaim: 'You know, these Yippies have something to say!'; to have ten thousand nude bodies floating on Lake Michigan—the list could go on."[36]

Today there are many social prophets who insist with complete certainty that *the* youth movement is this, that, or the other. In many cases these prophecies are very clearly made by radicals and radical sympathizers who are would-be leaders of a Second Great Children's Crusade

---

[36]Jerome H. Skolnick, *The Politics of Protest*, New York: Ballantine Books, 1969, pp. 285–86.

(though they presumably expect the Crusade to be more successful this time than the first time). They are generally trying to make themselves and others believe that at last the Mighty Host has arrived in the land to set men free from the iniquities of the materialistic life of hard work, competition, and repression. They use wild generalizations about the unity of "the youth movement" and its "totally revolutionary nature" to create an image of strength that will flag foundering spirits, urge the unconvinced to join up before the bandwagon leaves them in the dust (or the "dustbin of history"), and scare their ancient foes into submission: as the bumper sticker says, "America: *Change* It Or *Lose* It." These prophets have hailed the new *Swarmings* of rebellious youth, such as the vast swarming host that turned on and tuned in to the Woodstock Rock Festival, as a third coming, the rise of the New Christianity (only better than last time) that will sweep irresistibly across the land and down through the ages; and, in fact, the radical youth and their adult supporters and users do very frequently make precisely this parallel between the suppressed state of early Christians and the "suppressed" state of youth today (with Chicago as the modern Coliseum), a parallel which even so balanced an analyst as Daniel Moynihan has seen as worthy of consideration in his essay on "Nirvana Now."

At the other extreme, those who are committed to opposing and repressing the rebellious youth movement, as are a large percentage of the older generation and their official agents of control, see the rebellious youth movements as a rising tide of anarchy. They, too, make wild prophecies about the "anarchic hordes" and their growing strength, but for opposite purposes. Presumably, they seek to create a nightmare image of invading hordes that will galvanize the true bulwarks of social order and democracy to repress these hordes before it is too late, before they have overrun us all and—what? At this point, even the enemies of the movements cannot decide just what the enemy is like or just what he is after. Some are obviously simply fighting ancient enemies who have taken a new form and grown stronger: they see only Communist conspiracies in every nude party, every braless breast, every joint of marihuana, every strand of long hair or dirty feet exposed to public view. Others see a new religion. Some believers in the old religion see the revival of the old. Others see the final, long-delayed death rattles of the family.

This great buzzing confusion over the meanings of the rebellious youth subcultures, movements, and situational events only shows how fluid they are, how rapidly changing, how amorphous, how overlapping. But all of this does not mean that there are not some discernible patterns to them, however tentative we must be in evaluating those patterns. Most important it seems very clear that a generalized youth subculture involving significant elements of "alienation" and incipient "rebellion" has been growing throughout American society (and with vague relations to developments in other nations), though this subculture is only very situationally participated in or made use of (mainly on Rock occasions) by the great majority of American youth, who remain "straight"; and that this generalized youth culture is tied in with far more specific and far more rebellious youth subcultures, such as the leisure cults and the hippies, who provide many of the symbolic styles used by youth to set themselves off from the adult world and most of the ideas of rebellion. This generalized youth culture and even the rebellious youth cultures are not in themselves revolutionary in any way. That is, they are not setting out to overthrow the government or any other part of our society by concerted political action. For the most part, they have been apolitical. But they do flow into far more political subcultures with more revolutionary ideas and goals; they provide some of the ideas, styles, publicity-getting image, and (crossover) recruits (who can go both ways—that is, some revolutionaries go apolitical, just as the apoliticos can go politico). Very importantly, the generalized and slightly rebellious youth culture and, most especially, the rebellious youth cultures provide the vaguely favorable social context for the evolution of the more political protest movements. It is these rebellious cultural elements that are so widely shared that prepare a great number of American youth, especially college youth (for reasons we shall see), for the far more political protest movements when the situations that elicit and emotionalize these rebellious ideas arise; and it is this vague, generalized sense of rebellion against the adult world, especially against those seen as the official representatives of that adult world (the oppressors or suppressors), that provides an everyday social context for political protest that is implicitly supportive and rarely involves any informal controls. Without this generalized social context the student protest movements would prove ineffectual. With it, they have proven very effective in some ways, if not exactly in the ways intended.

11. SEX RAISES ITS REVOLUTIONARY HEAD

EDWARD SAGARIN

Lenny Bruce, who had few peers as social satirist, when asked his opinion of homosexuals, is reported to have said that they were all right, but he would not want one to marry his brother. Had the great humorist lived, however, he might today be under attack from two sides for this remark, which could easily be characterized as a pejorative sneer.

Borrowing from the language of politics—and what is more political than sex?—the right wing of the gay world would demand a retraction, for why should Bruce have objected if his brother wanted to be bound by clergy to another male, in a rite that could be dissolved only by God and that would hold them together till death do them part?

And from the left wing . . . well, that's where the Gay Liberation Front comes in, and it would lose no time and lack no words to show that Bruce is an agent of the imperialist-oppressive-antisexual-capitalist-militarist-psychiatric-industrial complex, whose denunciations of homosexuals are no different from the way they talk about and oppress blacks, women, workers and, in fact, people.

October 15, 1969 was a glorious day! God and the meteorologists were kind to the antiwar protesters on that sunny Wednesday, and they poured out in all parts of the country, students and teachers, hippies and apparent denizens of the square world, to celebrate Moratorium Day. They laughed, they marched, they shouted, they applauded, they shook their fists, and if only the war in Vietnam had ended, this might have gone down in history as the greatest argument that civilization had produced in favor of democracy and as proof of man's sanity.

And minor though it might have been among the events of that day, but certainly not ignored by press and television cameramen, was the surfacing of the Gay Liberation Front. In a very new and real sense, quite different from Mattachine and Daughters of Bilitis, organized homosexuals had decided to come out.

To come out. The phrase has so many meanings, and such new ones today, that we are apt to forget its history. For way back in the dim past

---

Reprinted from *The Realist*, May-June 1970, No. 87, by permission of the author.

when children played such innocent games as cops and robbers (and, incredibly, the kids always wanted to be the good guys, the cops!) and hide-and-go-seek, there was a time when the seeker had found his first victim and beaten him to the goal, and the kids would sing out happily—or shall we say gaily?—to those still undetected. "Come out, come out, wherever you are!"

Indeed it was, or appeared to be at least, the age of innocence. For imagine yourself walking down the streets of New York or San Francisco, and you pass a little group of gamins, and you overhear the prepubescent children talking about coming out. You step a little closer, lest your ears be deceiving you, and yes, the diminutive sophisticates are discussing latent homosexuals and closet queens, and guys who ought to know what they are and should decide to come out. Or, if they hesitate, one youngster adds, we'll bring them out.

So that while a church in the Mid-West, with a homosexual preacher, is performing the sacraments of marriage for two guys, only insisting that they swear on a stack of penises that they've known each other for at least six months (no one asks about premarital relations, and the bride may look grotesque in the white gown with veil and train, but at least one can be assured that neither principal in the ceremony is pregnant), at the same time all the bourgeois concepts of marriage and sex, fidelity and privacy, adultery (its evils) and adulthood (its necessity) are denounced in the language of the Weathermen by the Gay liberation Front, the Viet Cong of the homophiles.

"Up the ass of the ruling class," it proclaims, a lovely amalgam of sex and revolution, of youthful protest and contemporary expression of contempt for the powers that be, but a slogan that may betray as much doubt about oneself as about the enemy. More popular in GLF is the political slogan, "No revolution without us," and the explicitly homosexual one, "Out of the closets, into the streets."

Traditionally, it was to be expected that, when homosexual organizations were formed and then developed open meetings and legal publications, they would be ultraconformist, conventional, and middleclass in every respect, emphasizing that their members differed in no way, but *no* way, from the adherents of the local PTA or the suburban Elks club, except that they loved, formed lasting alliances, and incidentally had sex with someone of their own gender.

It is true that a few liberal leftists were active in the first organizations of homosexuals; in fact, if anybody remembers the name of Henry Wallace, it was a group of his followers who formed a Bachelors-for-Wallace club when Henry was campaigning for President, and the name was apparently the facade behind which there probably lurked a nice group of left wing gay guys.

Politics and sexuality notwithstanding, they were respectable people; in fact, from today's vantage point, it was hard to find anybody who didn't fit that sobriquet a generation ago. But when these people, the embarrassing "queer pinkos" as their enemies labeled them, finally awakened to reality on the first Wednesday after the first Tuesday after the first Monday in November, 1948 they decided to pick up their marbles and save something from the debacle.

Thus was born one of the first homosexual organizations in the United States; since then it has been a history of many groups, splits and splintering, proliferation and disappearance, growth and decline, and always a search for answers to some difficult questions. Foremost among them was how to organize and lead a movement for social acceptance when there was such an ease in concealment of one's own proclivities, such difficulties if one were to make a public proclamation.

By and large, the homophile groups, despite the Wallaceite club, were conservative and were respectable; that is, they were conservative in the sense that Martin Luther King could be so labeled, or the NAACP. If only society could be convinced that the homosexuals were really good boys and good girls, not promiscuous, very loving, always law-abiding, forever the victim and never the victimizer, they would be accepted.

They were loyal, excellent security risks, were no sissies and bull-dykes, and would make good soldiers and sailors, if only given the opportunity. In fact, had not Plato extolled the invincibility of an army made up of just such lovers, each soldier showing the greatest valor and courage because he would never want to appear in any but the most favorable light before his comrade?

But most Americans were not convinced; and the attitude of the armed forces as well as the gay youths could be summarized by the story of the Naval psychiatrist who, in rejecting a rather obvious kid, said, "You'd never make a good sailor," to which the lad replied, "Oh, you're wrong, dearie, I made three very good ones last week!"

All was not respectability, however, even in the public image of the homophile groups. On radio and television, they wanted to talk of the right of people to love one another and of the oppressive laws against this right, but in fact these organizations became involved—and for self-protection and to protect their constituency for whom they sought to have answers, they had to become involved—in defending "lovers" apprehended in what are euphemistically called subway and park tearooms.

And in order to keep the interest of the readers and attract more to the dull, repetitive, artless sheets, in which the occasional poetry served as unwitting and unintentional humor to lighten the otherwise drab scene, there were pictures that transcended the rules of respectability. At first only bulging crotches, then the material became less suggestive and more explicit, often openly depicting the attractions of sadomasochism (one of the publications was actually called *Black and Blue*), and finally embracing hard-core homosexual pornography.

But it all happened at a time when people were no longer getting uptight about pornography, so the lure of the pornographic, which blossomed despite the drive for respectability and in order to enhance the appeal to the specific audience, proved to be only the slightest obstacle in the effort to win support in the straight society. Actually, it soon became apparent that the homophile organizations were conducting both a public presentation and a soliloquy in which the actor is the audience: one could present one image to the world at large and another to appeal to a different constituency.

The peculiar thing about Mattachine, and so many of the similar organizations, was that it was so goddam straight! So that its members got on their knees, not to perform fellatio (unconsciously perhaps the desire or need, but not the explicitly expressed), but to beg the most conservative and Puritanical element in American society to accept them.

And that's how come it all ended up in a midwestern church, with the minister asking, "Do you solemnly swear . . . do you take this man for your lawfully wedded—" but then the cliche failed, and a word had to be found—your lawfully wedded *what?*—"your lawfully wedded spouse?" "I do." And he did. All right, Lenny, don't turn over in your grave, that guy wasn't your brother.

But he was, that's the funny thing, that's where we all failed, he *was* Lenny's brother, and mine and yours, if we really mean it that we're all brothers and sisters, black people and white, Jews and Arabs and the children of German Nazis, Vietnamese peasants and the American interventionists facing them, youths that the cops call dirty hippies and cops that the youths call fascist pigs: are we not all brothers?

And, if so, if we really mean it, then the guy walking down that aisle in drag, and the world of the straights, the sexual straights, not the Mattachine straights, and the gay Viet Cong of the U.S.A., calling itself the Gay Liberation Front, they are our brothers.

So, Lenny, that *was* your brother who was marrying the gay kid, and GLF is going to liberate us all from that bag, not from homosexuality, but from bourgeois marriage, straight or gay, from oppressive sex roles, and from being so uptight about who someone hops into bed with, or if no bed is around, who he makes out with in the public park.

Against all the expectations of sociological theory that would have and did predict the conservatism of homophile movements, GLF surfaced and announced its revolutionary program, demanding its place with Women's Lib and Black Panthers and Weatherpeople (once called Weathermen, but in deference to the attack on male chauvinism, the name has undergone a metamorphosis), as the vanguard of the Movement.

If there was special reason for GLF seeking alliance with the Panthers, because of the depth of the oppression and the militancy of the response, and perhaps on a less conscious level the admiration for supermasculinity that has been characteristic of homosexuals, there was also something special in the alliance with Women's Lib. For in this group GLF saw a common goal, an assault on the traditional concepts of masculine and feminine roles.

Protest movements tend on the one hand to be epidemic, one group suggesting by its very existence, and particularly the publicity that it today so quickly attracts, that another might be desirable.

At the same time, protest movements tend to form in a social climate conducive to them. From Karl Marx and Alexis de Tocqueville down to the most recent analysts in the technical journals of sociologists and political scientists, it has been pointed out that protests blossom forth when the oppressed social conditions are slightly ameliorated, when they seem to be on the road to improvement, offering hope and promise for change, but creating frustration in those impatient for the change and still suffering under less than tolerable conditions.

It is a formula that can account for GLF, even more than for some of the other groups in the movement today.

But this accounts for GLF; what about the search for alliances? Social movements have frequently faced the question of an alliance that strengthens by adding numbers against a common enemy or for a common cause, but that weakens because it leaves some of its adherents antagonized by the allies. Following the Civil War, the feminist counterparts of what is now called Women's Lib were demanding universal suffrage, as distinct from universal male suffrage.

They were supported by the powerful voice of Frederick Douglass, but many abolitionists, although hurrying to express their agreement with the aspirations of their female compatriots, urged that strategy and discretion be considered. The struggle for the ballot for the Negro, they argued, could only be weakened by giving the ballot to women.

Men, they claimed, by which they meant white men, the sole components of what came later to be called the power structure, were going to have a hard enough time accepting the notion that color of skin and status as slave or former slave (carrying with it illiteracy) should not be the determinant of voting rights; they would never accept the notion, and certainly not at the same time, that their wives, mistresses, and whores should decide the fate of the nation.

But the entry of GLF onto the revolutionary scene has implications that go beyond this, and that make the historical analogy of the feminist-abolitionist alliance seem disarmingly simple in comparison. For it would appear that the last thing that homosexuals might want is to be linked with the Panthers and Weatherpeople: in the public eye, bomb-throwing, irresponsible, antisocial, and terrorist.

It might build up the masculine ego of some gay men to have a revolutionary image of themselves, fantasies of barricades manned by those who had been scorned as weak, but most gay people felt that they had enough burdens, what with stigma and problems of identity and the management of concealment. Why should people who had to handle their lives in an atmosphere of hostility bring their already difficult movement into the center of the arena of disrespectability?

It is like the conversion to Judaism of Sammy Davis, Jr. People asked, didn't he have enough *tsurus*—did he have to be black *and* Jewish?

From the viewpoint of the Panthers, the Weatherpeople, Women's Lib and others, the GLF offered, or seemed to offer, few advantages and many disadvantages. In numbers, GLF could not aspire to be large, Kinsey's figures to the contrary notwithstanding. Even if Kinsey's rather doubtful statistics should be borne out (and recently no less an authority than Paul Gebhard, presently heading the Institute for Sex Research that was founded by Kinsey, has cast doubt on them), the one man in six, who with few exceptions had remained aloof from Mattachine and Daughters of Bilitis and the other respectables all these years, was not going to flock to GLF.

For all the talk about homosexuals being the nation's second largest minority (presumably this means after women, but before blacks), it is unlikely that their public banners will attract enough numbers to make the earth tremble or to add many decibels to the echoes of those shouting for the freedom of the Black Panthers. Or at least so I believe, but my friends in GLF smile at my naiveté, and in the youthful enthusiasm on which social movements thrive, they reply, "Wait and see."

At the same time, a movement like Panthers or Student Mobe or whatever else one may mention in the same breath is not likely to wish to project, even to its own constituency, the image brought forth in public minds by swishes and queers, faggots and kooks, whom they have embraced (albeit only symbolically, one hastens to add, not literally). In clear, practical, pragmatic terms, the arithmetic does not seem to add up; there is more to lose than to gain.

For the Panthers particularly, how true this would appear to be. For here are people claiming, and with considerable justification, that white America has robbed black men of their masculinity, has castrated these men even while being sexually envious of them, has degraded and seduced their females, and that they, the Panthers, represent the resurgence of the expression of strong masculine identification, unequivocal and assertive, among the blacks.

The militancy, the many beards, the shaking of the fists, the deep and resonant voices—somehow, it does not mingle well with the homosexual stereotypes, delicacy and daintiness and the demasculinizing process.

Homosexuality was just one of many things that the Panthers sneered at; among the blacks, when homosexuality did manifest itself, it was another sign of what the oppressive whites did to people of color; and among the whites, it was further evidence of the degradation, deterioration, demoralization and decay of bourgeois life in this country. The GLF hardly seemed like a welcome ally, nor were proponents of homosexuality as a way of life likely to be attracted to a program that rejected them.

More than that, the revolutionary movement was a haven for some who found therein an ability to live a less restrictive sexual life without the stern disapproval that one often met, and still meets, in less radical circles; but it was hardly the beckoning call for those whose chief interest was not in the political reorganization of society, but in the achievement of a new sexual freedom.

Whatever illusion the believers in and practitioners of free love (as it once was called) and homosexuality and other violations of the norms might have held in the early part of this century, the illusion that, comes the revolution and restrictions on human sexuality would go the way of other bourgeois-capitalist prejudices, how could they retain this vision after the Russian revolution, after Mao and Castro?

All societies, Kingsley Davis, a noted sociologist, has stated, require that the sexual urges be held in check by sets of norms and laws, and socialist societies have proved more restrictive, while totalitarian ones (including the socialist) have proved more repressive.

While the homosexuals fight against the raids on gay bars in the United States, they do not have to worry about such raids in Moscow, Leningrad, or Peking. This they do not deny, but simply argue that times have changed, or must. In America at least, the answer of GLF is embodied in its slogan: *No revolution without us!*

Yet, for all these forces that one could call anticentrifugal, factors that might have led one to expect that most left-wing homosexuals would spurn an alliance with the new young revolutionaries, and to further expect that the scorn would be mutual and reciprocal, there they were on Moratorium Day, proclaiming themselves the Gay Liberation Front, and again, as Spring 1970 was making its late debut in New York, marching under their own banners, demanding that the Black Panthers be freed, and not to be outdone in threat and invective and expression of anger against Judge John M. Murtagh.

And not scorned by other marchers, not vilified or laughed at, not causing embarrassment, but part of the radical scene.

What ostensibly unites these diverse and potentially hostile groups, or groups which when close to one another might be provocative of anxiety, is not merely the common cause of revolution (antiwar, black liberation, down with the pigs). The small increase in numbers is not being weighed; perhaps what is so attractive about the radical youth is that they are no longer as practical in a radical bureaucratic sense as were their fathers of the '30s.

Practicality is part of the system, and down with it. Who cares if one is embarrassed or provokes a sneer from some tomato-throwing fascist on a rooftop? We know why *he* hates fairies!

Nor is it that there is common cause against oppression: we fight against being oppressed, you fight against being oppressed, and together we support your fight and you support ours. It's a neat little calculus, once called the united front, and if it makes sense, it more often makes internecine warfare.

But this is not the way GLF sees the world today. The scene has changed, and GLF explains the willingness, albeit with some argument, of Women's Lib and Black Panthers and Weatherpeople to accept them, the most stigmatized of groups, because of what they claim is the high cost—ideologically, morally, if not practically—of their exclusion.

Basically, the question for them is one of struggle and oppression, of the old saw about a world half-slave and half-free, of the impossibility of any man or woman being free while one man or woman is not.

As I see it, however, there is still another explanation of this alliance, to be found neither in the common rejection of an oppressive ruling class, nor in the common struggle for goals that meet each others' support. Rather, I see a common interest in conducting one's struggles in a manner that upsets, offends, confronts, and in fact provokes something called the Establishment.

Whatever the reason, GLF is gaining entry, at least in some small way, into the world of revolutionary youth, and particularly its black militant contingent, for the straight youth (straight but not square, as against Mattachine, which is square but not straight) are not frightened at the alliance, but relish it as one more mechanism for expressing its contempt for the norms of society, the makers and enforcers of those norms, and for those who would reject them because in their ranks there march the homosexuals.

There is a negativism sweeping the left-wing youth today. Respectable is the most disrespectable word in the language, and if respectable people heap ridicule on the antiwar marchers, or the new breed of militant civil rights demonstrators, or on homosexuals, then let them throw their tomatoes and shout their filthy bourgeois prejudiced epithets: the more we provoke them, the better off we are.

Let the man in the gray flannel pants laugh at us, the youth feel, and one more reason to provoke his laughter is one more reason to believe that we have succeeded in our own task: to offend, to antagonize, to polarize, to confront, to sharpen the lines between ourselves and the enemy.

And then, just to add extra sauce to this delectable serving, the kids have learned a smattering of Freud and have heard about latency, and they laugh right back, certain that behind the fly of the gray flannel pants there lurks a limp penis that cannot express its own masculinity, or an erect one of a closet queen.

Come out, come out, wherever you are!

It is not quite clear what the name Gay Liberation Front means. The National Liberation Front, undoubtedly its inspiration, uses the last word in its name in the same sense that it was employed in the days of the united front; it is the amalgam, the spokesman, the "front" for several diverse groups that have united behind banner and program, while still retaining separate identities.

GLF, despite some factions and differences within it, is in no sense a front for a group of other organizations. If anything, its name implies that it is a self-proclaimed vanguard, in the front ranks of a struggle that has not yet been joined by some silent millions. If this is the case, the front is visible, but one does not know much about its rear.

This is the age of the radicalization of many once silent minorities, and while the homophile movement dates back many years, an event in New York City in the summer of 1969 served as the catalyst to turn homosexuals to the tactics of confrontation. It was the Stonewall incident, a police raid on a gay bar, accompanied by the usual amount of brutality real or alleged, but reacted to in an unexpected manner: a call to homosexuals and their friends and allies to demonstrate against the police action.

The call was heeded, a new militancy was born and in this event one can see the origins of GLF.

Today, the organization publishes a journal, called *Come Out,* and in its initial issue it proclaimed itself "a newspaper by and for the gay community." The paper appeared with an exclamation point after the title on the masthead, this same punctuation mark repeated on the pages within; by the second issue the exclamation point had disappeared, but it was the only sign of a flagging of militancy. If anything, the slogans had become leftier and heftier.

On the first page of issue number one, there were the well-known circles with protruding arrows and crosses, symbols of males and females, but the arrangement was, if anything, rather queer for a homosexual journal. There were three symbols, one a male, one a female, and a third carrying both pieces of apparatus, the latter being linked with each of the other two. By the second issue, this part of the logo had likewise disappeared, with the apparent and perhaps attractive bisexuality being interpreted as the not too pleasant apparition of hermaphroditism, and the slogan that proclaimed *Come Out!* as the newspaper by and for the gay community had also been replaced: it was now "a liberation forum for the gay community."

The format, size, and appearance of *Come Out* make it almost indistinguishable from *Rat, East Village Other,* and a long list of underground papers. And what else could it be? Here is the conformity that is always to be found in the world of the nonconformists.

In an early issue, there are two items on GLF that I should like to quote. The first is a statement of what the organization is; the second, of what the organization is, as supposedly paraphrased from a New York City Police Department report.

In its own words:

> Gay Liberation Front is a revolutionary homosexual group of men and women formed with the realization that complete sexual liberation for all people cannot come about unless existing social institutions are abolished. We respect society's attempt to impose sexual roles and definitions of our nature. We are stepping outside these roles and simplistic myths. We are going to be who we are. At the same time, we are creating new social forms and relations, that is, relations based upon brotherhood, cooperation, human love, and uninhibited sexuality. Babylon has forced us to commit ourselves to one thing . . . revolution.

The dots, may I add, are in the original. Nothing has been omitted, unless it was by the editors of *Come out,* and they are not in the habit of deleting the unprintable.

The second, the paraphrase of what purportedly was a police report on the GLF, sounds just too good to be true. Authentic, possibly, but if a GLF double agent in what once was called the Vice Squad of the NYPD wanted to express his contempt for the competition, he couldn't have done better:

> The Gay Liberation Front is a radical and revolutionary organization, based on anarchist guidelines, similar to the Black Panthers and Weathermen. The organization is worth watching, although there seems to be only one or two radical individuals present at any given time. There is no immediate threat. They represent themselves as a homophile organization but are unlike such respectable and dedicated organizations as Daughters of Bilitis and Mattachine.

So that, if fellow-revolutionaries frightened by the specter of homosexual comrades-in-arms should feel it necessary to rebuff GLF, they need just read this Police Department report, and know that, by proclamation of the common enemy, GLF is acceptable. "It's nice to know we're in good company," was the terse and complete comment of an editor following this paraphrased report. All that was lacking was the explicit message: "Black Panther and Weatherman papers, please copy."

Here is a page devoted to homosexuals in the movement, not the homophile movement, but the Movement, another to the Young Lords, another headed with the slogans: "Right on!" "All power to the people!" "Gay power to the gay people!"

But not all is unity in the ranks of the new partisans of militancy. A letter from the University of Toronto Homophile Association is signed by eleven persons; they are all students, one might assume, and perhaps some pseudonyms are among them, but one cannot be certain, and can only admire the courage while at the same time hoping that no one has stood up to be counted while still carrying on an inner struggle that might eventually lead to a different sexual orientation.

The letter protests GLF, or at least the newspaper speaking for it, because of its effort to link the homophile movement to communist revolution and its support of totalitarian anti-homosexual political systems. Don't the editors know what has happened to homosexuals in Cuba?

"After Castro's revolution, the previously large homosexual community in Cuba was systematically rounded up and imprisoned. Now, no homosexual social life or organizations are allowed, and homosexuality is officially nonexistent—considered a product of the decadent, bourgeois-capitalist system."

Don't they know that the Black Panthers are notoriously anti-homosexual, as any reader of Cleaver can easily discover?

Hannah Arendt is quoted by the students as having contended that homosexual revolutionaries are always among those who suffer most under communist and national socialist regimes, and then Milton Friedman is quoted as having stated that it is the free market that permits the state's restrictions on minority groups, including homosexuals, to be as small as they are.

Certainly Milton Friedman, arch rightwinger of American economics, is enough to anger any revolutionary, but the GLF people who responded to the students ignored Arendt and Friedman, and spoke of Cuba and the Panthers. Cuba has made great progress against disease, illiteracy, and malnutrition, it is pointed out, and the situation of the homosexuals on that island is not really as bad as the students say.

"We hope eventually out of our own dialogues, actions, and readings to work out an analysis of how we in Gay Liberation Front can relate to Cuba through both criticism and emulation."

(Criticism, it is hoped, for the sake of the safety of the GLFers, from the vantage point of the West Village.)

As for the black revolutionaries, those responding to the students chide them for thoughtlessly applying the word "terrorist" to the Panthers, and inform the Toronto youths that "we have found individual Black Panthers to embrace us and our cause after we worked, demonstrated & picketed with them. And it is in just this way, through working together with others on common causes that we can bring our cause to a realization of the wider support it must have to be successful."

All of this seems to have taken the respectable homophile movement by surprise, but there may have developed a symbiotic relationship of love and hate, acceptance and rejection, admiration and denunciation. While Mattachine and the numerous other groups demand security clearance for homosexuals, GLF denounces security clearances, defense contracts, and working for the war machine.

And while Mattachine and its allies fight for equal rights to be drafted, no discrimination in the right to be a soldier or sailor, and to be treated as well (or as badly) as any other young citizen, the GLF denounces the draft, and insists that no one, straight or gay, should be turned into cannon fodder for the purposes of imperialist oppression.

What may here be developing is a division of labor and one that has its analogue in the civil rights movement as well. The blacks, too, demand the right to enter the Army as equals, even while denouncing the armed forces and its war against colored peoples in Asia.

A division of labor, but although each group has its place and its task, sometimes this is difficult to accept by those caught up in the struggle. So that, at meetings of the conservative homophile factions, there is now strategy being mapped to prevent the takeover of their conventions by the leftwingers.

It is not an unfamiliar scene to those who have followed radical politics, and it is one that gives GLF important activities to plan. If planned well and carried out with the fervor that usually punctuates the youthful radical scene, the GLF is likely to make a big splash, but it might be in a very small pond.

The emergence of homosexuality as an issue for those fighting against oppression, and of GLF as an organization in that struggle, has not gone unnoticed, nor even unwelcome, in some sectors of the radical press. An entire issue of the organ of the War Resisters League, *Win,* is devoted to homosexuality.

Some might have argued that the matter was irrelevant, others that it would serve only to antagonize pacifists and those close to the WRL position. But today these arguments no longer prevail, and in *Win* one of the best known leaders of pacifism in America reveals his homosexuality.

But it is not GLF material, and it is hardly likely to please the homosexual revolutionists. Let us shift the focus from GLF to WRL, the former a group of homosexuals who happen to be in the Movement, the latter a group of pacifists a few of whom happen to be homosexuals. One of the latter is Dave McReynolds, and it is his statement that makes up the better part of the issue devoted to this theme.

It was a courageous statement that McReynolds made, and many of the gay kids will now claim him as one of their own, one more hero who made it, one more example to prove that a man need not be defeated by this adversity.

But it is also a pathetic story, one of longing and loneliness, and while it might be oppressive to read this and insist that the writer remain celibate or change his ways, to impose on him a psychiatrist that he cannot accept, to close the doors of the bars and to haunt the parks where he meets his comrades and companions; in short, to banish him, this most human of humans, from the halls of humanity—indeed, it is oppressive and unjust to do any or all such things—it is nevertheless far from unjust to state that the life described by this pacifist is not one that any society would want its young people to emulate.

"When I get tired of life and the struggle I retreat to a gay bar, secure that reality will never penetrate there," writes McReynolds. And as for those who see in all men latent homosexuality and are urging young people to recognize "what they are" and to come out, heed these words of McReynolds:

"Bar talk will persuade you that every man is queer while the fact is that *every queer is fighting against his heterosexuality*." (Emphasis in original.)

As for the slogan, "Gay is good," McReynolds makes a simple denial of that statement; for him gay is not good, "it is boring." To which he adds: "It is sick in a way that queerness is not." Exactly what this last statement means I am not sure, nor does the writer explain it.

Perhaps he is saying that he accepts being homosexual, which is called queer, but that he is not part of and could not belong to a community of people who are homosexuals and call themselves gay. Or, in very simple language, is he just rejecting the irony of the adjective gay when it is used to describe something so lacking in gaiety?

From this article and all else we know about this man, David McReynolds emerges as a full human being, a gentle man without being a gentleman, a person filled with love and compassion that drove him to find a home in socialism and in pacifism. He emerges as one who is dedicated to peace, but who has not come to peace with himself; he is hardly a man who can or will find homosexuality as a way of life that can offer love for others.

For those who see homosexuality as being intrinsically on a par with heterosexuality, read McReynolds. It is a fast and cheap cure, if not for the desires, then for the illusions about them.

But not for GLF. All that McReynolds says is true, but it simply illustrates that the pattern of life that our culture offers the homosexual is oppressive. Better that bars be left unmolested than raided, it is conceded; better that there be no entrapment in the parks. But homosexual life is stultifying because capitalism offers no opportunities to be free of socially and governmentally imposed roles.

For some people in GLF, homosexuality, even under capitalism, is evidently not on a par with heterosexuality (to use the phrase made popular by Mattachine and the old-line homophile group) but is superior to it. First they said that gay is good, later it became excellent. Now, the slogan could very well be, although it has not been explicitly articulated in this manner but the content is clearly in that direction: Gay is superior. One turns to a gay manifesto in another revolutionary publication, this time in *Liberation,* to see how this is stated.

The article is called "A Gay Manifesto" and is written by Carl Wittman; although it makes mention in a favorable way of GLF, it does not appear as an official statement of that group.

"Homosexuality," he writes, "is *not* a lot of things. It is not a makeshift in the absence of the opposite sex; it is not hatred or rejection of the opposite sex; it is not genetic; it is not the result of broken homes except inasmuch as we could see the sham of American marriage. *Homosexuality is the capacity to love someone of the same sex.*" (Emphasis in original.)

Whatever else one may think of this pronouncement, one would expect it to be followed by a similar statement about heterosexuality.

But, lo, heterosexuality "reflects a fear of people of the same sex, it's anti-homosexual, and it is frought [sic] with frustration. Heterosexual sex is fucked up, too; ask women's liberation about what straight guys are like in bed. Sex is aggressive for the male chauvinist; sex is obligation for traditional women. And among the young, the modern, the hip, it's only a subtle version of the same. For us to become heterosexual in the sense that our straight brothers and sisters are is not a cure, it is a disease."

The old fashioned gay groups do not like to talk about the apparently sordid aspects of the sex lives of their adherents. These things, whatever they may be, are sometimes denied, more often ignored, said to take place not more frequently than among straight people, and finally are blamed on the oppressive atmosphere created by a hostile society, in which loving sex between those of the same sex cannot easily flourish.

But GLF does not deny, does not blame, it simply interprets in a manner that will not be easy for straight revolutionists to buy: this is true of Wittman, at least; and GLF if he is writing for them or reflecting their view. In a section of the manifesto headed *Peversion,* he writes:

> We've been called perverts enough to be suspect of any usage
> of the word. Still many of us shrink from the idea of certain kinds

of sex: with animals, sado-masochism, dirty sex (involving piss or shit). Right off, even before we take the time to learn any more, there are some things to get straight.

1. We shouldn't be apologetic to straights about gays whose sex lives we don't understand or share;

2. It's not particularly a gay issue, except that gay people probably are less hung up about sexual experimentation.

3. Let's get perspective: even if we were to get into the game of deciding what's good for someone else, the harm done in the "perversions" is undoubtedly less dangerous or unhealthy than tobacco or alcohol.

4. While they can be reflections of neurotic or self-hating patterns, they may also be enactments of spiritual or important phenomena: e.g., sex with animals may be the beginning of interspecies communication: some dolphin-human breakthroughs have been made on the sexual level; e.g., one guy who says he digs shit during sex occasionally says it's not the taste or texture, but a symbol that's so far into sex that those things no longer bug him; e.g., sado-masochism, when consensual, can be described as a highly artistic endeavor, a ballet the constraints of which are the thresholds of pain and pleasure.

Amen, ah men!

GLF is striving to be, if anything, an anarchist group, which is like saying a nonorganization organization. There will be no officers, leaders, involuntary tasks, discipline; it is all part of the communitarian utopia that a few youths here and there in America have embraced. That it is almost the diametric reversal of the heterosexual groups that they emulate, particularly the Weatherpeople and the Panthers, does not seem to bother the GLFers. Each group has to have its own thing, and anarchist democracy is its.

But groups have a way of sprouting leadership, and particularly groups as unstructured as GLF, where unstructure most consciously becomes the striven-for structure, have a habit of forming themselves into factions, subgroups, and cliques. What starts out as a nonorganization not only becomes an organization, but then develops organizations within the organization, or non-organizations within the non-organization. Small and new as GLF is, it already has 10 or 15 of its own subgroups, each searching for the right answers.

One of these, called Red Butterfly, publishes its little mimeographed bulletin, called *Gay Liberation,* and a GLFer describes RB to me as a "cell" within the GLF (how I have always hated the word "cell" when used by radical groups). Red Butterfly, it is stated by my informant, is committed to defining a Marxist ideology of homosexuality.

"In practice," I am told, "it operates as an autonomous group of more professionally committed radicals within GLF," a perfectly legitimate practice according to GLF rules. In short, and the words are those of a GLF adherent, this is the "old left wing" of GLF.

Red Butterfly looks forward not only to a classless society, but a labelless society, and it calls for an end to all oppression. In a brief statement of its views, it states that homosexual acts between freely consenting partners are natural, and that the revolution cannot be just or complete if the rights of gay people as full human beings are not recognized.

So far, it could be Mattachine talking, except that words like "liberty" or "freedom" would have to be used in place of the frightening specter of revolution. But then, the oppression of homosexuals, it is said, is due not merely to ignorance and superstition, but to the interests and ideologies of an authoritarian capitalist society.

"Sexual liberation cannot succeed within the framework of reactionary society." Moscow papers: please copy.

The problems of GLF and Red Butterfly within it are many. Convince the revolutionary youth to accept them, convince the gay youth to come out and be revolutionary, and not the least, convince themselves that the revolution will bring sexual freedom, Russia and Cuba and China notwithstanding.

There may be some small successes simply because an organization that "salutes militant oppressed groups" and "offers aid" to them, that seeks to unify with "other oppressed groups into a cohesive body of people who do not find the enemy in each other," may have enough going for it to find a place in what is at this moment a very fragmented youthful revolutionary scene.

An organization that calls for the right of anyone to have sex with anyone else, with no age limit and no suggestion that public parks should not be turned into pubic ones ("Hell, yes, right here in Bryant Park, why not?") has an appeal to those who take revelry and ecstasy in offending the respectables and laughing at the institutions of society.

That such a group offers humane feelings, love and sympathy, that this comes out of the depths of their own degradations and humiliations and search for acceptance, that it speaks out against an injustice that is no less severe because it is universal, may be a force in contributing lovingness to a revolutionary youth that is caught in a whirlwind of an admixture of love and hate.

Nowhere is this warm hand of communitarian acceptance so evident as in the acceptance of the "swish" among the GLFers. Unlike Mattachine, always embarrassed, afraid that the straight world would be put off, denying that their members have limp wrists and concealing those who do ("Don't send *her* for the TV interview—what kind of an impression will *she* make?")—GLF finds all kinds acceptable.

Here there is no frantic denial of the stereotype: the male has a right to be "effeminate" and to be accepted as a full human being. It is a bold program, and even in this age of unisex, one that will gain not too many adherents. But that's just the point about the revolutionary youth: numbers don't count any more, it's recognizing the essential humanity of all of us.

So we come back to Lenny Bruce. What GLF is saying is that all men are our brothers, except some of them, who are our sisters.

I am reminded of a slogan that I once suggested be adopted by a revolutionary-Marxist group of transsexuals, who likewise wanted to convince the left-wing youth that transsexuals had a proper place within their movement. It was a simple paraphrase from the Communist Manifesto: "Transsexuals of the world, unite. You have a world to gain. You have nothing to lose but your balls and chains."

Talking to a City College student about the GLF recently, I think I stumbled across one of the basic difficulties, or contradictions, to use a favorite term of revolutionists, of this phase of the Movement. He was expressing his admiration for the gay revolutionists, his complete acceptance of their denunciation of the system, the capitalists, the pigs. But the pigs. "The thing I can't understand about myself," he confessed, "is that these pigs, these fascist pigs, in their nice blue uniforms, especially the younger ones. . . ."

And his voice dwindled off into a drool.

12. THE MAFIA AS A SOCIAL MOVEMENT

E. J. HOBSBAWM

Mafias—it is convenient to use the term for all phenomena of this kind—
have a number of special characteristics. *First,* they are never pure social
movements, with specific aims and programs. They are, as it were,
the meeting-places of all sorts of tendencies existing within their societies: the defence of the entire society against threats to its traditional
way of life, the aspirations of the various classes within it, the personal
ambitions and aspirations of individual energetic members. Hence they
are to some extent, like national movements, of which perhaps they are
a sort of embryo, fluid. Whether the tinge of social protest by the poor
determines their general color, as in Calabria, or that of the ambitions
of the local middle classes, as in Sicily, or pure crime, as in the American
Mafia, depends on circumstances. *Second,* they are to some extent unorganized. It is true that some *Mafias* are, at least on paper, centralized
and with proper "chains of command" and promotion, perhaps on the
model of masonic orders. But the most interesting situation is that in
which, as in the classical Sicilian *Mafia,* there is—or at one stage was—no
proper organization above local level and only very primitive organization
even there.

Under what conditions do *Mafias* arise? The question simply cannot be
answered, because we do not even know how many of them there are
or have been. Sicilian *Mafia* is the only body of its kind in modern Europe
which has provoked description and analysis in any quantity. Apart from
casual references to "delinquent associations," "secret associations of
robbers" and "protectors of robbers," and the like, we know hardly anything
about the situation in other places, and what we know allows us at best
to say that a situation out of which *Mafia could* have arisen, existed, not
whether it actually did.[1] We cannot conclude that absence of information
means that no such phenomenon existed. Thus, as we shall see, there is

From E. J. Hobsbawm, *Primitive Rebels: Studies in Archaic Forms of Social Movement in the 19th
and 20th Centuries.* New York: Praeger Publishers, Inc., 1963. First published by Manchester University Press, Manchester, England in 1959, reprinted in 1971. Reprinted by permission of the publishers.

[1]See Zugasti, *El Bandolerismo* (Madrid 1876–80), Introduction, vol. I for the *alcades'* reports on
the state of crime in their areas of Cordoba province, *c.* 1870; e.g., a "secret association of robbers"
in Baena, a "sociedad de ladrones" in Montilla, something that looks rather like *mafia* in the famous

absolutely no doubt of the existence of a body of *mafia*-type in Southern Calabria. But apart from a passing reference to such secret societies in Calabria and the Cilento (the region south of the gulf of Salerno) it seems to have been wholly unrecorded in the past.[2] This is less surprising than it might seem. Secret bodies composed largely of illiterate country-men work in obscurity. Middle-class townsmen are profoundly ignorant, and were normally profoundly contemptuous, of the low life under their feet. The only thing we can therefore do at present is to concentrate on one or two examples of known *Mafias* and hope that these may eventually throw light on the situation in hitherto uninvestigated areas.

Mafia is less well known than one might suppose. Though there is no dispute about the facts and a good deal of useful descriptive and analytical literature,[3] public discussion has been confused, partly by all manner of journalistic romancing, partly by the simple failure to recognize that "what appeared to the Piedmontese or the Lombard as "Sicilian delinquency" was in reality the law of a different society . . . a semi-feudal society."[4] It may, therefore, be as well to summarize what we know about it.

The word *Mafia* stands here for several distinct things. First, it represents a general attitude towards the State and the State's law which is not necessarily any more criminal than the very similar attitude of, let us say, public schoolboys towards their masters. A *mafioso* did not invoke State or law in his private quarrels, but made himself respected and safe by winning a reputation for toughness and courage, and settled his differences by fighting. He recognized no obligation except those of the code of honor or *omertà* (manliness), whose chief article forbade giving information to the public authorities. In other words *mafia* (which will be spelled with a small *m* when used in this sense) was the sort of code of behavior which always tends to develop in societies without effective public order, or in societies in which citizens regard the authorities as wholly or partly hostile (for instance in jails or in the underworld out-

---

smugglers' pueblo of Benameji, and the dumb opposition of Iznajar where 'according to the inveterate custom of this town, all these crimes have remained unpunished' (i.e., unsolved). I am inclined to accept Brenan's view that this was a proto-*mafia* rather than a *Mafia* situation. Cf. also Chapter V on Andalusian anarchism, below.

[2]G. Alongi, *La Camorra* (Turin 1890), 30. The note on La Camorra in Calabria (*Archivio di Psichiatria*, IV, 1883, 295) appears to deal exclusively with an organization of city crooks in Reggio Calabria, and appears to be quite unaware of the rural body. It may be noted that nobody was more passionately interested in this type of phenomenon than the Italian positivist (Lombroso) school of criminology, whose organ the Archivio was.

[3]The main sources used in this article, besides some personal conversations in Sicily, are N. Cola-janni, *La Delinquenza in Sicilia* (1885), *La Sicilia dai Borboni ai Sabaudi* (1900), A. Cutrera, *La Mafia ed i Mafiosi* (1900), G. Alongi, *La Maffia* (1887), G. Montalbane, "La Mafia" (*Nuovi Argomenti*, Nov.–Dec. 1953), various official enquiries and standard works on Sicilian economic and social conditions, of which L. Franchetti, *Condizioni Politiche e Amministrative della Sicilia* (1877), is a favourable specimen, and G. Mosca's articles in the *Giornale degli Economisti*, 1900 and the *Encyclopedia of Social Sciences*. The vast bulk of scholarly and sensible literature about *Mafia* appeared between 1880 and 1910, and the comparative dearth of more modern analyses is much to be deplored.

[4]E. Sereni, *El Capitalismo nelle Campagne, 1860–1900* (Turin 1948), 187.

side them), or as unappreciative of the things which really matter (for instance in schools), or as a combination of both. One should resist the temptation to link this code with feudalism, aristocratic virtues or the like. Its most complete and binding rule was among the *souteneurs* and minor hoodlums of the Palermo slums, whose conditions approximated most closely to "lawlessness," or rather to a Hobbesian state in which the relations between individuals or small groups are like those between sovereign powers. It has been rightly pointed out that in the really feudal parts of the island *omertà* tended to mean merely that only denunciation of the weak or defeated was permissible.[5] Where there is an established structure of power, "honor" tends to belong to the mighty.

In lawless communities power is rarely scattered among an anarchy of competing units, but clusters round local strong points. Its typical form is patronage, its typical holder the private magnate or boss with his body of retainers and dependants and the network of "influence" which surrounds him and causes men to put themselves under his protection. *Mafia,* in the second sense of the word, is almost a synonym for this, though it tended to be applied to the retainers (the "low *Mafia*") rather than to the patrons. Some of the forms of this system were certainly feudal, especially in the inland *latifundia;* and it is very probable that in Sicily (where legally feudal relations were not officially abolished until the 19th century, and their symbolism lives on even today in the painted battles between knights and Saracens on the sides of peasant carts) feudal forms of loyalty helped to shape it. However, this is a minor point, for retainership and patronage can come into existence without any feudal tradition. What characterized Sicily was the universal prevalence of such patronage and the virtual absence of any other form of constant power.

Mafia in the third, and most usual sense of the word, is not easy to distinguish from the second: it is the control of the community's life by a secret—or rather an officially unrecognized—system of gangs. So far as we know, this type of *Mafia* was never a single secret society, centrally organized, like the Neapolitan Camorra, though opinions about its degree of centralization have always differed.[6] The Palermo Procurator's report of 1931 probably expressed the situation best:

> The associations of the small localities normally exercise jurisdiction within these and the neighboring Communes. Those of the important centres are in relations with one another even to the most remote provinces, lending each other mutual aid and assistance.[7]

---

[5]Franchetti, 219–21.

[6]*Mafia* by Ed Reid, an American newspaper man (New York 1952), which holds the centralized view, is to be neglected, for the book—probably produced quickly to catch a market alerted by Sen. Kefauver's Crime Enquiry (which made vast accusations against *Mafia*)—shows a remarkable lack of appreciation of Sicilian problems. The strongest evidence for centralization comes from the post-1943 period, but even this is ambiguous.

[7]Quoted in Montalbane, *loc. cit.,* 179.

Indeed, being essentially a rural phenomenon to begin with, it is difficult to see how *Mafia* could have been hierarchically centralized, communications being what they were in the 19th century. It was rather a network of local gangs (*cosche*—today they seem to be called "families") sometimes two or three strong, sometimes much larger, each controlling a certain territory, normally a Commune or a *latifundium,* and linked with one another in various ways. Each *cosca* milked its territory; though some times, as during transhumance of cattle, the gangs of the territories through which the beasts travelled would co-operate. The migrations of harvest laborers, and especially the links between *latifundia* and the urban lawyers and the mass of cattle-markets and fairs all over the country, would provide other contacts between local groups.[8]

Their members recognized one another less by accepted secret signs and passwords than by bearing, dress, talk and behavior. Professional toughness and virility, professional parasitism and outlawry, breed their specialized behaviour, designed in a lawless society to impress the sheep— and perhaps also the lions—with the power of the wolves, as well as to set them apart from the herd. The *bravi* in Manzoni's *Betrothed* dress and behave very like the "lads" (*picciotti*) in Sicily two and a half centuries later. On the other hand each gang did have strikingly standardized initiation rituals and passwords in the 1870s, though these seem to have been allowed to lapse subsequently.[9] Whether or not, as Cutrera holds, they had been evolved long since in Milazzo jail, and popularized through songs and such pieces of literature as the *Life and Brave Deeds of the Bandit Pasquale Bruno,* I do not know. But they were clearly the rituals of an old-fashioned Mediterranean blood-brotherhood. The crucial ritual—normally (except where this was impossible as in jails) carried out in front of a saint's image—was that of piercing the candidate's thumb and extracting blood, which was daubed on the saint's image, which was then burnt. This last act may have been designed to bind the novice to the brotherhood by the ceremonial breaking of a taboo: a ritual involving the firing of a pistol at a statue of Jesus Christ is also reported.[10] Once initiated the *Mafioso* was a *compadre,* co-godparenthood being in Sicily, as elsewhere in the Mediterranean, the form of artificial kinship which implied the greatest and most solemn obligations of mutual help on the contracting parties. The passwords also seem to have been standardized. However this does not prove that the association was cen-

---

[8]Alongi, *op. cit.,* 70 ff.

[9]Montalbane, *loc. cit.* The fullest description of these is for the *Stoppaglieri* of Monreale and the neighbourhood, and the *Fratellanza* of Favara (prov. Agrigento) and the neighbourhood. These are printed in various places, e.g. Montalbane. See also F. Lestingi, 'L'Associazione della Fratellanza', in *Archivio di Psichiatria,* V (1884), 452 ff.

[10]Montalbane, 191.

tralized, for the Camorra—a purely Neapolitan organization without Sicilian links—also had a blood-brotherhood initiation of a similar type.[11]

So far as we can see, though standardized, each group seems to have regarded these rituals as its private bonds, rather as children adopt standardized forms of twisting words as strictly private languages. It is indeed probable that *Mafia* evolved some sort of quasi-national coordination; its central direction, if this term is not too precise, settling in Palermo. However, as we shall see this reflected the economic and political structure and evolution of Sicily rather than any criminal masterplan.[12]

Beneath the rule of the Bourbon or Piedmontese state, though sometimes living in strange symbiosis with it, *Mafia* (in all the three senses of the word) provided a parallel machine of law and organized power; indeed, so far as the citizen in the areas under its influence was concerned, the only effective law and power. In a society such as Sicily, in which the official government could not or would not exercise effective sway, the appearance of such a system was as inevitable as the appearance of gang-rule, or its alternative, private posses and vigilantes in certain parts of *laissez-faire* America. What distinguishes Sicily is the territorial extent and cohesion of this private and parallel system of power.

It was not, however, universal, for not all sections of Sicilian society were equally in need of it. Fishermen and sailors, for instance, never developed the code of *omertà* and—apart from the underworld—it was weakly developed in the towns, that is to say the real towns, not the great agglomerations in which Sicilian peasants lived in the midst of an empty, bandit-ridden or perhaps malarial countryside. Indeed, the urban artisans tended, especially during revolutions—as in Palermo in 1773 and 1820–1—to organize their own "train bands" or *ronde,* until the alliance of the ruling-classes, afraid of their revolutionary implications, imposed the socially more reliable National Guard and eventually the combination of policemen and *Mafiosi* on them after 1848.[13] On the other hand certain groups were in special need of private defences. Peasants on the large inland *latifundia,* and sulphur-miners, needed some means of mitigating their misery besides periodic jaqueries. For the owners of certain types of property—cattle, which was as easily rustled on the empty Sicilian ranges as in Arizona, and oranges and lemons, which invited thieves in the untended orchards of the coast—protection was vital. In fact, *Mafia* developed precisely in the three areas of this kind. It dominated the

---

[11]Ed Reid, *op. cit.,* for an initiation in New York 1917, 143–4; Algoni, 41.

[12]It is also probable that *Mafia* among the immigrants in America was more centralized than at home, because these were transferred to the new world along relatively few lanes, and settled in a handful of big cities. However, this need not concern us.

[13]Montalbane, 194–7, for a valuable discussion of the problem.

irrigated fruit-growing plain round Palermo, with its fertile, fragmented peasant tenancies, the sulphur-mining areas of the southern centre, and the open inland *latifundia*. Outside these areas it was weaker, and tended to disappear in the eastern half of the island.

It is a mistake to believe that institutions which look archaic are of great antiquity. They may, like public schools or the fancy dress part of English political life, have come into existence recently (though built of old or pseudo-ancient material) for modern purposes. *Mafia* is not a medieval, but a 19th- and 20th-century institution. Its period of greatest glory falls after 1890. No doubt Sicilian peasants have throughout history lived under the double régime of a remote and generally foreign central government and a local régime of slave or feudal lords; since theirs was *par excellence* the country of the *latifundium*. No doubt they were never, and could never be, in the habit of regarding the central government as a real State, but merely as a special form of brigand, whose soldiers, tax-gatherers, policemen and courts fell upon them from time to time. Their illiterate and isolated life was lived between the lord with his strong-arm mien and parasites and their own defensive customs and institutions. In a sense, therefore, something like the "parallel system" must always have existed, as it exists in all backward peasant societies.

Yet this was not *Mafia*, though it contained most of the raw material out of which *Mafia* grew. In fact it seems that *Mafia* in its full sense developed only after 1860. The word itself, in its modern connotation, does not occur before the early 1860s,[14] and had in any case previously been confined to the argot of one district in Palermo. A local historian from western Sicily—a hotbed of *Mafia*—finds no trace of it in his town before 1860.[15] On the other hand by 1866 the word is already used as a matter of course by Maggiorani, and by the 1870s it is common currency in political discussion. It is fairly clear that in some regions—perhaps mainly in Palermo province—a developed *Mafia* must have existed earlier. Nothing could be more typically *mafioso* than the career of Salvatore Miceli, the boss of Monreale, who brought his armed *squadre* to fight the Bourbons in Palermo in 1848, was pardoned and made a captain of arms by them in the 1850s (a characteristic touch), took his men to Garibaldi in 1860 and was killed fighting the Piedmontese in the Palermitan rising of 1866.[16] And by 1872 the Monreale *Mafia* was developed to the point where the first of the subsequently endemic revolts of the "young *Mafia*" against the "old *Mafia*" took place—aided by the police which sought to weaken the society—and produced the "sect" of the Stoppaglieri.[17] Never-

---

[14]G. Pitré, *Usi e costume . . . del popolo siciliano*, III, 287ff (1889); art. 'Mafia', in *Enc. Soc. Sciences*.

[15]S. Nicastro, *Dal Quarantotto a la Sessanta in Mazzara* (1913), 80–1.

[16]Cutrera, 170–4.

[17]*Giornale di Sicilia* 21.8.1877, quoted by Montalbane, 167–74.

theless, something pretty fundamental obviously happened to the "parallel system" after the official abolition of feudalism in Sicily (1812–38), and especially after its conquest by the northern middle-class; and this is, after all, no more than we should expect. The question is what? To answer it, we must summarize what is known of the composition and structure of the developed *Mafia*.

Its first, and by far its most important characteristic is, that *all* the heads of local *Mafias* were (and are) men of wealth, some ex-feudalists in the inland areas, but overwhelmingly men of the middle class, capitalist farmers and contractors, lawyers and the like. The evidence on this point seems conclusive.[18] Since *Mafia* was primarily a rural phenomenon, this in itself marks the beginnings of a revolution, for in mid-19th century Sicily bourgeois-owned land still amounted to only about 10 percent of the cultivated area. The backbone of *Mafia* were the *gabellotti*—wealthy middle-class persons who paid the absentee feudal owners a lump rent for their whole estate and sublet at a profit to the peasantry, and who virtually replaced them as the real ruling class. Virtually all of them, in the *Mafia* areas, seem to have been *mafiosi*. The rise of *Mafia* thus marks a transfer of power in the "parallel system" from feudal to rural middle class, an incident in the rise of rural capitalism. At the same time *Mafia* was one of the main engines of this transfer. For if the *gabellotto* used it to force terms on tenant and sharecropper, he also used it to force them on the absentee lord.

Because *Mafia* was in the hands of something like a local "businessmen's" class, it also developed a range of influence which it could never have done had it merely been an affair of "tough guys," whose horizon was bounded by the frontiers of their township. Most *gabellotti* were linked with Palermo, where the absentee barons and princes received their rents, as all Irish townlands in the 18th century were linked with Dublin. In Palermo lived the lawyers who settled major property transfers (and were as like as not educated sons and nephews of the rural bourgeoisie); the officials and courts which had to be "fixed"; the merchants who disposed of the ancient corn and cattle and the new cash crops of orange and lemon. Palermo was the capital in which Sicilian revolutions—i.e., the fundamental decisions about Sicilian politics—were traditionally made. Hence it is only natural that the local threads of *Mafia* should be tied into a single knot there, though—for obvious reasons—the existence of a Palermitan "high *Mafia*" has always been suspected rather than demonstrated.

The apparatus of coercion of the "parallel system" was as shapeless and decentralized as its political and legal structure; but it fulfilled its purpose

---

[18]Cutrera, 73, 88–9, 96. Franchetti, 170–2. The spectacle of gangsterism as a typically middle-class phenomenon amazed and troubled Franchetti.

of securing internal quiet and external power—i.e., of controlling the local inhabitants and harassing a foreign government. It is not easy to give a lucid and brief account of its structure. In any society as miserably poor and oppressed as that of the Sicilians there is a vast potential reserve of strong-arm men, as there is of prostitutes. The "bad man" is, in the expressive phrase of French criminal slang, *affranchi;* and there are no other individual methods of escaping the bondage of virtual serfdom but bullying and outlawry. In Sicily this great class consisted in the main of three groups: the retainers and private police-forces (such as the *guardiani* and *campieri* who guarded the orchards and ranges); the bandits and professional outlaws; and the strong and self-reliant among the legitimate laborers. We must bear in mind that the best chance the peasant or miner had of mitigating his oppression was to gain a reputation for being tough or a friend of toughs. The normal meeting place of all these was in the entourage of the local great man, who provided employment for men of daring and swagger and protected the outlaws—if only because his prestige required him to demonstrate his power to do so. Thus a local network, which enmeshed estate guards, goatherds, bandits, bullies, and strong men, with the local property-owners, already existed.

Two things were almost certainly responsible for turning this into *Mafia*. First, there was the attempt of the feeble Bourbons to set up the "Armed Companies." Like most other attempts by feeble governments to hand over the maintenance of public security to private enterprise, spurred on by the fear of financial loss, this failed. The "Armed Companies" which were set up independently in different areas, were responsible for making good what the thieves and robbers took. It follows, that under Sicilian conditions, each company had an overwhelming incentive to encourage its local bad men to rob elsewhere against the promise of local sanctuary, or to negotiate privately with them for the return of stolen goods. A small step separated this from the actual participation of the Armed Companies in crime, for they were naturally composed of the same kind of toughs as the brigands. Second, there was the increasing danger of urban and peasant discontent, especially after the abolition of feudalism. This, as usual, bore heavily on the peasants, and moreover involved them in the henceforth perennial tussle with the rural middle class about the ownership of the common and ecclesiastical lands, which the middle class tended to appropriate. At a period when revolutions occurred with terrifying frequency—four or five in 46 years—it was only natural that the rich tended to recruit retainers for the defence of their own interests—the so-called *contro-squadre*—as well as taking other measures to prevent the revolutions getting out of hand, and nothing lent itself to *mafioso* practices as well as such a combination of the (rural) rich and the toughs.

The relationship between the *Mafia*, the "lads" or retainers and the brigands was therefore somewhat complex. As property owners the *capi-mafia* had no interest in crime, though they had an interest in maintaining a body of armed followers for coercive purposes. The retainers, on the other hand, had to be allowed pickings, and a certain scope for private enterprise. The bandits, lastly, were an almost total nuisance, though they could occasionally be made use of to reinforce the power of the boss: the bandit Giuliano was called upon in 1947 to shoot up a May Day procession of peasants, the name of the influential Palermitan who arranged the transaction being known. However, in the absence of *central* state machinery, banditry itself could not be eliminated. Hence the peculiar compromise solution which is so typical of *Mafia:* a local monopoly of controlled extortion (often institutionalized so as to lose its character of naked force), and the elimination of interlopers. The orange-grower in the Palermo region would have to hire an orchard guard. If wealthy, he might from time to time have to contribute to the maintenance of the "lads"; if he had property stolen, he would have it returned minus a percentage, unless he stood specially well with *Mafia*. The private thief was excluded.[19]

The military formations of *Mafia* show the same mixture of retainers' loyalty and dependence, and private profit making by the fighting men. When war broke out, the local boss would raise his *squadre*—mainly, but perhaps not exclusively, composed of the members of the local *cosche*. The "lads" would join the *squadra*, partly to follow their patron (the more influential the *capo-mafia*, the larger his troop), partly to raise their personal prestige by the only way open to them, acts of bravery and violence, but also because war meant profit. In the major revolution the *capi-mafia* would arrange with the Palermo liberals for a daily stipend of four *tari* per man, as well as arms and munitions, and the promise of this wage (not to mention other pickings of war) swelled the numbers of the *squadre*.

Such, then, was the "parallel system" of the *Mafia*. One cannot say that it was imposed on the Sicilians by anyone. In a sense, it grew out of the needs of all rural classes, and served the purpose of all in varying degrees. For the weak—the peasants and the miners—it provided at least some guarantee that obligations between them would be kept,[20] some guarantee that the usual degree of oppression would not be habitually exceeded; it was the terror which mitigated traditional tyrannies. And perhaps, also, it satisfied a desire for revenge by providing that the rich were sometimes fleeced, and that the poor, if only as outlaws, could sometimes fight back.

---

[19]One of the commonest misconceptions about *Mafia*—perpetuated in such works as the ineffable Prefect Mori's *Last Battle of the Mafia* and in the first edition of Guercio's *Sicily*—is the confusion between it and banditry. *Mafia* maintained public order by private means. Bandits were, broadly speaking, what it protected the public from.

[20]See N. Colajanni, *Gli Avvenimenti di Sicilia* (1894), cap 5, on the function of *mafia* as a code governing the relations between different classes of sulphur-miners, esp. pp. 47–48.

It may even, on occasions, have provided the framework of revolutionary or defensive organization. (At any rate in the 1870s there seems to have been some tendency for Friendly Societies and quasi-*mafious* bodies like the *Fratellanza* of the sulphur-town of Favara, the *Fratuzzi* of Bagheria or the *Stoppaglieri* of Monreale to fuse.[21]) For the feudal lords it was a means of safeguarding property and authority: for the rural middle class a means of gaining it. For all, it provided a means of defence against the foreign exploiter—the Bourbon or Piedmontese government—and a method of national or local self-assertion. So long as Sicily was no more than a static feudal society subject to outside rule, *Mafia's* character as a national conspiracy of noncooperation gave it a genuinely popular basis. The *squadre* fought with the Palermo liberals (who included the anti-Bourbon Sicilian aristocracy) in 1820, 1848 and 1860. They headed the first great rising against the domination of northern capitalism in 1866. Its national, and to some extent popular character, increased the prestige of *Mafia*, and ensured it public sympathy and silence. Obviously it was a complex movement, including mutually contradictory elements. Nevertheless, however tiresome to the historian, he must resist the temptation to pigeon-hole *Mafia* more precisely at this stage of its development. Thus one cannot agree with Montalbane that the *picciotti* who then formed the revolutionary *squadre* were not really *Mafiosi* with a capital M but only *mafiosi* with a small m, while only the *contro-squadre,* already specialized strong-arm squads for the rich, were the "real" *Mafia*. That is to read the *Mafia* of the 20th century into a period were it does not belong.[22]

Indeed, we may suspect that *Mafia* began its real rise to major power (and abuse) as a Sicilian regional movement of revolt against the disappointments of Italian unity in the 1860s, and as a more effective movement than the parallel and contemporary guerilla warfare of the brigands in continental southern Italy. Its political links as we have seen were with the extreme Left, for the Garibaldian Radicals were the main Italian opposition party. Yet three things caused *Mafia* to change its character.

First, there was the rise of capitalist relationships in island society. The emergence of modern forms of peasant and labour movement in place of the old alternation of silent conspiratorial hatred and occasional massacre faced the *Mafia* with an unprecedented change. 1866 was the last time it fought against the authorities with arms. The great peasant rising of 1894—the *Fasci Siciliani*—saw it on the side of reaction, or at best neutral. Conversely, these risings were organized by new types of leaders—local socialists—connected with new types of organization, the *Fasci* or mutual defence societies, and independent of the "lads." The modern inverse pro-

---

[21]I am not convinced that the rise of these bodies in the 1870s can be interpreted purely in terms of the revolt of young against old *Mafia* elements, as Montalbane suggests; though this may have been the case in Monreale.

[22]Montalbane, 197.

portion between the strength of *Mafia* and revolutionary activity began to appear. Even then it was observed that the rise of the Fasci had diminished the hold of *Mafia* on the peasants.[23] By 1900 *Piana dei Greci*, the socialist stronghold, though surrounded by *Mafia* strongholds, was markedly less riddled with it.[24] It is only in politically backward and powerless communities that brigands and *mafiosi* take the place of social movements. However, in spite of such local setbacks, there can be no doubt that *Mafia* as a whole was still expanding in the western part of Sicily throughout this period. At least a comparison of the Parliamentary Enquiries of 1884 and 1910 leaves one with a strong impression that it was.[25] Second, the new ruling class of rural Sicily, the *gabellotti* and their urban partners, discovered a *modus vivendi* with northern capitalism. They did not compete with it, for they were not interested in manufacture, and some of their most important products, such as oranges, were hardly produced in the north; hence the transformation of the south into an agrarian colony of the trading and manufacturing north did not greatly trouble them. On the other hand the evolution of northern politics provided them with an unprecedented and invaluable means of gaining power: the vote. The great days of *Mafia's* power, but days which portended its decline, begin with the triumph of "Liberalism" in Italian politics and develop with the extension of the franchise.

From the point of view of the northern politicians, after the end of the conservative period which succeeded unification, the problem of the south was simple. It could provide safe majorities for whatever government gave sufficient bribes or concessions to the local bosses who could guarantee electoral victory. This was child's play for *Mafia*. Its candidates were always elected, in real strongholds almost unanimously. But the concessions and bribes which were small, from the point of view of northerners (for the south was poor) made all the difference to local power in a region as small as half Sicily. Politics made the power of the local boss; politics increased it, and turned it into big business.

Mafia won its new power, not merely because it could promise and intimidate, but because, in spite of the new competitors, it was still regarded as part of the national or popular movement; just as big city bosses in the

<hr>

[23]E. C. Calon, *La Mafia* (Madrid 1906), 11.

[24]See the invaluable *Mafia* distribution map in Cutrera. Piana, though apparently slow to adopt peasant organization, became the great stronghold of the 1893 Fasci, and has remained a fortress of socialism (and later communism) ever since. That it was previously impregnated by *Mafia* is suggested by the history of *Mafia* in New Orleans, whose Sicilian colony which arrived in the 1880s had, to judge by the occurrence of the characteristic Albanian family names—Schiro, Loyacano, Matranga—a strong contingent of Pianesi. The Matrangas—members of the Stoppaglieri—controlled the dockside rackets, and were prominent in the *Mafia* incidents of 1889 in New Orleans. (Ed. Reid, *op. cit.*, 100 ff.) The family apparently continued its *mafioso* activities, for in 1909 Lt. Petrosino of the New York police, later killed in Palermo—presumably by *Mafia*—was enquiring into the life of one of them (Reid, 122). I recall seeing the elaborate tomb of a Matranga in Piana in 1953, a man who had recently returned from emigration to the U.S.A. and had been found, in circumstances into which nobody was anxious to enquire, killed on a road a few years before.

[25]A. Damiani, *Inchiesta Agraria* (1884), Sicily, vol. III; G. Lorenzoni, *Inchiesta Parlamentare* (1910), Sicily, vol. VI, i–ii, esp. pp. 649–51.

United States won their original power not simply by corruption and force, but by being "our men" for thousands of immigrant voters: Irish men for the Irish, Catholics for the Catholic, Democrats (i.e., opponents of big business) in a predominantly Republican country. It is no accident that most American big city machines, however corrupt, belonged to the traditional party of minority opposition, as most Sicilians supported opposition to Rome, which, in the years after 1860, meant the Garibaldians. Thus the crucial turn in *Mafia's* fortunes could not come until the "Left" (or men who sported its slogans) became the government party after 1876. The "Left," as Colajanni put it, thus achieved "a transformation in Sicily and the south which could not otherwise have been brought about: the complete subjection of the mass to the government."[26] Sicilian political organization, i.e., *Mafia,* thus became part of the government system of patronage, and bargained all the more effectively because its illiterate and remote followers took time to realize that they were no longer voting for the cause of revolt. When they did (as for instance in the risings of the 1890s) it was too late. The tacit partnership between Rome with its troops and martial law and *Mafia* was too much for them. The true "kingdom of *Mafia*" had been established. It was now a great power. Its members sat as deputies in Rome and their spoons reached into the thickest part of the gravy of government: large banks, national scandals. Its influence and patronage was now beyond the dream of old-fashioned local captains like Miceli of Monreale. It was not to be opposed; but it was no longer a Sicilian popular movement as in the days of the *squadre* of 1848, 1860 and 1866.

Hence its decline. About this we know less than about its heyday, since no studies of importance about it appeared during Fascism and only very few since.[27] Some of the factors in the later history of *Mafia* may be briefly sketched.

First, there was the rise of the peasant leagues and the Socialists (later Communists), which provided the people with an alternative to *Mafia,* while at the same time alienating them from a body which became, with increasing openness and determination, a terrorist force directed against the Left.[28] The Fasci of 1893, the revival of agrarian agitation before the First World War, and in the disturbed years after 1918, were so many milestones on the roads which separated *Mafia* and the masses. The postfascist period with its open warfare between *Mafia* and the Socialist–Communists—the massacres of Villalba (1944) and Portella della Ginestra (1947), the attempted assassination of the leading Sicilian Communist

---

[26] *La Sicilia dai Borboni ai Sabaudi* (1951 ed.), 78.

[27] By far the most valuable, on which I have drawn heavily, is F. Renda, 'Funzione e basi sociali della Mafia', in *Il Movimento Contadino nella Società Siciliana* (Palermo 1956), and Montalbane, *loc. cit.*

[28] Prefect Mori, to do him justice, at least mentions this fact in passing.

Girolamo Li Causi, and the killing of various union organizers—widened the gap.[29] What mass basis *Mafia* had possessed among landless laborers, sulphur-miners, etc., has tended to diminish. There are still, according to Renda (a political organizer as well as a good scholar), a few places which remain generally and "spiritually" *mafiosi*, but "the spirit and custom of mafia survive on the margins of the great popular sentiments."

The rise of the Socialist–Communist vote has been marked in the most *Mafia*-riddled provinces, especially in the countryside. It is evident that the rise of the combined left wing vote in Palermo province from 11.8 percent in 1946 to 22.8 percent in 1953, or in Caltanissetta province from 29.1 percent in 1946 to 37.1 percent in 1953, marks a decline in the influence of the bitterly anti-left *Mafia*. The 29 percent of Socialist–Communist votes in Palermo City (1958 election) continue the trend; for the Sicilian city was always, and still is, much less kind to the left wing parties than the village, and *Mafia* is proverbially strong in Palermo.[30] The Left has provided Sicilians with an alternative and more up-to-date organization, and with some direct and indirect protection against *Mafia*, especially since 1945, if only because the more extreme forms of its political terror now tend to cause major rows in Rome. In the second place, since *Mafia* can no longer control elections, it has lost much of the power that comes from patronage. Instead of being a "parallel system," it is now only a very powerful pressure group, politically speaking.

Second, there were the internal divisions within *Mafia*. These took and take two forms: the rivalries between the "ins" (generally the old generation) and the "outs" (generally the "young") in a country in which pickings are limited and unemployment high, and the tension between the old generation of illiterate and parochially-minded *gabellotti*, barely removed (except in wealth) from the peasants on whom they batten, and their sons and daughters, of higher social status. The lads who become white-collar workers and lawyers, the girls who marry into "better" society —i.e., non-*Mafia* society—break up the family cohesion of *Mafia*, on which much of its strength depended. The first type of tension between "old" and "young" *Mafia* is old; as we have seen, it occurred in classic form in Monreale as early as 1872. The second is found in Palermo as early as 1875, but in the latifundist hinterland it has only developed in the last decades.[31] These ever-renewed rivalries between "old" and "young" *Mafia*,

---

[29]A certain Calogero Vizzini, a leading if not the leading *Mafioso*, was officially charged with the first and third of these crimes. The bandit Giuliano was put up to the second. (Montalbane, 186–7, quoting the 1946 report of Sig. Branca, General of the Carabiniere. Gavin Maxwell, *God Protect Me from My Friends*, 1956, for the relations between *Mafia* and Giuliano.)

[30]For election figures by provinces up to 1953, E. Caranti, *Sociologia e Statistica delle Elezioni Italiane* (Rome 1954). The 1958 figures are taken from the post-election Corriere della Sera, May 28th 1958. The total socialist-communist percentage for the four *Mafiose* provinces in 1958 was 33.9, against 43 for the Demochristians and most of the balance for the extreme right. (Palermo, Trapani, Agrigento, Caltanissetta electoral division.)

[31]Renda, *loc. cit.*, 219.

produce what Montalbane has called its "strange dialectic": sooner or later the young toughs, who cannot solve the problem of life by working—for there is no work—must solve it in some other manner, e.g. crime. But the older generation of the *Mafiosi* have the lucrative rackets under control and are reluctant to make way for the young men, who therefore organize rival gangs, generally on the same lines as the old *Mafia*, often with the help of the police, which hopes thereby to weaken the old *Mafia*, and which the young *Mafiosi* wish to use for the same purpose. Sooner or later, if neither side has been able to suppress the other—most *Mafia* killings are the outcome of such internecine quarrels—old and young combine, after a redistribution of the spoils.

However, it is widely felt that *Mafia* has suffered from abnormally profound internal dissensions since the First World War, and this may be due to tensions of the second kind, intensified by genuine policy differences which were bound to arise in an island whose economy, society and criminal horizons have changed with increasing rapidity. An example of such policy-differences may be given from America. There *Mafia* originally refused to deal with any but Sicilian immigrants, and fought notable battles against the rival (Neapolitan) *Camorristi*, e.g., the famous Matranga–Provenzano feuds in New Orleans in the 1880s, and similar battles in New York in the 1910s. It has been plausibly suggested that a purge of the "old" *Mafia* by the "young" took place about 1930, the old organization being replaced by a more up-to-date version ("Unione Siciliana") which was, unlike the old blood-brotherhood, prepared to cooperate with Neapolitan, or for that matter Jewish gangsters. The arguments about the survival or non-survival of *Mafia* among American gangsters are perhaps best explained in terms of such dissensions.[32] We shall consider the new "business" horizons of the modern *Mafia* below.

Thirdly, there was Fascism. Mussolini, according to the plausible account of Renda, found himself obliged to fight *Mafia*, since the non-fascist Liberal Party relied heavily on its backing. (The Palermo election of 1924 had shown Liberal-*Mafia* capacity to resist the normal Fascist process of political conquest.) Admittedly the Fascist campaigns against *Mafia* revealed its growing weakness more than they contributed to it, and ended with very much the same tacit working agreement between the local men of wealth and power and the central government as before. But by abolishing elections Fascism certainly deprived *Mafia* of its main currency for purchasing concessions from Rome, and the Blackshirt movement provided discontented *Mafiosi* or would-be *Mafiosi* with a wonderful opportunity for using the state apparatus to supplant their established rivals, and thus intensified the internal tensions of *Mafia*. Its roots re-

---

[32]For the old feuds, cf. Ed Reid, *The Mafia*, 100, 146. For the 1930 purge (unmentioned by Reid or Kefauver), Turkus & Feder, *Murder Inc.* (London 1953).

mained: after 1943 it re-emerged happily. However, the substantial shocks and shifts that were forced upon it had far from negligible social effects. The big *Mafiosi* could come to terms with Rome easily enough. For most Sicilians all that happened was that the "parallel system" and the official government merged into a single conspiracy to oppress; a step along the road opened in 1876 rather than a reversal of steps. The little *Mafiosi,* on the other hand, may well have suffered. It has even been argued that the Fascist campaigns "brought to a stop the long process by which the middle strata of the *Mafia* increasingly inserted themselves into the system of large landed property as small and medium proprietors."[33]

We do not know very well how *Mafia* re-emerged after 1943. It seems clear—according to Branca's report of 1946—that it was closely linked with the Sicilian separatist movement with which the Allies flirted somewhat rashly after their occupation of the island, and perhaps also with the old party of property and the *status quo,* the Liberals. Subsequently a drift towards the Monarchists and Demochristians seems to have taken place. At any rate the sharp decline of the Liberal and Independentist vote from half a million in 1947 to 220,000 in 1948 seems to indicate more than a long-term tendency among voters, especially as both parties have declined much more slowly since. The Demochristians gained most of these lost votes, but the Monarchists—the fact may not be insignificant— were quite unaffected and continued to grow slowly.[34] However, the straightforward political influence-peddling of *Mafia* has become much less important than it used to be.

In return, however, *Mafia* has in the post-war period discovered two new sorts of profitable economic activity. On the simple criminal side the horizons of certain *Mafia* groups have certainly become international, partly due to the vast pickings to be made in blackmarketing and wholesale smuggling in what historians will undoubtedly regard as the golden age in the world history of the organized criminals, partly because of the strong links between Sicily and the occupying American forces, strengthened by the expulsion to Italy of numerous well-known American gangsters. There seems little doubt that part of *Mafia* has taken to international drug-trafficking with enthusiasm. It is even possible—and a far cry from the old provincialism—that *Mafiosi* are prepared to subordinate themselves to criminal activities organized from elsewhere.[35]

---

[33]Renda, 213.

[34]The parties of the pre-fascist regime—Liberals and Monarchists—still remain remarkably strong in certain areas, which may perhaps serve as a rough index of "old *Mafia*" voting influence; in Trapani they run ahead of both Demochristians and Socialist-Communists, in Partinico-Monreale—an old *Mafia* fief—ahead of the Socialist-Communists, though in such typically Mafia areas as Corleone-Bagheria they have dropped well behind the Left and far behind the Demochristians. (1958 elections.)

[35]*Messagero* 6.9.1955, "Le geste dei fuorilegge in Sicilia," reports the killing by *Mafia on orders from Naples* of a tobacco smuggler in Palermo.

Far more important is the method by which *Mafia* has been able to resist the destruction of its former mainstay, the latifundist economy. The estates have gone, and many barons have sacked their *campieri*. But the position of the *Mafiosi* as local men of influence has enabled them to cash in on the vast body of land-sales to peasants under the various reform laws. "It may be affirmed," says Renda, "that practically all purchases of small peasant property have been negotiated through the mediation of *Mafioso* elements" to whose hands much of the land and other assets have therefore tended to cling. *Mafia* has thus once again played its part in the creation of a Sicilian middle class, and will undoubtedly survive the fall of the old economy. The typical *Mafioso*, who used to be a *campiere*, has merely been replaced by the *Mafioso* landowner or businessman.

How the organization of *Mafia* has changed in the course of this evolution, we do not know. One would guess that it may have become more centralized, partly because regional autonomy has made Palermo an even more vital centre for Sicily than it was in the past, partly because of the various "modernizing" tendencies in *Mafia's* business. How centralized, is anybody's guess, and so long as journalists simultaneously, and with equal confidence, indicate different people as "heads of *Mafia*" we shall be wise to confine ourselves to the modest proposition that, if there is any central direction it is almost certainly in Palermo, and probably in the hands of lawyers.

13. ECONOMIC ANALYSIS OF ORGANIZED CRIME

THOMAS C. SCHELLING

A useful distinction that we can borrow from the legitimate economy and apply to the economy of organized crime is the difference between an organized economy and an organized business. We should distinguish—within the organized underworld itself—between the organized economy within which criminal business operates and the highly organized criminal enterprise (firm), in particular the monopolistic enterprise.

Only some crime is organized in the second sense, in large-scale continuing firms with the internal organization of a large enterprise, and in particular with a conscious effort to control the market. Gambling syndicates and the better organized protection rackets qualify for this category.

Other criminal businesses, like "unorganized" robbery, would not meet the definition of "organized crime" in the restricted sense of a criminal firm. They nevertheless operate in, and participate in, a highly "organized" economic framework. That is, these "unorganized" but professional criminals are part of the underworld communication system, recruitment system, marketing system, and even diplomatic system (in relations with the world of law enforcement), and may consider themselves part of a highly organized criminal society.

Still other crimes, including those committed by amateur criminals but also apparently by abortionists, embezzlers, and ordinary dishonest businessmen, are outside the organized economy of the underworld. They may, however, have intermittent contact with it or make occasional use of the services available in it. In some cases the police themselves constitute part of this underworld society (at least from the point of view of the lone-operating prostitute or abortionist, or the regular purveyor of liquor to minors).

Our interest at this point will be in the firms and trade associations that qualify as "organized crime" in the more restricted sense. But the two can-

From "Economic Analysis and Organized Crime" by Thomas C. Schelling in *Task Force Report: Organized Crime* by the President's Commission on Law Enforcement and Administration of Justice. Washington, D.C.: Government Printing Office, 1967. Reprinted with permission of the author.

not be entirely separated. The organization of the underworld itself is undoubtedly affected, perhaps in a dominant way, by the occurrence of large-scale monopolist organizations and cartels. Indeed, the role of "government" within the underworld, including diplomatic relations with the legitimate world, may have to be played by large organizations originating from market forces, not political forces. It may require a large firm or cartel to represent the underworld in its relations with the legitimate world, to impose discipline and procedures for the adjudication of disputes, and to provide a source of recognizable leadership.

In fact, some of the central questions (to be investigated) about the functioning of the highly organized criminal firms are the extent to which they condition the underworld itself. This includes the extent to which organized crime lives off the underworld rather than directly off the upperworld, the extent to which the underworld benefits or loses by this kind of market dominance and leadership, and the extent to which relations of the underworld with the legitimate world depend on the emergence of some large, economically viable organization with the incentive and capability to centralize diplomatic and financial relations.

A closely related question is the extent to which organized crime itself depends on at least one major market occurring in which the returns to tight and complex organization are large enough to support a dominant monopoly firm or cartel. Not all businesses lend themselves to centralized organization; some do, and these may provide the nucleus of well-financed entrepreneurship and the extension of organizational talent into other businesses that would not, alone, support or give rise to an organized monopoly or cartel.

A strategic question is whether a few "core" criminal markets provide the organizational stimulus for organized crime. If the answer turns out to be yes, then a critical question is whether this particular market, so essential for the "economic development" of the underworld and the emergence of organized crime, is one of the black markets dependent on "protection" against legitimate competition; or is, instead, an inherently criminal activity? This question is critical because black markets always provide, in principle, the option of restructuring the market, or increasing competition as well as reducing it, of compromising the original prohibition in the larger interest of weakening organized crime, in addition to selectively relaxing the law or its enforcement. If, alternatively, the core industry is one that rests principally on violence, on the intimidation of customers (extortion) or competitors (monopoly), then compromise and relaxation of the law are likely to be both ineffectual and unappealing. Restructuring the market to the disadvantage of such criminal business is accordingly a good deal harder.

A TYPOLOGY OF UNDERWORLD BUSINESS

One of the interesting questions in analyzing organized crime is why some underworld business becomes organized and some remains unorganized; another is what kinds of organization we should expect to occur. These questions indicate that a workable classification of organizations has to be broader than simply "organized crime." A tentative breakdown is suggested as follows:

Black Markets. A large part of organized crime involves selling commodities and services contrary to law. In the underworld, this can include dope, prostitution, gambling, liquor under prohibition, abortion, contraceptives in some states, pornography, and contraband or stolen goods. Most of these tend to be consumer goods.

In what is not usually considered the underworld, black market goods and services include gold, rationed commodities and coupons in wartime, loans and rentals above controlled prices, theater tickets in New York, and a good many commodities that, though not illegal per se, are handled outside legitimate markets or are diverted from subsidized uses.

In some cases (i.e., gambling) the commodity is to be excluded from all consumers; in others (i.e., cigarettes) some consumers are legitimate and some (i.e., minors) not. In some cases what is illegal is the failure to pay a tax or duty. In some cases, it is the price of the transaction that makes it illegal. In some it is public hazard—carrying explosives through tunnels, producing phosphorus matches in disregard of safety regulations. In some cases (i.e., child labor, illegal immigrant labor) it is buying the commodity, not selling it, that is proscribed.

Some black markets tend to be "organized" and some not. In some black markets both parties to the transaction know that the deal is illegal; in others only one party to the transaction is aware of illegality. The innocent party to the transaction may have no way of knowing whether the goods were illegally obtained or are going into illegal channels.

Racketeering. Racketeering includes two kinds of business, both based on intimidation. One is extortion; the other, criminal monopoly.

"Criminal monopoly" means the use of criminal means to destroy competition. Whether one destroys a competitor, or merely threatens to make him go out of business, by deterring new competition, by the threat of violence or by other unfair practices, the object is to get protection from competition when the law will not provide it (by franchise, tariff protection). Such protection cannot be achieved through legal techniques (such as price wars, control of patents, or preclusive contracts).

We can distinguish altogether three kinds of "monopoly": Those achieved through legal means, including greater efficiency than one's competitors, or the inability of the market to support more than one firm; those achieved through means that are illegal only because of antitrust and other laws intended to make monopoly difficult; and monopolies achieved through means that are criminal by any standards, means that would be criminal whether or not they were aimed at monopolizing a business.

It is evident from the history of business abuses in the 19th and 20th centuries that "unfair competition" of a drastic sort, including violence, has not been confined to the underworld. So it is useful to distinguish between firms that, in excess of zeal and deficiency of scruples, engage when necessary in ruthless and illegal competition, and between the more strictly "racketeering" firms whose profitable monopoly rests entirely on the firm's propensity for criminal violence. It is the latter that I include under "criminal monopoly"; the object of law enforcement in the other case is not to destroy the firm but to curtail its illegal practices so that it will live within the law. If the whole basis of business success is the use of strong-arm methods that keep competition destroyed or scared away, it is a pure "racket."

"Extortion" means living off somebody else's business by the threat of criminal violence or by criminal competition. The protection racket lives off its victims, letting them operate and pay tribute. If one establishes a chain of restaurants and destroys competitors or scares them out of business, he is a monopolist. If one merely threatens to destroy people's restaurant business, taking part of their profits as the price for leaving them alone, he is an extortionist; he likes to see them prosper so that his share will be greater.

For several reasons it is difficult to distinguish between "extortion" that, like a parasite, wants a healthy host, and "criminal monopoly" that is dedicated to the elimination of competitors. First, one means of extortion is to threaten to cut off the supply of a monopolized commodity—labor on a construction site, trucking, or some illegal commodity provided through the black market. In other words, one can use a monopoly at one stage in the production process for extortionate leverage on the next.

Second, extortion itself can be used to secure a monopoly privilege. Instead of taking tribute in cash, a victim signs a contract for the high-priced delivery of beer or linen supplies. The result looks like monopoly but arose out of extortion. (To a competing laundry service this is "unfair" competition; criminal firm A destroys competitor B by intimidating customer C, gaining an exclusive right to his customers.)

Evidently extortion can be organized or not; there are bullies and petty blackmailers, whose business is localized and opportunistic. But in important cases extortion itself has to be monopolized. Vulnerable victims may have to be protected from other extortionists. A monopolistic laundry service, deriving from a threat to harm the business that does not subscribe, may have to destroy or intimidate not only competing legitimate laundry services but also other racketeers who would muscle in on the same victim. Thus, while organized criminal monopoly may not depend on extortion, organized extortion needs a large element of monopoly.

Black-Market Monopoly. Just as monopoly and extortion may go together in racketeering, monopoly and black markets go together. Indeed, any successful black marketeer enjoys a "protected" market in the same way that a domestic industry is protected by a tariff, or butter by a law against margarine. The black marketeer gets automatic protection, through the law itself, from all competitors unwilling to pursue a criminal career. The law gives a kind of franchise to those who are willing to break the law. But there is a difference between a "protected industry" and a "monopolized industry;" abortion quacks are protected by the laws against abortion, and charge prices accordingly, but apparently are seldom monopolized, while gambling and prostitution are often organized monopolies, locally if not regionally, within a market from which the bulk of their competitors are excluded by the law and the police. Thus abortion is a black-market commodity but not a black-market monopoly; a labor racket is a local monopoly but not a black-market one; the narcotics traffic has both elements: the monopolization of an illegal commodity.

Cartel. An interesting case is the "conspiracy in restraint of trade" that does not lead to single-firm monopoly but to collusive price fixing, and is maintained by criminal action. If the garment trade eliminates cutthroat competition by an agreement on prices and wages, hiring thugs to enforce the agreement, it is different from the monopoly racket discussed above. If the government would make such agreements enforceable (as it does with various retail-price-maintenance laws in some states) the businesses might be happy and in no need of criminally enforcing discipline on themselves. Similarly a labor organization can engage in criminal means to discipline its members, even to the benefit of its members, who may be better off working as a block rather than as competing individuals; if the law permits enforceable closed-shop agreements or dues collection, the criminal means becomes unnecessary.

Cheating. "Cheating" means all the things that a business can do to cheat customers, suppliers, tax authorities, and so forth. Tax evasion, adulteration of goods, some kinds of bankruptcy, are always available in greater or lesser degree to any business firm; all it takes is a dishonest or unscrupulous employee or proprietor and some cheating can occur. (The main distinction between cheating and straightforward stealing is that the victim—tax collector, customer, supplier—either does not realize that he has been cheated or has no recourse at law.) The only relation between this kind of dishonest business practice and the underworld, or organized crime, is that criminals have special needs and uses for businesses in which they can cheat. They may want a "front" in which to disguise other earnings; they may want to make money in legitimate business and, being criminally inclined, have a propensity to go into business where it is advantageous to cheat. If they already have connections by which to corrupt law enforcement, they will have a comparative advantage toward the kind of cheating that depends on bribery and intimidation.

Organized Criminal Services. A characteristic of all the businesses listed above is that they involve relations between the underworld and the upperworld. The ultimate victim or customer is not a career criminal, possibly not a criminal at all except insofar as the transaction in question is illegal. But just as businesses in the upperworld need legal services, financial advice and tax advice, credit, enforcement of contract, places to conduct their business, communication facilities, even advertising, so in the underworld there has to be a variety of business services that are "domestic" to the underworld itself. These can be organized or unorganized. They are in the underworld, but not because they do to the underworld, what the underworld does to the legitimate world. And, of course, they can operate in both worlds; the tax lawyer who advises a gambling casino can help them break the law and still have other customers in legitimate businesses.

Corruption of Police and Politics. Legitimate businesses have been known, through bribery and intimidation, to corrupt legislatures and public officials. Criminal organizations can do likewise and are somewhat like lobbies in that respect. The gambling rackets have as great a stake in antigambling laws as the dairy farmers in margarine laws or textile manufacturers in tariffs. But organized criminals have more need and more opportunity for corrupting officials whose job is law enforcement, especially the police. They need protection from the police; they can use police support in excluding competitors; they can even seek recruits among the police. What is special about the police is that they operate in both the upperworld and the underworld and do so in a more official capacity than the lawyers who have customers in both worlds.

THE INCENTIVES TO ORGANIZATION

Any firm prefers more business to less, a large share of a market to a small share. But the inducements to expansion and the advantages of large-scale over small are especially present in some markets rather than others.

The simplest explanation for a large-scale firm, in the underworld or anywhere else, is high costs of overhead or other elements of technology that make small-scale operation impractical. The need to utilize fully equipment or specialized personnel often explains at least the lower limit to the size of the firm.

Second is the prospect of monopolistic price increases. If most of the business can be cornered by a single firm, it does not merely multiply its profits in proportion to its expansion but can, if it keeps new competition from entering the market, raise the price at which it sells illegal services. Like any business, it does this at some sacrifice in size of the market; but if the demand for the goods is inelastic, the change in profit margin will be disproportionate to the reduction in output. Decentralized individual firms would have just as much to gain by pushing up the price at which they sell, but without discipline it will not work. Each firm will attempt to undercut its competitors, and profit margins will be shaved back to where they were. Thus where entry can be denied to newcomers, centralized price setting will yield monopoly rewards to whoever can organize the market. With discipline, a cartel can do it; in the absence of such discipline a merger may do it; but intimidation, too, can lead to the elimination of competition and the conquest of a monopoly position by a single firm.

Third, the larger the firm, and especially the larger its share in the whole market, the more "external" costs will become formal and attributable to the firm itself. "External costs" are those that fall on competitors, customers, by-standers, and others with whom the firm deals.

Collection of all the business within a single firm causes the costs that individual firms inflict on each other to show up as costs (or losses) to the larger centralized firm now doing the business. This is an advantage to it. It is an advantage because the costs were originally there but neglected; now there is incentive not to neglect them.

Spoiling the market in various ways is often an external cost. So is violence. While racketeers have a collective interest in curtailing violence in order to avoid trouble with the public and the police, the individual racketeer has little or no incentive to reduce the violence connected with his own crime. There is an analogy here with, say, the whaling industry, which has a collective interest in not killing off all the whales. The individual whaler will pay little attention to what he is doing to the future of the industry when he maximizes his own take. But a large organization will profit by imposing discipline, by holding down the violence if the business is crime, by holding down the slaughter of females if the business is whaling.

There are also other "external economies" that can become internalized to the advantage of the centralized firm. Lobbying has this characteristic, as does cultivating relations with the police. No small bookie can afford to spend money influencing gambling legislation, but an organized trade association or monopoly among those who live off illegal gambling can collectively afford to influence legislation to protect their monopoly from legitimate competition. Similarly with labor discipline: the small firm cannot afford to teach a lesson to the industry's labor force, since most of the lesson is lost on other people's employees, but a single large firm can expect the full benefit of its labor policy. Similarly with cultivating the market: if a boss cultivates the market for dope by hooking some customers, or cultivates a market for gambling in a territory where the demand is still latent, he cannot expect much of a return on his investment since opportunistic competitors will take advantage of the market he creates. Patent and copyright laws are based on the notion that the investment one makes in inventing something, or in writing a song, has to enjoy monopoly protection, or else the thing is not worth inventing or the song not worth writing. Anything that requires a long investment in cultivating a consumer interest, a labor market, and ancillary institutions or relations with the police can be undertaken only by a fairly large firm that has reason to expect enjoyment of most of the market and a return on its investment.

Finally, there is the attraction of not only monopolizing a particular market but also of achieving a dominant position in the underworld itself, and participating in its governing. To the extent that large criminal business firms provide governmental structure to the underworld, helping to maintain peace, setting rules, arbitrating disputes, and enforcing discipline, they are in a position to set up their own businesses and exclude competition. Constituting a kind of "corporate state," they can give themselves the franchise for various "state-sponsored monopolies." They can do this either by denying the benefits of the underworld government to their competitors or by using the equivalent of their "police power" to prevent competition. (They may even be able to use the actual police power if they can dominate diplomatic and financial relations with the agencies of law enforcement.) Where the line between business and government is indistinct, as it appears to be in the underworld, dominant business firms become regulators of their own industries, and developers of state monopolies.

THE RELATION OF ORGANIZED CRIME TO ENFORCEMENT

It is important to distinguish between the black-market monopolies dealing in forbidden goods, and the racketeering enterprises, like extortion and the criminal elimination of competition. It is the black-market monopolies that depend on the law itself. Without the law and some degree of enforcement, there is no presumption that the monopoly organization can survive competition—or, if it could survive competition once it is established, that it could have arisen in the first place as a monopoly in face of competition. Some rackets may also depend on the law itself, some labor rackets, some blackmail, even some threats to enforce the law with excessive vigor. But it is the black-market crimes—gambling, dope, smuggling, etc.—that are absolutely dependent on the law and on some degree of enforcement. That is, without a law that excludes legitimate competition, the basis for monopoly probably could not exist.

In fact, there must be an optimum degree of enforcement from the point of view of the criminal monopoly. With virtually no enforcement, either because enforcement is not attempted or because enforcement is infeasible, the black market could not be profitable enough to invite criminal monopoly (or not any more than any other market, legitimate or criminal.) With wholly effective enforcement, and no collusion with the police, the business would be destroyed. Between these extremes there may be an attractive black market profitable enough to invite monopoly.

Organized crime could not, for example, possibly corner the market on cigarette sales to minors. Every 21 year old is a potential source of supply to every 19 year old who is too young to buy his own cigarettes. No organization, legal or illegal, could keep a multitude of 21 year olds from buying cigarettes and passing them along to persons under 21. No black-market price differential great enough to make organized sale to minors profitable could survive the competition. And no organization, legal or illegal, could so intimidate every adult so that he would not be a source of supply to the youngsters. Without any way to enforce the law, organized crime would get no more out of selling cigarettes to children than out of selling them soft drinks.

The same is probably true with respect to contraceptives in those states where their sale is nominally illegal. If the law is not enforced, there is no scarcity out of which to make profits. And if one is going to intimidate every drugstore that sells contraceptives in the hope of monopolizing the business he may as well monopolize toothpaste or comic books unless the law can be made to intimidate the druggists with respect to the one commodity that organized crime is trying to monopolize.

What about abortions? Why are they not organized? The answer is not easy, and there may be too many special characteristics of this market to permit a selection of the critical one. First, the consumer and the product have unusual characteristics; nobody is a regular consumer the the way a person may regularly gamble, drink, or take dope. A woman may repeatedly need the services of an abortionist, but each occasion is once-for-all. Second, consumers are probably more secret about dealing with this black market, and secret especially among intimate friends and relations, than are the consumers of most banned commodities. Third, it is a dirty business and too many of the customers die; and while organized crime might drastically reduce fatalities, it may be afraid of getting involved with anything that kills and maims so many customers in a way that might be blamed on the criminal himself rather than just on the commodity that is sold. We probably don't know which reason or reasons are crucial here, but it would be interesting to know. (In particular it would be worth knowing whether organized abortion is less harmful than unorganized.)

Black Markets and Competition. An important difference between black-market crimes and most of the others, like racketeering and robbery, is that they are "crimes" only because we have chosen to legislate against the commodity or service they provide. We single out certain consumer goods and services as harmful or sinful; for reasons of history and tradition, as well as for other reasons, we forbid dope but not tobacco, forbid gambling in casinos but not on the stock market, forbid extramarital sex but not gluttony, forbid erotic stories but not mystery stories. We do this for reasons different from those behind the laws against robbery, parking in front of fire hydrants, and tax evasion.

It is, in other words, a matter of policy that determines the black markets. Cigarettes and firearms are two borderline cases. We can, as a matter of policy, make the sales of guns and cigarettes illegal. We can also, as a matter of policy, make contraceptives and abortion illegal. Times change, policies change, and what was banned yesterday can become legitimate today; what was freely available yesterday can be banned tomorrow. Evidently there are changes in policy on birth control; there may be changes on abortion and homosexuality, and there may be legislation restricting the sale of firearms.

The pure black markets, in other words, in contrast to rackets, tend to reflect some moral tastes, economic principles, paternalistic interests, and notions of personal freedom in a way that the rackets do not. A good example is contraception. We can change our policy on birth control in a way that we would not change our policy on armed robbery. And evidently we are changing our policy on birth control. The usury laws may to some extent be a holdover from medieval economics; and some of the laws on prostitution, abortion, and contraception were products of the Victorian era and reflect the political power of various church groups. One cannot even deduce from the existence of abortion laws that a majority of the voters, especially a majority of enlightened voters, opposes abortion; and the wise money would probably bet that the things that we shall be forbidding in 50 years will differ substantially from the things we forbid now.

One of the important questions is what happens when a forbidden industry is subjected to legitimate competition. We need more study of this matter. Legalized gambling is a good example. What has happened to Las Vegas is hardly reassuring. But the legalization of liquor in the early 1930s rather swamped the criminal liquor industry with competition.

Criminals are alleged to have moved into church bingo, but they have never got much of a hold on the stockmarket. What happens when a forbidden industry is legitimized needs careful analysis; evidently criminals cannot always survive competition, evidently sometimes they can. A better understanding of market characteristics would be helpful. The question is important in the field of narcotics. We could easily put insulin and antibiotics into the hands of organized crime by forbidding their sale; we could do the same with a dentist's novocaine. (We could, that is, if we could sufficiently enforce the prohibition. If we cannot enforce it, the black market would be too competitive for any organized monopoly to arise.) If narcotics were not illegal, there could be no black market and no monopoly profits, and the interest in "pushing" it would probably be not much greater than the pharmaceutical interest in pills to reduce the symptoms of common colds. This argument cannot by itself settle the question of whether, and which narcotics or other evil commodities, ought to be banned, but it is an important consideration.

The greatest gambling enterprise in the United States has not been significantly touched by organized crime. That is the stockmarket. (There has been criminal activity in the stockmarket, but not on the part of what we usually call "organized crime.") Nor has organized crime succeeded in controlling the foreign currency black markets around the world. The reason is that the market works too well. Furthermore, Federal control over the stockmarket, designed mainly to keep it honest and informative, and aimed at maximizing the competitiveness of the market and the information for the consumer, makes tampering difficult. Ordinary gambling ought to be one of the hardest industries to monopolize, because almost anybody can compete, whether in taking bets or providing cards, dice, or racing information. Wire services could not stand the ordinary competition of radio and Western Union; bookmakers could hardly be intimidated if the police were not available to intimidate them. If ordinary brokerage firms were encouraged to take accounts of customers and buy and sell bets by telephone for their customers, it is hard to see how racketeers could get any kind of grip on it. And when any restaurant or bar or country club or fraternity house can provide tables and sell fresh decks of cards, it is hard to see how gambling can be monopolized any more than the soft drink business, the television business, or any other. Even the criminal-skilled-labor argument probably would not last once it became recognized that the critical skills were in living outside the law, and those skills became obsolete with legalization.

We can still think gambling is a sin and try to eliminate it; we should probably try not to use the argument that it would remain in the hands of criminals if we legalize it. Both reason and evidence seem to indicate the contrary.

Essentially the question is whether the goal of somewhat reducing the consumption of narcotics, gambling, prostitution, abortion, or anything else that is forced by law into the black market, is or is not outweighed by the costs to society of creating a criminal industry. In all probability, though not with certainty, consumption of the proscribed commodity or service is reduced. Evidently it is not anywhere near to being eliminated because the estimates of abortion run to about a million a year, the turnover from gambling is estimated in the tens of billions of dollars per year, and dope addiction seems to be a serious problem. The costs to society of creating these black markets are several.

First, it gives the criminal the same kind of protection that a tariff might give a domestic monopoly: it guarantees the absence of competition from people who are unwilling to be criminal, and guarantees an advantage to those whose skill is in evading the law.

Second, it provides a special incentive to corrupt the police, because the police not only may be susceptible to being bought off, but also can be used to eliminate competition.

Third, a large number of consumers who are probably not ordinary criminals—the conventioneers who visit houses of prostitution, the housewives who bet on horses, the women who seek abortion—are taught contempt, even enmity, for the law, by being obliged to purchase particular commodities and services from criminals in an illegal transaction.

Fourth, dope addiction may so aggravate poverty for certain desperate people that they are induced to commit crimes or can be urged to commit crimes because the law arranges that the only (or main) source for what they desperately demand will be a criminal source.

Fifth, these big black markets may guarantee enough incentive and enough profit for organized crime so that the large-scale criminal organization comes into being and maintains itself. It may be—this is an important question for research—that without these important black markets crime would be substantially decentralized, lacking the kind of organization that makes it enterprising, safe, and able to corrupt public officials. In economic development terms, these black markets may provide the central core (or infrastructure) of underworld business, capable of branching out into other lines.

A good economic history of prohibition in the 1920s has never been attempted, so far as I know. By all accounts, though, prohibition was a mistake. Even those who do not like drinking and want to prohibit it have to reach the conclusion that prohibition was a mistake. It merely turned the liquor industry over to organized crime. In the end we gave up—probably not only because there was disagreement whether drinking was bad, or, if it were, whether it was properly a political question—but also because the attempt was an evident failure and an exceedingly costly one in its social byproducts. It may have given underworld business in the United States what economic developers call the takeoff into self-sustained growth.

Institutional Practices. A variety of institutional practices in the underworld needs to be better understood. What, for example, is the effect of the tax laws on extortion? Why does an extortionist put cigarette machines in a restaurant or provide linen service? Do the tax laws make it difficult to disguise the payment of tribute in cash but easy to disguise it (and make it tax deductible) if the tribute takes the form of a concession or the purchase of high-priced services? Why does a gambling syndicate bother to provide "wire services" when evidently its primary economic function is to shake down bookies by the threat of hurting their businesses or themselves, possibly with the collusion of the police? The Kefauver hearings indicate that the wire service syndicate in Miami took a standard 50 percent from the bookies. The 50 percent figure is itself remarkable. Equally remarkable is the fact that the figure was uniform. Similarly remarkable is the fact that the syndicate went through the motions of providing a wire service when it perfectly well could have taken cash tribute instead. There is an analogy here with the car salesman who refuses to negotiate the price of a new car but is willing to negotiate quite freely the allowance on the used car that one turns in. The underworld seems to need institutions, conventions, traditions, and recognizable standard practices much like the upper world of business.

14. NEW POLITICAL CRIMES AND THE EMERGENCE OF REVOLUTIONARY NATIONALIST IDEOLOGIES

ROBERT J. KELLY

INTRODUCTION

In this paper, I hope to examine and appraise the relationships between crimes and political ideologies, with special focus on "Third World" nations. The theses advanced, and the modes of analyses used, draw their methodological and theoretical substance from familiar approaches and sources: most notably C. Wright Mills, whose work consistently retained a reformist-radical set of political motivations. The argument presented will tend to stress the proposition that policy in large modern societies and in newly developed nations does not stem from rational debate—by soldiers, cold-war scholars, or defense intellectuals. Rather, foreign and domestic policy develops from the subtle interplay among large, fluid interest groups, both public and private, jockeying for the measures most immediately beneficial to their own purpose. Much discussion has been devoted to the massive economic, political, and demographic dislocations in contemporary society as "exercises in problem-solving."[1] Within this bureaucratic frame of reference, dissent, protest, and the articulation of critical perspectives are not perceived as profound attempts to reorganize society, but as the occurrence of persistent but nonetheless manageable problems created by outside forces adept at manipulating the apathetic and ignorant peasants whose parochialism and gullibility render them vulnerable to agitation. What is required in these circumstances to insure the preservation or restoration of order and stability is adequate diagnosis and the subsequent application of remedial action.

The social diagnostician-bureaucrat is a sociopolitical therapist armed, in Gouldner's words, with

> . . . some confidence that his knowledge and technical skill are sufficient to aid the client more than the latter could do for himself. The

This article was reproduced from F. Alder and G. O. W. Mueller (eds.), *Politics, Crime and the International Scene: An Interamerican Focus* (1972), with the permission of the copyright holders, North-South Press, North South Center for Technical and Cultural Interchange, P.O. Box 1058, 542 Ponce de Leon, Hato Rey, Puerto Rico 00919.

[1]S. Wolin and J. Schaar, "Berkeley: The Battle of People's Park," *New York Review*, 12(12): 29, June 1969.

diagnostician's morale is, in part, a function of the extent to which he believes his own skill and knowledge will suffice to provide a remedy.[2]

The services of the diagnostician are most urgently needed in times and under circumstances when life for large segments of a population becomes ahistorical and noninstitutional. Men, in this dramaturgic view, see themselves moving through a succession of situations linked only by mere propinquity or surface symbolic consistency; the movement and rhythm of life sprawls and lacks the familiar punctuations provided by the larger architecture of culture which preserves meanings and structures events, thereby attenuating if not preventing the dissolution of social action into episodic shreds. In a word, the diagnostician's job is to shore up a collapsing social system, and often his remedies and proposals take the form of mass coercion organized around a police state. Connected to these practices, and underlying the assumptions of order, stability, development, and progress, lies the basic article of faith cutting across the ideological cleavages of capitalism and communism: the belief that the key to progress and development lies in a technological-managerial elite. American and Soviet technocrats concur perfectly in their emphasis on the crucial role of technology and its major corollary: the unchallenged prerogatives of the "national security managers."

In Asia, Latin America, and Africa, people's war and its advocates have stood as the primary resource against the advancement and implementation of American-Soviet models of society. More importantly, people's war has played a critical role in national unity. In the course of such wars local communities have been effectively integrated into national movements.[3]

CONTEMPORARY NATIONALIST IDEOLOGIES: SOME HISTORICAL CONSIDERATIONS

Most of the major writers on nationalism and nationalist movements have suggested that the growth of nationalist forms of government, especially in Western Europe, had been preceded by the centralizing tendencies of the Holy Roman Empire, the establishment of strong absolute monarchies, and eventually the evolution of a national bourgeoisie.[4] Common territory, distinctive, and generally shared cultural characteristics (languages, customs, and historical traditions) served to produce national consciousness

---

[2]A. W. Gouldner, *Enter Plato* (New York, Basic Books, 1965), 256.

[3]M. Selden, "People's War and the Transformation of Peasant Society: China & Vietnam," in E. Friedman and M. Selden, eds., *America's Asia* (New York, Pantheon, 1971); also F. Fanon, *A Dying Colonialism* (New York, Grove, 1967); P. Boudieu and A. M. Sayad, *Le deracinement: La crise de l'agriculture traditionelle en Algerie* (Paris, Minuit, 1964); and J. Womack, *Zapata and the Mexican Revolution* (New York, Knopf, 1969).

[4]H. Kohn, *The Idea of Nationalism* (New York, Macmillan, 1958).

and sentiment. At the end of the 18th and the beginning of the 19th centuries, revolution and war in Europe stimulated national feeling everywhere. War, conquest, and oppression by one nation meant the rise of national consciousness and loyalty among conquered and oppressed peoples. Hope, fear, and hate in a time of insecurity and disintegrating values were fundamental factors nourishing the growth of nationalism. The nation became an answer to men's anxieties, a solution for their frustrations, and a refuge in time of trouble. For example, the French conquests in Prussia and Austria stimulated a national patriotism that finally achieved its goal of an independent German nation in 1871. Also, the growing nationalist feelings sweeping the continent during the period of the French Revolution and its aftermath arose, in part, directly out of individual frustration. Men like Rousseau, Robespierre, Fichte, and Arndt found in nationalism a way to realize their visions and ideals of society. Nationalism from 1709 to about 1815 offered patriots a way of identifying themselves with the community and thus of finding security, status, and authority in a time of extreme uncertainty. Arising out of revolution, war, and diplomacy, one new state after another was created on the basis of nationality.

By the 20th century, four general forces made the nation the supreme community and nationalism the supreme sentiment: (a) the desire to unify the success in unifying territory and people; (b) the extension of the power of the nation-state; (c) the growth of, and increasing awareness of, national cultures; and (d) the power conflict among the nations which further stimulated national feeling. All through the 19th and into the 20th century, economic and technological advances tended further to unify groups already possessing a common territory and state. In modern times in much of Europe the cultural needs and the economic and social problems became so vast and complex that only an institution like the nation-state was capable of—if not solving—then at least handling them. The political ideology of liberalism played an immensely important role in the growth of nationalism—it was through the nation-state that an individual acquired his freedom and obtained his vote. As dictatorial regimes arose in the 20th century, out of a variety of conditions, part of their success was attributable to their shrewd use of symbols and propaganda through which they identified themselves, the nation, and the people.[5]

In many ways contemporary nationalism has replaced religion in its organization and attractiveness. One authority has asserted that "modern and contemporary nationalism appeals to man's 'religious sense.' It offers a substitute for, or supplement to, historic supernatural religion."[6] It should come as no surprise, then, that much of the intellectual and ideo-

---

[5]B. Shafer, *Nationalism, Myth and Reality* (New York, Harcourt, Brace, 1955).
[6]C. J. H. Hayes, *Nationalism: A Religion* (New York, Columbia U. Press, 1963), 168.

logical resistance to modernization, of which nationalism is an integral part, has come from advocates of the traditional faiths. In southern and eastern Asia this means Buddhism, Hinduism, and sometimes Islam; in the middle east Islam, or sometimes Eastern Orthodoxy; in Latin America, Roman Catholicism—although here some changes in policy and attitude are beginning to materialize. In all of these areas, religious leaders have often been leaders in conservative and traditionalist movements as well.

In Third World countries, widely diverse politically and economically, in which religion has played a significant role in the resistance to modernization, there seems to be evolving a generally shared set of similar values: the desire to increase and improve their output while simultaneously ensuring a more fair distribution of goods and services.[7] This aspiration, however, has been the subject of sharp conflicts and differences. The most prevalent view toward the attainment of these goals has argued that a modicum of national unity coupled with a nationally integrated political system is essential both to the implementation of programs instituted by government and to the expression and involvement of the interests and needs of the people in government.

The coming of independence in many Third World countries has not meant the restoration of earlier indigenous political structures, but the suppression of a foreign bureaucracy by one staffed and run by nationals.[8] Not that tribal authorities and native systems of control and influence were ever totally abolished by colonial regimes and law; for example, the national bureaucracy in many new African states seeks to keep chiefs out of politics while preserving their traditional rights. When independence occurs old divisions have made their appearance. Ethnic or cultural groups may then contend with one another for power and privilege within the national political arena. Black Africa (Nigeria, for example) epitomizes this state of internal strife, but marked dissension and internecine conflict are common throughout the underdeveloped world. Rose points out that "India is not yet a nation in a sociological or psychological sense. It is still a collection of mutually suspicious and mutually hostile extended families."[9]

In taking over the government from colonial powers, nationals typically found themselves in short supply of administrative talent and trained bureaucrats. Thus, the tendency has been for the anticolonialist leader or party to become the government without the stability and support offered by a developed civil service and party system.[10] As most of the nationalist ideologies organizing the movement toward independence tend to be so-

---

[7] R. Aron, *The Industrial Society* (New York, Clarion, 1968), 44–46.
[8] L. Mair, *New Nations* (Chicago, U. of Chicago, 1967), 111–13.
[9] A. M. Rose, "Sociological Factors Affecting Economic Development in India," *Studies in Comparative International Development*, 3 (9): 171 (1967–68).
[10] A. A. Said, *The African Phenomenon* (Boston, Allyn & Bacon, 1968).

cialist in aspiration and format—though not necessarily—insofar as they appeal to desires for a centrally administered national plan of rapid development, espouse a collective orientation to the solution of problems, and promise the reduction of income inequality and class privilege,[11] they precipitate a peculiarly non-Western type of political and social activity. Under these types of political programs attempts are made to mobilize the "voiceless masses" through democratic ideas and institutions and at the same time provide these masses with the amenities of the "welfare state." This means that all of the cleavages of the social structure are given political articulation simultaneously, while governments attempt to plan economic development and provide the minimum essentials of a welfare state. If it is argued that such governments possess only an uncertain authority and relatively little experience, it is usually answered that they must make the attempt nevertheless because only on this basis will the mobilized masses positively identify themselves with the new government or nation. If they don't, revolution on an almost perpetual scale will ensue. As a consequence of these conditions ideological controversy is waged with unparalleled intensity, while political leaders attempt to establish a functioning governmental machinery and protect it against the assaults of politics and corruption. The coup d'etat, "colonels' revolts," and palace revolutions, have been regular events throughout the Third World. And, increasingly, military coups and regimes have turned out or aborted constitutionally elected governments, often as not with the approval or even support of the United States.[12]

Historically, the power vacuums left by departing colonial regimes and changing administrations dominating such societies have culminated in the ascendancy of cultist groups, secret sodalities, and what Hobsbawm has called "archaic social movements."[13] Hobsbawm distinguishes between three types of rural archaic social movements. The first is social banditry or Robin Hoodism which is usually a local reaction against the agents of government, the rich, or the foreigners who threaten to "destroy and transform" a static community.[14] The second is the "mafia" phenomenon. This type of movement initially develops in rural societies in which there is no effective law or respect for the authority of the state. "In lawless communities power . . . clusters around local strong points. Its typical form is patronage, its typical holder the private magnate or boss with his body of retainers and dependents and the network of 'influence' which

<hr/>

[11] I. L. Horowitz, *Three Worlds of Development* (New York, Oxford, 1966), Chapter 1.

[12] F. Goff and M. Locker, "The Violence of Domination: U.S. Power and the Dominican Republic," in I. L. Horowitz, J. DeCastro, and J. Gerassi, eds., *Latin American Radicalism* (New York, Random, 1969), 249–91.

[13] E. J. Hobsbawm, *Primitive Rebels: Studies in Archaic Forms of Social Movements in the 19th and 20th Centuries* (New York, Norton, 1965).

[14] *Op. cit.*, p. 24.

surrounds him and causes men to put themselves under his protection."[15]

Mafias tend to be decentralized gangs, each of which has its own private rituals and behavior binding its members together. Mafia gangs prove "a machine of law and organized power" which is parallel to the state's and, for the members, a substitute for the state's.[16]

A mafia develops when the state is unable to keep public order or when people consider the authorities to be hostile or indifferent to their welfare. A mafia provides "the effective law and power" that the state has failed to supply. This is not to say that mafias have egalitarian political goals or seek to replace decaying and declining political administrations with munificent and democratically oriented governments. Rather, such gangs arise in times of crisis and transition when the effectiveness of indigenous or colonial administrations slackens, creating power vacuums. In no cases where mafias have come to power in parts of Sicily, Vietnam, or elsewhere, have they ushered in reforms or initiated massive land reorganization programs. In their continuation of subjugation, mafiosi replaced absentee feudal landowners and introduced direct terror and violence into the methods of exploiting the peasantry.

Hobsbawm's third type is millenarianism. Millenarian movements usually regard the existing world as fundamentally bad. They seek or expect the overthrow of the present order and its replacement by a utopia.[17] Millenarian, messianic movements are primarily religious in character; they also demand and strive to secure for their followers certain riches without which life itself is scarcely worth living. These riches are freedom and salvation; freedom from subjection and servitude to foreign powers as well as from adversity, and salvation from the possibility of having the traditional culture destroyed and the native society wiped out as an historical entity. In his studies of modern messianic cults, Lanternari has observed:

> The increasingly close contacts between whites and natives that have developed in the course of the last hundred years, especially under the stress of two world wars, have given rise to nativistic religious movements in almost every part of the globe. Two factors have contributed most substantially to this: the intensified efforts of imperialism to bring the aborigines under control, and the grow-

---

[15]Many of the loansharking operations in American urban areas still retain this form of organization: a local capo (boss) underwrites an individual or group offering friendship (protection) and security (provisions for forceful collection of "vigs" [indebted money]) for a percentage of the profits. Reluctance to join him or attempts to circumvent his authority are usually met with violence and the subsequent failure of the enterprise.

[16]Hobsbawm, op. cit., pp. 32–35.

[17]Ibid., pp. 57–59.

ing awareness on the part of the native peoples of the economic and cultural lags in their own societies as compared to the civilization of the West. Therefore, it is the impact made upon so-called "primitive" societies by the colonial powers that has brought about conditions favoring the rise of messianic movements.[18]

Messianic cults all involve a belief in society's return to its sources, usually expressed in terms of the expectation of the millenium and the cataclysms and catastrophes that are to precede it, and also embody a belief in the reversal of the existing social order, and in the ejection of the white man.

In the southwestern section of the United States, the Alianza Federal de Mercedes comes closest in its chiliastic doctrinal program to messianic-type movements. Led by its fiery leader, Reies Lopez Tijerina, the Alianza, representing the rural Chicano populations of south Texas and New Mexico, exhibits many of the characteristics of a revitalization movement, especially in its emphasis on the elimination of alien persons, customs, values, and materiel. The chief aim of the Alianza, articulated by its charismatic leader Tijerina, is to press for the return of, or get compensation for, millions of acres of land which he claims were wrongfully acquired by the federal government. In June 1967, the Alianza burst into the national spotlight in the so-called insurrection at Tierra Amarilla, a small county seat in northern New Mexico where Aliancistas attempted a citizen arrest of a district attorney who had allegedly violated the rights of Alianza members. In many similar ways the life-styles of a sizable portion of the masses of lower-class blacks living in the ghettoes of American cities may best be described by reference to the typologies of cultist movements described by Lanternari and others. Such studies suggest that the social stoicism rampant in the black ghettoes might be analyzed as a reaction to the political and economic void produced by feeble governmental policies ostensibly aimed at relieving the economic and social misery of blacks. Along these lines, McCord and his associates have depicted several life-styles in the black ghetto which bear striking resemblances to the anthropological and historical studies of non-Western messianic movements. For example, McCord found large segments of black urban populations uninvolved, resigned, passive, indifferent, to politics or participation in the civil rights movement; believing that fate or luck rather than planning determined one's lot in life; and sharing a conviction that their destiny is largely controlled either by "higher forces" or, at least, by circumstances beyond their control. Such attitudes have led to widespread involvement in "Other-Worldly Churches" whose clergy preaches for-

---

[18]V. Lanternari, *The Religions of the Oppressed: A Study of Modern Messianic Cults* (New York, Knopf, 1965), 142.

bearance in this world as a prerequisite to justice and salvation in the next.[19]

POLITICIZATION

Authority, writes Bierstedt, is a property of social organization:

> When there is no organization there is no authority. Authority appears only in organized groups—the associations—of society, never in unorganized groups, or in the unorganized community.[20]

Following the decay and removal of traditional agencies of social control, including the village landed elite and the territorial administration upon which the cohesion of peasant and rural society depends, there occurs a process of fragmentation in which sects and movements arise and flourish; movements which Hobsbawm and Lanternari view as essentially transitional. As traditional institutions become dysfunctional, village and national elites lose their authority and power over mechanisms of coercion and control, with the result that the peasantry drifts into cultism and banditry. These coalitions provoke a crisis of authority conferring only nominal legitimacy on the extant government. The question—What forces occasioned these social and political upheavals and generated the ferment for revolution?—may be engaged in terms of the processes of modernization and development. The social imbalances created by primitive accumulation wherein the expanding capitalist system ransacked the world in its search for capital and later converted the tribesmen and peasants into millhands, rubber-tappers, cane-cutters, and miners, composed a "world" as a social system by converting human labor and natural resources into "free-floating" factors of production. In addition, the development of the market brought about a rapid circulation of the elite. The manipulators of the new free-floating resources—labor bosses, merchants, industrial entrepreneurs—challenged the inherited power of the controllers of fixed social resources—the tribal chief, the mandarin, the landed nobleman.[21] Moreover, as Wolfe has observed, in those societies in which rural populations have participated in revolutions, both capitalist mobilization of resources through the pressure of taxation and resource conversion into commodity production coupled with population increases of considerable magnitude coincided, disrupting the hinterland and deranging the numerous middle-level ties between urban and rural sec-

---

[19]W. McCord, J. Howard, B. Friedberg, and E. Harwood, *Life Styles in the Black Ghetto* (New York, Norton, 1969), Chapter 6.
[20]R. Bierstedt, "The Problem of Authority," in M. Berger, T. Abel, and C. H. Page, eds., *Freedom and Control in Modern Society* (New York, Van Nostrand, 1954), 68.
[21]S. N. Eisenstadt: *Modernization: Protest and Change* (Englewood Cliffs, N.J., Prentice-Hall, 1966).

tors.[22] Prior to the convergence of these three factors: rapid economic mobilization and expansion, population explosion, and political unrest triggered by the first two, peasants were merely passive spectators watching governments passing in and out of the marble halls of power more concerned with self-perpetuation than with the plight of their peoples. A cursory analysis of the political face of South America will show the effects of capitalist economic policy: seven of South America's 13 republics are governed by military dictatorships—governments which are right-wing in their orientation and policy. With the exception of nationalistic Peru which is veering to the left with a system of "social democracy," and "Marxist" Chile, the other nations are ruled by elected civilian heads of state or still under colonial domination and hence ripe for revolution.

What political conditions of this sort reflect is the consolidation of power among a few, limited constituencies and coalitions which exploit the mass of the population and the natural wealth of the country. The consequences of these types of power alignments for the peasant are usually dislocation and disorder. Against the strain of the disorder of his everyday existence, the peasant seeks relief in ideological and religious movements which proffer intervention and deliverance; rescuing the peasant, as it were, from the pandemonium of his existence. Through the appropriation of cultist theodicies of happiness and suffering which serve as precursors for the revolution, in that such movements constitute opportunities for which alternatives to present conditions may be imagined, the believer may experiment mentally with alternative forms of organization, thus preparing the population for the changes and innovations to come. In short, messianic movements are the mental rehearsals of the forthcoming revolutionary transformations.

It seems that changes in perception and understanding of the world one inhabits are prerequisites for major organizational changes as the courses of several 20th century revolutions testify: the formulation of new cognitive and emotive mazeways, new Weltanschauungen, antecedes the organizational patterns of exegesis of contemporary ideological apparatuses. For example, the Mexican revolution was preceded by the widespread circulation of anarchist ideas; in Algiers, prior to the operations of the FLN, the Badissa, a reformist Islamic movement, attracted a large following; the Chinese revolution of 1911 occurred after the Taiping, Nien, and

---

[22]E. R. Wolfe, "Peasant Rebellion and Revolution," in N. Miller and R. Aya, eds., *National Liberation: Revolution in the Third World* (New York, Free Press, 1971), pp. 48–67. Wolfe provides interesting statistics relating rapid population growth, economic expansion, and political ferment: "Mexico had a population of 5.8 million at the beginning of the nineteenth century; in 1910—at the outbreak of the Revolution—it had 16.5 million. European Russia had a population of 20 million in 1725; at the turn of the twentieth century it had 87 million. China numbered 265 million in 1775, 430 million in 1850, and close to 600 million at the time of the revolution. Vietnam . . . sustained a population of between 6 and 14 million in 1820; it had 30.5 million in 1963, representing a considerable increase. . . . Algeria numbered 10.5 million in 1963, representing a fourfold increase since the beginnings of French occupation in the first part of the 19th century. [Finally] Cuba had 550,000 inhabitants in 1800; by 1953, it had 5.8 million" (pp. 51–52).

Boxer rebellions; and the mushrooming of heterodox secret societies, the groundwork for the Russian revolution, was prepared by the secession of the Old Believers and the spread of millenarian ideology among the peasantry. More recently, the Vietnamese revolution in the south followed the growth of novel sects, such as the Cao Dai and the Hoa Hao.[23] These movements and sects appear to be of crucial importance in shaping a receptive sociocultural climate for more sophisticated ideological socialization.

Returning to the question posed above concerning the forces which engender revolutionary movements, I would argue with Gusfield that contrary to much theorizing and polemical writing, mass society makes available sources of direct attachment—however tenuous—to supralocal, supraethnic, and suprareligious institutions. In so doing, mass society can reduce the intensity of social and cultural conflicts by evolving frameworks for consensus.[24] It is, on the contrary, in pluralistic social systems undergoing rapid economic and social change, in which groups and classes are disenfranchised or adversely affected by these processes, that allegiance and loyalty flag—especially in countries where the political order is clearly structured to represent select interest groups at the exclusion of all others. Furthermore, the assumption is made among many of the advocates of political pluralism that the ideological dynamics of pluralism insure attachment to larger national institutions and structures through commitment to intermediate structures; it is perhaps more reasonable to maintain that as a group or class perceives an external threat to its integrity, promoting its sense of solidarity, such circumstances not only augment group identity and organization but exacerbate its shared sense of alienation from the total political order.

Into this atmosphere of disaffection and despair in which the peasant resorts to sectism and cultism seeking opportunities for popular participation and involvement denied him as the traditional village disintegrates, the national revolutionary ideologists move: articulating peasant protest, organizing land reform policies, and setting up parallel hierarchies of government and political administrations discrediting thereby ruling regimes that have refused or ignored popular aspirations for change and fundamental reform. In a sense, the revolutionary ideologists fix upon the pervasive rapport among the discontented as the basis for mobilization.[25]

---

[23]M. Nomad, *Aspects of Revolt* (New York, Farrar, Straus, 1960); J. R. McLane, "Archaic Movements and Revolution in South Vietnam," in *National Liberation, op. cit.,* pp. 68–101.

[24]J. R. Gusfield, "Mass Society and Extremist Politics," in P. Orleans, ed., *Social Structure and Social Process* (Boston, Allyn & Bacon, 1969), 512–28.

[25]As noted earlier fragmentation of traditional institutions, and experience in sect and cultist groups, activate the peasantry to alternative modes of thinking and acting. An audience for revolutionary propaganda and appeals has been made available by the breakdown of traditional rural insulation accelerated by such factors as economic depression, rapid secularization, and the enervation of familial ties. This general decline in the relevance and efficacy of traditional ways and persons conspires to make men available for revolutionary appeal. Then, too, political and military considerations dictate that revolutionists operate in the more inaccessible rural areas. Often, regimes ignore or simply cannot staff rural installations.

Besides promulgating ideals and themes of national progress, the fulfillment of a national mission, and utilizing didactic techniques of education and propaganda to infuse the population with a sense of social solidarity by alluding to folk heroes, history (real or fictitious), myths of common descent and racial unity, the ideological cadres must build a network of institutions that not only parallel but replace those of the established government (an "infrastructure" or "parallel hierarchy") which serves several interrelated ends: first, the rebels must construct an administrative structure to collect taxes, to provide some education and social welfare, and to maintain a modicum of economic activity. The major task here is not to outfight but to outadminister the government; second, in order to establish organic ties with the population, the movement must accede to the demands of the local population. For example, in South Vietnam the NLF encouraged the peasants to unite in order to reduce excessive landlord rent exactions. Characteristically, the NLF offered no uniform national guidelines for appropriate rent levels, allowing these to be determined in each area on the basis of local conditions.[26] Third, by enjoining the population to play an active role in the rebel government or people's government, the movement speeds the rise of leaders from the peasantry itself, intensifying the fusion between peasantry and leadership which sparked the revolutionary effort. Also, opposition between the old and the young, men and women, the intellectuals and the masses, is softened through these participatory structures, deepening the cleavage between the traditional cultural forms and the new.[27] Fourth—and for our purposes one of the most important functions of a revolutionary infrastructure—it sets up models and examples for defiance and challenge of established authority, breaking the inhibitions of habitual or reflexive obedience. Examples of overt resistance help establish new standards of defiance.

The central objective underlying the elaboration and use of all of these devices is to heighten the moral isolation of the government from the people, forcing the government to issue decrees, instructions, and legislation in a void which degrades its authoritative posture and tarnishes its image of legitimacy.

POLITICAL CRIMES AND CRIMINALITY: I

In September 1971, Uruguay's anti-government Tupamaro guerrillas freed British Ambassador G. Jackson in front of a Roman Catholic church eight months after a group of gunmen abducted the dip-

---

[26]M. Selden, "People's War and the Transformation of Peasant Society," in N. Miller and R. Aya, *op. cit.*, p. 225.

[27]Frantz Fanon declares that the war against the French not only welded traditionally hostile elements of Arab society together, but transformed Algerian family life into a more satisfying unit of expressivity and compassion. Fanon, *op. cit.*, Chapter 3.

lomat on his way to work. Jackson was returned in excellent health despite his months of detainment in what guerrillas called their "people's prison." (UPI)

No practicing revolutionary would disagree with Che Guevara's general proposition that "terrorism is a negative weapon which produces in no way the desired effects, which can turn a people against a given revolutionary movement, and which brings with it a loss of lives among those taking part that is much greater than the return."[28]

An outstanding feature of guerrilla training is the stress on scrupulously correct and just behavior toward civilians. The rebel army code carries severe punishment for rape, robbery, and damage to property and crops. Political work, believes General Giap, is "the soul of the Army," and a Chinese guerrilla expert explains that "army indoctrination is primarily aimed at training the troops to act in such a way that they will gain the total support of the people." The guerrilla's use of terror, therefore, must be sociologically and psychologically selective. At one stage of its application, the insurgent's employment of terror is designed to disrupt the inertial relationship between incumbent ruling bodies and the mass of the population. By attacking the symbols of the state (e.g., blowing up governmental buildings, sabotaging transportation systems, and assassinating political leaders), the rebels reveal the weakness of the framework in its capacity to ensure protection and security for the population. Tactical considerations, however, require discrimination in the use of terror, so it must ultimately be limited to those who are popularly defined as the enemies of the people—officials, landlords, and informers. In order for terror to be effective, it must be regarded by the people as an extra-governmental effort to dispense justice long overdue. Part of the revolutionary ideology's content, therefore, must contain an elaborate labelling and defining machinery, a set of codes which can be invoked to explain and interpret both insurgent and governmental action. As Pye observes:

> Any government faced with a violent challenge to its authority must provide a public interpretation of the causes of the insurrection. The hypothesis about the causes of insurgency must not only be plausible but they must leave the government in an effective position to carry on the struggle. Few governments can accept the view that their own policy deficiencies drove people to violence. Governments prefer to picture insurrections as caused by misguided people lured by false prophets or evil conspiracy.

> Such a characterization has the virtue of making officials appear to be on the side of reason and their enemies essentially fools.[29]

---

[28]E. Guevara, *Che Guevara on Guerrilla Warfare* (New York, Praeger, 1961).
[29]L. W. Pye, "The Roots of Insurgency and the Commencement of Rebellions," in H. Eckstein, ed., *Internal War* (New York, Praeger, 1964).

Counteracting these strategies which enable the government to define the conflict and thus, in many ways, to control it, the revolutionary ideologists must be capable of initiating a campaign of their own which either discredits or minimizes the effects of criminal labelling by recasting the actors in opposite roles. Propaganda is instituted which portrays the government and its agents as villains and criminals (whose wickedness points up the goodness of the guerrilla-hero); and, as Klapp writes, "a David–Goliath encounter (is manufactured) in which a little man upsets a big man."[30] This point is well illustrated by Martin Luther King's organization of the strike against the bus companies of Montgomery, Alabama. Here, a small hero is pitted against a large villain.

The government, its policies, agents, and allies, are refracted through rebel propaganda machines and depicted as criminals, freeing the guerrilla-activist from guilt and culpability for his actions. Through this mechanism of symbolic reversal, acts of violence and criminality are transformed and become acts of liberation—blows against the empire; and conversely, the actions and policies of the government take on criminal and traitorous dimensions.

Many rebel activities defined by the government as criminal and traitorous do not result in killing and murder; they originate in the need to sabotage the government's belated efforts to gain popular support, and thus perpetuate its isolation from the people. The rebel's account of reality, his definitions of situations, gain currency and cumulative support if their hierarchies and infrastructures carry out education and welfare programs, implement land reforms, and generally relieve conditions of privation and misery. To insure that these policies can materialize, terror is directed against selected governmental agents and administrators. Eqbal Ahmad reports that government schoolteachers and health workers were favorite targets of the Vietcong. Many of these people were kidnapped or underwent indoctrination. "In June 1962, a South Vietnamese observer at the UN informed UNESCO that the Vietcong had kidnapped more than 1200 teachers; the government's malaria eradication program collapsed after 22 health officers had been killed and 60 kidnapped."[31]

Often, if not invariably, psychopathic types who join liberation movements pursue their criminal careers under its protective canopy—especially when the movement enjoys widespread sympathy and tacit support in the population. Others, men like Lee Harvey Oswald and Sirhan Sirhan, seek through criminal acts, presumably motivated by their political convictions, the fulfillment of an unsuccessful or inconclusive life. For these

---

[30]O. Klapp, "Dramatic Encounters," in J. R. Gusfield, ed., *Protest, Reform, and Revolt* (New York, Wiley, 1970), p. 382.
[31]E. Ahmad, "Revolutionary Warfare and Counterinsurgency," in N. Miller and R. Aya, *op. cit.*, p. 162.

men, personal failure is dramatically transcended in one long, supreme, "political" gesture. Doubtless, a great number of violent acts against the police and other representatives of government are simply reactions to power and privilege, the chief offenders usually being members of the lower classes who are merely expressing latent hostility toward those in power and not proceeding deliberately and consciously from resolute political principles. Blind lashing out only enhances the power of the clandestine services of police administrations and expands the role of governmental agencies over which legislative bodies are able to exercise little or no control.

Characteristics of the Political Criminal. Typically, the political criminal has no criminal self-concept. He violates the law more often than not out of conscience, out of a set of convictions that arise from a desire to create a better society, correct perceived injustices, and change the nature of society. The political offender ordinarily has no established history of criminal behavior or a criminal career. Merton, in making a distinction between "nonconforming" and "aberrant" behavior, has provided some guidelines to understanding the career of the political criminal.[32] According to Merton, the nonconformer, in contrast to the aberrant, (a) announces his dissent publicly, (b) challenges the legitimacy of the norms and the laws he violates, (c) aims to change the norms he is denying in practice, (d) is acknowledged by conventional members of the society to depart from prevailing norms for disinterested purposes and not for what he personally can get out of it, and (e) lays claim to a higher morality and to ultimate values rather than to the particular norms of the society. Political criminals are usually committed to a larger social order. This order may differ from the existing one so that they are, in their commitment to it, willing to engage in criminal behavior. In this connection, Elliott has noted that:

> Although some political offenders are persons without integrity who have yielded to the extensive bribes paid either by foreign powers or by local groups, the vast majority are conscientious adherents to a political philosophy which threatens the existence of the government they are opposing. Political offenders represent a paradox for they are criminals who carry on their illegal activities in pursuit of their ideals. They are not imbued with sordid schemes for extracting vast sums of money from unsuspecting victims, nor are they motivated by basic desires to kill or destroy, although these crimes may be necessary in the pursuit of their ideals. They are generally idealists devoted to a cause.[33]

---

[32]R. K. Merton, "Social Problems and Sociological Theory," in R. K. Merton and R. A. Nisbet, eds., *Contemporary Social Problems*, 2nd ed. (New York, Harcourt, Brace, 1966), 808–811.
[33]M. A. Elliott, *Crime in Modern Society* (New York, Harper & Row, 1951), 180.

The Black Panthers, Young Lords, and Brown Berets seem to fit both Merton's classificatory scheme as nonconformist and Elliott's description of the political offender. The recent sensational political trials and armed confrontations with urban police forces have brought the Panthers and similar groups into national attention. The Panther leaders, many of whom are now dead, imprisoned, tangled up in litigation, or exiled, are self-made intellectuals or, in Kilson's terms, "paraintellectuals."[34] The Panthers have had to purge people who turned out to be basically criminals (in Merton's sense of aberrant) or racists unable to relate to the party's political and intellectual program. Point #8 of the party's 10-point program of black liberation is of interest. It states: "We want freedom for all black men held in federal, state, county, and city prisons and jails," suggesting that all black men are victims (political prisoners) of a system of justice designed neither to protect them as citizens nor guarantee their constitutional rights. Even those persons convicted of assaults on black people, even with regard to depredations by blacks against blacks, the Panthers persist in their contentions that basically black men in prison are the victims of a racist society geared either to killing them or, if they protest vigorously and defend themselves against the system, reducing them to criminals. In any case, many of their claims point implicitly to a growing tendency in law enforcement regarding various methods of political suppression and arrest. Political crime can also consist of behavior by agents of the government as well as behavior directed against government. The attitudes and actions of representatives of Southern political power toward the civil rights movement in the early sixties is a case in point.[35]

Depending upon one's perceptions of situations, related mainly to well-structured sets of values and norms (ideologies), what constitutes criminal behavior from one perspective may be filtered through a different or disparate aggregate of categories, and perceived and conceptualized as acts of liberation and freedom. In the Watts riots of 1965, where the police saw black criminals tearing apart law and order with a cascade of Molotov cocktails, many of the black inhabitants of Watts saw freedom fighters liberating themselves with blood and fire. The most distinctive and generally shared feeling among blacks about the riots was that they were not

---

[34]Kilson has written: "Unlike the established elements in the Negro intelligentsia, the paraintellectuals share a cultural experience similar to that of the black lower-classes. They share too the lower classes' brutalizing experience with the coercive arm of white-controlled cities, especially the police power. These common experiences enabled the paraintellectuals to be spokesmen for the Negro masses as they emerged into a militant politicization through riots. The paraintellectuals came onto the scene as legitimate and *natural* leaders. Moreover, they advance the politicalization of the black urban masses, after a fashion, by formulating descriptions of black-white relations, past and present, and policies for altering these relationships that the Negro lower-class finds meaningful. Few of the established elements among the black intelligentsia have, until very recently, had such success" (M. Kilson, "The New Black Intellectuals," *Dissent* [July–August 1969], 307).

[35]For additional examples, see J. C. Mouledous, "Political Crime and the Negro Revolution," in R. Quinney and M. Clinard, eds., *Criminal Behavior Systems: A Typology* (New York, Holt, Rinehart, Winston, 1967), 217–231.

criminal. To some, they were the explosion of anger created by oppression; to others, rationally planned demonstration against sustained injustice; to still others, a full-scale rebellion, an assertion of racial pride, a protest against intolerable poverty. For few indeed were the riots "bad" or "criminal" in the sense in which these words are used and acted upon by the police and judicial administrations.

To argue, as some criminologists do, that crime is any act punishable by the state is to imply strongly that government and law are one; that is, that all which government punishes is necessarily unlawful. Kadish has argued that disorderly conduct and vagrancy laws function, in many instances, as delegations of discretion to the police to act in ways which formally we decline to extend to them because it would be inconsistent with certain fundamental principles with respect to the administration of criminal justice. Kadish asserts that

> . . . disorderly-conduct laws constitute, in effect, a grant of authority to the police to intervene in a great range of minor conduct, difficult or impossible legally to specify in advance, in which the police find it desirable to act. The vagrancy laws similarly delegate an authority to hold a suspect, whom police could not hold under the laws of arrest, for purposes of investigation and interrogation.[36]

To this, one might add: to hold and interrogate for the purposes of harassment—a charge frequently leveled at police by militant political groups, many of whose leaders have been intimidated by the police under the cover of such statutes. Entrapment is another example of efforts by government or police administrations to suppress political activity by luring activists and militants into the commission of crimes.[37] In their structural aspects, police and court intimidation, where the weapons of defamation, perjury, and contempt are manipulated in an effort to repudiate and malign a political foe, are no different than the ruthless actions of military forces and police toward revolutionaries in Third World countries caught up in revolution.

POLITICAL CRIME AND CRIMINALITY: II

With the development of new technologies of production, distribution, and, it must be added, destruction, through which new, more efficient thresholds of achievement are reached, the institutions which successfully incorporate these advances are enormously expanded. And it follows that

---

[36]S. H. Kadish, "The Crisis of Overcriminalization," in J. H. Skolnick and E. Currie, eds.: *Crisis in American Institutions* (Boston, Little Brown, 1970), 438.

[37]For an extended treatment of this phenomenon, see "The Problem of Entrapment," by E. Sagarin and D. E. J. MacNamara, *Crime and Delinquency* (October 1970), 368–78.

as new technologies evolve, new forms of criminal activity appear. Outside of a specific ideological context, however, air piracy, hijackings, wiretappings, and the surreptitious exchange of classified information, may be distinguished as nonpolitical criminal acts with reference to the criteria proposed by Merton and Elliott.

A special stratum of the population that cuts across all classes is the bewildering young, especially the affluent, politically conscious youth in whom radical political ideas have found their most rigorous adherents. A phenomenon that is increasingly widespread among them is stealing and shoplifting, carried off under the rubric of "ripping off" the system, or revolutionary reappropriation of goods and services. Tactically, ripping off is designed to serve two purposes: free the thief from the responsibility of his actions, and torment the establishment. Many of those who steal and pilfer genuinely feel themselves to be part of a revolutionary vanguard whose role is to subvert an allegedly debased and hopelessly philistinized world.

The psychological and intellectual underpinnings legitimating these types of criminal acts might be understood as based upon an "individual ideology" as a parallel to the "collective" ideology I have been discussing. The thief, kidnapper, hijacker, and air pirate, like the collectivity, tends to justify himself (as Freud says, he "rationalizes" his motivations and "projects" inacceptable motives onto the objects which he confronts), and he builds up a personally acceptable image of his own identity.

The individual ideology enables the person to maintain his self-esteem in the face of a possible challenge (arrest) from without. It provides him with a cognitive map of society which includes his conception of personal identity, and thus aids in the reduction of emotionally intolerable uncertainty and anxiety. Hostile impulses are channeled through the individual ideology into "acceptable" directions (ripping off the system), and the choice of action alternatives in other domains is facilitated as well. Where the structural focus of the collective ideology is the authority system, the organization of individual ideologies is structured by contrast around the conception of individual identity. The differences of these foci make for certain irreducible divergencies between the individual and collective levels of legitimation. In no case can the analysis of collectivities avoid the assessment of the sometimes complex relations among the various collective and individual ideologies.

SUMMARY

Many of the revolutionary nationalist ideologies emerging in Third World countries contain within their corpus of knowledge and action-agendas reality constructs and value-orientations—ontologies—which legitimate claims for power and prestige and justify the behavior of participants. At one level, ideologies of this sort function as legitimating symbolizations; that is, they equip a group or an individual with justificatory devices, enabling them to proceed in their actions (systematic destruction of a government) unencumbered by traditional cultural constraints. As symbolic instruments, these doctrines have been successfully used in the achievement of political unification by mobilizing the energies of disparate millenarian movements and social-bandit groups as well as channeling hostility and anguish against a clearly defined "enemy of the people."

It has been observed that complex labelling and explanatory apparatuses constitute a major part of the ideology furnishing its practitioners with constructs of imaginary reference groups (utopias) of wider scope than the established system. Moreover, such alienative radicalisms have been able to incorporate escapist sectarianism by appeals to more comprehensive values as well as implement frontal attacks on existing political regimes deemed unworthy of further continuity.

Revolutionary nationalist ideologies are in some ways unreflecting totalizations in which no component or sector of social life is alien to its purview, the consuming ambition of ideological thought being to symbolize everything. These political and social grammars codify actions in moral terms as they apply to the people and their "enemies." All of the flaws and contradictions of social life are inspected and subjected to sociopolitical evaluation; through an ideology's conceptual and labelling machinery, ruling regimes, landed aristocracies, and impoverished peasants are cast in their appropriate roles and portrayed as either heroes or criminals. Perhaps the most important social data communicated by contemporary revolutionary ideologies are its models of defiance and rebellion.

PART FOUR: PROCESSES OF INTEREST GROUP CONFLICT

Individuals occupy numerous positions in society. In these social locations, whether occupational, religious, or political, people experience life in different ways. Much of their interaction is normative, that is, the common assumptions of everyday life are not violated or disrupted. However, some events are outside of the "common sense world" or expected "definition of the situation." Many of these occurrences are dismissed as merely manifestations of insanity or some other freakishness. But some unique events, as the philosopher John Dewey and others have noted, may impinge upon what is considered as acceptable or correct. It is in this context that laws may be passed or revolutions born. Karl Mannheim (1936: 64) observes:

> Only in a world in upheaval, in which fundamental new values are being created and old ones destroyed, can intellectual conflict go so far that antagonists will seek to annihilate not merely the specific beliefs and attitudes of one another but also the intellectual foundations upon which these beliefs and attitudes rest.

The "consciousness of dysfunction" (Rush and Denisoff, 1971:185–191) refers to a problem that a group in society desires to correct. The location of a social group, according to conflict theorists, will in part determine the type of solution desired. Karl Marx, in his famous concept of "class consciousness," argued that the working class, because of its unique position, would see the contradictions of capitalist society and strive to change them. The workers' special position lay in the fact that *they* were being exploited by the system. What was necessary, according to Marx, was that they become aware of this position *and* desirous of changing it. Consequently, Marx said that *objective* social position must be complemented by *subjective* awareness of this location. The objective position was called "a class *in* itself" and subjective awareness "a class *for* itself." As summarized by C. Wright Mills (1951:325), class consciousness must include:

> 1) A rational awareness and identification with one's own class interests; 2) an awareness of and rejection of other class interests as illegitimate; and 3) an awareness of and a readiness to use collective political means to the collective political end of realizing one's interests.

Ralf Dahrendorf (1959:187) transformed this definition to connote *manifest interests,* that is "that emotion, will, and desire" be directed toward a goal. Manifest interests are articulated as programs of action by organized groups.

Thus, class consciousness and manifest interests, the essential ingredients of conflict, involve the awareness of one group that a problem exists that is to be solved only through the political and legislative process. If this process cannot rectify the situation, the implication is that the system itself must be changed. Chalmers Johnson (1964:5) in his explanation of political revolution notes that "social change is action undertaken to alter the structure of the system for the purpose of relieving the condition of dysfunction." In revolutionary rhetoric, Johnson is saying: If the system will not respond to the people, the people will change that system.

Earlier, we presented some of these same theoretical perspectives as they applied to the process of criminalization. Vold, Turk, and Quinney postulate that the application of criminal definitions to individuals and behavior is a manifestation of conflict within a society. The legislation and enforcement of law are stigmatizing procedures designed to protect and perpetuate the interests of certain groups with the power to influence public policy. The selections in Part Four present specific examples of the influence of interest groups: how they instigate, alter, or restrain the enactment of law, and how the differential enforcement of law is indicative of a conflict of interests.

Howard S. Becker, who is generally not considered a "conflict" theorist but is placed in the "interactionist" or "labelling"[1] school, underlines the impact of consciousness in relation to deviance. In this sense his premises are consistent with those of the conflict perspectives:

> Factions within [a society or social group] disagree and maneuver to have their own definition of the group's function [goal] accepted.

---

[1]For a comprehensive explication and systematization of the labelling approach, see Schur (1971).

The function of the group or organization, then, is decided in political conflict, not given in the nature of the organization. If this is true, then it is likewise true that the questions of what rules are to be enforced, what behavior regarded as deviant, and which people labelled as outsiders must also be regarded as political (Becker, 1963:7).

And:

Social groups create deviance by making the rules whose infraction constitutes deviance (Becker, 1963:9).

The selection by Becker sets the tone for this part by pointing out instances of how interest groups or "moral entrepreneurs" are instrumental in obtaining legislation, prohibition and the sex psychopath laws being cases in point. He also reinforces an important distinction between *rule creation* and *rule enforcement*. The road to procuring the state's assistance in recognizing the "legitimacy" of one's interests is perilous and uncertain. But even success in the creation of a law carries no assurances. The enforcers' more pragmatic view of things based on community expectations, their own particular brand of bias, and a wide latitude of discretion all may conspire to effectively nullify the law's intent. In short, enforcers are yet another dimension of the conflict situation in society. This factor will be further explored in Part Five.

Moral crusaders are in fact groups acting on their basic interests as defined by their social location. Chambliss, Molotch, McCaghy and Denisoff examine the interaction of objective and subjective definitions of the situation and how they may be translated into the "creation of rules." Chambliss analyzes the role of "vested interest" groups in the formulating and altering of laws concerning vagrancy. In recent times the content of these laws has come under increasing attack. In February 1972 the United States Supreme Court dealt vagrancy laws a severe blow when it ruled an ordinance unconstitutional in the case of *Papachristou et al. v. City of Jacksonville, Florida.* The Court took issue with the law's vagueness as to the exact conduct that is forbidden and with the "unfettered discretion it places in the hands of police." The decision pointed out that:

Those generally implicated by the imprecise terms of the ordinance —poor people, nonconformists, dissenters, idlers—may be required to comport themselves according to the life-style deemed appropriate by the Jacksonville police and courts.

A contemporary example of interest group conflict is presented by Molotch in his description of reactions toward an oil spill in Santa Barbara Channel. It is a chronicle of a struggle over decision-making power: the issues, the parties involved, and the evolution of the forms of conflict. The usual targets of legislation or those whose interests are neglected in legislation usually can be described as politically impotent minority groups. The Santa Barbara case is unique in that it involved elites. Both opposing groups apparently possessed sufficient political strength to gain concessions. But for all their affluence and political unity the Santa Barbarans were no match for the oil companies. The companies' interests proved to be indistinguishable from those of the authority structure.

The problematic process of obtaining legislation to protect one's interests is further illustrated in the article by McCaghy and Denisoff. This selection primarily concerns the conflicts involved in the actual lawmaking process itself; that is, when the interest groups take their case into the legislative arena.[2] It is evident from the history of attempts to obtain federal protection against record piracy that legislative action against even a politically powerless opponent is not a matter of simply requesting it. Superficially, at least, there was little disagreement that the pirates were "wrong" and that protection for record manufacturers was needed. But political realities operated to forestall legislation for decades.

As pointed out by Turk and Quinney (see Part Two) and later by Becker, the creation of law is only one aspect of the criminalization process. The implementation of law is delegated to the police and courts. While the law may provide direction, its ultimate application rests with these enforcement agents who may or may not have a commitment to the interests of those originally responsible for the law. The discretionary power of these agents enables them to act in their own interests against politically powerless groups the authorities wish to control. Just as law is the product of interest group conflict, so too is its enforcement. The final article in this part portrays such a conflict: that between authorities and hippies as it is manifested by rigorous application of law, harassment, illegal search practices, and the selective use of unwarranted violence.

The articles in Part Four indicate that while lines of conflict may appear to be clearly drawn between interest groups, the outcomes of the conflict rest on any number of intricate contingencies. The propositions to consider are:

1. Specific social positions exhibit interests endemic to them.
2. Social location alone is not enough to motivate interest group behavior.
3. For conflict to occur manifest interests must be present.
4. The initiation of the criminalization process is a product of manifest interest group behavior.
5. Interest group conflict is present at every level of the criminalization process.

---

[2] For a somewhat similar analysis of the prostitution law in New York State, see Roby (1969).

6. For the criminalization process to be completed, the interests of the law enforcers must concur with those of the law creators.

REFERENCES

BECKER, H. S., *Outsiders: Studies in the Sociology of Deviance.* New York: Free Press of Glencoe, 1963.

DAHRENDORF, R., *Class and Class Conflict in Industrial Society.* Stanford: Stanford University Press, 1959.

JOHNSON, C., *Revolution and the Social System.* Stanford: Hoover Institution Studies, 1964.

MANNHEIM, K., *Ideology and Utopia: An Introduction to the Sociology of Knowledge.* New York: Harcourt, Brace and World, 1936.

MILLS, C. W., *White Collar: The American Middle Class.* New York: Oxford University Press, 1951.

ROBY, P. A., "Politics and Criminal Law: Revision of the New York State Penal Law on Prostitution," *Social Problems,* 17 (Summer 1969): 83–109.

RUSH, G. B., and R. SERGE DENISOFF, *Social and Political Movements.* New York: Appleton-Century-Crofts, 1971.

SCHUR, E. M., *Labelling Deviant Behavior: Its Sociological Implications.* New York: Harper and Row, 1971.

HOWARD S. BECKER

Rules are the products of someone's initiative and we can think of the people who exhibit such enterprise as *moral entrepreneurs*. Two related species—rule creators and rule enforcers—will occupy our attention.

RULE CREATORS

The prototype of the rule creator, but not the only variety as we shall see, is the crusading reformer. He is interested in the content of rules. The existing rules do not satisfy him because there is some evil which profoundly disturbs him. He feels that nothing can be right in the world until rules are made to correct it. He operates with an absolute ethic; what he sees is truly and totally evil with no qualification. Any means is justified to do away with it. The crusader is fervent and righteous, often self-righteous.

It is appropriate to think of reformers as crusaders because they typically believe that their mission is a holy one. The prohibitionist serves as an excellent example, as does the person who wants to suppress vice and sexual delinquency or the person who wants to do away with gambling.

These examples suggest that the moral crusader is a meddling busybody, interested in forcing his own morals on others. But this is a one-sided view. Many moral crusades have strong humanitarian overtones. The crusader is not only interested in seeing to it that other people do what he thinks right. He believes that if they do what is right it will be good for them. Or he may feel that his reform will prevent certain kinds of exploitation of one person by another. Prohibitionists felt that they were not simply forcing their morals on others, but attempting to provide the conditions for a better way of life for people prevented by drink from realizing a truly good life. Abolitionists were not simply trying to prevent slave owners from doing the wrong thing; they were trying to help slaves to achieve a better life. Because of the importance of the humanitarian motive, moral crusaders (despite their relatively single-minded devotion to their particular cause) often lend their support to other humanitarian crusades. Joseph Gusfield has pointed out that:

> The American temperance movement during the 19th century was part of a general effort toward the improvement of the worth of the human being through improved morality as well as economic conditions. The mixture of the religious, the equalitarian, and the humanitarian was an outstanding facet of the moral reformism of many movements. Temperance supporters formed a large segment of movements such as sabbatarianism, abolition, woman's rights, agrarianism, and humanitarian attempts to improve the lot of the poor. . . .
> In its auxiliary interests the WCTU revealed a great concern for the improvement of the welfare of the lower classes. It was active in campaigns to secure penal reform, to shorten working hours and raise wages for workers, and to abolish child labor and in a number of other humanitarian and equalitarian activities. In the 1880's the WCTU worked to bring about legislation for the protection of working girls against the exploitation by men.[1]

As Gusfield says, "Moral reformism of this type suggests the approach of a dominant class toward those less favorably situated in the economic and social structure."[2] Moral crusaders typically want to help those beneath them to achieve a better status. That those beneath them do not always like the means proposed for their salvation is another matter. But this fact—that moral crusades are typically dominated by those in the upper levels of the social structure—means that they add to the power they derive from the legitimacy of their moral position, the power they derive from their superior position in society.

Naturally, many moral crusades draw support from people whose motives are less pure than those of the crusader. Thus, some industrialists supported Prohibition because they felt it would provide them with a more manageable labor force.[3] Similarly, it is sometimes rumored that Nevada gambling interests support the opposition to attempts to legalize gambling in California because it would cut so heavily into their business, which depends in substantial measure on the population of Southern California.[4]

---

[1]Joseph R. Gusfield, "Social Structure and Moral Reform: A Study of the Woman's Christian Temperance Union," *American Journal of Sociology*, LXI (November, 1955), 223.

[2]*Ibid.*

[3]See Raymond G. McCarthy, editor, *Drinking and Intoxication* (New Haven and New York: Yale Center of Alcohol Studies and The Free Press of Glencoe, 1959), pp. 395–96.

[4]This is suggested in Oscar Lewis, *Sagebrush Casinos: The Story of Legal Gambling in Nevada* (New York: Doubleday and Co., 1953), pp. 233–234.

The moral crusader, however, is more concerned with ends than with means. When it comes to drawing up specific rules (typically in the form of legislation to be proposed to a state legislature or the Federal Congress), he frequently relies on the advice of experts. Lawyers, expert in the drawing up of acceptable legislation, often play this role. Government bureaus in whose jurisdiction the problem falls may also have the necessary expertise, as did the Federal Bureau of Narcotics in the case of the marihuana problem.

As psychiatric ideology, however, becomes increasingly acceptable, a new expert has appeared—the psychiatrist. Sutherland, in his discussion of the natural history of sexual psychopath laws, pointed to the psychiatrist's influence.[5] He suggests the following as the conditions under which the sexual psychopath law, which provides that a person "who is diagnosed as a sexual psychopath may be confined for an indefinite period in a state hospital for the insane,"[6] will be passed.

> First, these laws are customarily enacted after a state of fear has been aroused in a community by a few serious sex crimes committed in quick succession. This is illustrated in Indiana, where a law was passed following three or four sexual attacks in Indianapolis, with murder in two. Heads of families bought guns and watch dogs, and the supply of locks and chains in the hardware stores of the city was completely exhausted. . . .
>
> A second element in the process of developing sexual psychopath laws is the agitated activity of the community in connection with the fear. The attention of the community is focused on sex crimes, and people in the most varied situations envisage dangers and see the need of and possibility for their control. . . .
>
> The third phase in the development of these sexual psychopath laws has been the appointment of a committee. The committee gathers the many conflicting recommendations of persons and groups of persons, attempts to determine "facts," studies precedures in other states, and makes recommendations, which generally include bills for the legislature. Although the general fear usually subsides within a few days, a committee has the formal duty of following through until positive action is taken. Terror which does not result in a committee is much less likely to result in a law.[7]

In the case of sexual psychopath laws, there usually is no government agency charged with dealing in a specialized way with sexual deviations. Therefore, when the need for expert advice in drawing up legislation

---

[5]Edwin H. Sutherland, "The Diffusion of Sexual Psychopath Laws," *American Journal of Sociology,* LVI (September, 1950), 142–148.

[6]*Ibid.*, p. 142.

[7]*Ibid.*, pp. 143–45.

arises, people frequently turn to the professional group most closely associated with such problems:

> In some states, at the committee stage of the development of a sexual psychopath law, psychiatrists have played an important part. The psychiatrists, more than any others, have been the interest group back of the laws. A committee of psychiatrists and neurologists in Chicago wrote the bill which became the sexual psychopath law of Illinois; the bill was sponsored by the Chicago Bar Association and by the state's attorney of Cook County and was enacted with little opposition in the next session of the State Legislature. In Minnesota all the members of the governor's committee except one were psychiatrists. In Wisconsin the Milwaukee Neuropsychiatric Society shared in pressing the Milwaukee Crime Commission for the enactment of a law. In Indiana the attorney-general's committee received from the American Psychiatric Association copies of all of the sexual psychopath laws which had been enacted in other states.[8]

The influence of psychiatrists in other realms of the criminal law has increased in recent years.

In any case, what is important about this example is not that psychiatrists are becoming increasingly influential, but that the moral crusader, at some point in the development of his crusade, often requires the services of a professional who can draw up the appropriate rules in an appropriate form. The crusader himself is often not concerned with such details. Enough for him that the main point has been won; he leaves its implementation to others.

By leaving the drafting of the specific rule in the hands of others, the crusader opens the door for many unforeseen influences. For those who draft legislation for crusaders have their own interests, which may affect the legislation they prepare. It is likely that the sexual psychopath laws drawn up by psychiatrists contain many features never intended by the citizens who spearheaded the drives to "do something about sex crimes," features which do however reflect the professional interests of organized psychiatry.

THE FATE OF MORAL CRUSADES

A crusade may achieve striking success, as did the Prohibition movement with the passage of the Eighteenth Amendment. It may fail completely, as has the drive to do away with the use of tobacco or the anti-vivisection movement. It may achieve great success, only to find its gains whittled

---

[8]*Ibid.*, pp. 145–46.

away by shifts in public morality and increasing restrictions imposed on it by judicial interpretations; such has been the case with the crusade against obscene literature.

One major consequence of a successful crusade, of course, is the establishment of a new rule or set of rules, usually with the appropriate enforcement machinery being provided at the same time. I want to consider this consequence at some length later. There is another consequence, however, of the success of a crusade which deserves mention.

When a man has been successful in the enterprise of getting a new rule established—when he has found, so to speak, the Grail—he is out of a job. The crusade which has occupied so much of his time, energy, and passion is over. Such a man is likely, when he first began his crusade, to have been an amateur, a man who engaged in a crusade because of his interest in the issue, in the content of the rule he wanted established. Kenneth Burke once noted that a man's occupation may become his preoccupation. The equation is also good the other way around. A man's preoccupation may become his occupation. What started as an amateur interest in a moral issue may become an almost full-time job; indeed, for many reformers it becomes just this. The success of the crusade, therefore, leaves the crusader without a vocation. Such a man, at loose ends, may generalize his interest and discover something new to view with alarm, a new evil about which something ought to be done. He becomes a professional discoverer of wrongs to be righted, of situations requiring new rules.

When the crusade has produced a large organization devoted to its cause, officials of the organization are even more likely than the individual crusader to look for new causes to espouse. This process occurred dramatically in the field of health problems when the National Foundation for Infantile Paralysis put itself out of business by discovering a vaccine that eliminated epidemic poliomyelitis. Taking the less constraining name of The National Foundation, officials quickly discovered other health problems to which the organization could devote its energies and resources.

The unsuccessful crusade, either the one that finds its mission no longer attracts adherents or the one who achieves its goal only to lose it again, may follow one of two courses. On the one hand, it may simply give up its original mission and concentrate on preserving what remains of the organization that has been built up. Such, according to one study, was the fate of the Townsend Movement.[9] Or the failing movement may adhere rigidly to an increasingly less popular mission, as did the Prohibition Movement. Gusfield has described present-day members of the WCTU

---

[9]Sheldon Messinger, "Organizational Transformation: A Case Study of a Declining Social Movement," *American Sociological Review*, XX (February, 1955), 3–10.

as "moralizers-in-retreat."[10] As prevailing opinion in the United States becomes increasingly anti-temperance, these women have not softened their attitude toward drinking. On the contrary, they have become bitter at the formerly "respectable" people who no longer will support a temperance movement. The social class level from which WCTU members are drawn has moved down from the upper-middle class to the lower-middle class. The WCTU now turns to attack the middle class it once drew its support from, seeing this group as the locus of acceptance of moderate drinking. The following quotations from Gusfield's interviews with WCTU leaders give some of the flavor of the "moralizer-in-retreat":

> When this union was first organized, we had many of the most influential ladies of the city. But now they have got the idea that we ladies who are against taking a cocktail are a little queer. We have an undertaker's wife and a minister's wife, but the lawyer's and doctor's wives shun us. They don't want to be thought queer.
> We fear moderation more than anything. Drinking has become so much a part of everything—even in our church life and our colleges.
> It creeps into the official church boards. They keep it in their ice-boxes. . . . The minister here thinks that the church has gone far, that they are doing too much to help the temperance cause. He's afraid that he'll stub some influential toes.[11]

Only some crusaders, then, are successful in their mission and create, by creating a new rule, a new group of outsiders. Of the successful, some find they have a taste for crusades and seek new problems to attack. Other crusaders fail in their attempt and either support the organization they have created by dropping their distinctive mission and focusing on the problem of organizational maintenance itself or become outsiders themselves, continuing to espouse and preach a doctrine which sounds increasingly queer as time goes on.

RULE ENFORCERS

The most obvious consequence of a successful crusade is the creation of a new set of rules. With the creation of a new set of rules we often find that a new set of enforcement agencies and officials is established. Sometimes, of course, existing agencies take over the administration of the new rule, but more frequently a new set of rule enforcers is created. The passage of the Harrison Act presaged the creation of the Federal Narcotics

---

[10]Gusfield, *op. cit.*, pp. 227–28.
[11]*Ibid.*, pp. 227, 229–30.

Bureau, just as the passage of the Eighteenth Amendment led to the creation of police agencies charged with enforcing the Prohibition Laws.

With the establishment of organizations of rule enforcers, the crusade becomes institutionalized. What started out as a drive to convince the world of the moral necessity of a new rule finally becomes an organization devoted to the enforcement of the rule. Just as radical political movements turn into organized political parties and lusty evangelical sects become staid religious denominations, the final outcome of the moral crusade is a police force. To understand, therefore, how the rules creating a new class of outsiders are applied to particular people we must understand the motives and interests of police, the rule enforcers.

Although some policemen undoubtedly have a kind of crusading interest in stamping out evil, it is probably much more typical for the policeman to have a certain detached and objective view of his job. He is not so much concerned with the content of any particular rule as he is with the fact that it is his job to enforce the rule. When the rules are changed, he punishes what was once acceptable behavior just as he ceases to punish behavior that has been made legitimate by a change in the rules. The enforcer, then, may not be interested in the content of the rule as such, but only in the fact that the existence of the rule provides him with a job, a profession, and a *raison d'être*.

Since the enforcement of certain rules provides justification for his way of life, the enforcer has two interests which condition his enforcement activity: first, he must justify the existence of his position and, second, he must win the respect of those he deals with.

These interests are not peculiar to rule enforcers. Members of all occupations feel the need to justify their work and win the respect of others. Musicians, as we have seen, would like to do this but have difficulty findings ways of successfully impressing their worth on customers. Janitors fail to win their tenants' respect, but develop an ideology which stresses the quasi-professional responsibility they have to keep confidential the intimate knowledge of tenants they acquire in the course of their work.[12] Physicians, lawyers, and other professionals, more successful in winning the respect of clients, develop elaborate mechanisms for maintaining a properly respectful relationship.

In justifying the existence of his position, the rule enforcer faces a double problem. On the one hand, he must demonstrate to others that the problem still exists: the rules he is supposed to enforce have some point, because infractions occur. On the other hand, he must show that his attempts at enforcement are effective and worthwhile, that the evil he is supposed to deal with is in fact being dealt with adequately. Therefore, enforcement organizations, particularly when they are seeking funds,

---

[12]See Ray Gold, "Janitors Versus Tenants: A Status-Income Dilemma," *American Journal of Sociology*, LVII (March, 1952), 486–93.

typically oscillate between two kinds of claims. First, they say that by reason of their efforts the problem they deal with is approaching solution. But, in the same breath, they say the problem is perhaps worse than ever (though through no fault of their own) and requires renewed and increased effort to keep it under control. Enforcement officials can be more vehement than anyone else in their insistence that the problem they are supposed to deal with is still with us, in fact is more with us than ever before. In making these claims, enforcement officials provide good reason for continuing the existence of the position they occupy.

We may also note that enforcement officials and agencies are inclined to take a pessimistic view of human nature. If they do not actually believe in original sin, they at least like to dwell on the difficulties in getting people to abide by rules, on the characteristics of human nature that lead people toward evil. They are skeptical of attempts to reform rule-breakers.

The skeptical and pessimistic outlook of the rule enforcer, of course, is reinforced by his daily experience. He sees, as he goes about his work, the evidence that the problem is still with us. He sees the people who continually repeat offenses, thus definitely branding themselves in his eyes as outsiders. Yet it is not too great a stretch of the imagination to suppose that one of the underlying reasons for the enforcer's pessimism about human nature and the possibilities of reform is the fact that if human nature were perfectible and people could be permanently reformed, his job would come to an end.

In the same way, a rule enforcer is likely to believe that it is necessary for the people he deals with to respect him. If they do not, it will be very difficult to do his job; his feeling of security in his work will be lost. Therefore, a good deal of enforcement activity is devoted not to the actual enforcement of rules, but to coercing respect from the people the enforcer deals with. This means that one may be labeled as deviant not because he has actually broken a rule, but because he has shown disrespect to the enforcer of the rule.

Westley's study of policemen in a small industrial city furnishes a good example of this phenomenon. In his interview, he asked policemen, "When do you think a policeman is justified in roughing a man up?" He found that "at least 37% of the men believed that it was legitimate to use violence to coerce respect."[13] He gives some illuminating quotations from his interviews:

> Well, there are cases. For example, when you stop a fellow for a routine questioning, say a wise guy, and he starts talking back to you and telling you you are no good and that sort of thing. You know you can take a man in on a disorderly conduct charge, but you can practically never make it stick. So what you do in a case like

---

[13]William A. Westley, "Violence and the Police," *American Journal of Sociology*, LIX (July, 1953), 39.

that is to egg the guy on until he makes a remark where you can justifiably slap him and, then, if he fights back, you can call it resisting arrest.

Well, a prisoner deserves to be hit when he goes to the point where he tries to put you below him.

You've gotta get rough when a man's language becomes very bad, when he is trying to make a fool of you in front of everybody else. I think most policemen try to treat people in a nice way, but usually you have to talk pretty rough. That's the only way to set a man down, to make him show a little respect.[14]

What Westley describes is the use of an illegal means of coercing respect from others. Clearly, when a rule enforcer has the option of enforcing a rule or not, the difference in what he does may be caused by the attitude of the offender toward him. If the offender is properly respectful, the enforcer may smooth the situation over. If the offender is disrespectful, then sanctions may be visited on him. Westley has shown that this differential tends to operate in the case of traffic offenses, where the policeman's discretion is perhaps at a maximum.[15] But it probably operates in other areas as well.

Ordinarily, the rule enforcer has a great deal of discretion in many areas, if only because his resources are not sufficient to cope with the volume of rule-breaking he is supposed to deal with. This means that he cannot tackle everything at once and to this extent must temporize with evil. He cannot do the whole job and knows it. He takes his time, on the assumption that the problems he deals with will be around for a long while. He establishes priorities, dealing with things in their turn, handling the most pressing problems immediately and leaving others for later. His attitude toward his work, in short, is professional. He lacks the naïve moral fervor characteristic of the rule creator.

If the enforcer is not going to tackle every case he knows at once, he must have a basis for deciding when to enforce the rule, which persons committing which acts to label as deviant. One criterion for selecting people is the "fix." Some people have sufficient political influence or know-how to be able to ward off attempts at enforcement, if not at the time of apprehension then at a later stage in the process. Very often, this function is professionalized; someone performs the job on a full-time basis, available to anyone who wants to hire him. A professional thief describes fixers this way:

There is in every large city a regular fixer for professional thieves. He has no agents and does not solicit and seldom takes any case

---

[14]*Ibid.*
[15]See William A. Westley, "The Police: A Sociological Study of Law, Custom, and Morality" (unpublished Ph.D. dissertation, University of Chicago, Department of Sociology, 1951).

except that of a professional thief, just as they seldom go to anyone except him. This centralized and monopolistic system of fixing for professional thieves is found in practically all of the large cities and many of the small ones.[16]

Since it is mainly professional thieves who know about the fixer and his operations, the consequence of this criterion for selecting people to apply the rules to is that amateurs tend to be caught, convicted, and labeled deviant much more frequently than professionals. As the professional thief notes:

> You can tell by the way the case is handled in court when the fix is in. When the copper is not very certain he has the right man, or the testimony of the copper and the complainant does not agree, or the prosecutor goes easy on the defendant, or the judge is arrogant in his decisions, you can always be sure that someone has got the work in. This does not happen in many cases of theft, for there is one case of a professional to twenty-five or thirty amateurs who know nothing about the fix. These amateurs get the hard end of the deal every time. The coppers bawl out about the thieves, no one holds up his testimony, the judge delivers an oration, and all of them get credit for stopping a crime wave. When the professional hears the case immediately preceding his own, he will think, "He should have got ninety years. It's the damn amateurs who cause all the heat in the stores." Or else he thinks, "Isn't it a damn shame for that copper to send that kid away for a pair of hose, and in a few minutes he will agree to a small fine for me for stealing a fur coat?" But if the coppers did not send the amateurs away to strengthen their records of convictions, they could not sandwich in the professionals whom they turn loose.[17]

Enforcers of rules, since they have no stake in the content of particular rules themselves, often develop their own private evaluation of the importance of various kinds of rules and infractions of them. This set of priorities may differ considerably from those held by the general public. For instance, drug users typically believe (and a few policemen have personally confirmed it to me) that police do not consider the use of marihuana to be as important a problem or as dangerous a practice as the use of opiate drugs. Police base this conclusion on the fact that, in their experience, opiate users commit other crimes (such as theft or prostitution) in order to get drugs, while marihuana users do not.

Enforcers, then, responding to the pressures of their own work situation, enforce rules and create outsiders in a selective way. Whether a

---

[16]Edwin H. Sutherland (editor), *The Professional Thief* (Chicago: University of Chicago Press, 1937), pp. 87–88.
[17]*Ibid.*, pp. 91–92.

person who commits a deviant act is in fact labeled a deviant depends on many things extraneous to his actual behavior: whether the enforcement official feels that at this time he must make some show of doing his job in order to justify his position, whether the misbehaver shows proper deference to the enforcer, whether the "fix" has been put in, and where the kind of act he has committed stands on the enforcer's list of priorities.

The professional enforcer's lack of fervor and routine approach to dealing with evil may get him into trouble with the rule creator. The rule creator, as we have said, is concerned with the content of the rules that interest him. He sees them as the means by which evil can be stamped out. He does not understand the enforcer's long-range approach to the same problems and cannot see why all the evil that is apparent cannot be stamped out at once.

When the person interested in the content of a rule realizes or has called to his attention the fact that enforcers are dealing selectively with the evil that concerns him, his righteous wrath may be aroused. The professional is denounced for viewing the evil too lightly, for failing to do his duty. The moral entrepreneur, at whose instance the rule was made, arises again to say that the outcome of the last crusade has not been satisfactory or that the gains once made have been whittled away and lost.

DEVIANCE AND ENTERPRISE: A SUMMARY

Deviance—in the sense I have been using it, of publicly labeled wrong-doing—is always the result of enterprise. Before any act can be viewed as deviant, and before any class of people can be labeled and treated as outsiders for committing the act, someone must have made the rule which defines the act as deviant. Rules are not made automatically. Even though a practice may be harmful in an objective sense to the group in which it occurs, the harm needs to be discovered and pointed out. People must be made to feel that something ought to be done about it. Someone must call the public's attention to these matters, supply the push necessary to get things done, and direct such energies as are aroused in the proper direction to get a rule created. Deviance is the product of enterprise in the largest sense; without the enterprise required to get rules made, the deviance which consists of breaking the rule could not exist.

Deviance is the product of enterprise in the smaller and more particular sense as well. Once a rule has come into existence, it must be applied to particular people before the abstract class of outsiders created by the rule can be peopled. Offenders must be discovered, identified, apprehended and convicted (or noted as "different" and stigmatized for their noncon-formity, as in the case of legal deviant groups such as dance musicians).

This job ordinarily falls to the lot of professional enforcers who, by enforcing already existing rules, create the particular deviants society views as outsiders.

It is an interesting fact that most scientific research and speculation on deviance concerns itself with the people who break rules rather than with those who make and enforce them. If we are to achieve a full understanding of deviant behavior, we must get these two possible foci of inquiry into balance. We must see deviance, and the outsiders who personify the abstract conception, as a consequence of a process of interaction between people, some of whom in the service of their own interests make and enforce rules which catch others who, in the service of their own interests, have committed acts which are labeled deviant.

16. A SOCIOLOGICAL ANALYSIS
OF THE LAW OF VAGRANCY

WILLIAM J. CHAMBLISS

With the outstanding exception of Jerome Hall's analysis of theft[1] there has been a severe shortage of sociologically relevant analyses of the relationship between particular laws and the social setting in which these laws emerge, are interpreted, and take form. The paucity of such studies is somewhat surprising in view of widespread agreement that such studies are not only desirable but absolutely essential to the development of a mature sociology of law.[2] A fruitful method of establishing the direction and pattern of this mutual influence is to systematically analyze particular legal categories, to observe the changes which take place in the categories and to explain how these changes are themselves related to and stimulate changes in the society. This paper is an attempt to provide such an analysis of the law of vagrancy in Anglo-American Law.

LEGAL INNOVATION: THE EMERGENCE OF
THE LAW OF VAGRANCY IN ENGLAND

There is general agreement among legal scholars that the first full-fledged vagrancy statute was passed in England in 1349. As is generally the case with legislative innovations, however, this statute was preceded by earlier laws which established a climate favorable to such change. The most significant forerunner to the 1349 vagrancy statute was in 1274 when it was provided:

Reprinted from *Social Problems* 12 (Summer 1964), 67–77 by permission of The Society for the Study of Social Problems and the author.
For a more complete listing of most of the statutes dealt with in this report the reader is referred to Burn, *The History of the Poor Laws.* Citations of English statutes should be read as follows: 3 Ed. 1. c. 1. refers to the third act of Edward the first, chapter one, etc.

[1]Hall, J., *Theft, Law and Society,* Bobbs-Merrill, 1939. See also, Alfred R. Lindesmith, "Federal Law and Drug Addiction," *Social Problems,* Vol. 7, No. 1, 1959, p. 48.

[2]See, for example, Rose, A., "Some Suggestions for Research in the Sociology of Law," *Social Problems,* Vol. 9, No. 3, 1962, pp. 281–283, and Geis, G., "Sociology, Criminology, and Criminal Law," *Social Problems,* Vol. 7, No. 1, 1959, pp. 40–47.

Because that abbies and houses of religion have been overcharged and sore grieved, by the resort of great men and other, so that their goods have not been sufficient for themselves, whereby they have been greatly hindered and impoverished, that they cannot maintain themselves, nor such charity as they have been accustomed to do; it is provided, that none shall come to eat or lodge in any house of religion, or any other's foundation than of his own, at the costs of the house, unless he be required by the governor of the house before his coming hither.[3]

Unlike the vagrancy statutes this statute does not intend to curtail the movement of persons from one place to another, but is solely designed to provide the religious houses with some financial relief from the burden of providing food and shelter to travelers.

The philosophy that the religious houses were to give alms to the poor and to the sick and feeble was, however, to undergo drastic change in the next fifty years. The result of this changed attitude was the establishment of the first vagrancy statute in 1349 which made it a crime to give alms to any who were unemployed while being of sound mind and body. To wit:

Because that many valiant beggars, as long as they may live of begging, do refuse to labor, giving themselves to idleness and vice, and sometimes to theft and other abominations; it is ordained, that none, upon pain of imprisonment shall, under the colour of pity or alms, give anything to such which may labour, or presume to favour them towards their desires; so that thereby they may be compelled to labour for their necessary living.[4]

It was further provided by this statute that:

. . . every man and woman, of what condition he be, free or bond, able in body, and within the age of threescore years, not living in merchandize nor exercising any craft, nor having of his own whereon to live, nor proper land whereon to occupy himself, and not serving any other, if he in convenient service (his estate considered) be required to serve, shall be bounded to serve him which shall him require . . . And if any refuse, he shall on conviction by two true men, . . . be committed to gaol till he find surety to serve.

And if any workman or servant, of what estate or condition he be, retained in any man's service, do depart from the said service without reasonable cause or license, before the term agreed on, he shall have pain of imprisonment.[5]

---

[3] 3 Ed. 1. c. 1.
[4] 35 Ed. 1. c. 1.
[5] 23 Ed. 3.

There was also in this statute the stipulation that the workers should receive a standard wage. In 1351 this statute was strengthened by the stipulation:

> And none shall go out of the town where he dwelled in winter to serve the summer, if he may serve in the same town.[6]

By 34 Ed 3 (1360) the punishment for these acts became imprisonment for fifteen days and if they "do not justify themselves by the end of that time, to be sent to gaol till they do."

A change in official policy so drastic as this did not, of course, occur simply as a matter of whim. The vagrancy statutes emerged as a result of changes in other parts of the social structure. The prime mover for this legislative innovation was the Black Death which struck England about 1348. Among the many disastrous consequences this had upon the social structure was the fact that it decimated the labor force. It is estimated that by the time the pestilence had run its course at least fifty per cent of the population of England had died from the plague. This decimation of the labor force would necessitate drastic innovations in any society but its impact was heightened in England where, at this time, the economy was highly dependent upon a ready supply of cheap labor.

Even before the pestilence, however, the availability of an adequate supply of cheap labor was becoming a problem for the landowners. The crusades and various wars had made money necessary to the lords and, as a result, the lord frequently agreed to sell the serfs their freedom in order to obtain the needed funds. The serfs, for their part, were desirous of obtaining their freedom (by "fair means" or "foul") because the larger towns which were becoming more industrialized during this period could offer the serf greater personal freedom as well as a higher standard of living. This process is nicely summarized by Bradshaw:

> By the middle of the 14th century the outward uniformity of the manorial system had become in practice considerably varied . . . for the peasant had begun to drift to the towns and it was unlikely that the old village life in its unpleasant aspects should not be resented. Moreover the constant wars against France and Scotland were fought mainly with mercenaries after Henry III's time and most villages contributed to the new armies. The bolder serfs either joined the armies or fled to the towns, and even in the villages the free men who held by villein tenure were as eager to commute their services as the serfs were to escape. Only the amount of "free" labor available enabled the lord to work his demense in many places.[7]

---

[6]25 Ed. 3 (1351).
[7]Bradshaw, F., *A Social History of England*, p. 54.

And he says regarding the effect of the Black Death:

> . . . in 1348 the Black Death reached England and the vast mortality
> that ensued destroyed that reserve of labour which alone had made
> the manorial system even nominally possible.[8]

The immediate result of these events was of course no surprise: Wages
for the "free" man rose considerably and this increased, on the one hand,
the landowner's problems and, on the other hand, the plight of the unfree
tenant. For although wages increased for the personally free laborers, it
of course did not necessarily add to the standard of living of the serf; if
anything it made his position worse because the landowner would be
hard pressed to pay for the personally free labor which he needed and
would thus find it more and more difficult to maintain the standard of
living for the serf which he had heretofore supplied. Thus the serf had
no alternative but flight if he chose to better his position. Furthermore,
flight generally meant both freedom and better conditions since the possibility of work in the new weaving industry was great and the chance of
being caught small.[9]

It was under these conditions that we find the first vagrancy statutes
emerging. There is little question but that these statutes were designed
for one express purpose: to force laborers (whether personally free or
unfree) to accept employment at a low wage in order to insure the landowner an adequate supply of labor at a price he could afford to pay. Caleb
Foote concurs with this interpretation when he notes:

> The anti-migratory policy behind vagrancy legislation began as an
> essential complement of the wage stabilization legislation which ac-
> companied the breakup of feudalism and the depopulation caused
> by the Black Death. By the Statutes of Labourers in 1349–1351,
> every ablebodied person without other means of support was re-
> quired to work for wages fixed at the level preceding the Black
> Death; it was unlawful to accept more, or to refuse an offer to work,
> or to flee from one county to another to avoid offers to work or to
> seek higher wages, or to give alms to able-bodied beggars who re-
> fused to work.[10]

In short, as Foote says in another place, this was an "attempt to make the
vagrancy statutes a substitute for serfdom."[11] This same conclusion is
equally apparent from the wording of the statute where it is stated:

> Because great part of the people, and especially of workmen and
> servants, late died in pestilence; many seeing the necessity of mas-

---

[8]*Ibid.*
[9]*Ibid.*, p. 57.
[10]Foote, C., "Vagrancy Type Law and Its Administration," *Univ. of Pennsylvania Law Review*
(104), 1956, p. 615.
[11]*Ibid.*

ters, and great scarcity of servants, will not serve without excessive wages, and some rather willing to beg in idleness than by labour to get their living: it is ordained, that every man and woman, of what condition he be, free or bond, able in body and within the age of threescore years, not living in merchandize, (etc.) be required to serve. . .

The innovation in the law, then, was a direct result of the aforementioned changes which had occurred in the social setting. In this case these changes were located for the most part in the economic institution of the society. The vagrancy laws were designed to alleviate a condition defined by the lawmakers as undesirable. The solution was to attempt to force a reversal, as it were, of a social process which was well underway; that is, to curtail mobility of laborers in such a way that labor would not become a commodity for which the landowners would have to compete.

Statutory Dormancy: A Legal Vestige. In time, of course, the curtailment of the geographical mobility of laborers was no longer requisite. One might well expect that when the function served by the statute was no longer an important one for the society, the statutes would be eliminated from the law. In fact, this has not occurred. The vagrancy statutes have remained in effect since 1349. Furthermore, as we shall see in some detail later, they were taken over by the colonies and have remained in effect in the United States as well.

The substance of the vagrancy statutes change very little for some time after the first ones in 1349–1351 although there was a tendency to make punishments more harsh than originally. For example, in 1360 it was provided that violators of the statute should be imprisoned for fifteen days[12] and in 1388 the punishment was to put the offender in the stocks and to keep him there until "he find surety to return to his service."[13] That there was still, at this time, the intention of providing the landowner with labor is apparent from the fact that this statute provides:

> and he or she which use to labour at the plough and cart, or other labour and service of husbandry, till they be of the age of 12 years, from thenceforth shall abide at the same labour without being put to any mastery or handicraft: and any covenant of apprenticeship to the contrary shall be void.[14]

The next alteration in the statutes occurs in 1495 and is restricted to an increase in punishment. Here it is provided that vagrants shall be "set in stocks, there to remain by the space of three days and three nights, and there to have none other sustenance but bread and water; and after the

---

[12]34 Ed. 3 (1360).
[13]12 R. 2 (1388).
[14]*Ibid.*

said three days and nights, to be had out and set at large, and then to be commanded to avoid the town."[15]

The tendency to increase the severity of punishment during this period seems to be the result of a general tendency to make finer distinctions in the criminal law. During this period the vagrancy statutes appear to have been fairly inconsequential in either their effect as a control mechanism or as a generally enforced statue.[16] The processes of social change in the culture generally and the trend away from serfdom and into "free" economy obviated the utility of these statutes. The result was not unexpected. The judiciary did not apply the law and the legislators did not take it upon themselves to change the law. In short, we have here a period of dormancy in which the statute is neither applied nor altered significantly.

A SHIFT IN FOCAL CONCERN

Following the squelching of the Peasant's Revolt in 1381, the services of the serfs to the lord " . . . tended to become less and less exacted, although in certain forms they lingered on till the seventeenth century. . . . By the sixteenth century few knew that there were any bondmen in England . . . and in 1575 Queen Elizabeth listened to the prayers of almost the last serfs in England . . . and granted them manumission."[17]

In view of this change we would expect corresponding changes in the vagrancy laws. Beginning with the lessening of punishment in the statute of 1503 we find these changes. However, instead of remaining dormant (or becoming more so) or being negated altogether, the vagrancy statutes experienced a shift in focal concern. With this shift the statutes served a new and equally important function for the social order of England. The first statute which indicates this change was in 1530. In this statute (22 H.8.c. 12 1530) it was stated:

> If any person, being whole and mighty in body, and able to labour, be taken in begging, or be vagrant and can give no reckoning how he lawfully gets his living; . . . and all other idle persons going about, some of them using divers and subtil crafty and unlawful games and plays, and some of them feigning themselves to have knowledge of . . . crafty sciences . . . shall be punished as provided.

What is most significant about this statute is the shift from an earlier concern with laborers to a concern with *criminal* activities. To be sure, the stipulation of persons "being whole and mighty in body, and able to

---

[15]11 H. & C. 2 (1495).

[16]As evidence for this note the expectation that ". . . the common gaols of every shire are likely to be greatly pestered with more numbers of prisoners than heretofore . . . " when the statutes were changed by the statute of 14 Ed. c. 5 (1571).

[17]Bradshaw, *op. cit.*, p. 61.

labour, be taken in begging, or be vagrant" sounds very much like the concerns of the earlier statutes. Some important differences are apparent however when the rest of the statute includes those who " . . . can give no reckoning how he lawfully gets his living"; "some of them using divers subtil and unlawful games and plays." This is the first statute which specifically focuses upon these kinds of criteria for adjudging someone a vagrant.

It is significant that in this statute the severity of punishment is increased so as to be greater not only than provided by the 1503 statute but the punishment is more severe than that which had been provided by *any* of the pre-1503 statutes as well. For someone who is merely idle and gives no reckoning of how he makes his living the offender shall be:

> . . . had to the next market town, or other place where they [the constables] shall think most convenient, and there to be tied to the end of a cart naked, and to be beaten with whips throughout the same market town or other place, till his body be bloody by reason of such whipping.[18]

But, for those who use "divers and subtil crafty and unlawful games and plays," etc., the punishment is " . . . whipping at two days together in manner aforesaid."[19] For the second offense, such persons are:

> . . . scourged two days, and the third day to be put upon the pillory from nine of the clock till eleven before noon of the same day and to have one of his ears cut off.[20]

And if he offend the third time " . . . to have like punishment with whipping, standing on the pillory and to have his other ear cut off."

This statute (1) makes a distinction between types of offenders and applies the more severe punishment to those who are clearly engaged in "criminal" activities, (2) mentions a specific concern with categories of "unlawful" behavior, and (3) applies a type of punishment (cutting off the ear) which is generally reserved for offenders who are defined as likely to be a fairly serious criminal.

Only five years later we find for the first time that the punishment of death is applied to the crime of vagrancy. We also note a change in terminology in the statute:

> and if any ruffians . . . after having been once apprehended . . . shall wander, loiter, or idle use themselves and play the vagabonds . . . shall be eftfoons not only whipped again, but shall have the gristle of his right ear clean cut off. And if he shall again offend, he shall be

---

[18]22 H. 8. c. 12 (1530).
[19]*Ibid.*
[20]*Ibid.*

committed to gaol till the next sessions; and being there convicted upon indictment, he shall have judgment to suffer pains and execution of death, as a felon, as an enemy of the commonwealth.[21]

It is significant that the statute now makes persons who repeat the crime of vagrancy a felon. During this period then, the focal concern of the vagrancy statutes becomes a concern for the control of felons and is no longer primarily concerned with the movement of laborers.

These statutory changes were a direct response to changes taking place in England's social structure during this period. We have already pointed out that feudalism was decaying rapidly. Concomitant with the breakup of feudalism was an increased emphasis upon commerce and industry. The commercial emphasis in England at the turn of the sixteenth century is of particular importance in the development of vagrancy laws. With commercialism came considerable traffic bearing valuable items. Where there were 169 important merchants in the middle of the fourteenth century there were 3,000 merchants engaged in foreign trade alone at the beginning of the sixteenth century.[22] England became highly dependent upon commerce for its economic support. Italians conducted a great deal of the commerce of England during this early period and were held in low repute by the populace. As a result, they were subject to attacks by citizens and, more important, were frequently robbed of their goods while transporting them. "The general insecurity of the times made any transportation hazardous. The special risks to which the alien merchant was subjected gave rise to the royal practice of issuing formally executed covenants of safe conduct through the realm."[23]

Such a situation not only called for the enforcement of existing laws but also called for the creation of new laws which would facilitate the control of persons preying upon merchants transporting goods. The vagrancy statutes were revived in order to fulfill just such a purpose. Persons who had committed no serious felony but who were suspected of being capable of doing so could be apprehended and incapacitated through the application of vagrancy laws once these laws were refocused so as to include " . . . any ruffians . . . [who] shall wander, loiter, or idle use themselves and play the vagabonds . . . "[24]

The new focal concern is continued in 1 Ed. 6. c. 3 (1547) and in fact is made more general so as to include:

> Whoever man or woman, being not lame, impotent, or so aged or diseased that he or she cannot work, not having whereon to live, shall be lurking in any house, or loitering or idle wandering by the

---

[21]27 H. 8. c. 25 (1535).
[22]Hall, *op. cit.*, p. 21.
[23]*Ibid.*, p. 23.
[24]27 H. 8. c. 25 (1535).

highway side, or in streets, cities, towns, or villages, not applying themselves to some honest labour, and so continuing for three days; or running away from their work; every such person shall be taken for a vagabond. And . . . upon conviction of two witnesses . . . the same loiterer (shall) be marked with a hot iron in the breast with the letter V, and adjudged him to the person bringing him, to be his slave for two years.

Should the vagabond run away, upon conviction, he was to be branded by a hot iron with the letter S on the forehead and to be thenceforth declared a slave forever. And in 1571 there is modification of the punishment to be inflicted, whereby the offender is to be "branded on the chest with the letter V" (for vagabond). And, if he is convicted the second time, the brand is to be made on the forehead. It is worth noting here that this method of punishment, which first appeared in 1530 and is repeated here with somewhat more force, is also an indication of a change in the type of person to whom the law is intended to apply. For it is likely that nothing so permanent as branding would be applied to someone who was wandering but looking for work, or at worst merely idle and not particularly dangerous *per se*. On the other hand, it could well be applied to someone who was likely to be engaged in other criminal activities in connection with being "vagrant."

By 1571 in the statute of 14 El. C. 5 the shift in focal concern is fully developed:

All rogues, vagabonds, and sturdy beggars shall . . . be committed to the common gaol . . . he shall be grievously whipped, and burnt thro' the gristle of the right ear with a hot iron of the compass of an inch about; . . . And for the second offense, he shall be adjudged a felon, unless some person will take him for two years in to his service. And for the third offense, he shall be adjudged guilty of felony without benefit of clergy.

And there is included a long list of persons who fall within the statute: "proctors, procurators, idle persons going about using subtil, crafty and unlawful games or plays; and some of them feigning themselves to have knowledge of . . . absurd sciences . . . and all fencers, bearwards, common players in interludes, and minstrels . . . all juglers, pedlars, tinkers, petty chapmen . . . and all counterfeiters of licenses, passports and users of the same." The major significance of this statute is that it includes all the previously defined offenders and adds some more. Significantly, those added are more clearly criminal types, counterfeiters, for example. It is also significant that there is the following qualification of this statute: "Provided also, that this act shall not extend to cookers, or harvest folks, that travel for harvest work, corn or hay."

That the changes in this statute were seen as significant is indicated by the following statement which appears in the statute:

> And whereas by reason of this act, the common gaols of every shire are like to be greatly pestered with more number of prisoners than heretofore hath been, for that the said vagabonds and other lewd persons before recited shall upon their apprehension be committed to the said gaols; it is enacted . . . [25]

And a provision is made for giving more money for maintaining the gaols. This seems to add credence to the notion that this statute was seen as being significantly more general than those previously.

It is also of importance to note that this is the first time the term *rogue* has been used to refer to persons included in the vagrancy statutes. It seems, *a priori*, that a "rogue" is a different social type than is a "vagrant" or a "vagabond"; the latter terms implying something more equilvalent to the idea of a "tramp" whereas the former (rogue) seems to imply a more disorderly and potentially dangerous person.

The emphasis upon the criminalistic aspect of vagrants continues in Chapter 17 of the same statute:

> Whereas divers *licentious* persons wander up and down in all parts of the realm, to countenance their *wicked behavior;* and do continually assemble themselves armed in the highways, and elsewhere in troops, *to the great terror* of her majesty's true subjects, *the impeachment of her laws,* and the disturbance of the peace and tranquility of the realm; and whereas many outrages are daily committed by these dissolute persons, and more are likely to ensue if speedy remedy be not provided. [Italics added]

With minor variations (*e.g.,* offering a reward for the capture of a vagrant) the statutes remain essentially of this nature until 1743. In 1743 there was once more an expansion of the types of persons included such that "all persons going about as patent gatherers, or gatherers of alms, under pretense of loss by fire or other casualty; or going about as collectors for prisons, gaols, or hospitals; all persons playing or betting at any unlawful games; and all persons who run away and leave their wives or children . . . all persons wandering abroad, and lodging in alehouses, barns, outhouses, or in the open air, not giving good account of themselves," were types of offenders added to those already included.

By 1743 the vagrancy statutes had apparently been sufficiently reconstructed by the shifts of concern so as to be once more a useful instrument in the creation of social solidarity. This function has apparently continued down to the present day in England and the changes from 1743 to the

---

[25] 14 Ed. c. 5. (1571).

present have been all in the direction of clarifying or expanding the categories covered but little has been introduced to change either the meaning or the impact of this branch of the law.

We can summarize this shift in focal concern by quoting from Halsbury. He has noted that in the vagrancy statutes:

> . . . elaborate provision is made for the relief and incidental control of destitute wayfarers. These latter, however, form but a small portion of the offenders aimed at by what are known as the Vagrancy Laws, . . . many offenders who are in no ordinary sense of the word vagrants, have been brought under the laws relating to vagrancy, and the great number of the offenses coming within the operation of these laws have little or no relation to the subject of poor relief, but are more properly directed towards the prevention of crime, the preservation of good order, and the promotion of social economy.[26]

Before leaving this section it is perhaps pertinent to make a qualifying remark. We have emphasized throughout this section how the vagrancy statutes underwent a shift in focal concern as the social setting changed. The shift in focal concern is not meant to imply that the later focus of the statutes represents a completely new law. It will be recalled that even in the first vagrancy statute there was reference to those who "do refuse labor, giving themselves to idleness and vice and sometimes to theft and other abominations." Thus the possibility of criminal activities resulting from persons who refuse to labor was recognized even in the earliest statute. The fact remains, however, that the major emphasis in this statute and in the statutes which followed the first one was always upon the "refusal to labor" or "begging." The "criminalistic" aspect of such persons was relatively unimportant. Later, as we have shown, the criminalistic potential becomes of paramount importance. The thread runs back to the earliest statute but the reason for the statutes' existence as well as the focal concern of the statutes is quite different in 1743 than it was in 1349.

VAGRANCY LAWS IN THE UNITED STATES

In general, the vagrancy laws of England, as they stood in the middle eighteenth century, were simply adopted by the states. There were some exceptions to this general trend. For example, Maryland restricted the application of vagrancy laws to "free" Negroes. In addition, for *all* states the vagrancy laws were even more explicitly concerned with the control of criminals and undesirables than had been the case in England.

---

[26]Earl of Halsbury, *The Laws of England*, Butterworth & Co., Bell Yard, Temple Bar, 1912, pp. 606–07.

New York, for example, explicitly defines prostitutes as being a category of vagrants during this period. These exceptions do not, however, change the general picture significantly and it is quite appropriate to consider the U.S. vagrancy laws as following from England's of the middle eighteenth century with relatively minor changes. The control of criminals and undesirables was the *raison d'être* of the vagrancy laws in the U.S. This is as true today as it was in 1750. As Caleb Foote's analysis of the application of vagrancy statutes in the Philadelphia court shows, these laws are presently applied indiscriminately to persons considered a "nuisance." Foote suggests that " . . . the chief significance of this branch of the criminal law lies in its quantitative impact and administrative usefulness."[27] Thus it appears that in America the trend begun in England in the sixteenth, seventeenth and eighteenth centuries has been carried to its logical extreme and the laws are now used principally as a mechanism for "clearing the streets" of the derelicts who inhabit the "skid rows" and "Bowerys" of our large urban areas.

Since the 1800's there has been an abundant source of prospects to which the vagrancy laws have been applied. These have been primarily those persons deemed by the police and the courts to be either actively involved in criminal activities or at least peripherally involved. In this context, then, the statutes have changed very little. The functions served by the statutes in England of the late eighteenth century are still being served today in both England and the United States. The locale has changed somewhat and it appears that the present day application of vagrancy statutes is focused upon the arrest and confinement of the "down and outers" who inhabit certain sections of our larger cities but the impact has remained constant. The lack of change in the vagrancy statutes, then, can be seen as a reflection of the society's perception of a continuing need to control some of its "suspicious" or "undesirable" members.[28]

A word of caution is in order lest we leave the impression that this administrative purpose is the sole function of vagrancy laws in the U.S. today. Although it is our contention that this is generally true it is worth remembering that during certain periods of our recent history, and to some extent today, these laws have also been used to control the movement of workers. This was particularly the case during the depression years and California is of course infamous for its use of vagrancy laws to restrict the admission of migrants from other states.[29] The vagrancy

---

[27]Foote, *op. cit.*, p. 613. Also see in this connection, Irwin Deutscher, "The Petty Offender," *Federal Probation*, XIX, June, 1955.

[28]It is on this point that the vagrancy statutes have been subject to criticism. See for example, Lacey, Forrest W., "Vagrancy and Other Crimes of Personal Condition," *Harvard Law Review* (66), p. 1203.

[29]Edwards v California. 314 S: 160 (1941).

statutes, because of their history, still contain germs within them which make such effects possible. Their main purpose, however, is clearly no longer the control of laborers but rather the control of the undesirable, the criminal and the "nuisance."

DISCUSSION

The foregoing analysis of the vagrancy laws has demonstrated that these laws were a legislative innovation which reflected the socially perceived necessity of providing an abundance of cheap labor to landowners during a period when serfdom was breaking down and when the pool of available labor was depleted. With the eventual breakup of feudalism the need for such laws eventually disappeared and the increased dependence of the economy upon industry and commerce rendered the former use of the vagrancy statutes unnecessary. As a result, for a substantial period the vagrancy statutes were dormant, undergoing only minor changes and, presumably, being applied infrequently. Finally, the vagrancy laws were subjected to considerable alteration through a shift in the focal concern of the statutes. Whereas in their inception the laws focused upon the "idle" and "those refusing to labor," after the turn of the sixteenth century the emphasis came to be upon "rogues," "vagabonds," and others who were suspected of being engaged in criminal activities. During this period the focus was particularly upon "roadmen" who preyed upon citizens who transported goods from one place to another. The increased importance of commerce to England during this period made it necessary that some protection be given persons engaged in this enterprise and the vagrancy statutes provided one source for such protection by re-focusing the acts to be included under these statutes.

Comparing the results of this analysis with the findings of Hall's study of theft we see a good deal of correspondence. Of major importance is the fact that both analyses demonstrate the truth of Hall's assertion that "The functioning of courts is significantly related to concomitant cultural needs, and this applies to the law of procedure as well to substantive law."[30]

Our analysis of the vagrancy laws also indicates that when changed social conditions create a perceived need for legal changes these alterations will be effected through the revision and refocusing of existing statutes. This process was demonstrated in Hall's analysis of theft as well as in our analysis of vagrancy. In the case of vagrancy, the laws were dormant when the focal concern of the laws was shifted so as to provide control over potential criminals. In the case of theft the laws were re-

---

[30]Hall, *op. cit.*, p. XII.

interpreted (interestingly, by the courts and not by the legislature) so as to include persons who were transporting goods for a merchant but who absconded with the contents of the packages transported.

It also seems probable that when the social conditions change and pre-viously useful laws are no longer useful there will be long periods when these laws will remain dormant. It is less likely that they will be officially negated. During this period of dormancy it is the judiciary which has prin-cipal responsibility for *not* applying the statutes. It is possible that one finds statutes being negated only when the judiciary stubbornly applies laws which do not have substantial public support. An example of such laws in contemporary times would be the "Blue Laws." Most states still have laws prohibiting the sale of retail goods on Sunday yet these laws are rarely applied. The laws are very likely to remain but to be dormant unless a recalcitrant judge or a vocal minority of the population insist that the laws be applied. When this happens we can anticipate that the statutes will be negated.[31] Should there arise a perceived need to curtail retail selling under some special circumstances, then it is likely that these laws will undergo a shift in focal concern much like the shift which character-ized the vagrancy laws. Lacking such application the laws will simply remain dormant except for rare instances where they will be negated.

This analysis of the vagrancy statutes (and Hall's analysis of theft as well) has demonstrated the importance of "vested interest" groups in the emergence and/or alteration of laws. The vagrancy laws emerged in order to provide the powerful landowners with a ready supply of cheap labor. When this was no longer seen as necessary and particularly when the land-owners were no longer dependent upon cheap labor nor were they a powerful interest group in the society the laws became dormant. Finally a new interest group emerged and was seen as being of great importance to the society and the laws were then altered so as to afford some pro-tection to this group. These findings are thus in agreement with Weber's contention that "status groups" determine the content of the law.[32] The findings are inconsistent, on the other hand, with the perception of the law as simply a reflection of "public opinion" as is sometimes found in the literature.[33] We should be cautious in concluding, however, that either of these positions is necessarily correct. The careful analysis of other laws, and especially of laws which do not focus so specifically upon the "crimi-nal," are necessary before this question can be finally answered.

---

[31]Negation, in this instance, is most likely to come about by the repeal of the statute. More gen-erally, however, negation may occur in several ways including the declaration of a statute as uncon-stitutional. This later mechanism has been used even for laws which have been "on the books" for long periods of time. Repeal is probably the most common, although not the only, procedure by which a law is negated.

[32]M. Rheinstein, *Max Weber on Law in Economy and Society*, Cambridge, Mass.: Harvard Uni-versity Press, 1954.

[33]Friedman, N., *Law in a Changing Society*, Berkeley and Los Angeles: University of California Press, 1959.

In conclusion, it is hoped that future analyses of changes within the legal structure will be able to benefit from this study by virtue of (1) the data provided and (2) the utilization of a set of concepts (innovation, dormancy, concern and negation) which have proved useful in the analysis of the vagrancy law. Such analyses should provide us with more substantial grounds for rejecting or accepting as generally valid the description of some of the processes which appear to characterize changes in the legal system.

HARVEY MOLOTCH

More than oil leaked from Union Oil's Platform A in the Santa Barbara Channel—a bit of truth about power in America spilled out along with it. It is the thesis of this paper that this technological "accident," like all accidents, provides clues to the realities of social structure (in this instance, arrangements) not otherwise available to the outside observer. Further, it is argued, the response of the aggrieved population (the citizenry of Santa Barbara) provides insight into the more general process which shapes disillusionment and frustration among those who come to closely examine and be injured by existing power arrangements.

A few historical details concerning the case under examination are in order. For over fifteen years, Santa Barbara's political leaders had attempted to prevent despoliation of their coastline by oil drilling on adjacent federal waters. Although they were unsuccessful in blocking eventual oil leasing (in February 1968) of *federal* waters beyond the three-mile limit, they were able to establish a sanctuary within *state* waters (thus foregoing the extraordinary revenues which leases in such areas bring to adjacent localities—e.g., the riches of Long Beach). It was therefore a great irony that the one city which voluntarily exchanged revenue for a pure environment should find itself faced, on January 28, 1969, with a massive eruption of crude oil—an eruption which was, in the end, to cover the entire city coastline (as well as much of Ventura and Santa Barbara County coastline as well) with a thick coat of crude oil. The air was soured for many hundreds of feet inland and the traditional economic base of the region (tourism) was under threat. After ten days of unsuccessful attempts, the runaway well was brought under control, only to be followed by a second eruption on February 12. This fissure was

Reprinted from *Sociological Inquiry* 40 (Winter 1970), 131–44 by permission of the publisher.
    This paper was written as Working Paper No. 8, Community and Organization Research Institute, University of California, Santa Barbara. It was delivered at the 1969 Annual Meeting of the American Sociological Association, San Francisco. A shorter version has been published in *Ramparts*, November 1969. The author wishes to thank his wife, Linda Molotch, for her active collaboration and Robert Sollen, reporter for the *Santa Barbara News-Press*, for his cooperation and critical comments on an early draft.

closed on March 3, but was followed by a sustained "seepage" of oil—a leakage which continues, at this writing, to pollute the sea, the air, and the famed local beaches. The oil companies had paid $603,000,000 for their lease rights and neither they nor the federal government bear any significant legal responsibility toward the localities which these lease rights might endanger.

If the big spill had occurred almost anywhere else (e.g., Lima, Ohio; Lompoc, California), it is likely that the current research opportunity would not have developed. But Santa Barbara is different. Of its 70,000 residents, a disproportionate number are upper class and upper middle class. They are persons who, having a wide choice of where in the world they might live, have chosen Santa Barbara for its ideal climate, gentle beauty and sophisticated "culture." Thus a large number of worldly, rich, well-educated persons—individuals with resources, spare time, and contacts with national and international elites—found themselves with a commonly shared disagreeable situation: the pollution of their otherwise near-perfect environment. Santa Barbarans thus possessed none of the "problems" which otherwise are said to inhibit effective community response to external threat: they are not urban villagers (cf. Gans, 1962); they are not internally divided and parochial like the Springdalers (cf. Vidich and Bensman, 1960); nor emaciated with self-doubt and organizational naiveté as is supposed of the ghetto dwellers. With moral indignation and high self-confidence, they set out to right the wrong so obviously done to them.

Their response was immediate. The stodgy *Santa Barbara News-Press* inaugurated a series of editorials, unique in uncompromising stridency. Under the leadership of a former State Senator and a local corporate executive, a community organization was established called "GOO" (Get Oil Out!) which took a militant stand against any and all oil activity in the Channel.

In a petition to President Nixon (eventually to gain 110,000 signatures), GOO's position was clearly stated:

> With the seabed filled with fissures in this area, similar disastrous oil operation accidents may be expected. And with one of the largest faults centered in the channel waters, one sizeable earthquake could mean possible disaster for the entire channel area.
>
> Therefore, we the undersigned do call upon the state of California and the Federal Government to promote conservation by:
>
> 1. Taking immediate action to have present offshore oil operations cease and desist at once.
> 2. Issuing no further leases in the Santa Barbara Channel.
> 3. Having all oil platforms and rigs removed from this area at the earliest possible date.

The same theme emerged in the hundreds of letters published by the *News-Press* in the weeks to follow and in the positions taken by virtually every local civic and government body. Both in terms of its volume (372 letters published in February alone) and the intensity of the revealed opinions, the flow of letters was hailed by the *News-Press* as "unprecedented." Rallies were held at the beach, GOO petitions were circulated at local shopping centers and sent to friends around the country; a fund-raising dramatic spoof of the oil industry was produced at a local high school. Local artists, playwrights, advertising men, retired executives and academic specialists from the local campus of the University of California (UCSB) executed special projects appropriate to their areas of expertise.

A GOO strategy emerged for a two-front attack. Local indignation, producing the petition to the President and thousands of letters to key members of Congress and the executive would lead to appropriate legislation. Legal action in the courts against the oil companies and the federal government would have the double effect of recouping some of the financial losses certain to be endured by the local tourist and fishing industries while at the same time serving notice that drilling would be a much less profitable operation than it was supposed to be. Legislation to ban drilling was introduced by Cranston in the U.S. Senate and Teague in the House of Representatives. Joint suits by the city and County of Santa Barbara (later joined by the State) for $1 billion in damages were filed against the oil companies and the federal government.

All of these activities—petitions, rallies, court action and legislative lobbying—were significant for their similarity in revealing faith in "the system." The tendency was to blame the oil companies. There was a muck-raking tone to the Santa Barbara response: oil and the profit-crazy executives of Union Oil were ruining Santa Barbara—but once our national and state leaders became aware of what was going on, and were provided with the "facts" of the case, justice would be done.

Indeed, there was good reason for hope. The quick and enthusiastic responses of Teague and Cranston represented a consensus of men otherwise polar opposites in their political behavior: Democrat Cranston was a charter member of the liberal California Democratic Council; Republican Teague was a staunch fiscal and moral conservative (e.g., a strong Vietnam hawk and unrelenting harasser of the local Center for the Study of Democratic Institutions). Their bills, for which there was great optimism, would have had the consequence of effecting a "permanent" ban on drilling in the Channel.

But from other quarters there was silence. Santa Barbara's representatives in the state legislature either said nothing or (in later stages) offered minimal support. It took several months for Senator Murphy to introduce Congressional legislation (for which he admitted to having little hope) which would have had the consequence of exchanging the oil companies' leases in the Channel for comparable leases in the under-exploited Elk Hills oil reserve in California's Kern County. Most disappointing of all to Santa Barbarans, Governor Reagan withheld support for proposals which would end the drilling.

As subsequent events unfolded, this seemingly inexplicable silence of the democratically elected representatives began to fall into place as part of a more general problem. American democracy came to be seen as a much more complicated affair than a system in which governmental officials actuate the desires of the "people who elected them" once those desires come to be known. Instead, increasing recognition came to be given to the "all-powerful oil lobby"; to legislators "in the pockets of Oil"; to academicians "bought" by Oil and to regulatory agencies which lobby for those they are supposed to regulate. In other words, Santa Barbarans became increasingly *ideological,* increasingly *sociological,* and in the words of some observers, increasingly *"radical."*[1] Writing from his lodgings in the area's most exclusive hotel (the Santa Barbara Biltmore), an irate citizen penned these words in his published letter to the *News-Press:*

> We the people can protest and protest and it means nothing because the industrial and military junta are the country. They tell us, the People, what is good for the oil companies is good for the People. To that I say, Like Hell! . . .
>
> Profit is their language and the proof of all this is their history (*SBNP,*[2] Feb. 26, 1969, p. A-6).

As time wore on, the editorials and letters continued in their bitterness.

THE EXECUTIVE BRANCH AND THE REGULATORY AGENCIES: DISILLUSIONMENT

From the start, Secretary Hickel's actions were regarded with suspicion. His publicized associations with Alaskan Oil interests did his reputation no good in Santa Barbara. When, after a halt to drilling (for "review" of procedures) immediately after the initial eruption, Hickel one day later ordered a resumption of drilling and production (even as the oil continued to gush into the channel), the government's response was seen as unbelievingly consistent with conservationists' worst fears. That he backed down within 48 hours and ordered a halt to drilling and production was taken as a response to the massive nationwide media play then being given to the Santa Barbara plight and to the citizens' mass outcry just then beginning to reach Washington.

---

[1]See the report of Morton Mintz in the June 29, 1969 *Washington Post.* The conjunction of these three attributes is not, in my opinion, coincidental.

[2]*SBNP* will be used to denote *Santa Barbara News-Press* throughout this paper.

Disenchantment with Hickel and the executive branch also came through less spectacular, less specific, but nevertheless genuine activity. First of all, Hickel's failure to support any of the legislation introduced to halt drilling was seen as an *action* favoring Oil. His remarks on the subject, while often expressing sympathy with Santa Barbarans[3] (and for a while placating local sentiment) were revealed as hypocritical in light of the action not taken. Of further note was the constant attempt by the Interior Department to minimize the extent of damage in Santa Barbara or to hint at possible "compromises" which were seen locally as near-total capitulation to the oil companies.

Volume of Oil Spillage. Many specific examples might be cited. An early (and continuing) issue in the oil spill was the *volume* of oil spilling into the Channel. The U.S. Geological Survey (administered by Interior), when queried by reporters, broke its silence on the subject with estimates which struck as incredible in Santa Barbara. One of the extraordinary attributes of the Santa Barbara locale is the presence of a technology establishment among the most sophisticated in the country. Several officials of the General Research Corporation (a local R & D firm with experience in marine technology) initiated studies of the oil outflow and announced findings of pollution volume at a "minimum" of ten fold the Interior estimate. Further, General Research provided (and the *News-Press* published) a detailed account of the methods used in making the estimate (cf. Allan, 1969). Despite repeated challenges from the press, Interior both refused to alter its estimate or to reveal its method for making estimates. Throughout the crisis, the divergence of the estimates remained at about ten fold.

The "seepage" was estimated by the Geological Survey to have been reduced from 1,260 gallons per day to about 630 gallons. General Research, however, estimated the leakage at the rate of 8,400 gallons per day at the same point in time as Interior's 630 gallon estimate. The lowest estimate of all was provided by an official of the Western Oil and Gas Association, in a letter to the *Wall Street Journal*. His estimate: "Probably less than 100 gallons a day" (SBNP, August 5, 1969:A-1).

Damage to Beaches. Still another point of contention was the state of the beaches at varying points in time. The oil companies, through various public relations officials, constantly minimized the actual amount of damage and maximized the effect of Union Oil's cleanup activity. What surprised (and most irritated) the locals was the fact that Interior statements implied the same goal. Thus Hickel referred at a press conference to the "recent" oil spill, providing the impression that the oil spill was over, at a time when freshly erupting oil was continuing to stain local

---

[3]Hickel publicly stated and wrote (personal communication) that the original leasing was a mistake and that he was doing all within discretionary power to solve the problem.

beaches. President Nixon appeared locally to "inspect" the damage to beaches, and Interior arranged for him to land his helicopter on a city beach which had been cleaned thoroughly in the days just before, but spared him a close-up of much of the rest of the County shoreline which continued to be coverd with a thick coat of crude oil. (The beach visited by Nixon has been oil stained on many occasions subsequent to the President's departure.) Secret servicemen kept the placards and shouts of several hundred demonstrators safely out of Presidential viewing or hearing distance.

Continuously, the Oil and Interior combine implied the beaches to be restored when Santa Barbarans knew that even a beach which looked clean was by no means restored. The *News-Press* through a comprehensive series of interviews with local and national experts on wildlife and geology made the following points clear:

(1) As long as oil remained on the water and oil continued to leak from beneath the sands, all Santa Barbara beaches were subject to continuous doses of oil—subject only to the vagaries of wind change. Indeed, all through the spill and up to the present point in time, a beach walk is likely to result in tar on the feet. On "bad days" the beaches are unapproachable.

(2) The damage to the "ecological chain" (a concept which has become a household phrase in Santa Barbara) is of unknown proportions. Much study will be necessary to learn the extent of damage.

(3) The continuous alternating natural erosion and building up of beach sands means that "clean" beaches contain layers of oil at various sublevels under the mounting sands; layers which will once again be exposed when the cycle reverses itself and erosion begins anew. Thus, it will take many years for the beaches of Santa Barbara to be completely restored, even if the present seepage is halted and no additional pollution occurs.

Damage to Wildlife. Oil on feathers is ingested by birds; continuous preening thus leads to death. In what local and national authorities called a hopeless task, two bird-cleaning centers were established to cleanse feathers and otherwise administer to damaged wild-fowl. (Oil money helped to establish and supply these centers.) Both spokesmen from Oil and the federal government then adopted these centers as sources of "data" on the extent of damage to wild-fowl. Thus, the number of dead birds due to pollution was computed on the basis of number of fatalities at the wild-fowl centers.[4] This of course is preposterous given the fact

---

[4]In a February 7 letter to Union Oil shareholders, Fred Hartley informed them that the bird refuge centers had been "very successful in their efforts." In fact, by April 30, 1969, only 150 birds (of thousands treated) had been returned to the natural habitat as "fully recovered" and the survival rate of birds treated was estimated as a miraculously high (in light of previous experience) 20 per cent (cf. *SBNP*, April 30, 1969, F-3).

that dying birds are provided with very inefficient means of propelling themselves to such designated places. The obviousness of this dramatic understatement of fatalities was never acknowledged by either Oil or Interior—although noted in Santa Barbara.

At least those birds in the hands of local ornithologists could be confirmed as dead—and this fact could not be disputed by either Oil or Interior. Not so, however, with species whose corpses are more difficult to produce on command. Several observers at the Channel Islands (a national wildlife preserve containing one of the country's largest colonies of sea animals) reported sighting unusually large numbers of dead sea-lion pups—on the oil stained shores of one of the islands. Statement and counter-statement followed with Oil's defenders arguing that the animals were not dead at all—but only appeared inert because they were sleeping. Despite the testimony of staff experts of the local Museum of Natural History and the Museum Scientist of UCSB's Biological Sciences Department that the number of "inert" sea-lion pups was far larger than normal and that field trips had confirmed the deaths, the position of Oil, as also expressed by the Department of the Navy (which administers the stricken island) remained adamant that the sea animals were only sleeping (cf. *Life,* June 13, 1969; July 4, 1969). The dramatic beaching of an unusually large number of dead whales on the beaches of Northern California— whales which had just completed their migration through the Santa Barbara Channel—was acknowledged, but held not to be caused by oil pollution. No direct linkage (or nonlinkage) with oil could be demonstrated by investigating scientists (cf. *San Francisco Chronicle,* March 12, 1969:1-3).

In the end, it was not simply Interior, its U.S. Geological Survey and the President which either supported or tacitly accepted Oil's public relations tactics. The regulatory agencies at both national and state level, by action, inaction and implication had the consequence of defending Oil at virtually every turn. Thus at the outset of the first big blow, as the ocean churned with bubbling oil and gas, the U.S. Coast Guard (which patrols Channel waters regularly) failed to notify local officials of the pollution threat because, in the words of the local commander, "the seriousness of the situation was not apparent until late in the day Tuesday and it was difficult to reach officials after business hours" (*SBNP,* January 30, 1969: A-1, 4). Officials ended up hearing of the spill from the *News-Press.*

The Army Corps of Engineers must approve all structures placed on the ocean floor and thus had the discretion to hold public hearings on each application for a permit to build a drilling platform. With the exception of a single *pro forma* ceremony held on a platform erected in 1967, requests for such hearings were never granted. In its most recent handling of these matters (at a point long after the initial eruption and as oil still leaks into the ocean) the Corps changed its criteria for public hearings by restricting written objections to new drilling to "the effects of the proposed exploratory drilling on *navigation or national defense*" (*SBNP*, August 17, 1969:A-1, 4). Prior to the spill, effects on *fish and wildlife* were specified by the Army as possible grounds for objection, but at that time such objections, when raised, were more easily dismissed as unfounded.

The Federal Water Pollution Control Administration consistently attempted to understate the amount of damage done to waterfowl by quoting the "hospital dead" as though a reasonable assessment of the net damage. State agencies followed the same pattern. The charge of "Industry domination" of state conservation boards was levelled by the State Deputy Attorney General, Charles O'Brien (*SBNP*, February 9, 1969:A-6). Thomas Gaines, a Union Oil executive, actually sits as a member on the State Agency Board most directly connected with the control of pollution in Channel waters. In correspondence with complaining citizens, N. B. Livermore, Jr., of the Resources Agency of California refers to the continuing oil spill as "minor seepage" with "no major long-term effect on the marine ecology." The letter adopts the perspective of Interior and Oil, even though the state was in no way being held culpable for the spill (letter, undated to Joseph Keefe, citizen, University of California, Santa Barbara Library, on file).

With these details under their belts, Santa Barbarans were in a position to understand the sweeping condemnation of the regulatory system as contained in a *News-Press* front page, banner-headlined interview with Rep. Richard D. Ottenger (D-NY), quoted as follows: "And so on down the line. Each agency has a tendency to become the captive of the industry that it is to regulate" (*SBNP*, March 1, 1969:A-1).

THE CONGRESS: DISILLUSIONMENT

Irritations with Interior were paralleled by frustrations encountered in dealing with the Congressional establishment which had the responsibility of holding hearings on ameliorative legislation. A delegation of Santa Barbarans was scheduled to testify in Washington on the Cranston bill. From the questions which Congressmen asked of them, and the manner in which they were "handled," the delegation could only conclude that the Committee was "in the pockets of Oil." As one of the returning delegates put it, the presentation bespoke of "total futility."

At this writing, six months after their introduction, both the Cranston and Teague bills lie buried in committee with little prospect of surfacing. Cranston has softened his bill significantly—requiring only that new drilling be suspended until Congress is convinced that sufficient technological safeguards exist. But to no avail.

SCIENCE AND TECHNOLOGY: DISILLUSIONMENT

From the start, part of the shock of the oil spill was that such a thing could happen in a country with such sophisticated technology. The much overworked phrase, "If we can send a man to the moon. . . ." was even more overworked in Santa Barbara. When, in years previous, Santa Barbara's elected officials had attempted to halt the original sale of leases, "assurances" were given from Interior that such an "accident" could not occur, given the highly developed state of the art. Not only did it occur, but the original gusher of oil spewed forth completely out of control for ten days and the continuing "seepage" which followed it remains uncontrolled to the present moment, seven months later. That the government would embark upon so massive a drilling program with such unsophisticated technologies, was striking indeed.

Further, not only were the technologies inadequate and the plans for stopping a leak, should it occur, nonexistent, but the area in which the drilling took place was known to be ultrahazardous from the outset. That is, drilling was occurring on an ocean bottom known for its extraordinary geological circumstances—porous sands lacking a bedrock "ceiling" capable of containing runaway oil and gas. Thus the continuing leakage through the sands at various points above the oil reservoir is unstoppable, and could have been anticipated with the data *known to all parties involved.*

Another peculiarity of the Channel is the fact that it is located in the heart of earthquake activity in that region of the country which, among all regions, is among the very most earthquake prone.[5] Santa Barbarans are now asking what might occur in an earthquake: if pipes on the ocean floor and casings through the ocean bottom should be sheared, the damage done by the Channel's *thousands* of potential producing wells would be devastating to the entire coast of Southern California.[6]

Recurrent attempts have been made to ameliorate the continuing seep by placing floating booms around an area of leakage and then having workboats skim off the leakage from within the demarcated area.[7] Chemical dispersants, of various varieties, have also been tried. But the oil bounces over the sea booms in the choppy waters; the work boats suck up only a drop in the bucket and the dispersants are effective only when used in quantities which constitute a graver pollution threat than the oil they are designed to eliminate. Cement is poured into suspected fissures

---

[5]Cf. "Damaging Earthquakes of the United States through 1966," Fig. 2, National Earthquake Information Center, Environmental Science Services Administration, Coast and Geodetic Survey.

[6]See Interview with Donald Weaver, Professor of Geology, UCSB, *SBNP*, Feb. 21, 1969, p. A-1, 6. (Also, remarks by Professor Donald Runnells, UCSB geologist, *SBNP*, Feb. 23, 1969, p. B-2.) Both stress the dangers of faults in the Channel and potential earthquakes.

[7]More recently, plastic tents have been placed on the ocean floor to trap seeping oil; it is being claimed that half the runaway oil is now being trapped in these tents.

in an attempt to seal them up. Oil on beaches is periodically cleaned by dumping straw over the sands and then raking up the straw along with the oil it absorbs.

This striking contrast between the sophistication of the means used to locate and extract oil compared to the primitiveness of the means to control and clean it up was widely noted in Santa Barbara. It is the result of a system which promotes research and development which leads to strategic profitability rather than to social utility. The common sight of men throwing straw on miles of beaches within sight of complex drilling rigs capable of exploiting resources thousands of feet below the ocean's surface, made the point clear.

The futility of the clean-up and control efforts was widely noted in Santa Barbara. Secretary Hickel's announcement that the Interior Department was generating new "tough" regulations to control off-shore drilling was thus met with great skepticism. The Santa Barbara County Board of Supervisors was invited to "review" these new regulations—and refused to do so in the belief that such participation would be used to provide the fraudulent impression of democratic responsiveness—when, in fact, the relevant decisions had been already made. In previous years when they were fighting against the leasing of the Channel, the Supervisors had been assured of technological safeguards; now, as the emergency continued, they could witness for themselves the dearth of any means for ending the leakage in the Channel. They had also heard the testimony of a high-ranking Interior engineer who, when asked if such safeguards could positively prevent future spills, explained that "no prudent engineer could ever make such a claim" (SBNP, February 19, 1969:A-1). They also had the testimony of Donald Solanas, a regional supervisor of Interior's U.S. Geological Survey, who had said about the Union Platform eruption:

> I could have had an engineer on that platform 24 hours a day, 7 days a week and he couldn't have prevented the accident.

His "explanation" of the cause of the "accident": "Mother earth broke down on us" (SBNP, February 28, 1969: C-12).

Given these facts, as contained in the remarks of Interior's own spokesmen, combined with testimony and information received from non-Interior personnel, Interior's new regulations and the invitation to the County to participate in making them, could only be a ruse to preface a resumption of drilling. In initiating the County's policy of not responding to Interior's "invitation," a County Supervisor explained: "I think we may be falling into a trap" (SBNP, April 1, 1969).

The very next day, the Supervisor's suspicions were confirmed. Interior announced a selective resumption of drilling "to relieve pressures." (News-Press letter writers asked if the "pressure" was geological or political.)

The new tough regulations were themselves seriously flawed by the fact that most of their provisions specified those measures, such as buoyant booms around platforms, availability of chemical dispersants, etc., which had proven almost totally useless in the current emergency. They fell far short of minimum safety requirements as enumerated by UC Santa Barbara geologist Robert Curry who criticized a previous version of the same regulations as "relatively trivial" and "toothless"[8] (*SBNP*, March 5, 1969: C-9).

On the other hand, the new regulations did specify that oil companies would henceforth be financially responsible for damages resulting from pollution mishaps. (This had been the *de facto* reality in the Union case; the company had assumed responsibility for the clean-up, and advised stockholders that such costs were covered by "more than adequate" insurance.)[9] The liability requirement has been vociferously condemned by the oil companies—particularly by those firms which have failed to make significant strikes on their Channel leases (*SBNP*, March 14, 1969). Several of these companies have now entered suit (supported by the ACLU) against the federal government charging that the arbitrary changing of lease conditions renders Channel exploitation "economically and practically impossible," thus depriving them of rights of due process (*SBNP*, April 10, 1969:A-1).

The weaknesses of the new regulations came not as a surprise to people who had already adapted to thinking of Oil and the Interior Department as the same source. There was much less preparation for the results of the Presidential Committee of "distinguished" scientists and engineers (the Du Bridge Panel) which was to recommend means of eliminating the seepage under Platform A. Given the half-hearted, inexpensive and primitive attempts by Union Oil to deal with the seepage, feeling ran high that at last the technological sophistication of the nation would be harnessed

---

[8]Curry's criticism is as follows:
These new regulations make no mention at all about in-pipe safety valves to prevent blowouts, or to shut off the flow of oil deep in the well should the oil and gas escape from the drill hole region into a natural fissure at some depth below the wellhead blowout preventers. There is also no requirement for a backup valve in case the required preventer fails to work. Remember, the runaway well on Union Platform A was equipped with a wellhead blowout preventer. The blowout occurred some 200 feet below that device.

Only one of the new guidelines seems to recognize the possible calamitous results of earthquakes which are inevitable on the western offshore leases. None of the regulations require the minimization of pollution hazards during drilling that may result from a moderate-magnitude, nearby shallow-focus earthquake, seismic sea wave (tsunami) or submarine landslide which could shear off wells below the surface.

None of the regulations state anything at all about onshore oil and gas storage facilities liable to release their contents into the oceans upon rupture due to an earthquake or seismic seaway.

None of the new regulations stipulate that wells must be cased to below a level of geologic hazard, or below a depth of possible open fissures or porous sands, and, as such, none of these changes would have helped the present situation in the Santa Barbara Channel or the almost continuous blowout that has been going on since last year in the Bass Straits off Tasmania, where one also finds porous sands extending all the way up to the sea floor in a tectonically active region—exactly the situation we have here.

[9]Letter from Fred Hartley, President of Union Oil, to "all shareholders," dated February 7, 1969.

to solve this particular vexing problem. Instead, the panel—after a two-day session and after hearing testimony from no one not connected with either Oil or Interior—recommended the "solution" of drilling an additional 50 wells under Platform A in order to pump the area dry as quickly as possible. The process would require ten to twenty years, one member of the panel estimated.[10]

The recommendation was severely terse, requiring no more than one and a half pages of type. Despite an immediate local clamor, Interior refused to make public the data or the reasoning behind the recommendations. The information on Channel geological conditions was provided by the oil companies; the Geological Survey routinely depends upon the oil industry for the data upon which it makes its "regulatory" decisions. The data, being proprietary, could thus not be released. Totally inexplicable, in light of this "explanation," is Interior's continuing refusal to immediately provide the information given a recent clearance by Union Oil for public release of all the data. Santa Barbara's local experts have thus been thwarted by the counter-arguments of Oil-Interior that "if you had the information we have, you would agree with us."

Science was also having its non-neutral consequences on the other battlefront being waged by Santa Barbarans. The chief Deputy Attorney General of California, in his April 7 speech to the blue-ribbon Channel City Club of Santa Barbara, complained that the oil industry

> is preventing oil drilling experts from aiding the Attorney General's office in its lawsuits over the Santa Barbara oil spill (SBNP, Aug. 8, 1969).

Complaining that his office has been unable to get assistance from petroleum experts at California universities, the Deputy Attorney General further stated:

> The university experts all seem to be working on grants from the oil industry. There is an atmosphere of fear. The experts are afraid that if they assist us in our case on behalf of the people of California, they will lose their oil industry grants.

At the Santa Barbara Campus of the University, there is little Oil money in evidence and few, if any, faculty members have entered into proprietary research arrangements with Oil. Petroleum geology and engineering is simply not a local specialty. Yet it is a fact that Oil interests did contact several Santa Barbara faculty members with offers of funds for studies of

---

[10]Robert Curry of the geography department of the University of California, Santa Barbara, warned that such a tactic might in fact accelerate leakage. If, as he thought, the oil reservoirs under the Channel are linked, accelerated development of one such reservoir would, through erosion of subterranean linkage channels, accelerate the flow of oil into the reservoir under Platform A, thus adding to the uncontrolled flow of oil through the sands and into the ocean. Curry was not asked to testify by the DuBridge Panel.

the ecological effects of the oil spill, with publication rights stipulated by Oil.[11] It is also the case that the Federal Water Pollution Control Administration explicitly requested a UC Santa Barbara botanist to withhold the findings of his study, funded by that Agency, on the ecological consequences of the spill (*SBNP*, July 29, 1969:A-3).

Except for the Deputy Attorney General's complaint, none of these revelations received any publicity outside of Santa Barbara. But the Attorney's allegation became something of a statewide issue. A professor at the Berkeley campus, in his attempt to refute the allegation, actually confirmed it. Wilbur H. Somerton, Professor of petroleum engineering, indicated he could not testify against Oil

> because my work depends on good relations with the petroleum industry. My interest is serving the petroleum industry. I view my obligation to the community as supplying it with well-trained petroleum engineers. We train the industry's engineers and they help us. (*SBNP*, April 12, 1969, as quoted from a *San Francisco Chronicle* interview.)

Santa Barbara's leaders were incredulous about the whole affair. The question—one which is more often asked by the downtrodden sectors of the society—was asked: "Whose University is this, anyway?" A local executive and GOO leader asked, "If the truth isn't in the universities, where is it?" A conservative member of the State Legislature, in a move reminiscent of SDS demands, went so far as to ask an end to all faculty "moonlighting" for industry. In Santa Barbara, the only place where all of this publicity was occurring, there was thus an opportunity for insight into the linkages between knowledge, the University, government and Oil and the resultant non-neutrality of science. The backgrounds of many members of the DuBridge Panel were linked publicly to the oil industry. In a line of reasoning usually the handiwork of groups like SDS, a *News-Press* letter writer labeled Dr. DuBridge as a servant of Oil interests because, as a past President of Cal Tech, he would have had to defer to Oil in generating the massive funding which that institution requires. In fact, the relationship was quite direct. Not only has Union Oil been a contributor to Cal Tech, but Fred Hartley (Union's President) is a Cal Tech trustee. The impropriety of such a man as DuBridge serving as the key "scientist" in determining the Santa Barbara outcome seemed more and more obvious.

---

[11]Oral communication from one of the faculty members involved. The kind of "studies" which oil enjoys is typified by a research conclusion by Professor Wheeler J. North of Cal Tech, who after performing a one week study of the Channel ecology under Western Oil and Gas Association sponsorship, determined that it was the California winter floods which caused most of the evident disturbance and that (as quoted from the Association Journal) "Santa Barbara beaches and marine life should be back to normal by summer with no adverse impact on tourism." Summer came with oil on the beaches, birds unreturned, and beach motels with unprecedented vacancies.

TAXATION AND PATRIOTISM: DISILLUSIONMENT

From Engler's detailed study of the politics of Oil, we learn that the oil companies combat local resistance with arguments that hurt: taxation and patriotism (cf. Engler, 1961). They threaten to take their operations elsewhere, thus depriving the locality of taxes and jobs. The more grandiose argument is made that oil is necessary for the national defense; hence, any weakening of "incentives" to discover and produce oil plays into the hands of the enemy.

Santa Barbara, needing money less than most locales and valuing environment more, learned enough to know better. Santa Barbara wanted oil to leave, but oil would not. Because the oil is produced in federal waters, only a tiny proportion of Santa Barbara County's budget indirectly comes from oil, and virtually none of the city of Santa Barbara's budget comes from oil. *News-Press* letters and articles disposed of the defense argument with these points: (1) oil companies deliberately limit oil production under geographical quota restrictions designed to maintain the high price of oil by regulating supply; (2) the federal oil import quota (also sponsored by the oil industry) which restricts imports from abroad, weakens the country's defense posture by forcing the nation to exhaust its own finite supply while the Soviets rely on the Middle East; (3) most oil imported into the U.S. comes from relatively dependable sources in South America which foreign wars would not endanger; (4) the next major war will be a nuclear holocaust with possible oil shortages a very low level problem.

Just as an attempt to answer the national defense argument led to conclusions the very opposite of Oil's position, so did a closer examination of the tax argument. For not only did Oil not pay very much in local taxes, Oil also paid very little in *federal* taxes. In another of its front-page editorials the *News-Press* made the facts clear. The combination of the output restrictions, extraordinary tax write-off privileges for drilling expenses, the import quota, and the 27.5 per cent depletion allowance, all created an artificially high price of U.S. oil—a price almost double the world market price for the comparable product delivered to comparable U.S. destinations.[12] The combination of incentives available creates a situation where some oil companies pay no taxes whatever during extraordinarily profitable years. In the years 1962–1966, Standard of New Jersey paid less

---

[12]Cf. Walter J. Mead, "The Economics of Depletion Allowance," testimony presented to Assembly Revenue and Taxation Committee, California Legislature, June 10, 1969, mimeo: "The System of Government Subsidies to the Oil Industry," testimony presented to the U.S. Senate Subcommittee on Antitrust and Monopoly, March 11, 1969. The ostensible purpose of the depletion allowance is to encourage oil companies to explore for new oil reserves. A report to the Treasury Department by Consad Research Corp. concluded that *elimination* of the depletion allowance would decrease oil reserves by only 3 per cent. The report advised that more efficient means could be found than a system which causes the government to pay $10 for every $1 in oil added to reserves. (Cf. Leo Rennert, "Oil Industry's Favors," *SBNP*, April 27, 1969, pp. A-14, 15 as reprinted from the *Sacramento Bee*.)

than 4 per cent of profits in taxes, Standard of California, less than 3 per cent, and 22 of the largest oil companies paid slightly more than 6 per cent (*SBNP*, February 16, 1969:A-1). It was pointed out, again and again to Santa Barbarans, that it was this system of subsidy which made the relatively high cost deep-sea exploration and drilling in the Channel profitable in the first place. Thus, the citizens of Santa Barbara, as federal taxpayers and fleeced consumers were subsidizing their own demise. The consequence of such a revelation can only be *infuriating*.

THE MOBILIZATION OF BIAS

The actions of Oil and Interior and the contexts in which such actions took place can be reexamined in terms of their function in diffusing local opposition, disorienting dissenters, and otherwise limiting the scope of issues which are potentially part of public controversies. E. E. Schatt-schneider (1960:71) has noted:

> All forms of political organization have a bias in favor of the ex-ploitation of some kinds of conflict and the suppression of others because *organization is the mobilization of bias.* Some issues are or-ganized into politics while others are organized out.

Expanding the notion slightly, certain techniques shaping the "mobiliza-tion of bias" can be said to have been revealed by the present case study.

1. The Pseudo-event. Boorstin (1962) has described the use of the pseudo-event in a large variety of task accomplishment situations. A pseudo-event occurs when men arrange conditions to simulate a certain kind of event, such that certain prearranged consequences follow as though the actual event had taken place. Several pseudo-events may be cited. *Local participation in decision making.* From the outset, it was obvious that national actions vis-à-vis Oil in Santa Barbara had as their strategy the freezing out of any local participation in decisions affecting the Channel. Thus, when in 1968 the federal government first called for bids on a Channel lease, local officials were not even informed. When subsequently queried about the matter, federal officials indicated that the lease which was advertised for bid was just a corrective measure to pre-vent drainage of a "little old oil pool" on federal property adjacent to a state lease producing for Standard and Humble. This "little old pool" was to draw a high bonus bid of $21,189,000 from a syndicate headed by Phillips (*SBNP*, February 9, 1969:A-17). Further, local officials were not notified by any government agency in the case of the original oil spill, nor (except after the spill was already widely known) in the case of any of the previous or subsequent more "minor" spills. Perhaps the thrust of the federal government's colonialist attitude toward the local community was contained in an Interior Department engineer's memo written to J. Cordell Moore, Assistant Secretary of Interior, explaining the policy of refusing public hearings prefatory to drilling: "We preferred not to stir up the natives any more than possible."[13] (The memo was released by Senator Cranston and excerpted on page 1 of the *News-Press*.)

Given this known history, the Santa Barbara County Board of Supervisors refused the call for "participation" in drawing up new "tougher" drilling regulations, precisely because they knew the government had no intention of creating "safe" drilling regulations. They refused to take part in the pseudo-event and thus refused to let the consequences (in this case the appearance of democratic decision-making and local assent) of a pseudo-event occur.

Other attempts at the staging of pseudo-events may be cited. Nixon's "inspection" of the Santa Barbara beachfront was an obvious one. Another series of pseudo-events were the Congressional hearings staged by legislators who were, in the words of a local well-to-do lady leader of GOO, "kept men." The locals blew off steam—but the hearing of arguments and the proposing of appropriate legislation based on those arguments (the presumed essence of the Congressional hearing as a formal event) certainly did not come off. Many Santa Barbarans had a similar impression of the court hearings regarding the various legal maneuvers against oil drilling; legal proceedings came to be similarly seen as ceremonious arrangements for the accomplishing of tasks not revealed by their formally-stated properties.

2. The Creeping Event. A creeping event is, in a sense, the opposite of a pseudo-event. It occurs when something *is* actually taking place, but when the manifest signs of the event are arranged to occur at an inconspicuously gradual and piecemeal pace, thus eliminating some of the consequences which would otherwise follow from the event if it were to be perceived all-at-once to be occurring. Two major creeping events were arranged for the Santa Barbara Channel. Although the great bulk of the bidding for leases in the Channel occurred simultaneously, the first lease was, as was made clear earlier, advertised for bid prior to the others and prior to any public announcement of the leasing of the Channel. The federal waters' virginity was thus ended with only a whimper. A more salient example of the creeping event is the resumption of production and drilling after Hickel's second moratorium. Authorization to resume *production* on different specific groups of wells occurred on these dates in 1969: February 17; February 21; February 22; and March 3. Authorization to resume *drilling* of various groups of new wells was announced by In-

---

[13]Cranston publicly confronted the staff engineer, Eugene Standley, who stated that he could neither confirm nor deny writing the memo. (Cf. *SBNP*, March 11, 1969, p. A-1.)

terior on these dates in 1969: April 1, June 12, July 2, August 2, and August 16. (This is being written on August 20.) Each time, the resumption was announced as a safety precaution to relieve pressures, until finally on the most recent resumption date, the word "deplete" was used for the first time as the reason for granting permission to drill. There is thus no *particular* point in time in which production and drilling were reauthorized for the Channel—and full resumption has still not been officially authorized.

A creeping event has the consequences of diffusing resistance to the event by holding back what journalists call a "time peg" on which to hang "the story." Even if the aggrieved party should get wind that "something is going on," strenuous reaction is inhibited. Non-routine activity has as its prerequisite the crossing of a certain threshold point of input; the dribbling out of an event has the consequence of making each of the revealed inputs fall below the threshold level necessary for non-routine activity. By the time it becomes quite clear that "something *is* going on" both the aggrieved and the sponsors of the creeping event can ask why there should be a response *"now"* when there was none previously to the very same kind of stimulus. In such manner, the aggrieved has resort only to frustration and a gnawing feeling that "events" are sweeping him by.

3. The "Neutrality" of Science and the "Knowledge" Producers. I have already dealt at some length with the disillusionment of Santa Barbarans with the "experts" and the University. After learning for themselves of the collusion between government and Oil and the use of secret science as a prop to that collusion, Santa Barbarans found themselves in the unenviable position of having to demonstrate that science and knowledge were, in fact, not neutral arbiters. They had to demonstrate, by themselves, that continued drilling was not safe, that the "experts" who said it was safe were the hirelings directly or indirectly of Oil interests and that the report of the DuBridge Panel recommending massive drilling was a fraudulent document. They had to document that the University *petroleum* geologists were themselves in league with their adversaries and that knowledge unfavorable to the Oil interests was systematically withheld by virtue of the very structure of the knowledge industry. As the SDS has learned in other contexts, this is no small task. It is a long story to tell, a complicated story to tell, and one which pits lay persons (and a few academic renegades) against a profession and patrons of a profession. An illustration of the difficulties involved may be drawn from very recent history. Seventeen Santa Barbara plaintiffs, represented by the ACLU, sought a temporary injunction against additional Channel drilling at least until the information utilized by the DuBridge Panel was made public and a hearing could be held. The injunction was not granted and, in the end, the presiding federal judge ruled in favor of what he termed the "expert" opinions available to the Secretary of the Interior. It was a function of limited time for re-buttal, the disorienting confusions of courtroom procedures, and also per-haps the desire to not offend the Court, that the ACLU lawyer could not make his subtle, complex and highly controversial case that the "experts" were partisans and that their scientific "findings" follow from that par-tisanship.

4. Constraints of Communication Media. Just as the courtroom setting was not amenable to a full reproduction of the details surrounding the basis for the ACLU case, so the media in general—through restrictions of time and style—prevent a full airing of the details of the case. A more cynical analysis of the media's inability to make known the Santa Barbara "problem" in its full fidelity might hinge on an allegation that the media are constrained by fear of "pressures" from Oil and its allies; Metromedia, for example, sent a team to Santa Barbara which spent several days docu-menting, interviewing and filming for an hour-long program—only to suddenly drop the whole matter due to what is reported by locals in touch with the network to have been "pressures" from Oil. Such blatant inter-ventions aside, however, the problem of full reproduction of the Santa Barbara "news" would remain problematic nonetheless.

News media are notorious for the anecdotal nature of their reporting; even so-called "think pieces" rarely go beyond a stringing together of proximate "events." There are no analyses of the "mobilization of bias" or linkages of men's actions and their pecuniary interests. Science and learn-ing are assumed to be neutral; regulatory agencies are assumed to function as "watchdogs" for the public. Information to the contrary of these as-sumptions is treated as exotic exception; in the manner of Drew Pearson columns, exception piles upon exception without intellectual combination, analysis or ideological synthesis. The complexity of the situation to be reported, the wealth of details needed to support such analyses require more time and effort than journalists have at their command. Their recita-tion would produce long stories not consistent with space requirements and make-up preferences of newspapers and analogous constraints of the other media. A full telling of the whole story would tax the reader/viewer and would risk boring him.

For these reasons, the rather extensive media coverage of the oil spill centered on a few dramatic moments in its history (e.g., the initial gusher of oil) and a few simple-to-tell "human interest" aspects such as the pathetic deaths of the sea birds struggling along the oil-covered sands. With increasing temporal and geographical distance from the initial spill, national coverage became increasingly rare and increasingly sloppy. In-terior statements on the state of the "crisis" were reported without local rejoinders as the newsmen who would have gathered them began leaving the scene. It is to be kept in mind that, relative to other local events, the

Santa Barbara spill received extraordinarily extensive national coverage.[14] The point is that this coverage is nevertheless inadequate in both its quality and quantity to adequately inform the American public.

5. The Routinization of Evil.   An oft quoted American cliché is that the news media cover only the "bad" things; the everyday world of people going about their business in conformity with American ideals loses out to the coverage of student and ghetto "riots," wars and crime, corruption and sin. The grain of truth in this cliché should not obfuscate the fact that there are *certain kinds of evil* which, partially for reasons cited in the preceding paragraphs, also lose their place in the public media and the public mind. Pollution of the Santa Barbara Channel is now routine; the issue is not whether or not the Channel is polluted, but *how much* it is polluted. A recent oil slick discovered off a Phillips Platform in the Channel was dismissed by an oil company official as a "routine" drilling byproduct which was not viewed as "obnoxious." That "about half" of the current oil seeping into the Channel is allegedly being recovered is taken as an improvement sufficient to preclude the "outrage" that a big national story would require.

Similarly, the pollution of the "moral environment" becomes routine; politicians are, of course, on the take, in the pockets of Oil, etc. The depletion allowance issue becomes not whether or not such special benefits should exist at all, but rather whether it should be at the level of 20 or 27.5 per cent. "Compromises" emerge such as the 24 per cent depletion allowance and the new "tough" drilling regulations, which are already being hailed as "victories" for the reformers (cf. *Los Angeles Times*, July 14, 1969:17). Like the oil spill itself, the depletion allowance debate becomes buried in its own disorienting detail, its ceremonious pseudo-events and in the triviality of the "solutions" which ultimately come to be considered as the "real" options. Evil is both banal and complicated; both of these attributes contribute to its durability.[15]

THE STRUGGLE FOR THE MEANS TO POWER

It should (although it does not) go without saying that the parties competing to shape decisionmaking on oil in Santa Barbara do not have equal access to the means of "mobilizing bias" which this paper has discussed. The same social structural characteristics which Michels has asserted make for an "iron law of oligarchy" make for, in this case, a series

---

[14]Major magazine coverage occurred in these (and other) national publications: *Time* (Feb. 14, 1969); *Newsweek* (March 3, 1969); *Life* (June 13, 1969); *Saturday Review* (May 10, 1969); *Sierra Club Bulletin; Sports Illustrated* (April 10, 1969). The last three articles cited were written by Santa Barbarans.

[15]The notion of the banality of evil is adapted from the usage of Arendt, 1963.

of extraordinary advantages for the oil-government combine. The ability to create pseudo-events such as Nixon's Santa Barbara inspection or controls necessary to bring off well-timed creeping events are not evenly distributed throughout the social structure. Lacking such ready access to media, lacking the ability to stage events at will, lacking a well-integrated system of arrangements for goal attainment (at least in comparison to their adversaries) Santa Barbara's leaders have met with repeated frustrations.

Their response to their relative powerlessness has been analogous to other groups and individuals who, from a similar vantage point, come to see the system up close. They become willing to expand their repertoire of means of influence as their cynicism and bitterness increase concomitantly. Letter writing gives way to demonstrations, demonstrations to civil disobedience. People refuse to participate in "democratic procedures" which are a part of the opposition's event-management strategy. Confrontation politics arise as a means of countering with "events" of one's own, thus providing the media with "stories" which can be simply and energetically told. The lesson is learned that "the power to make a reportable event is . . . the power to make experience" (Boorstin, 1962:10).

Rallies were held at local beaches; Congressmen and state and national officials were greeted by demonstrations. (Fred Hartley, of Union Oil, inadvertently landed his plane in the midst of one such demonstration, causing a rather ugly name-calling scene to ensue.) A "sail-in" was held one Sunday with a flotilla of local pleasure boats forming a circle around Platform A, each craft bearing large anti-oil banners. (Months earlier boats coming near the platforms were sprayed by oil personnel with fire hoses.) City-hall meetings were packed with citizens reciting "demands" for immediate and forceful local action.

A City Council election in the midst of the crisis resulted in the landslide election of the Council's bitterest critic and the defeat of a veteran Councilman suspected of having "oil interests." In a rare action, the News-Press condemned the local Chamber of Commerce for accepting oil money for a fradulent tourist advertising campaign which touted Santa Barbara (including its beaches) as restored to its former beauty. (In the end, references to the beaches were removed from subsequent advertisements, but the oil-financed campaign continued briefly.)

In the meantime, as a Wall Street Journal reporter was to observe, "a current of gloom and despair" ran through the ranks of Santa Barbara's militants. The president of Sloan Instruments Corporation, an international R & D firm with headquarters in Santa Barbara, came to comment:

> We are so God-damned frustrated. The whole democratic process
> seems to be falling apart. Nobody responds to us, and we end up
> doing things progressively less reasonable. This town is going to

blow up if there isn't some reasonable attitude expressed by the Federal Government—nothing seems to happen except that we lose.

Similarly, a well-to-do widow, during a legal proceeding in Federal District Court in which Santa Barbara was once again "losing," whispered in the author's ear:

> Now I understand why those young people at the University go around throwing things. . . . The individual has no rights at all.

One possible grand strategy for Santa Barbara was outlined by a local public relations man and GOO worker:

> We've got to run the oil men out. The city owns the wharf and the harbor that the company has to use. The city has got to deny its facilities to oil traffic, service boats, cranes and the like. If the city contravenes some federal navigation laws (which such actions would unquestionably involve), to hell with it.

> The only hope to save Santa Barbara is to awaken the nation to the ravishment. That will take public officials who are willing to block oil traffic with their bodies and with police hoses, if necessary. Then federal marshals or federal troops would have to come in. This would pull in the national news media (*SBNP*, July 6, 1969, p. 7).

This scenario has thus far not occurred in Santa Barbara, although the use of the wharf by the oil industries has led to certain militant actions. A picket was maintained at the wharf for two weeks, protesting the conversion of the pier from a recreation and tourist facility to a heavy industrial plant for the use of the oil companies.[16] A boycott of other wharf businesses (e.g., two restaurants) was urged. The picket line was led by white, middle-class adults—one of whom had almost won the mayoralty of Santa Barbara in a previous election. Hardly a "radical" or a "militant," this same man was several months later representing his neighborhood protective association in its opposition to the presence of a "Free School" described by this man (somewhat ambivalently) as a "hippie hotel."

Prior to the picketing, a dramatic Easter Sunday confrontation (involving approximately 500 persons) took place between demonstrators and city police. Unexpectedly, as a wharf rally was breaking up, an oil service truck began driving up the pier to make delivery of casing supplies for oil drilling. There was a spontaneous sit-down in front of the truck. For the first time since the Ku Klux Klan folded in the 1930's, a group of Santa Barbarans (some young, some "hippie," but many hard-working middle-class adults), was publicly taking the law into its own hands. After much lengthy discussion between police, the truck driver and the demonstrators,

---

[16]As a result of local opposition, Union Oil was to subsequently move its operations from the Santa Barbara wharf to a more distant port in Ventura County.

the truck was ordered away and the demonstrators remained to rejoice their victory. The following day's *News-Press* editorial, while not supportive of such tactics, found much to excuse—noteworthy given the paper's long standing *bitter* opposition to similar tactics when exercised by dissident Northern blacks or student radicals.

A companion demonstration on the water failed to materialize; a group of Santa Barbarans was to sail to the Union platform and "take it"; choppy seas, however, precluded a landing, causing the would-be conquerors to return to port in failure.

It would be difficult to speculate at this writing what forms Santa Barbara's resistance might take in the future. The veteran *News-Press* reporter who has covered the important oil stories has publicly stated that if the government fails to eliminate both the pollution and its causes "there will, at best be civil disobedience in Santa Barbara and at worst, violence." In fact, talk of "blowing up" the ugly platforms has been recurrent—and is heard in all social circles.

But just as this kind of talk is not completely serious, it is difficult to know the degree to which the other kinds of militant statements are serious. Despite frequent observations of the "radicalization"[17] of Santa Barbara, it is difficult to determine the extent to which the authentic grievances against Oil have generalized to a radical analysis of American society. Certainly an SDS membership campaign among Santa Barbara adults would be a dismal failure. But that is too severe a test. People, especially basically contented people, change their world-view only very slowly, if at all. Most Santa Barbarans go about their comfortable lives in the ways they always did; they may even help Ronald Reagan to another term in the statehouse. But I do conclude that large numbers of persons have been moved, and that they have been moved in the directions of the radical left. They have gained insights into the structure of power in America not possessed by similarly situated persons in other parts of the country. The claim is thus that some Santa Barbarans, especially those with most interest and most information about the oil spill and its surrounding circumstances, have come to view power in America more intellectually, more analytically, more sociologically—more *radically*—than they did before.

I hold this to be a general sociological response to a series of concomitant circumstances, which can be simply enumerated (*again!*) as follows:

1. Injustice. The powerful are operating in a manner inconsistent with the normatively sanctioned expectations of an aggrieved population. The aggrieved population is deprived of certain felt needs as a result.

2. Information. Those who are unjustly treated are provided with rather complete information regarding this disparity between expectations

---

[17]Cf. Morton Mintz, "Oil Spill 'Radicalizes' a Conservative West Coast City," *Washington Post*, June 29, 1969, pp. C-1, 5.

and actual performances of the powerful. In the present case, that information has been provided to Santa Barbarans (and only to Santa Barbarans) by virtue of their own observations of local physical conditions and by virtue of the unrelenting coverage of the city's newspaper. Hardly a day has gone by since the initial spill that the front page has not carried an oil story; everything the paper can get its hands on is printed. It carries analyses; it makes the connections. As an appropriate result, Oil officials have condemned the paper as a "lousy" and "distorted" publication of "lies."[18]

3. Literacy and Leisure. In order for the information relevant to the injustice to be assimilated in all its infuriating complexity, the aggrieved parties must be, in the larger sense of the terms, literate and leisured. They must have the ability and the time to read, to ponder and to get upset.

My perspective thus differs from those who would regard the radical response as appropriate to some form or another of social or psychological freak. Radicalism is not a subtle form of mental illness (cf. recent statements of such as Bettelheim) caused by "rapid technological change" or increasing "impersonality" in the modern world; radicals are neither "immature," "underdisciplined," nor "anti-intellectual." Quite the reverse. They are persons who most clearly live under the conditions specified above and who make the most rational (and moral) response, given those circumstances. Thus radical movements draw their membership disproportionately from the most leisured, intelligent and informed of the white youth (cf. Flacks, 1967), and from the young blacks whose situations are most analogous to these white counterparts.

THE ACCIDENT AS A RESEARCH METHODOLOGY

If the present research effort has had as its strategy anything pretentious enough to be termed a "methodology," it is the methodology of what could be called "accident research." I define an "accident" as an occasion in which miscalculation leads to the breakdown of customary order. It has as its central characteristic the fact that an event occurs which is, to some large degree, unanticipated by those whose actions caused it to occur. As an event, an accident is thus crucially dissimilar both from the pseudo-event and the creeping event. It differs from the pseudo-event in that it bespeaks of an authentic and an unplanned happening; it differs from the creeping event in its suddenness, its sensation, in the fact that it brings to light a series of preconditions, actions and consequences all at

---

[18]Union Oil's public relations director stated: "In all my long career, I have never seen such distorted coverage of a news event as the *Santa Barbara News-Press* has foisted on its readers. It's a lousy newspaper." (*SBNP*, May 28, 1969, p. A-1.)

once. It is "news"—often sensational news. Thresholds are reached; attentions are held.

The accident thus tends to have consequences which are the very opposite of events which are pseudo or creeping. Instead of being a deliberately planned contribution to a purposely developed "social structure" (or, in the jargon of the relevant sociological literature, "decisional outcome"), it has as its consequence the revelation of features of a social system, or of individuals' actions and personalities, which are otherwise deliberately obfuscated by those with the resources to create pseudo- and creeping events. A resultant convenience is that the media, at the point of accident, may come to function as able and persistent research assistants.

At the level of everyday individual behavior, the accident is an important lay methodological resource of gossipers—especially for learning about those possessing the personality and physical resources to shield their private lives from public view. It is thus that the recent Ted Kennedy accident functioned so well for the purpose (perhaps useless) of gaining access to that individual's private routines and private dispositions. An accident such as the recent unprovoked police shooting of a deaf mute on the streets of Los Angeles provides analogous insights into routine police behavior which official records could never reveal. The massive and unprecedented Santa Barbara oil spill has similarly led to important revelations about the structure of power. An accident is thus an important instrument for learning about the lives of the powerful and the features of the social system which they deliberately and quasi-deliberately create. It is available as a research focus for those seeking a comprehensive understanding of the structure of power in America.

FINALE

Bachrach and Baratz (1962) have pointed to the plight of the pluralist students of community power who lack any criteria for the inevitable *selecting* of the "key political decisions" which serve as the basis for their research conclusions. I offer accident as a criterion. An accident is not a decision, but it does provide a basis for insight into whole series of decisions and non-decisions, events and pseudo-events which, taken together, might provide an explanation of the structure of power. Even though the local community is notorious for the increasing triviality of the decisions which occur within it (cf. Schulze, 1961; Vidich and Bensman, 1958; Mills, 1956), accident research at the local level might serve as "micro"-analyses capable of revealing the "second face of power" (Bachrach and Baratz), ordinarily left faceless by traditional community studies which fail to concern themselves with the processes by which bias is mobilized and thus how "issues" rise and fall.

The present effort has been the relatively more difficult one of learning not about community power, but about national power—and the relationship between national and local power. The "findings" highlight the extraordinary intransigence of national institutions in the face of local dissent, but more importantly, point to the processes and tactics which undermine that dissent and frustrate and radicalize the dissenters.

The relationship described between oil, government, and the knowledge industry does not constitute a unique pattern of power in America. All major sectors of the industrial economy lend themselves to the same kind of analysis as oil in Santa Barbara. Where such analyses have been carried out, the results are analogous in their content and analogous in the outrage which they cause. The nation's defeat in Vietnam, in a sense an accident, has led to analogous revelations about the arms industry and the manner in which American foreign policy is waged.[19] Comparable scrutinies of the agriculture industry, the banking industry, etc., would, in my opinion, lead to the same infuriating findings as the Vietnam defeat and the oil spill.

The national media dwell upon only a few accidents at a time. But across the country, in various localities, accidents routinely occur—accidents which can tell much not only about local power, but about national power as well. Community power studies typically have resulted in relevations of the "pluralistic" squabbles among local sub-elites which are stimulated by exogenous interventions (cf. Walton, 1968). Accident research at the local level might bring to light the larger societal arrangements which structure the parameters of such local debate. Research at the local level could thus serve as an avenue to knowledge about *national* power. Sociologists should be ready when an accident hits in their neighborhood, and then go to work.

REFERENCES

ALLEN, ALLAN A., "Santa Barbara oil spill." Statement presented to the U.S. Senate Interior Committee, Subcommittee on Minerals, Materials and Fuels, May 20, 1969.

ARENDT, HANNAH, *Eichmann in Jerusalem: A Report on the Banality of Evil.* New York: The Viking Press, 1963.

BACHRACH, PETER and MORTON BARATZ, "The two faces of power." *American Political Science Review* 57 (December 1962): 947–952.

---

[19] I have in mind the exhaustively documented series of articles by I. F. Stone in the *New York Review of Books* over the course of 1968 and 1969, a series made possible, in part, by the outrage of Senator Fulbright and others at the *mistake* of Vietnam.

BOORSTIN, DANIEL J., *The Image*. New York: Atheneum Press, 1961.

ENGLER, ROBERT, *The Politics of Oil*. New York: Macmillan, 1961.

FLACKS, RICHARD, "The liberated generation." *Journal of Social Issues* 22 (December 1967): 521–43.

GANS, HERBERT, *The Urban Villagers*. New York: The Free Press of Glencoe, 1962.

MILLS, C. WRIGHT, *The Power Elite*. New York: Oxford University Press, 1956.

SCHATTSCHNEIDER, E. E., *The Semisovereign People*. New York: Holt, Rinehart & Winston, 1960.

SCHULZE, ROBERT O., "The bifurcation of power in a satellite city." Pp. 19–81 in Morris Janowitz (ed.), *Community Political Systems*. New York: The Free Press of Glencoe, 1961.

VIDICH, ARTHUR, and JOSEPH BENSMAN, *Small Town in Mass Society*. Princeton: Princeton University Press, 1958.

WALTON, JOHN, "The vertical axis of community organization and the structure of power." Pp. 353–67 in Willis D. Hawley and Frederick M. Wirt (eds.), *The Search for Community Power*. Englewood Cliffs, N.J.: Prentice-Hall, 1968.

18. PIRATES AND POLITICS: AN ANALYSIS OF INTEREST GROUP CONFLICT

CHARLES H. McCAGHY
and R. SERGE DENISOFF

A persisting issue in the study of deviance is the relationship between social conflict and the emergence and enforcement of legal norms. The process of criminalization is essentially political: the application of legal sanctions is based less on a consensus over norms than on a differential ability of interest groups to implement their own particular values as matters of public policy. With the possible exceptions of certain behaviors involving overt assault on persons or property, it cannot be assumed that popular perceptions of acts are congruent with the legal definitions of those acts.

Fundamental to a conflict theory of criminalization is the existence of a struggle between interest groups prior to legislative action (Vold 1959, pp. 207–209; Turk 1966, pp. 347–348 and 1969, pp. 54–64; Quinney 1970, pp. 16–18). If conditions are appropriate, the struggle is moved into a legislative arena where one opponent attempts to neutralize another by causing his behavior to be defined as criminal. Even if successful in this endeavor, the struggle will continue through every stage of the judicial process. There will be bargaining and compromises based at least partially on positions of strength throughout the enforcement levels from arrest through sentencing (Vold 1958, p. 209; Turk 1966, pp. 349–351 and 1969, pp. 64–70; Quinney 1970, pp. 18–20). In short, criminality is a status conferred within the context of conflicting social units.

Conflict in the structural model generally has been addressed within sociopolitical institutions. Dahrendorf (1959) portrays conflict as fundamentally political along an axis of power; that is, as a differential distribution of authority. Associations, whether corporations, political parties, or movements, compete for authority positions on the basis of latent and manifest interests. Latent interests are those inherent in any social position while manifest interests are those *perceived* by the groups. For conflict to emerge units must act as "interest groups" possessing awareness

From a paper presented at the Interamerican Congress of the American Society of Criminology and the Interamerican Association of Criminology, Caracas, Venezuela, November 19–27, 1972.
Copyright © 1972 by Charles H. McCaghy and R. Serge Denisoff.

of their basis or latent interests. According to Dahrendorf's model, groups struggle only when aware of their interests and when willing to engage in a struggle to obtain goals.

However, the existence of manifest interests and a consciousness of threats to values or scarce resources are not sufficient to generate rules or rule enforcement. Opposing interest groups and/or existing rule enforcing agencies may view the conflict as being within a "legitimate" framework; it is seen as a form of "competition" which, if not encouraged, is tolerated. For the process of criminalization to be initiated there must be at least a perception by one or more of the opposing parties that the conflict situation has exceeded acceptable limits and that manifest interests are threatened beyond a manageable point. It is at this point that one group attempts to label its opponent as deviant in order to facilitate legislation. The ultimate outcome of the rule-making process is subject to contingencies and is therefore problematic. The purpose of this study is to analyze an economic conflict and the contingencies which affected attempts to obtain legislation. It concerns the nearly 70-year attempt by the phonograph record industry to obtain copyright protection for its products.

VICTIMS IN SEARCH OF A LAW

Since its beginning, the phonograph record industry has faced the problem of piracy: the unauthorized duplication of its products for the purpose of sale.[1] Despite the evident contribution of manufacturers to the reproduction of sound such as engineering, promotion, and distribution, they have encountered inordinate difficulties in protecting their products, unlike other sectors of American industry and the published arts.

The first attempt to make sound reproductions copyrightable was in 1906, during hearings on revising the copyright law. After testimony by representatives of the sound reproduction industry a bill was introduced to the Committee on Patents specifying that copyrights could be obtained for "devices, appliances, and contrivances for reproducing to the ear, speech, or music." Due to a Supreme Court decision, the constitutionality of copyrighting products which were not intelligible writings became an

---

[1] "Piracy," when more precisely used in the music industry, refers to the unauthorized use of sound reproductions from one or more legitimate records when producing a record to be passed off as an original. "Counterfeiting" involves the unauthorized production of a record in which the genuine article is copied in all respects including label, jacket, etc. "Bootlegging" refers to the unauthorized manufacture and distribution of what is otherwise a legitimate record; the usual case is when a record pressing plant deliberately overruns an order to a consumer and disposes of the excess copies without permission (*Billboard* November 4, 1967, p. 3; Diamond 1968, p. 856n). The most recent practice of marketing unauthorized reproductions of live performances is also referred to as "bootlegging" in the industry. The term "piracy" will be used in this article as a general term to cover these and all forms of unauthorized duplication of sound reproductions. Entertainment industry publications frequently use the term "disklegging" in this sense.

issue. As a result, the enacted bill of 1909 (Title 17, United States Code) contained no provision concerning sound reproductions and the Copyright Office consistently refused to register them.

This first aborted attempt to find a remedy for piracy is indicative of the pattern to follow for the next 60 years.[2] Despite a general recognition that record manufacturers had a right to product protection and that there was some urgency for this protection, several attempts to gain appropriate legislation were thwarted. In 1925, amidst the rise of radio shows featuring gramophone records, another attempt was mounted to include sound reproduction under the protection of the copyright law. This bill (H.R. 11258, 68th Congress, 2nd Session, 1925), as would others in the next 30 years, met with increasing opposition from performers, publishers, broadcasters, jukebox concessionaires, and film producers. The opponents contended the common law concerning unfair competition was sufficient to combat piracy and the extension of copyright privileges to manufacturers would jeopardize their own interests.

Without protection from the Federal copyright statute record manufacturers were not completely lacking means of legal recourse. Protection could be sought under common law which recognizes a property right in assets gained through the expenditure or investment of money, skill, time, and effort. This protection, however, had numerous drawbacks such as limited jurisdiction, lack of uniformity, and uncertainty of case outcome (Ringer 1961, p. 47). Since no criminal violation was involved, pirates had to be tracked down to face civil actions by the companies themselves. This was both a fruitless and expensive operation. In some cases, after difficult detective work located a pirate, he simply disappeared leaving the manufacturer little to show for his effort (Billboard, May 19, 1951).

Although common law protection against piracy was a poor substitute for that possible under statutory law, the record industry obviously lacked the political strength to overcome the array of interest groups opposed to manufacturer control over sound recordings. Of the 31 bills introduced in Congress between 1906 and 1951 which offered statutory protection at the federal level, none passed. Furthermore, no state was to give such protection until the mid-1960's.

1952 marked a turning point in the quest for copyright protection. In this year, Columbia Records Inc. filed a complaint with the New York Supreme Court against Dante Bollentino of Paradox Industries Inc. for re-recording under misleading brand labels records made by Columbia between 1925 and 1932. Shortly after Columbia obtained an injunction against further pirating of these records, publishers holding copyrights

---

[2] A detailed discussion of manufacturers' attempts to acquire legislation during the period up to 1955 will be found in a study by Ringer (1961).

sued Bollentino for damages stemming from infringement since he had neither secured licenses to use the music nor paid royalties.

The Bollentino case marked a new phase in the piracy battle: another group besides the manufacturers was showing concern over lost revenues. Unlike manufacturers, the publishers had some recourse through the copyright law, but the resulting awards for damages from the Bollentino case and others proved trivial. Consequently, publishers began to favor copyright protection for manufacturers.

In the meantime the manufacturers themselves were consolidating their efforts through trade associations. The Record Industry Association of America, Inc. (RIAA), comprised of the largest and many medium-sized record manufacturers, had been seeking state legislation against piracy as early as 1952. The American Record Manufacturers and Distributors Association (ARMADA), formed in 1959 and comprised of smaller and medium-sized manufacturers and large distributors from major cities, considered the combating of piracy a principal goal. Both organizations actively initiated several civil suits and supplied evidence in actions in piracy cases. But their principal goal was intimated by ARMADA president, Art Talmadge, when he claimed that stiff federal legislation was the "ultimate remedy:" "The answer is a clear federal law, possibly an amendment to the Copyright Act, which would put the fear of the Lord and the F.B.I. into the hearts of the bootleggers" (*Billboard,* October 10, 1960).

In mid-1962, hearings began on a bill (H.R. 6354) to provide up to $10,000 fine or up to 10 years imprisonment for interstate transport of recordings with forged or counterfeited labels, and for interstate transport of recordings "reproduced without the permission or authorization of the owner of the master recording." The bill would also amend the copyright law to provide damages on counterfeited records. Unlike previous hearings on the copyrighting of records, manufacturers, publishers, and composers were in accord favoring the bill's passage.

Despite the final agreement among warring parties after some 35 years, the manufacturers still could not gain the victory they wanted. Opposition to the bill was expressed by the Register of Copyrights and the Librarian of Congress. While favoring the intent of the bill, these opponents argued that a number of complicated copyright issues concerning sound recordings were unresolved. Furthermore, the opponents felt that since a general revision of the copyright law was in progress, the bill was a kind of piecemeal legislation which should be avoided at this juncture.

Another probable factor operating against the record industry was the memory of Congress. The entire entertainment industry had just emerged from the television quiz show scandals in the late 1950's. These were shortly followed by the payola scandals within the record industry itself. The effect of payola was to strain the industry's image of integrity. The degree to which this tempered the legislators' enthusiasm for copyright revision in 1962 is impossible to say. The fact is, however, the copyright law remained untouched when a revised bill was eventually passed: Public Law 87-773. The bill's passage represented only a minor victory for the manufacturers since it provided penalties solely for interstate commerce in recordings with forged or counterfeited labels. Also the initially harsh penalties were diluted to a maximum fine of $1,000 and/or not more than one year imprisonment.

By 1971, piracy was perceived to be assuming alarming proportions and copyright protection via passage of a complete revision bill still appeared far away. In June of that year House hearings convened on another bill, already passed in the Senate without hearings, to amend the copyright law as it applied to sound recordings. The proponents were a formidable array: Librarian of Congress, Deputy Attorney General, Copyright Office, American Federation of Musicians, RIAA, National Association of Record Merchandisers, Inc.; and National Music Publishers Association, Inc.

In addition, support for the bill came from two new sources. The Department of State was in the process of negotiating an international treaty on record piracy and felt that the passage of the bill would enhance the United States' bargaining position. Since the treaty negotiations had implications for international trade relations, the Department of Commerce also urged the bill's passage.

In October of 1971 Congress passed Public Law 92-140, an amendment to the copyright law making illegal the unauthorized reproduction and sale of copyrighted records. The law also allowed criminal prosecution for unauthorized use of copyrighted musical works in recordings; the original law had specially excluded criminal action and only allowed the musical copyright owner to collect royalties through a civil action. Thus, after nearly 70 years the manufacturers finally obtained statutory law to protect their products.[3]

THE EMERGENCE OF MANIFEST INTERESTS

Although piracy in sound reproductions is nearly as old as sound reproducing devices themselves, its volume did not accelerate appreciably until after 1945. The consumerism boom greatly benefited the recording industry. The soaring expense of live entertainment plus technological improvements in recording material and reproducing equipment available for home use spurred an unprecedented demand for recordings. With this demand emerged a multimillion dollar piracy business.

Collectors' Pirates. Up through 1920, record piracy was comparatively limited in both sales volume and scope. The immediate post-war pirate

---

[3]The law affects only those recordings made between February 15, 1972 and January 1, 1975 on the assumption a general copyright revision will be in effect by the later date.

appealed almost exclusively to the record collectors interested in jazz, blues, and swing: his products were essentially obscure and otherwise unavailable pre-war recordings. Hundreds of such collectors' items were available on various "pirate" labels (e.g., Wax, Jazz-Time, Jolly Roger, The Hot Jazz Club of America). But they seldom sold more than 1,000 copies of any one item (*Variety*, July 5, 1950). Given the restricted market and difficulties in obtaining legal redress, the operations of these "collectors' pirates" did not particularly concern the record companies.

In 1951, the record industry took note of a new phenomenon in piracy: current hits were being issued under counterfeit labels with one pirate pressing 50,000 records per week in four plants (*Billboard*, September 1, 1951). But the initial targets of the companies were collectors' pirates. The first case concerned recordings of Metropolitan Opera Saturday matinee broadcasts and the second, in 1951, concerned Dante Bollentino, who marketed pirate jazz records.

Bollentino's operation was destroyed by Columbia's injunction and by publishers later filing suits for damages on unpaid royalties. Following this case, there was a decline in jazz pirating perhaps due less to pirates' fear than to a greater effort by the industry to reissue out-of-print jazz records during the fifties.

The collectors' pirates did not disappear, their products changed. In the early fifties they began to issue folk and classical music, and more currently operatic music. As with the jazz collectors' pirates of the late forties, record companies evidently feel they can afford to ignore the opera pirates since the products are not in direct competition. Such is likely to remain the case until companies, for whatever reason, begin marketing reissues of the same products.

Entrepreneurial Pirates. The operations of collectors' pirates are marginal: they provide a small public with a product otherwise unavailable, their profits are generally minimal, and their economic impact on legitimate record companies is negligible. The opposite of these characteristics describe the "entrepreneurial pirates." Like buccaneers of the 17th century, the success of these pirates depends on the success of others. A flourishing market must be already established for a product before they will enter into the competition. They have no intention of establishing a monopoly, for to drive record companies out of business would only defeat their own sources of income.

It is impossible to accurately assess the magnitude of the economic impact of entrepreneurial piracy on the record industry. All estimates by industry spokesmen must be considered in the context that they are given, namely, in attempt to justify legislative action. By 1959, industry spokesmen were estimating that 20 percent of hit records (*Billboard*, December 14, 1959) and one-third of all records sold (*Billboard*, June 15, 1959) were pirated. The following year, Art Talmadge, president of ARMADA, claimed that five percent of the record industry's annual gross or $20 million per year was being siphoned off by pirates (*Billboard*, October 10, 1960).

The most serious inroads of piracy into the record business came with the development and rapid popularity of tapes and cartridges. Again, there was a flurry of estimates of the damage. By 1969 it was claimed that one-third of the retail sales in prerecorded tapes represented pirated goods (*Billboard*, May 10, 1969). By the 1971 House hearings on amending the copyright law, the generally accepted estimates were that one of every four prerecorded tapes, representing $100 million in sales, was a pirate product; five percent of the records were pirates' and represented sales of $60 million. At the same hearings members of the industry provided examples of the wide range of pirates' works: popular, hard rock, country and western, and folk. The types of performers ranging from Tom Jones to Janis Joplin to Buck Owens had one common trait: their record sales were large enough to encourage pirating.

Counterculture Pirates. In the summer of 1969, a new type of pirate emerged. His first product was a set of two unmarked records packaged in a white double sleeve with the words *Great White Wonder* rubber stamped in a corner. The records contained 26 performances by Bob Dylan, 25 of which were taken from private tapes never heard before in public. The records' release had not been approved by Dylan and certainly not by his record company, Columbia. The *Great White Wonder* was a precedent for a series of albums to follow as Dylan had produced a number of tapes containing unreleased songs.

Although the new pirates were providing the public with unreleased material, they were unlike the collectors' pirates in two important respects. First, the demand for their products was much greater, hence potentially more profitable. Second, rationales associated with the products were to go beyond the simple service theme of the collectors' pirates. It was a complex amalgam drawing upon both Marxist and utopian socialist writers and translated into the rhetoric of the New Left.

THE POLITICALIZATION OF RECORD PIRACY

Rock music has been bestowed with an elaborate ideology by the counter-culture.[4] This ideology possesses two major tenets in direct opposition to

---

[4]The term "counterculture" is synonymous with "contraculture" as defined by Yinger (1960, p. 629): ". . . The normative system of a group contains, as a primary element, a theme of conflict with the values of the total society, where personality variables are directly involved in the development and maintenance of the group's values, and wherever its norms can be understood only by reference to the relationships of the group to a surrounding dominant culture." Cf. Parsons' (1951, p. 355) "counter-ideology" and Roszak's (1969, pp. 48–49) "counter-culture."

the dominant value system. The first posits that rock music is a revolutionary force which will destroy the dominant social structure of "Amerika" or the "death culture." The most elaborate explication of this proposition has been articulated by John Sinclair, founder of the White Panther Party, who portrayed rock as the core of the new culture providing "inspiration and the breath to go on." "Everything was built up on the music, and it was going to be the force that would carry us through to the glorious world of the future" (*Creem,* Vol. 2 #17, 1971). Rock music was to reveal the manifest interests of young people and contribute unity and purpose to them.

The second tenet of the rock ideology has already been implied by Sinclair. He argued that the people's culture was being exploited by the creators and manufacturers of the music through over-pricing records, concerts, and festivals and "selling out" the people. Indicative of the feelings of many radicals are those of A. J. Weberman, the founder of the Dylan Liberation Front, when he shouted at the singer: ". . . you *used* the struggle of the black people to get yourself ahead . . . you ripped-off their music. *You owe them quite a bit*" (*Rolling Stone,* March 4, 1971:44).

Dylan was the first victim of the counterculture pirates. In the late summer of 1969 *Great White Wonder* appeared in selected record stores in the Los Angeles area. According to one Columbia executive and lawyer, the company at first did not take *GWW* seriously and dismissed it as of little consequence.[5] But *GWW* proved to be a success, selling an estimated 60,000 to 100,000 copies, and it generated other Dylan pirate recordings. At this point the company began to exhibit concern.

After the Dylan tapes had been exhausted, the "live" or concert facsimile became the standard pirate product. The first rock concert album was *LIVEr Than You'll Ever Be,* containing live performances of the Rolling Stones. This was nearly a year prior to the release of many of the same performances, *Get Yer Ya Ya's Out,* by London Records. *LIVEr* is as significant as *GWW* in that it was the prototype of a major aspect of the underground pirating: it established that "any kid can take his tape recorder to a Rolling Stones' performance and become a millionaire" (*Time,* 1971:72).

The rock and underground press partially supported the pirate phenomenon arguing that the record conglomerates were not sympathetic to the needs of the people. Griel Marcus reviewed a number of unauthorized recordings in *Rolling Stone* (February 7, 1970:36) and noted: "In a way, the bootleg phenomenon may well force artists to respond to what the public wants—or lose a lot of bread. One obvious way to squelch the *Great*

---

[5]During the Spring of 1972, the second author conducted a series of interviews with executives and attorneys at the following record companies: Columbia, Capitol, Warner/Reprise, United Artists, Elektra, and A&M. These interviews were designed in part to verify statements found in trade journals concerning pirating and to obtain other information on the companies' reactions toward pirating.

White Wonder album, without arousing any bad feelings, would have been to issue the basement tape; the way to kill the new live Stones' album would be to release a similar LP that was even better."

The pirates themselves presented their operations as merely public services:

> I explain it mainly through the failure of the establishment record companies to provide the listener with anything stimulating, innovative, and worthwhile. After all, the summer of 1969, when the underground record industry began, was an incredible period of record industry hype and shuck. Such utterly atrocious jive as "Grand Funk," "Ten Wheel Drive," "Blind Faith," "Santana," and "Chicago" were served up to the listening public (*Los Angeles Free Press,* April 10, 1970:10).

The counterculture pirate was thus an artifact of the alternative life-style. Like the collectors' pirate, he furnished a service not provided by the major record companies, but his product had acquired political significance.

Many of the Dylan pirate albums were considered by critics to be of superior aesthetic merit to his later efforts on Columbia Records. "Early" Dylan was in fact competing with the "new" Dylan for consumers' dollars. It is difficult to measure the exact value of the pirate records since their sales were confined to the larger urban areas and to university and college towns. However, Bob Johnston, producer of several of Dylan's Columbia albums, told one reporter that he had been offered $200,000 for any unreleased material he had in his possession (*Rolling Stone,* July 27, 1971:19).

Record companies were at first hesitant to respond to the counterculture pirates. One reason for this reluctance was that the record industry considered the album a unique phenomenon, one which was not immediately understood in terms of its long-range consequences. "If we ignore it perhaps it will just go away," was the comment of one Columbia executive. Even when the success of the album became apparent the company reaction was mild and based on a sense of corporate morality. The same Columbia executive noted: "It was not so much the fact that we were losing X dollars, but that it was wrong. It seemed to be morally wrong to them [company policy makers] and that seemed to be the thing that annoyed them more than anything else."

But the production of *LIVEr* was the catalyst for sterner reaction. This album was not merely a collection of otherwise unavailable tapes but a product that was directly competitive. The plans for the 1969 Rolling Stones' American tour had included an album from the outset. The pirate album was cheaply produced but with surprisingly high quality. As a result, both the group and their recording company were financially affected. This album was the vanguard of a series of competitive pirate recordings which according to a company executive evoked a response:

> Nothing fostered moral indignation as much as having it hit you in the money belt. . . . As the albums followed upon albums, and as the volume started to increase, they became increasingly aware of the total impact of them, and it became a major problem to them. Then they decided that perhaps there was a moral indignation on top of economic indignation.

This change in reaction toward the counterculture pirating is best illustrated by the change in record company tactics regarding retail outlets. When *GWW* was marketed a technique of gentle persuasion was employed: store owners were approached and warned of poorer service if they handled the pirate goods. This tactic did not have universal appeal, however. One record executive claimed it was not in their interest to alienate business associates over a few "hippie kids" selling Dylan tapes. The companies' perceptions of pirate records as direct competition appears to have altered this posture. In 1971, owners were being specifically told that they would no longer receive any promotional or advertising money from Warner Brothers or Columbia. One owner told *Rolling Stone* (October 14, 1971:10): "I was also instructed by the Warner-Elecktra-Atlantic group that if I carried a single bootleg, they wouldn't sell me any more records. They were unwilling to put this in writing." These informal enforcement practices, of questionable functionality, were not initiated; the recording industry was finally successful in petitioning Congress to legislate protection.

DISCUSSION

It is paradoxical that eventual Federal intervention into record piracy required over a half century of effort. The targets of legislation possessed the requisites to be legally stigmatized: their actions were labelled as "deviant," with even an appropriate set of appellations—pirates, bootleggers, etc.—and they were politically powerless. Conversely, the record manufacturers as legitimate businessmen seemingly had significant lobbying resources. Despite this power differential, the criminalization process was stalled for decades.[6] A number of contingencies were operative during the process of obtaining legal sanctions.

---

[6]Turk (1969, pp. 69–70) has pointed out that in law enforcement, a situation analogous but not similar to law enactment, wide disparity in power serves to moderate the use of official processing of deviants:

> [W]here the opposition is seen to be virtually powerless, normal legal procedures are likely to be unofficially abrogated in favor of more summary and less costly procedures. . . . The greater the power difference in favor of norm enforcers over resisters, the greater the probability of criminalization—with the proviso that criminality rates derived from official records are likely to show a curvilinear instead of a linear relationship.

Conflicting manifest interests. While piracy obviously posed an economic threat to the record industry, the means of meeting this threat was subject to contention. Companies' attempts to revise the copyright law were openly opposed, not by pirates but by other legitimate media groups who perceived such legislation as jeopardizing their own economic concerns. Fearing manufacturers' control over sound reproductions, these interest groups neutralized the companies' lobbying efforts by claiming that existent legal norms were sufficient. The legal stigmatization of pirates was consequently delayed. Only when the opposing groups perceived piracy as a threat to their own interests did they support manufacturers' legislative efforts. But until this time the lack of a united front effectively negated the ability of one interest group to criminalize the activities of a deviant group.

Uncrystallized manifest interests. Pirates posed a threat to the latent interests of the music industry as a whole; however, only the recording companies—the most vulnerable—acted in their manifest concern as the others ignored the problem. Nor did all recording companies consistently approach the matter with the same sense of urgency. The behavior of the companies toward pirates was episodic, depending more on perceived interests of individual companies than of the industry as a whole. During the post-World War II period through 1960, the pirates neither questioned the legitimacy of the companies nor consistently affected their income. Only when a pirate produced a directly competitive product did companies act. Furthermore, the marginal operations of such pirates were vulnerable if the companies cared to expend enough time and money.

Even with the emergence of the competitive, mass volume entrepreneurial pirates who were difficult to prosecute, companies often failed to interpret them as a threat toward the industry as a whole. Major companies in particular preferred to believe that their less affluent competitors suffered more. Pirates were seen as a variable form of competition. The extent to which they were taken seriously depended upon whose products were being appropriated. Thus, the manufacturers did not always present a unified front against a common foe. It was not until the early 1960's that they coalesced in the form of trade associations to face an outside threat to their collective interests.

Failure of legitimation. The final realization of common interests and the presentation of a unified front before Congress did not ensure completion of the criminalization process. In 1962 the only opposition to proposed legislation was from the register of Copyrights and the Librarian of Congress. Although promises of forthcoming copyright revision may have influenced Congress to delay action, it is noteworthy that penalties in the enacted counterfeit record law were reduced to inconsequential levels. The music industry, following the payola scandals of the early 1960's, was itself being considered for sanctions by Congress. The industry's image was tainted. This conspired against persuading Congress that the industry's interests needed protection on their own merits, or that the public's interests were significantly endangered by pirates.

Political interests and legitimation. Conflict theorists have indicated that historically the questioning of dominant ideology engenders an awareness of latent economic interests among the power holders. Such appears to be the case for Congress when political radicals condoned the exploitation of the music industry in ideological terms. Record companies became legitimized as part of the "Establishment" with their ascendency to the posture of a billion dollar industry and by the assaults from youthful political radicals. With the shadow of payola far behind, the industry was free of stigma. It and its allies could present themselves as part of the free enterprise system sorely beset by unfair competition from both economic *and* political deviants.

The climate for legislation was also enhanced by international politics. The Departments of State and Commerce urged passage of a copyright revision to facilitate participation in an international treaty. Under these circumstances Congress swiftly legitimated the interests of the record industry.

Thus, while the criminalization process begins within the context of conflicting social units, each successive step in the process is highly problematic. Rule-making requires not only that the legitimacy of an opponent be put in question, but also that power holders be convinced that stigmatized individuals should and can be neutralized by the suggested means.

REFERENCES

DAHRENDORF, R., *Class and Class Conflict in Industrial Society.* Stanford: Stanford University, 1959.

DIAMOND, S. A., "Sound Recordings and Copyright Revision." *Iowa Law Review* 53 (February 1968): 839–869.

PARSONS, T., *The Social System.* Glencoe, Ill.: Free Press, 1951.

QUINNEY, R., *The Social Reality of Crime.* Boston: Little, Brown, 1970.

RINGER, B. A., *The Unauthorized Duplication of Sound Recordings.* Study No. 26, February, 1957, in Senate Committee Print, *Copyright Law Revision,* Studies Prepared for the Subcommittee on Patents, Trademarks, and Copyrights of the Committee on the Judiciary. Washington: Government Printing Office, 1961.

Roszak, T., *The Making of a Counter Culture*. Garden City. New York: Doubleday, 1969.

Turk, A. T., "Conflict and Criminality." *American Sociological Review* 31 (June 1966): 338–52.

————, *Criminality and Legal Order*. Chicago: Rand McNally, 1969.

Vold, G., *Theoretical Criminology*. New York: Oxford, 1958.

Yinger, J. M., "Contraculture and Subculture." *American Sociological Review* 25 (October 1960): 625–35.

19. THE CONDEMNATION AND
PERSECUTION OF HIPPIES

MICHAEL E. BROWN

This article is about persecution and terror. It speaks of the Hippie and the temptations of intimacy that the myth of Hippie has made poignant, and it does this to discuss the institutionalization of repression in the United States.

When people are attacked as a group, they change. Individuals in the group may or may not change, but the organization and expression of their collective life will be transformed. When the members of a gathering believe that there is a grave danger imminent and that opportunities for escape are rapidly diminishing, the group loses its organizational quality. It becomes transformed in panic. This type of change can also occur outside a situation of strict urgency: When opportunities for mobility or access to needed resources are cut off, people may engage in desperate collective actions. In both cases, the conversion of social form occurs when members of a collectivity are about to be hopelessly locked into undesired and undesirable positions.

The process is not, however, automatic. The essential ingredient for conversion is social control exercised by external agents on the collectivity itself. The result can be benign, as a panic mob can be converted into a crowd that makes an orderly exit from danger. Or it can be cruel.

The transformation of groups under pressure is of general interest; but there are special cases that are morally critical to any epoch. Such critical cases occur when pressure is persecution, and transformation is destruction. The growth of repressive mechanisms and institutions is a key concern in this time of administrative cruelty. Such is the justification for the present study.

SOCIAL CONTROL AS TERROR

Four aspects of repressive social control such as that experienced by Hippies are important. First, the administration of control is suspicious. It

Published by permission of Transaction Inc. from *transaction*, Vol. 6 (September 1969). © 1969 by Transaction Inc.

projects a dangerous future and guards against it. It also refuses the risk of inadequate coverage by enlarging the controlled population to include all who might be active in any capacity. Control may or may not be administered with a heavy hand, but it is always a generalization applied to specific instances. It is a rule and thus ends by pulling many fringe innocents into its bailiwick; it creates as it destroys.

Second, the administration of control is a technical problem which, depending on its site and object, requires the bringing together of many different agencies that are ordinarily dissociated or mutually hostile. A conglomerate of educational, legal, social welfare, and police organizations is highly efficient. The German case demonstrates that. Even more important, it is virtually impossible to oppose control administered under the auspices of such a conglomerate since it includes the countervailing institutions ordinarily available. When this happens control is not only efficient and widespread, but also legitimate, commanding a practical, moral and ideological realm that is truly "one-dimensional."

Third, as time passes, control is applied to a wider and wider range of details, ultimately blanketing its objectives' lives. At that point, as Hilberg suggests in his *The Destruction of the European Jews*, the extermination of the forms of lives leads easily to the extermination of the lives themselves. The line between persecution and terror is thin. For the oppressed, life is purged of personal style as every act becomes inexpressive, part of the struggle for survival. The options of a life-style are eliminated at the same time that its proponents are locked into it.

Fourth, control is relentless. It develops momentum as organization accumulates, as audiences develop, and as unofficial collaborators assume the definition of tasks, expression and ideology. This, according to W. A. Westley's "The Escalation of Violence Through Legitimation," is the culture of control. It not only limits the behaviors, styles, individuals and groups toward whom it is directed, it suppresses all unsanctioned efforts. As struggle itself is destroyed, motivation vanishes or is turned inward.

These are the effects of repressive control. We may contrast them with the criminal law, which merely prohibits the performance of specific acts (with the exception, of course, of the "crime without victims"—homosexuality, abortion, and drug use). Repression converts or destroys an entire social form, whether that form is embodied in a group, a style or an idea. In this sense, it is terror.

These general principles are especially relevant to our understanding of tendencies that are ripening in the United States day by day. Stated in terms that magnify it so that it can be seen despite ourselves, this is the persecution of the Hippies, a particularly vulnerable group of people who are the cultural wing of a way of life recently emerged from its quiet and individualistic quarters. Theodore Roszak, describing the Hippies in terms of their relationship to the culture and politics of dissent, notes that "the underlying unity of youthful dissent consists . . . in the effort of beat-hip bohemianism to work out the personality structure, the total life-style that follows from New Left social criticism." This life-style is currently bearing the brunt of the assault on what Roszak calls a "counter-culture"; it is an assault that is becoming more concentrated and savage every day. There are lessons for the American future to be drawn from this story.

PERSECUTION

Near Boulder, Colorado, a restaurant sign says "Hippies not served here." Large billboards in upstate New York carry slogans like "Keep America Clean: Take a Bath." and "Keep America Clean: Get a Haircut." These would be as amusing as ethnic jokes if they did not represent a more systematic repression.

The street sweeps so common in San Francisco and Berkeley in 1968 and 1969 were one of the first lines of attack. People were brutally scattered by club-wielding policemen who first closed exits from the assaulted area and then began systematically to beat and arrest those who were trapped. This form of place terror, like surveillance in Negro areas and defoliation in Vietnam, curbs freedom and forces people to fight or submit to minute inspection by hostile forces. There have also been one-shot neighborhood pogroms, such as the police assault on the Tompkins Square Park gathering in New York's Lower East Side on Memorial Day, 1967: "Sadistic glee was written on the faces of several officers," wrote the *East Village Other*. Some women became hysterical. The police slugged Frank Wise, and dragged him off, handcuffed and bloody, crying, "My God, my God, where is this happening? Is this America?" The police also plowed into a group of Hippies, Yippies, and straights at the April, 1968, "Yip-in" at Grand Central Station. The brutality was as clear in this action as it had been in the Tompkins Square bust. In both cases, the major newspapers editorialized against the police tactics, and in the first the Mayor apologized for the "free wielding of nightsticks." But by the summer of 1968, street sweeps and busts and the continuous presence of New York's Tactical Police Force had given the Lower East Side an ominous atmosphere. Arrests were regularly accompanied by beatings and charges of "resistance to arrest." It became clear that arrests rather than subsequent procedures were the way in which control was to be exercised. The summer lost its street theaters, the relaxed circulation of people in the neighborhood and the easy park gatherings.

Official action legitimizes nonofficial action. Private citizens take up the cudgel of law and order newly freed from the boundaries of due process and respect. After Tompkins Square, rapes and assaults became common as local toughs assumed the role, with the police, of defender of the faith. In Cambridge, Massachusetts, following a virulent attack on Hippies by the Mayor, *Newsweek* reported that vigilantes attacked Hippie neighborhoods in force.

Ultimately more damaging are the attacks on centers of security. Police raids on "Hippie pads," crash pads, churches and movement centers have become daily occurrences in New York and California over the past two and a half years. The usual excuses for raids are drugs, runaways and housing violations, but many incidents of unlawful entry by police and the expressions of a more generalized hostility by the responsible officials suggest that something deeper is involved. The Chief of Police in San Francisco put it bluntly; quoted in *The New York Times* magazine in May, 1967, he said:

> Hippies are no asset to the community. These people do not have the courage to face the reality of life. They are trying to escape. Nobody should let their young children take part in this hippy thing.

The Director of Health for San Francisco gave teeth to this counsel when he sent a task force of inspectors on a door-to-door sweep of the Haight-Ashbury—"a two-day blitz" that ended with a strange result, again according to *The Times:* Very few of the Hippies were guilty of housing violations.

Harassment arrests and calculated degradation have been two of the most effective devices for introducing uncertainty to the day-to-day lives of the Hippies. Cambridge's Mayor's attack on the "hipbos" (the suffix stands for body odor) included, said *Newsweek* of October 30, 1967, a raid on a "hippie pad" by the Mayor and "a platoon of television cameramen." They "seized a pile of diaries and personal letters and flushed a partially clad girl from the closet." In Wyoming, *The Times* reported that two "pacifists" were "jailed and shaved" for hitchhiking. This is a fairly common hazard, though Wyoming officials are perhaps more sadistic than most. A young couple whom I interviewed were also arrested in Wyoming during the summer of 1968. They were placed in solitary confinement for a week during which they were not permitted to place phone calls and were not told when or whether they would be charged or released. These are not exceptional cases. During the summer of 1968, I interviewed young hitchhikers throughout the country; most of them had similar stories to tell.

In the East Village of New York, one hears countless stories of apartment destruction by police (occasionally reported in the newspapers), insults from the police when rapes or robberies are reported, and cruel speeches and even crueler bails set by judges for arrested Hippies.

In the light of this, San Francisco writer Mark Harris' indictment of the Hippies as paranoid seems peculiar. In the September 1967 issue of *The Atlantic,* he wrote,

> The most obvious failure of perception was the hippies' failure to discriminate among elements of the Establishment, whether in the Haight-Ashbury or in San Francisco in general. Their paranoia was the paranoia of all youthful heretics.

This is like the demand of some white liberals that Negroes acknowledge that they (the liberals) are not the power structure, or that black people must distinguish between the good and the bad whites despite the fact that the black experience of white people in the United States has been, as the President's Commission on Civil Disorder suggested, fairly monolithic and racist.

Most journalists reviewing the "Hippie scene" with any sympathy at all seem to agree with *Newsweek* that "the hippies do seem natural prey for publicity-hungry politicians—if not overzealous police," and that they have been subjected to varieties of cruelty that ought to be intolerable. This tactic was later elaborated in the massive para-military assault on Berkeley residents and students during a demonstration in support of Telegraph Avenue's street people and their People's Park. The terror of police violence, a constant in the lives of street people everywhere, in California carries the additional threat of martial law under a still-active state of extreme emergency. The whole structure of repression was given legitimacy and reluctant support by University of California officials. Step by step, they became allies of Reagan's "dogs of war." Roger W. Heyns, chancellor of the Berkeley campus, found himself belatedly reasserting the university's property in the lot. It was the law and the rights of university that trapped the chancellor in the network of control and performed the vital function of providing justification and legitimacy for Sheriff Madigan and the National Guard. Heyns said: "We will have to put up a fence to re-establish the conveniently forgotten fact that this field is indeed the university's, and to exclude unauthorized personnel from the site. . . . The fence will give us time to plan and consult. We tried to get this time some other way and failed—hence the fence." And hence "Bloody Thursday" and the new regime.

And what of the Hippies? They have come far since those balmy days of 1966–67, days of flowers, street-cleaning, free stores, decoration and love. Many have fled to the hills of Northern California to join their brethren who had set up camps there several years ago. Others have fled to communes outside the large cities and in the Middle West. After the Tompkins Square assault, many of the East Village Hippies refused to follow the lead of those who were more political. They refused to develop organizations of defense and to accept a hostile relationship with the police and neighborhood. Instead, they discussed at meeting after meeting, how they could show their attackers love. Many of those spirits have fled; others have been beaten or jailed too many times; and still others have modified their outlook in ways that reflect the struggle. Guerrilla theater, Up Against the Wall Mother Fucker, the Yippies, the urban communes; these are some of the more recent manifestations of the alternative culture. One could see these trends growing in the demonstrations mounted by Hippies against arrests of runaways or pot smokers, the community organizations, such as grew in Berkeley for self-defense and politics, and the beginnings of the will to fight back when trapped in street sweeps.

It is my impression that the Hippie culture is growing as it recedes from the eye of the media. As a consequence of the destruction of their urban places, there has been a redistribution of types. The flower people have left for the hills and become more communal; those who remained in the city were better adapted to terror, secretive or confrontative. The Hippie culture is one of the forms radicalism can take in this society. The youngsters, 5,000 of them, who came to Washington to counter-demonstrate against the Nixon inaugural showed the growing amalgamation of the New Left and its cultural wing. The Yippies who went to Chicago for guerrilla theater and learned about "pigs" were the multi-generational expression of the new wave. A UAWMF (Up Against the Wall Mother Fucker) drama, played at Lincoln Center during the New York City garbage strike—they carted garbage from the neglected Lower East Side and dumped it at the spic 'n' span cultural center—reflected another interpretation of the struggle, one that could include the politically militant as well as the culturally defiant. Many Hippies have gone underground—in an older sense of the word. They have shaved their beards, cut their hair, and taken straight jobs, like the secret Jews of Spain; but unlike those Jews, they are consciously an underground, a resistance.

What is most interesting and, I believe, a direct effect of the persecution, is the enormous divergence of forms that are still recognizable by the outsider as Hippie and are still experienced as a shared identity. "The Yippies," says Abbie Hoffman, "are like Hippies, only fiercer and more fun." The "hippie types" described in newspaper accounts of drug raids on colleges turn out, in many cases, to be New Leftists.

The dimensions by which these various forms are classified are quite conventional: religious-political, visible-secret, urban-hill, communal-individualistic. As their struggle intensifies, there will be more efforts for unity and more militant approaches to the society that gave birth to a real alternative only to turn against it with a mindless savagery. Yippie leader Jerry Rubin, in an "emergency letter to my brothers and sisters in the movement" summed up:

Huey Newton is in prison.
Eldridge Cleaver is in exile.
Oakland Seven are accused of conspiracy.
Tim Leary is up for 30 years and how many of our brothers are in court and jail for getting high?
. . .
Camp activists are expelled and arrested.
War resisters are behind bars.
Add it up!

Rubin preambles his summary with:

From the Bay Area to New York, we are suffering the greatest depression in our history. People are taking bitterness in their coffee instead of sugar. The hippie-yippie-SDS movement is a "white nigger" movement. The American economy no longer needs young whites and blacks. We are waste material. We fulfill our destiny in life by rejecting a system which rejects us.

He advocates organizing "massive mobilizations for the spring, nationally coordinated and very theatrical, taking place near courts, jails, and military stockades."

An article published in a Black Panther magazine is entitled "The Hippies Are Not Our Enemies." White radicals have also overcome their initial rejection of cultural radicals. Something clearly is happening, and it is being fed, finally, by youth, the artists, the politicos and the realization, through struggle, that America is not beautiful.

SOME HISTORICAL ANALOGIES

The persecution of the Jews destroyed both a particular social form and the individuals who qualified for the Jewish fate by reason of birth. Looking at the process in the aggregate, Hilberg describes it as a gradual coming together of a multitude of loose laws, institutions, and intentions, rather than a program born mature. The control conglomerate that resulted was a refined engine "whose devices," Hilbert writes, "not only trap a larger number of victims; they also require a greater degree of specialization, and with that division of labor, the moral burden too is fragmented among the participants. The perpetrator can now kill his victims without touching them, without hearing them, without seeing them. . . . This ever growing capacity for destruction cannot be arrested anywhere." Ultimately, the persecution of the Jews was a mixture of piety, repression and mobilization directed against those who were in the society but suddenly not of it.

The early Christians were also faced with a refined and elaborate administrative structure whose harsh measures were ultimately directed at their ways of life: their social forms and their spiritual claims. The rationale was, and is, that certain deviant behaviors endanger society. Therefore, officials are obligated to use whatever means of control or persuasion they consider necessary to strike these forms from the list of human possibilities. This is the classical administrative rationale for the suppression of alternative values and world views.

As options closed and Christians found the opportunities to lead and explore Christian lives rapidly struck down, Christian life itself had to become rigid, prematurely closed and obsessed with survival.

The persecution of the early Christians presents analogies to the persecution of European Jews. The German assault affected the quality of Jewish organizations no less than it affected the lives of individual Jews, distorting communities long before it destroyed them. Hilberg documents some of the ways in which efforts to escape the oppression led on occasion to a subordination of energies to the problem of simply staying alive—of finding some social options within the racial castle. The escapist mentality that dominated the response to oppression and distorted relationships can be seen in some Jewish leaders in Vienna. They exchanged individuals for promises. This is what persecution and terror do. As options close and all parts of the life of the oppressed are touched by procedure, surveillance and control, behavior is transformed. The oppressed rarely retaliate (especially where they have internalized the very ethic that rejects them), simply because nothing is left untouched by the persecution. No energy is available for hostility, and, in any case, it is impossible to know where to begin. Bravery is stoicism. One sings to the cell or gas chamber.

The persecution of Hippies in the United States involves, regardless of the original intentions of the agencies concerned, an assault on a way of life, an assault no less concentrated for its immaturity and occasional ambivalence. Social, cultural and political resources have been mobilized to bring a group of individuals into line and to prevent others from refusing to toe the line.

The attractiveness of the Hippie forms and the pathos of their persecution brought into being an impressive array of defenders. Nevertheless theirs has been a defense of gestures, outside the realm of politics and social action essential to any real protection. It has been verbal, scholarly and appreciative, with occasional expressions of horror at official actions and attitudes. But unfortunately the arena of conflict within which the Hippies, willy-nilly, must try to survive is dominated not by the likes of

Susan Sontag, but by the likes of Daniel Patrick Moynihan whose apparent compassion for the Hippies will probably never be translated into action. For even as he writes (in the *American Scholar*, Autumn, 1967) that these youths are "trying to tell us something" and that they are one test of our "ability to survive," he rejects them firmly, and not a little *ex cathedra*, as a "truth gone astray." The Hippie remains helpless and more affected by the repressive forces (who will probably quote Moynihan) than by his own creative capacity or the sympathizers who support him in the journals. As John Kifner reported in *The Times*, " 'This scene is not the same anymore,' said the tall, thin Negro called Gypsy. ' . . . There are some very bad vibrations.' "

SOCIAL FORM AND CULTURAL HERESY

> But it's just another murder. A hippie being killed is just like a housewife being killed or a career girl being killed or a hoodlum being killed. None of these people, notice, are persons; they're labels. Who cares who Groovy was; if you know he was a 'hippie,' then already you know more about him than he did about himself.
> See, it's hard to explain to a lot of you what a hippie is because a lot of you really think a hippie IS something. You don't realize that the word is just a convenience picked up by the press to personify a social change thing beginning to happen to young people (*Paul Williams, in an article entitled "Label Dies—But Not Philosophy,"* Open City, *Los Angeles, November 17–23, 1967*).

Because the mass media have publicized the growth of a fairly well-articulated Hippie culture, it now bears the status of a social form. Variously identified as "counter-culture," "Hippie-dom," "Youth" or "Underground," the phenomenon centers on a philosophy of the present and takes the personal and public forms appropriate to that philosophy. Its values constitute a heresy in a society that consecrates the values of competition, social manipulation and functionalism, a society that defines ethical quality by long-range and general consequences, and that honors only those attitudes and institutions that affirm the primacy of the future and large-scale over the local and immediately present. It is a heresy in a society that eschews the primary value of intimacy for the sake of impersonal service to large and enduring organizations, a society that is essentialist rather than existentialist, a society that prizes biography over interactive quality. It is a heresy in a country whose President could be praised for crying, "Ask not what your country can do for you, but what you can do for your country!" Most important, however, it is heresy in a society whose official values, principles of operation and officials themselves are threatened domestically and abroad.

For these reasons the Hippie is available for persecution. When official authority is threatened, social and political deviants are readily conjured up as demons requiring collective exorcism and thus a reaffirmation of that authority. Where exorcism is the exclusive province of government, the government's power is reinforced by the adoption of a scapegoat. Deviant style and ideals make a group vulnerable to exploitation as a scapegoat, but it is official action which translates vulnerability into actionable heresy.

By contrast, recent political developments within black communities and the accommodations reached through bargaining with various official agencies have placed the blacks alongside the Viet Cong as an official enemy, but not as a scapegoat. As an enemy, the black is not a symbol but a source of society's troubles. It is a preferable position. The Hippie's threat lies in the lure of his way of life rather than in his political potential. His vulnerability as well as his proven capacity to develop a real alternative life permits his selection as scapegoat. A threatened officialdom is all too likely to take the final step that "brings on the judge." At the same time, by defining its attack as moderate, it reaffirms its moral superiority in the very field of hate it cultivates.

A PLAUSIBLE FORCE

We are speaking of that which claims the lives, totally or in part, of perhaps hundreds of thousands of people of all ages throughout the United States and elsewhere. The number is not inconsiderable.

The plausibility of the Hippie culture and its charisma can be argued on several grounds. Their outlook derives from a profound mobilizing idea: Quality resides in the present. Therefore, one seeks the local in all its social detail—not indulgently and alone, but openly and creatively. Vulnerability and improvisation are principles of action, repudiating the "rational" hierarchy of plans and stages that defines, for the grounded culture, all events as incidents of passage and means to an indefinitely postponable end—as transition. The allocation of reality to the past and the future is rejected in favor of the present, and a present that is known and felt immediately, not judged by external standards. The long run is the result rather than the goal of the present. "Psychical distance," the orientation of the insulated tourist to whom the environment is something forever foreign or of the administrator for whom the world is an object of administration, is repudiated as a relational principle. It is replaced by a principal of absorption. In this, relationships are more like play, dance or jazz. Intimacy derives from absorption, from spontaneous involvement, to use Erving Goffman's phrase, rather than from frequent contact or attraction, as social psychologists have long argued.

This vision of social reality makes assumptions about human nature. It sees man as only a part of a present that depends on all its parts. To be a "part" is not to play a stereotyped role or to plan one's behavior prior to entering the scene. It is to be of a momentum. Collaboration, the overt manifestation of absorption, is critical to any social arrangement because the present, as experience, is essentially social. Love and charisma are the reflected properties of the plausible whole that results from mutual absorption. "To swing" or "to groove" is to be of the scene rather than simply at or in the scene. "Rapping," an improvised, expansive, and collaborative conversational form, is an active embodiment of the more general ethos. Its craft is humor, devotion, trust, openness to events in the process of formation, and the capacity to be relevant. Identity is neither strictly personal nor something to be maintained, but something always to be discovered. The individual body is the origin of sounds and motions, but behavior, ideas, images, and reflective thought stem from interaction itself. Development is not of personalities but of situations that include many bodies but, in effect, one mind. Various activities, such as smoking marijuana, are disciplines that serve the function of bringing people together and making them deeply interesting to each other.

The development of an authentic "counter-culture," or, better, "alternative culture," has some striking implications. For one, information and stress are processed through what amounts to a new conceptual system—a culture that replaces, in the committed, the intrapersonal structures that Western personality theories have assumed to account for intrapersonal order. For example, in 1966, young Hippies often turned against their friends and their experience after a bad acid trip. But that was the year during which "the Hippie thing" was merely one constructive expression of dissent. It was not, at that point, an alternative culture. As a result, the imagery cued in by the trauma was the imagery of the superego, the distant and punitive authority of the Western family and its macrocosmic social system. Guilt, self-hatred and the rejection of experience was the result. Many youngsters returned home filled with a humiliation that could be forgotten, or converted to a seedy and defensive hatred of the dangerously deviant. By 1968 the bad trip, while still an occasion for reconversion for some, had for others become something to be guarded against and coped with in a context of care and experienced guidance. The atmosphere of trust and new language of stress-inspired dependence rather than recoil as the initial stage of cure. One could "get high with a little help from my friends." Conscience was purged of "authority."

Although the ethos depends on personal contact, it is carried by underground media (hundreds of newspapers claiming hundreds of thousands of readers), rock music, and collective activities, artistic and political, which deliver and duplicate the message; and it is processed through a generational flow. It is no longer simply a constructive expression of dissent and thus attractive because it is a vital answer to a system that destroys vitality; it is culture, and the young are growing up under the wisdom of its older generations. The ethos is realized most fully in the small communes that dot the American urbscape and constitute an important counter-institution of the Hippies.

This complex of population, culture, social form, and ideology is both a reinforcing environment for individuals and a context for the growth and elaboration of the complex itself. In it, life not only begins, it goes on; and, indeed, it must go on for those who are committed to it. Abbie Hoffman's *Revolution for the Hell of It* assumes the autonomy of this cultural frame of reference. It assumes that the individual has entered and has burned his bridges.

As the heresy takes an official definition and as the institutions of persecution form, a they-mentality emerges in the language which expresses the relationship between the oppressor and the oppressed. For the oppressed, it distinguishes life from nonlife so that living can go on. The they-mentality of the oppressed temporarily relieves them of the struggle by acknowledging the threat, identifying its agent, and compressing both into a quasi-poetic image, a cliché that can accommodate absurdity. One young man said, while coming down from an amphetamine high: "I'm simply going to continue to do what I want until they stop me."

But persecution is also structured by the they-mentality of the persecutors. This mentality draws lines around its objects as it fits them conceptually for full-scale social action. The particular uses of the term "hippie" in the mass media—like "Jew," "Communist," "Black Muslim," or "Black Panther"—cultivates not only disapproval and rejection but a climate of opinion capable of excluding Hippies from the moral order altogether. This is one phase of a subtle process that begins by locating and isolating a group, tying it to the criminal, sinful or obscene, developing and displaying referential symbols at a high level of abstraction which depersonalize and objectify the group, defining the stigmata by which members are to be known and placing the symbols in the context of ideology and readiness for action.

At this point, the symbols come to define public issues and are, consequently, sources of strength. The maintenance of power—the next phase of the story—depends less on the instruction of reading and viewing publics than on the elaboration of the persecutory institutions which demonstrate and justify power. The relationship between institution and public ceases to be one of expression or extension (of a public to an institution) and becomes one of transaction or dominance (of a public with or by an institution). The total dynamic is similar to advertising or the growth of the military as domestic powers in America.

An explosion of Hippie stories appeared in the mass media during the summer of 1967. Almost every large-circulation magazine featured articles on the Hippie "fad" or "subculture." *Life's* "The Other Culture" set the tone. The theme was repeated in *The New York Times Magazine,* May 14, 1967, where Hunter Thompson wrote that "The 'Hashbury' (Haight-Ashbury in San Francisco) is the new capital of what is rapidly becoming a drug culture." *Time's* "wholly new subculture" was "a cult whose mystique derives essentially from the influences of hallucinogenic drugs." By fall, while maintaining the emphasis on drugs as the cornerstone of the culture, the articles had shifted from the culturological to a "national character" approach, reminiscent of the World War II anti-Japanese propaganda, as personal traits were piled into the body of the symbol and objectification began. The Hippies were "acid heads," "generally dirty," and "visible, audible and sometimes smellable young rebels."

As "hippie" and its associated terms ("long-haired," "bearded") accumulated pejorative connotation, they began to be useful concepts and were featured regularly in news headlines: for example, "Hippie Mother Held in Slaying of Son, 2" (*The New York Times,* Nov. 22, 1967); "S Squad Hits Four Pads" (*San Francisco Chronicle,* July 27, 1967). The articles themselves solidified usage by dwelling on "hippie types," "wild drug parties" and "long-haired, bearded" youths (see, for example, *The New York Times* of Feb. 13, 1968, Sept. 16, 1968 and Nov. 3, 1967).

This is a phenomenon that R. H. Turner and S. J. Surace described in 1956 in order to account for the role of media in the development of hostile consciousness toward Mexicans. The presentation of certain symbols can remove their referents from the constraints of the conventional moral order so that extralegal and extramoral action can be used against them. Political cartoonists have used the same device with less powerful results. To call Mexican-Americans "zootsuiters" in Los Angeles, in 1943, was to free hostility from the limits of the conventional, though fragile, antiracism required by liberal ideology. The result was a wave of brutal anti-Mexican assaults. Turner and Surace hypothesized that:

> To the degree, then, to which any symbol evokes only one consistent set of connotations throughout the community, only one general course of action with respect to that object will be indicated, and the union of diverse members of the community into acting crowd will be facilitated . . . or it will be an audience prepared to accept novel forms of official action.

First the symbol, then the accumulation of hostile connotations, and finally the action-issue: Such a sequence appears in the news coverage of Hippies from the beginning of 1967 to the present. The amount of coverage has decreased in the past year, but this seems less a result of sympathy or sophistication and more one of certainty: The issue is decided and certain truths can be taken for granted. As this public consciousness finds official representation in the formation of a control conglomerate, it heralds the final and institutional stage in the growth of repressive force, persecution and terror.

The growth of this control conglomerate, the mark of any repressive system, depends on the development of new techniques and organizations. But its momentum requires an ideological head of steam. In the case of the Hippie life the ideological condemnation is based on several counts: that it is dangerous and irresponsible, subversive to authority, immoral, and psychopathological.

Commenting on the relationship between beliefs and the development of the persecutory institutions for witch-control in the 16th century, Trevor-Roper, in an essay on "Witches and Witchcraft," states:

> In a climate of fear, it is easy to see how this process could happen: how individual deviations could be associated with a central pattern. We have seen it happen in our own time. The "McCarthyite" experience of the United States in the 1950's was exactly comparable: Social fear, the fear of an incompatible system of society, was given intellectual form as a heretical ideology and suspect individuals were persecuted by reference to that heresy.

The same fear finds its ideological expression against the Hippies in the statement of Dr. Stanley F. Yolles, director of the National Institute of Mental Health, that "alienation," which he called a major underlying cause of drug abuse, "was wider, deeper and more diffuse now than it has been in any other period in American history." The rejection of dissent in the name of mental health rather than moral values or social or political interest is a modern characteristic. Dr. Yolles suggested that if urgent attention is not given the problem:

> there are serious dangers that large proportions of current and future generations will reach adulthood embittered towards the larger society, unequipped to take on parental, vocational and other citizen roles, and involved in some form of socially deviant behavior.

Dr. Seymour L. Halleck, director of student psychiatry at the University of Wisconsin, also tied the heresy to various sources of sin: affluence, lack of contact with adults, and an excess of freedom. Dr. Henry Brill, director of Pilgrim State Hospital on Long Island and a consultant on drug use to federal and state agencies, is quoted in *The New York Times*, Sept. 26, 1967:

> It is my opinion that the unrestricted use of marijuana type substances produces a significant amount of vagabondage, dependency, and psychiatric disability.

Drs. Yolles, Halleck, and Brill are probably fairly representative of psychiatric opinion. Psychiatry has long defined normality and health in terms of each other in a "scientific" avoidance of serious value questions. Psychiatrists agree in principle on several related points which could constitute a medical rational foundation for the persecution of Hippies: They define the normal and healthy individual as patient and instrumental. He plans for the long range and pursues his goals temperately and economically. He is an individual with a need for privacy and his contacts are moderate and respectful. He is stable in style and identity, reasonably competitive and optimistic. Finally, he accepts reality and participates in the social forms which constitute the givens of his life. Drug use, sexual pleasure, a repudiation of clear long-range goals, the insistence of intimacy and self-affirmation, distrust of official authority and radical dissent are all part of the abnormality that colors the Hippies "alienated" or "disturbed" or "neurotic."

This ideology characterizes the heresy in technical terms. Mental illness is a scientific and medical problem, and isolation and treatment are recommended. Youth, alienation and drug use are the discrediting characteristics of those who are unqualified for due process, discussion or conflict. The genius of the ideology has been to separate the phenomenon under review from consideration of law and value. In this way the mutual hostilities that ordinarily divide the various agencies of control are bypassed and the issue endowed with ethical and political neutrality. Haurek and Clark, in their "Variants of Integration of Social Control Agencies," described two opposing orientations among social control agencies, the authoritarian-punitive (the police, the courts) and the humanitarian-welfare (private agencies, social workers), with the latter holding the former in low esteem. The Hippies have brought them together.

The designation of the Hippie impulse as heresy on the grounds of psychopathology not only bypasses traditional enmity among various agencies of social control, but its corollaries activate each agency. It is the eventual coordination of their efforts that constitutes the control conglomerate. We will briefly discuss several of these corollaries before examining the impact of the conglomerate. Youth, danger and disobedience are the major themes.

Dominating the study of adolescence is a general theory which holds that the adolescent is a psychosexual type. Due to an awakening of the instincts after a time of relative quiescence, he is readily overwhelmed by them. Consequently, his behavior may be viewed as the working out of intense intrapsychic conflict—it is symptomatic or expressive rather than rational and realistic. He is idealistic, easily influenced, and magical. The idealism is the expression of a threatened superego; the susceptibility to influence is an attempt to find support for an identity in danger of diffusion; the magic, reflected in adolescent romance and its rituals, is an attempt to get a grip on a reality that shifts and turns too much for comfort. By virtue of his entrance into the youth culture, he joins in the collective expression of emotional immaturity. At heart, he is the youth of Golding's *Lord of the Flies,* a fledgling adult living out a transitional status. His idealism may be sentimentally touching, but in truth he is morally irresponsible and dangerous.

YOUTH

As the idealism of the young is processed through the youth culture, it becomes radical ideology, and even radical practice. The attempts by parents and educators to break the youth culture by rejecting its symbols and limiting the opportunities for its expression (ranging from dress regulations in school to the censorship of youth music on the air) are justified as a response to the dangerous political implications of the ideology of developed and ingrown immaturity. That these same parents and educators find their efforts to conventionalize the youth culture (through moderate imitations of youthful dress and attempts to "get together with the kids") rejected encourages them further to see the young as hostile, unreasonable and intransigent. The danger of extremism (the New Left and the Hippies) animates their criticism, and all intrusions on the normal are read as pointing in that direction. The ensuing conflict between the wise and the unreasonable is called (largely by the wise) the "generation gap."

From this it follows that radicalism is the peculiar propensity of the young and, as Christopher Jencks and David Riesman have pointed out in *The Academic Revolution,* of those who identify with the young. At its best it is not considered serious; at its worst it is the "counter-culture." The myth of the generation gap, a myth that is all the more strongly held as we find less and less evidence for it, reinforces this view by holding that radicalism ends, or should end, when the gap is bridged—when the young grow older and wiser. While this lays the groundwork for tolerance or more likely, forbearance, it is a tolerance limited to youthful radicalism. It also lays the groundwork for a more thorough rejection of the radicalism of the not-so-young and the "extreme."

Thus, the theory of youth classifies radicalism as immature and, when cultivated, dangerous or pathological. Alienation is the explanation used to account for the extension of youthful idealism and paranoia into the realm of the politically and culturally adult. Its wrongness is temporary and trivial. If it persists, it becomes a structural defect requiring capture and treatment rather than due process and argument.

Once a lifestyle and its practices are declared illegal, its proponents are by definition criminal and subversive. On the one hand, the very dangers presupposed by the legal proscriptions immediately become clear and present. The illegal lifestyle becomes the living demonstration of its alleged dangers. The ragged vagabondage of the Hippie is proof that drugs and promiscuity are alienating, and the attempts to sleep in parks, gather and roam are the new "violence" of which we have been reading. Crime certainly is crime, and the Hippies commit crime by their very existence. The dangers are: (1) crime and the temptation to commit crime; (2) alienation and the temptation to drop out. The behaviors that, if unchecked, become imbedded in the personality of the suspectible are, among others, drug use (in particular marijuana), apparel deviance, dropping out (usually of school), sexual promiscuity, communal living, nudity, hair deviance, draft resistance, demonstrating against the feudal oligarchies in cities and colleges, gathering, roaming, doing strange art and being psychedelic. Many of these are defused by campaigns of definition; they become topical and in fashion. To wear bell-bottom pants, long side-burns, flowers on your car and beads, is, if done with taste and among the right people, stylish and eccentric rather than another step toward the brink or a way of lending aid and comfort to the enemy. The disintegration of a form by co-opting only its parts is a familiar phenomenon. It is tearing an argument apart by confronting each proposition as if it had no context, treating a message like an intellectual game.

Drugs, communalism, gathering, roaming, resisting and demonstrating, and certain styles of hair have not been defused. In fact, the drug scene is the site of the greatest concentration of justificatory energy and the banner under which the agencies of the control conglomerate unite. That their use is so widespread through the straight society indicates the role of drugs as temptation. That drugs have been pinned so clearly (despite the fact that many Hippies are nonusers) and so gladly to the Hippies, engages the institutions of persecution in the task of destroying the Hippie thing.

The antimarijuana lobby has postulated a complex of violence, mental illness, genetic damage, apathy and alienation, all arising out of the ashes of smoked pot. The hypothesis justifies a set of laws and practices of great harshness and discrimination, and the President recently recommended that they be made even more so. The number of arrests for use, possession or sale of marijuana has soared in recent years: Between 1964 and 1966 yearly arrests doubled from 7,000 to 15,000. The United States Narcotics Commissioner attributed the problem to "certain groups" which give marijuana to young people, and to "false information" about the danger of the drug.

Drug raids ordinarily net "hippie-type youths" although lately news reports refer to "youths from good homes." The use of spies on campuses, one of the bases for the original protest demonstrations at Nanterre prior to the May revolution, has become common, with all its socially destructive implications. Extensive spy operations were behind many of the police raids of college campuses during 1967, 1968 and 1969. Among those hit were Long Island University's Southampton College (twice), State University College at Oswego, New York, the Hun School of Princeton, Bard College, Syracuse University, Stony Brook College and Franconia College in New Hampshire; the list could go on.

It is the "certain groups" that the Commissioner spoke of who bear the brunt of the condemnation and the harshest penalties. The laws themselves are peculiar enough, having been strengthened largely since the Hippies became visible, but they are enforced with obvious discrimination. Teenagers arrested in a "good residential section" of Naugatuck, Connecticut, were treated gently by the circuit court judge:

> I suspect that many of these youngsters should not have been arrested. . . . I'm not going to have these youngsters bouncing around with these charges hanging over them.

They were later released and the charges dismissed. In contrast, after a "mass arrest" in which 15 of the 25 arrested were charged with being in a place where they knew that others were smoking marijuana, Washington's Judge Halleck underscored his determination "to show these long-haired ne'er-do-wells that society will not tolerate their conduct" (*Washington Post,* May 21, 1967).

The incidents of arrest and the exuberance with which the laws are discriminatorily enforced are justified, although not explained, by the magnifying judgment of "danger." At a meeting of agents from 74 police departments in Connecticut and New York, Westchester County Sheriff John E. Hoy, "in a dramatic stage whisper," said, "It is a frightening situation, my friends . . . marijuana is creeping up on us."

One assistant district attorney stated that "the problem is staggering." A county executive agreed that "the use of marijuana is vicious," while a school superintendent argued that "marijuana is a plague-like disease, slowly but surely strangling our young people." Harvard freshmen were warned against the "social influences" that surround drugs and one chief of police attributed drug use and social deviance to permissiveness in a slogan which has since become more common (*St. Louis Post-Dispatch,* Aug. 22, 1968).

Bennett Berger has pointed out that the issue of danger is an ideological ploy (*Denver Post,* April 19, 1968): "The real issue of marijuana is ethical and political, touching the 'core of cultural values.'" *The New York Times* of Jan. 11, 1968, reports "Students and high school and college officials agree that 'drug use has increased sharply since the intensive coverage given to drugs and the Hippies last summer by the mass media.'" It is also supported by other attempts to tie drugs to heresy: *The New York Times* of Nov. 17, 1968, notes a Veterans Administration course for doctors on the Hippies which ties Hippies, drugs, and alienation together and suggests that the search for potential victims might begin in the seventh or eighth grades.

The dynamic relationship between ideology, organization and practice is revealed both in President Johnson's "Message on Crime to Insure Public Safety" (delivered to Congress on February 7, 1968) and in the gradual internationalizing of the persecution. The President recommended "strong new laws," an increase in the number of enforcement agents, and the centralization of federal enforcement machinery. At the same time, the United Nations Economic and Social Council considered a resolution asking that governments "deal effectively with publicity which advocates legalization or tolerance of the nonmedical use of cannabis as a harmless drug." The resolution was consistent with President Johnson's plan to have the Federal Government of the United States "maintain worldwide operations . . . to suppress the trade in illicit narcotics and marijuana." The reasons for the international campaign were clarified by a World Health Organization panel's affirmation of its intent to prevent the use or sale of marijuana because it is "a drug of dependence, producing health and social problems." At the same time that scientific researchers at Harvard and Boston University were exonerating the substance, the penalties increased and the efforts to proscribe it reached international proportions. A number of countries, including Laos and Thailand, have barred Hippies, and Mexico has made it difficult for those with long hair and serious eyes to cross its border.

DISOBEDIENCE

The assumption that society is held together by formal law and authority implies in principle that the habit of obedience must be reinforced. The details of the Hippie culture are, in relation to the grounded culture, disobedient. From that perspective, too, their values and ideology are also explicitly disobedient. The disobedience goes far beyond the forms of social organization and personal presentation to the conventional systems of healing, dietary practice and environmental use. There is virtually no system of authority that is not thrown into question. Methodologically, the situationalism of pornography, guerrilla theater and place conversion is not only profoundly subversive in itself; it turns the grounded culture around. By coating conventional behavioral norms with ridicule and obscenity, by tying radically different meanings to old routines, it challenges our sentiments. By raising the level of our self-consciousness it allows us to become moral in the areas we had allowed to degenerate into habit (apathy or gluttony). When the rock group, the Fugs, sings and dances "Group Grope" or any of their other songs devoted brutally to "love" and "taste," they pin our tender routines to a humiliating obscenity. We can no longer take our behavior and our intentions for granted. The confrontation enables us to disobey or to reconsider or to choose simply by forcing into consciousness the patterns of behavior and belief of which we have become victims. The confrontation is manly because it exposes both sides in an arena of conflict.

When questions are posed in ways that permit us to disengage ourselves from their meaning to our lives, we tolerate the questions as a moderate and decent form of dissent. And we congratulate ourselves for our tolerance. But when people refuse to know their place, and, what is worse, our place, and they insist on themselves openly and demand that we re-decide our own lives, we are willing to have them knocked down. Consciousness permits disobedience. As a result, systems threatened from within often begin the work of reassertion by an attack on consciousness and chosen forms of life.

Youth, danger and disobedience define the heresy in terms that activate the host of agencies that, together, comprise the control conglomerate. Each agency, wrote Trevor-Roper, was ready: "The engine of persecution was set up before its future victims were legally subject to it." The conglomerate has its target. But it is a potential of the social system as much as it is an actor. Trevor-Roper comments further that:

> once we see the persecution of heresy as social intolerance, the intellectual difference between one heresy and another becomes less significant.

And the difference, one might add, between one persecutor and another becomes less significant. Someone it does not matter who tells Mr. Blue (in Tom Paxton's song): "What will it take to whip you into line?"

How have I ended here? The article is an analysis of the institutionalization of persecution and the relationship between the control conglomerate which is the advanced form of official persecution and the Hippies as an alternative culture, the target of control. But an analysis must work within a vision if it is to move beyond analysis into action. The tragedy of America may be that it completed the technology of control before it developed compassion and tolerance. It never learned to tolerate history, and now it is finally capable of ending history by ending the change that political sociologists and undergroups understand. The struggle has always gone on in the mind. Only now, for this society, is it going on in the open among people. Only now is it beginning to shape lives rather than simply sh ping individuals. Whether it is too late or not will be worked out in the attempts to transcend the one-dimensionality that Marcuse described. That the alternative culture is here seems difficult to doubt. Whether it becomes revolutionary fast enough to supersede an officialdom bent on its destruction may be an important part of the story of America.

As an exercise in over-estimation, this essay proposes a methodological tool for going from analysis to action in areas which are too easily absorbed by a larger picture but which are at the same time too critical to be viewed outside the context of political action.

The analysis suggests several conclusions:

● Control usually transcends itself both in its selection of targets and in its organization.

● At some point in its development, control is readily institutionalized and finally institutional. The control conglomerate represents a new stage in social organization and is an authentic change-inducing force for social systems.

● The hallmark of an advanced system of control (and the key to its beginning) is an ideology that unites otherwise highly differing agencies.

● Persecution and terror go in our society. The Hippies, as a genuine heresy, have engaged official opposition to a growing cultural-social-political tendency. The organization of control has both eliminated countervailing official forces and begun to place all deviance in the category of heresy. This pattern may soon become endemic to the society.

PART FIVE: TOWARD THE REDUCTION OF CONFLICT

The criminalization process is an attempt by conflicting parties to neutralize opponents by means of the legal machinery of the state. It is a step toward terminating conflict. For all the threat that the legal system connotes in terms of the sanctions it can bring to bear, the system is remarkably inefficient in accomplishing its task, especially within the context of a nontotalitarian society. The law as a political tool is effective only to the extent it is supported by enforcers and does not intrude into the area of valuative conflict. Indeed, the criminalization process may even exacerbate conflict. As Herbert L. Packer (1968:364–65) tells us:

> Crime is a sociopolitical artifact, not a natural phenomenon. We can have as much or as little crime as we please, depending on what we choose to count as criminal. . . . The criminal sanction is the best device we have for dealing with gross and immediate harms and threats of harm. It becomes less useful as the harms become less gross and immediate. It becomes largely inefficacious when it is used to enforce morality rather than to deal with conduct that is generally seen as harmful. Efficacy aside, the less threatening the conduct with which it is called upon to deal, the greater the social costs that enforcement incurs. We alienate people from the society in which they live. We drive enforcement authorities to more extreme measures of intrusions and coercion. We taint the quality of life for free men.

The classic example of the inefficiency of using law to resolve conflict is the case of the Volstead Act. The prohibition law did not end the conflict between the "wets" and the "drys" but elevated it to even greater intensity, which proved to be the ultimate undoing of the "drys."

Lewis Coser in this part stresses the need for supportive sentiments for the resolution of conflict:

> In order to end a conflict, the parties must agree upon rules and norms allowing them to assess their respective power position in the struggle. Their common interest leads them to accept rules which enhance their mutual dependence in the very pursuit of their antagonistic goals.

John Martin's paper makes a similar case. Martin feels that conflict in the realm of juvenile delinquency can be resolved if the contending groups are equally represented and thus have a similar stake in the system. This, he argues, is not currently possible because of the present composition of powerholders where those legislated against are excluded from the decision-making processes. His solution is a redistribution of power through Youth Service Bureaus.

The statements of Coser and Martin are important ones, but their positions neglect an important dimension: the differentiation between rule makers and rule enforcers.

Rule makers and moral entrepreneurs are those who apply the deviant label and act to obtain the legislative means to deal with those so labelled. But, as Becker indicates in Part Four, those who must interpret and apply the law are less concerned with the content of the law than with the fact that it is their job to enforce it. The following statement from a police officer provides an explanation of the distinction between the two roles:

> I think the "two hat" approach is easily recognizable by any layman. He [the policeman] is only the enforcer of the law and his enforcement policy comes from above, but he is caught up in the web when the legislative and judicial branches fail. Every society has a system of taboos, but for the police officer this is an exceptionally limiting condition. . . . He is an ass for arresting a drunk according to the sympathizing public and derelict in duty for not arresting him according to his employers.[1]

As certain observers (Westley, 1953; Niederhoffer, 1969; and Chevigny, 1969) of police conduct have noted, police often tailor enforcement policies in accordance with their own occupational norms. Westley (1953:35) concludes that occupational status is an important determining factor:

> He [the policeman] regards the public as his enemy, feels his occupation to be in conflict with the community, and regards himself to be a pariah. The experience and the feeling give rise to a collective emphasis on secrecy, an attempt to coerce respect from the public,

---

[1]Personal correspondence to the senior editor.

and a belief that almost any means are legitimate in completing an important arrest.

Obviously the strict and uniform enforcement of law is not only impractical but undesirable (LaFave, 1965:63–82). Police must use discretion in the application of their authority. Selectivity in law enforcement depends upon the contingencies of the situation and the characteristics of persons involved (LaFave, 1965: *passim* and Bittner, 1967), but the interpretation of situations and persons is, in turn, dependent to varying degrees on the ideology of the police. The greater the extent to which this ideology determines the use of authority, the greater the likelihood that a conflict situation will develop.

The "clean-cut" but drunken college student may be transported to his dorm and released; the derelict is more apt to be jailed. Despite the policeman's selectivity in these instances, his actions in both cases are not likely to engender a conflict situation. However, the jailing of middle-class youth engaged in "political protest" exposes the police to inconsistent societal reaction. When the application of the criminal label is resisted and opposed by relatively powerful segments of society, police find themselves in the untidy situation of choosing "whose side" they are on. As Michael Brown indicated in the previous section, police tend to ally with tradition and the maintenance of the *status quo*. As Lipset (1969:82) observes:

> Police understand as normal the problems of dealing with crime or vice. They may resent violence stemming from minority ghettos, but this, too, is understandable and part of police work. But to take provocative behavior from youths who are socially and economically much better off than they and their children is more than the average policeman can tolerate.

Thus, law enforcement authorities who have interests of their own are parties to a conflict situation. Law enforcement is a form of conflict between authorities and "law breakers." Although there may exist a great degree of congruency between enforcement procedures and legislative intent, it is not inevitably so. Because enforcement authorities exercise discretion, however limited, the *interpretation* of what constitutes law breaking is a factor that can compromise or even distort the original intent of the lawmakers. Discretion is a means by which law enforcement authorities can enlarge, contract, and alter the lines of conflict.

A second difficulty in attempting to terminate conflict is suggested by John Martin's discussion of juvenile delinquency laws. His thesis has been a central one throughout this book: The poor and powerless are legislated against by a government acting in the interest of a few powerful groups. The result, claims Martin, is a series of laws and agencies that ignore the essential ingredients of the behavior labelled delinquent. The imbalance of power has produced a system of juvenile justice that is ineffective in terms of its presumed goals: It fails to alter behavior patterns in acceptable directions, it makes a mockery of the concept "justice," and it has neither favor nor support among those it is supposedly designed to "help." In short, the response of authorities to a "problem" has failed to remedy it.

Taken one step further, an inappropriate response by authorities to a conflict situation may not only be ineffective but may engender greater conflict. The response may become counterproductive and dysfunctional if it causes a group to deny the legitimacy of authorities' actions. For example, studies of student protests found that authorities' insistence on a repressive response rather than dealing with root causes resulted in an aggravation of the conflict (Foster and Long, 1970; Skolnick, 1970:105–24; and Stark, 1972:139–58). The termination of conflict requires a mutual appreciation of law and its enforcers. Disenfranchised persons and groups outside the power structure of society will not be convinced of the system's legitimacy by mere legislative edict.

Short of total repression, legislation and its enforcement are not sufficient to stabilize society. At best they can create the ground rules under which conflict may take place; at worst they can create anarchy.

Any interpretation of conflict is tied to one's particular perspective, as pointed out in Part One. Durkheim and other "order" theorists deplore conflict as disrupting to the consensual fabric of society. Consequently, they place great stress upon terminating conflict by means of mutual consensus. Coser's arguments are consistent with this perspective. Writers concerned with the "conflict" model have come to see conflict as an inevitable social force guiding the hand of history. It is only through conflict that social betterment occurs. As the French writer Albert Camus observed, "I rebel—therefore we exist."

The propositions to consider in this part are:

1. To reduce conflict, interested group participation must exist at every level of the criminalization process.
2. For law to reduce conflict, consensus concerning legislation must exist at every societal level.

REFERENCES

BITTNER, E., "The Police on Skid-Row: A Study of Peace Keeping," *American Sociological Review*, 32 (October 1967): 699–715.

CHEVIGNY, P., *Police Power: Police Abuses in New York City*. New York: Vintage Books, 1969.

FOSTER, J. and D. LONG, *Protest! Student Activism in America.* New York: William Morrow and Co., 1970.

LaFAVE, W. R., *Arrest: The Decision to Take a Suspect Into Custody.* Boston: Little, Brown and Co., 1965.

LIPSET, S. M., "Why Cops Hate Liberals—and Vice Versa," *Atlantic,* 223 (September 1969): 76–83.

NIEDERHOFFER, A., *Behind the Shield: The Police in Urban Society.* Garden City: Doubleday and Co., 1969.

PACKER, H. L., *The Limits of the Criminal Sanction.* Stanford, California: Stanford University Press, 1968.

SKOLNICK, J., *The Politics of Protest.* New York: Simon and Schuster, 1970.

STARK, R., *Police Riots: Collective Violence and Law Enforcement.* Belmont, California: Wadsworth Publishing Co., 1972.

WESTLEY, W., "Violence and the Police," *American Journal of Sociology,* 59 (July 1953): 34–41.

20. THE TERMINATION OF CONFLICT

LEWIS A. COSER

Certain social processes are finite, i.e., they are defined by their transitory character and the manner of their termination is institutionally prescribed. Courtship ends when union with the beloved has been attained in marriage; formal education ends when the educational goal has been reached and examinations or commencement exercises mark completion of the process. Other social processes, however, such as friendship or love, have no precise termination point. They follow a law of social inertia insofar as they continue to operate if no explicit provision for stopping their course is made by the participants. Social conflict is such a process. While in a game, for example, the rules for the process include rules for its ending, in social conflict explicit provisions for its termination must be made by the contenders. If no mutual agreements are made at some time during the struggle, it "ceaseth only in death" or in total destruction of at least one of the antagonists. The termination of conflict hence presents problems that do not arise in finite processes.

Various types of conflicts can be classified according to the degree of their normative regulation. Fully institutionalized conflicts, such as duels, may be said to constitute one extreme of a continuum while absolute conflicts, in which the goal is the total destruction of the enemy rather than a mutually agreed-upon settlement fall at the other extreme. In the second type, agreement is reduced to a minimum; the struggle ceases only upon the extermination of one or both of the contenders. As Hans Speier has said, "peace terminating an absolute war is established *without* the enemy" (9, p. 223).

It stands to reason that conflicts of this kind—at least between contenders with a rough equality of strength—are exceedingly costly and exhausting. If the contenders wish to prevent their struggle from becoming a zero sum game in which the outcome can only be total defeat or

"The Termination of Conflict," by Lewis A. Coser is reprinted from *Journal of Conflict Resolution*, Vol. V, No. 4 (December 1961), pp. 347–353, by permission of the publisher, Sage Publications, Inc.

This paper was written while the author was carrying out research at the Institute for Social Research, Oslo, Norway, under a Fulbright grant.

total victory, they have a common interest in establishing mechanisms which can lead to an agreed-upon termination of the struggle. The fact is that most conflicts do indeed end long before the defeated has been totally crushed. "Resistance to the last man" is almost always a phrase. As long as one belligerent survives in one's camp further resistance is always possible; yet combat usually ceases long before this point is reached. This is so because both parties agree upon norms for the termination of the conflict.

While absolute conflicts allow practically no agreements as to their termination, certain types of highly institutionalized conflicts have built-in termination points. Trials by ordeal, duels and other agonistic struggles are centered upon symbolic endings which give them game-like features and determine the outcome automatically. A score is kept, a goal line established, maximum injury is conventionally fixed. When the score adds up to a certain number, when a certain type of injury has been established, or the goal line has been crossed, the conflict is over and the loser as well as the winner can easily perceive the outcome of the contention.

In conflicts not fully institutionalized, assessment of relative strength is not an easy matter so that the loser may not in fact concede that he has lost, nor may he even be aware of it. Therefore, it is to the interest of both contenders that the point at which victory is attained or the point beyond which no more gains can be anticipated, be marked as clearly as possible so as to avoid unnecessary exertions on both sides. Termination of conflict becomes a problem to be solved by both parties.

The termination of conflict is a social process dependent upon, but not directly deducible from its pursuits. It is, as Georg Simmel has noted, "a specific enterprise. It belongs neither to war nor to peace, just as a bridge is different from either bank it connects" (8, p. 110). To be sure, the outcome of a conflict is related to the goals of the antagonists and to the means by which it is fought; its duration and intensity will depend on objectives and available resources plus the time and effort required to achieve a decision. But the termination of the conflict, that is agreement as to what constitutes a true decision, highlights some factors which are not deducible from its pursuit and must hence be studied separately.

For all except absolute conflict, termination involves a reciprocal activity and cannot be understood simply as an unilateral imposition of the will of the stronger on the weaker. Therefore, contrary to what common sense might suggest, not only the potential victor but also the potential vanquished makes crucial contributions to the termination. As a military commentator has pointed out, "war is pressed by the victor, but peace is made by the vanquished. Therefore, to determine the causes of peace, it is always necessary to take the vanquished's point of view. Until the vanquished quits, the war goes on" (1, p. 18). Victory, in other words, involves the yielding of the vanquished. By the very act of declaring himself beaten, he achieves a last assertion of power. With this act, as Georg Simmel has said, "he actually makes a gift to the victor" (8, p. 114). The capacity of making gifts is a measure of autonomy.

If both victor and vanquished are to make a contribution to the termination of their conflict they must arrive at some agreement. Thomas Schelling has recently argued persuasively that "limited war requires limits . . . but limits require agreement or at least some kind of mutual recognition and acquiescence" (7, p. 53). This applies not only to the conduct but also to the termination of conflicts. In order to end a conflict the parties must agree upon rules and norms allowing them to assess their respective power position in the struggle. Their common interest leads them to accept rules which enhance their mutual dependence in the very pursuit of their antagonistic goals. Such agreements make their conflict, so to speak, self-liquidating. To the degree that such rules are provided, the conflict is partly institutionalized and acquires some of the features of the agonistic struggle alluded to earlier.

Agreements as to goals and determination of outcome shorten the conflict. Once a goal has been reached by one of the parties and this accepted as a clue to the acceptance of defeat by the other, the conflict is ended. The more restricted the object of contention and the more visible for both parties the clues to victory, the higher the chances that the conflict be limited in time and extension. Emile Durkheim's dictum concerning human needs, "The more one has, the more one wants, since satisfaction received only stimulates instead of filling needs" is applicable in this connection. Agreed-upon limits upon the "appetites" of the contenders place normative restrictions upon a process which does not inherently contain self-limiting properties. The history of trade unionism provides interesting examples.

Struggles engaged in by business unionism, given its limited goals, provide for the contending parties an opportunity for settlement and furnish them at the same time with recognizable signals as to the opportune moment for ending a conflict. Revolutionary syndicalism, on the other hand, has always been plagued by the problem of ending strike action. Since its goal is the overthrow of the capitalist order rather than improvements within it, it cannot accept as the end of the conflict outcomes which would constitute victories from the point of view of business unionism. Revolutionary syndicalism is faced with the dilemma that no outcome of a strike, short of the overthrow of capitalism, can be considered an acceptable form of conflict resolution so that its strategy is foredoomed to failure. Not sensitized to clues which would allow them to conclude that a victory has been reached, unable to recognize peace overtures or concessions from the adversary, revolutionary syndicalists are not in a position to take advantage of partial gains. Paradoxically, in this case, those who are under ordinary conditions the *weaker* party demand "unconditional surrender" of the stronger so that they make it inevitable that the struggle can cease only upon total exhaustion.

The above examples illustrate how closely specific outcomes are related to the aims of the contenders. The smaller the sacrifice a party demands from the opponent, the more limited the aims, the higher the chances that the potential loser will be ready to give up battle. The loser must be led to decide that peace is more attractive than the continuation of the conflict; such a decision will be powerfully enhanced if the demands made upon him are not exorbitant (1, p. 253 *et passim*). When the war aims of the winning side are limited as, say, in the Spanish-American war or the Russo-Japanese conflict of 1905, the making of peace is relatively easy. Once the Japanese war aims—the stopping of Russian penetration into the Far East—had been reached, Japan could afford to make the first move for peace by appealing to Theodore Roosevelt to act as a mediator. Once Cuba was liberated and the Spanish fleet defeated, American war aims were attained and the United States had no interest in continuing the war through an attack upon the Spanish mainland.

It remains, however, that no matter how the activities of the potential winner have facilitated an early termination of the conflict, the final decision to end the war remains with the potential loser. How, then, is the loser moved to decide that he has, in fact, lost? Not only the objective situation but the perception of the situation is crucially important since only the latter will bring forth the requisite admission of defeat. "If an opponent," writes Clausewitz, "is to be made to comply with our will, we must place him in a situation which is more oppressive to him than the sacrifice we demand" (2, vol. 1, p. 5). This elegantly phrased dictum is, however, meaningless unless the criteria be specified that determine how the antagonist will in fact assess the situation. Different contenders might arrive at variant estimates as to the degree of oppressiveness of a situation and of the value of the sacrifice demanded. Since such assessments are difficult to make and do not depend on rational calculations alone, they are greatly facilitated by the availability of symbolic signposts.

Whenever wars have been strictly limited, as in eighteenth-century warfare, some visible event, such as the taking of a particular fortress, the reaching of some natural barrier and the like, symbolized to both parties that the desired objective had been reached by one of them and that the conflict could now be considered solved through the subsequent acquiescence of the loser. When such mutually acceptable symbolic clues are not available, the resolution of the conflict will be more difficult.

The nature of such symbolic clues may vary considerably[1] and it is hence important that the potential winner ascertain which clues will be accepted by the potential loser as symbols of defeat. If in the common consciousness of the citizens, the capital symbolizes the very existence of the nation, then its fall will be perceived as defeat and will lead to the acceptance of the terms of the victor. The Fall of Paris in 1871 and 1940 symbolized to the bulk of Frenchmen the end of the war despite the fact that Gambetta had rallied significant numbers of undefeated troops in the provinces, and that de Gaulle appealed for the continuation of the war from London. Only a relatively small number of Frenchmen refused to accept the Fall of Paris as a symbol of defeat. In less centralized nations, however, where the capital has no such symbolic significance, its fall is not perceived as a decisive event. Pretoria and Bloemfontein fell to the British in 1900, yet Boer resistance, rather to the surprise of the British, continued for two more years. The British failed to understand that, to the rural Boers, the vast countryside rather than the cities symbolized the nation; to them the war ended only when want of forage, capture, and overwork decimated the Boer horses. In a country in which men were bred in the saddle, the decimation of horses symbolized defeat (1, p. 114). Similarly, the sacking of Washington in 1812 did not signal defeat to Americans for whom the open spaces of the country rather than the federal capital symbolized national independence. In other situations the capture of charismatic war lords rather than any taking of a locality will symbolize defeat.

The structure of the opposing camp furnishes clues as to meaningful symbols of defeat and victory. It is hence of the utmost importance for both sides to have as much knowledge as possible about the characteristic features of their respective structure and symbols. When ignorant armies clash at night, their pluralistic ignorance militates against their ability to come to terms short of mutual exhaustion.

The contenders' ability to make use of one another's symbols of defeat and victory does not only depend on their awareness of the structure of the opposing camp, but also on the dynamics within each camp. Internal struggles may be waged over what set of events may be considered a decisive symbol of defeat. A minority may consider that resistance can be continued even though the majority has accepted defeat. Subgroups may consider that the decision-makers have betrayed the cause by agreeing to end the conflict. Peace terms provide ample material for internal conflict within each of the contending camps. These terms are, moreover, likely to

---

[1]One must further distinguish between purely symbolic events, such as the capture of a flag, and events which, as in the examples that follow, have realistic as well as symbolic significance.

be defined and redefined in the course of the conflict in tune with the fortunes of battle. Different parties may disagree violently on whether a given event is to be considered decisive or of only incidental significance. Such contentions are likely to be the more deepgoing the less integrated the social structure. In integrated structures internal contentions may vitalize and strengthen the groups' energies, but if divergencies as to appropriate action affect the basic layers of common belief, symbolizations of victory and defeat are also likely to be basically divergent (3, pp. 72–80). In highly polarized social systems where a number of internal conflicts of different sorts are superimposed upon one another, there exists hardly any common definition of the situation binding all members of the society to commonly held perceptions (3, p. 76 ff., 4, pp. 213 ff.). To the extent that a society or group is rent into rival camps so that there is no community of ends between the parties, if one party is not willing to accept the definition of the situation which the other propounds, the making of peace becomes an almost impossible enterprise. In such situations a prior settlement of scores within, an unambiguous definition or redefinition of the balance of power between contending groups, may be the precondition for concluding peace without. The Russian provisional government after the March 1917 revolution being continuously goaded and challenged by the growing Bolshevik Party, was unable either to wage war effectively or to conclude peace; once the Bolsheviks had seized power their definition of the situation prevailed and peace could be concluded at Brest Litovsk.

Even when such deep going fissures are not present in a social structure, the everpresent divergencies between the perspectives of the leaders and the led, between those in authority and those submitted to it (4, ch. 5), require considerable effort on the part of the leaders to make the led accept their definition of the situation. Just as at the beginning of the struggle the leaders must convince the led that the sacrifice demanded of them will redound to their benefit and that the conflict concerns wide interests of all rather than the narrow interests of the top stratum, so the leaders must also be able to convince the led that the acceptance of defeat is warranted and even desirable from the point of view of the total system rather than in terms of special leadership interests. To make defeat palatable may require as much effort as to make war desirable.

Leaders will typically differ from the led not only in terms of social perspectives but also in regard to their cognitive horizon so that leaders may be able to assess consequences and relative advantages more rationally than the led. A leader foreseeing a defeat which is not as yet visible to his followers must adjust his strategy to the need of convincing the followers. In such an effort it might be advantageous to him to construe partial defeat in such a way as to make it appear as at least a partial victory. Often the led, like the mark in a con game, might have to be cooled out by being told that what they experience as a loss is "really" a partial victory (5).

Contentions within enemy camps as to the proper definition of the situation once again highlight the importance of symbolizations. The leader will have to rely on his ability to manipulate the symbolic system by which the led define the situations if he is to soften the blow that defeat implies. In labor-management conflicts, for example, events which may appear to an outsider as having only peripheral importance may in fact have highly charged emotional significance to the participants. The return to work of a few strikers or, alternatively, the success of a demonstration or the support of public officials or the reactions of an organ of public opinion, may be invested by the rank and file with high symbolic significance and trigger off a return to work or a revival of the will to victory. This is why it is important for the leaders to manage the symbols that structure the perception of the led. The strike leader must know how to end a strike at the opportune moment, but his knowledge would serve him but little if he did not also have the ability to communicate his knowledge to the led. This may often involve the highlighting for the rank and file of a partially attained victory in order to divert attention from a partially suffered defeat.

This is the stuff of which compromises are made. Often seen by the rank and file as a "betrayal" by the leaders, they actually derive from the structural circumstance that the leaders' position allows them a view of the total situation which is denied to the led. Moreover, leadership roles require to so manage intragroup tensions as to keep the group united in adversity even though this might entail certain sacrifices insofar as the attainment of the group's goals are concerned. "System maintenance," to use Parsons' terminology, may sometimes require lowered task performance.

Indeed, most conflicts end in compromises in which it is often quite hard to specify which side has gained relative advantage. Hence, one must distinguish between the will to make peace and the will to accept defeat. Quite often the former may be present although the latter is not. The parties to the conflict may be willing to cease the battle when they recognize that their aims cannot be attained or that they can be attained only at a price which they are not willing to pay, or, more generally, when they conclude that continuation of the conflict is less attractive than the making of peace. In neither of these cases would they be willing to accept defeat although they are willing to stop short of victory. In such situations they may be impelled to explore the chances for a compromise. The willingness to negotiate a compromise, that is to stop chasing the mirage of victory, will, of course, depend on correct assessment of the situation and such assessment, just as in the cases discussed earlier, will be facilitated by the availability of indices of relative standing in the battle. It is one of the key functions of the mediator to make such indices readily available to both parties. To the extent that the contenders share a common system of symbols allowing them to arrive at a common assessment, to that extent they will be able to negotiate. Symbols of defeat and victory thus turn out to be of relevance in order to stop short of either.

Relative appraisal of power is difficult before the contenders have measured their respective strength in conflict. But accommodation may be reached once such an assessment has been achieved. Such redefinitions in the course of a struggle often bring to the fore elements which remained hidden during its onset. Accommodation is facilitated if criteria are available which allow the contenders to gauge the situation. The chance of attaining peace without victory depends on the possibility of achieving consensus as to relative strength and on the ability to make this new definition "stick" within each camp. When the United States chose the neck of Korea as their symbolic standing place in the Korean war, they succeeded in conveying to the other side as well as to the American people their determination to hold it. When enough blood had been let and it became clear to both sides that the other could be beaten only at a cost that neither was willing to incur, negotiations got down to a compromise that took into account the real balance of political and military power and proved acceptable at home. "Peace through stalemate," writes B. H. Liddell-Hart, "based on a coincident recognition by each side of the opponent's strength, is at least preferable to peace through common exhaustion" (6, p. 370).

Although it is true that in many cases an assessment of the relative strength of the opponents is possible only in conflict, it is also true that their travail may be shortened if clear symbolizations of outcome and relative strength are readily available. When recourse to such measures of success or failure has been highly institutionalized, the duration of the conflict can be shortened and its intensity limited. In this sense, research directed toward an understanding of those symbols which move men to accept compromise or even defeat might be as valuable as research to uncover symbols which incite to war.

REFERENCES

1. CALAHAN, H. A. *What Makes a War End*. New York: Vanguard Press, 1944.
2. CLAUSEWITZ, KARL VON. *On War*. London: Routledge and Kegan Paul, 1956.
3. COSER, LEWIS A. *The Functions of Social Conflict*. Glencoe, Ill.: Free Press, 1956.

4. DAHRENDORF, RALF. *Class and Class Conflict in Industrial Society.* Stanford, Calif.: Stanford University Press, 1959.
5. GOFFMAN, ERVING. "On Cooling the Mark Out," *Psychiatry,* 15 (November, 1952), 451–63.
6. LIDDELL-HART, B. H. *Strategy, the Indirect Approach.* London: Faber and Faber, 1955.
7. SCHELLING, THOMAS C. *The Strategy of Conflict.* Cambridge, Mass.: Harvard University Press, 1960.
8. SIMMEL, GEORG. *Conflict.* Trans. Kurt H. Wolff. Glencoe, Ill.: Free Press, 1955.
9. SPEIER, HANS. *Social Order and the Risks of War.* New York: George W. Stewart, 1952.

21. TOWARD A POLITICAL DEFINITION
OF JUVENILE DELINQUENCY

JOHN M. MARTIN

Fairness and justice, many argue, are not often found in juvenile courts, in the practices of the Nation's training schools, or in other aspects of what may be called the juvenile justice system. The problems connected with this condition are massive. Howard James, writing in *The Christian Science Monitor* last year,[1] called the situation a national scandal. Martin, Fitzpatrick, and Gould recently defined the issue in sharply political terms:

> A central difficulty is that of introducing into law enforcement and the administration of justice a real, not hypothetical, balance of power between individuals who are on the receiving end of justice and the officials who administer it. The crucial task will be that of building a public policy which both recognizes and understands the inherent conflicts of interest between those groups and collectivities in society against which the law is enforced and those in whose name and for whose benefit it is enforced.[2]

The difficulty is essentially political. It cannot be accounted for in terms of the malicious intent of judges, probation officers, training school superintendents, and others employed by the juvenile justice system. If this were so, the remedy would be relatively simple: Properly motivated people could be put in as replacements. The real problem lies in the very way the institutions of the system are organized, in the specification of their goals, and in the manner in which they function. Far more is involved than the lack of money, crowded court calendars, huge case loads, and the lack of trained caseworkers and legally trained judges.

Much more crucial to a fuller understanding of the situation is an appreciation of the narrow ideological and theoretical foundations upon

---

Reprinted from *Toward a Political Definition of Juvenile Delinquency* by John M. Martin, a monograph sponsored by U.S. Department of Health, Education, and Welfare, Social and Rehabilitation Service, Youth Development and Delinquency Prevention Administration, Washington, D.C.: Government Printing Office, 1970. Reprinted with permission of the author.

[1]Howard James, *Children in Trouble: A National Scandal.* Boston: The Christian Science Publishing Society, 1969.

[2]John M. Martin, Joseph P. Fitzpatrick, and Robert E. Gould, M.D., *The Analysis of Delinquent Behavior: A Structural Approach.* New York: Random House, 1970.

which the juvenile justice apparatus rests. The system is grossly conservative in that it accepts little or no active responsibility for winning social justice for the children with whom it deals. It remains wedded to the idea that what is wrong in delinquency is limited to that which is presumed to be wrong with the youngster himself or with his family.

But far deeper organizational difficulties also exist which may prove to be far more significant than any of its other characteristics for understanding the unfairness and injustice which taint the system. Essentially the problem boils down to this: When decisions about the lives and careers of powerless people and their children are made by a large and remote bureaucratic system, which by design has made very little provision for establishing a balance of power between the two camps, unfairness and injustice inevitably follow.

Before considering further this central imbalance of power in the operations of the juvenile justice system, it may be helpful to explicate some of the criticisms which have been leveled at the system.

CRITICISMS OF THE JUVENILE JUSTICE SYSTEM

At present, few in public life are satisfied with the capacity of the juvenile justice system to fulfill its mandate; many also disagree about what the mandate should be. Few academicians and few informed officials find the system useful or beneficial to the youth involved in it. Today for example, in State after State, an informed consensus is rather vigorously maintaining that juvenile courts, and especially training schools, are a "mess." There is widespread conviction that the juvenile justice system is, in large part, an outright failure. It not only frequently fails to rehabilitate, but it also fails to live up to ordinary standards of human decency. Even agency personnel, as professional agents of the larger society, find the system of juvenile justice highly problematic. Many feel that the agencies in which they work are badly financed, poorly staffed, and lacking a relevant program model. The present model, involving in its idealized form individual case adjustment, wins no constituency in the ghettos from which the usual urban agency draws its clientele; it has no viable political prospects at a time when the political roots of the delinquency question are becoming more apparent to all concerned; it "turns on" few governors or legislators; and it is increasingly avoided by the various professions. Most significantly, perhaps, ghetto residents themselves are unhappy about the system. The propertied among them are left unprotected by it, while the poor among them suffer its various injustices.

Criticism of the juvenile justice system is neither simple nor new. Rather it stems from a set of interrelated intellectual developments which have grown rapidly and become more intricate over the last 30 years.

Historically speaking, the first link in the chain of criticism was that which revolved around commentaries of closed institutions, starting with prisons and mental hospitals, and finally narrowing in focus to those institutions, notably training schools, which house a juvenile population. The most significant literature in this link is that by Clemmer, Sykes, Cloward, Cressey, Goffman, Polsky, and Giallombardo, all of which points to the totalitarian social organizations of such institutions and the pathology-ridden, antitherapeutic nature of their inmate subcultures.[3]

The second link in the chain began to develop shortly after the first and focused on the malfunctioning and injustice of the juvenile court, another of the institutions designed to handle society's delinquents. While the first link attacked the institutions to which delinquents were sent, the second sought to make clear the problems inherent in the court which, in the name of "help," committed gross injustices upon children, their parents, and the social class and ethnic groups from which they came. This link can most easily be traced to Paul W. Tappan's now classic, sociolegal critique of the juvenile court. From there, it can be traced through the writings of Goffman, Matza-Sykes, Wheeler-Cottrell, various contributors to *The Challenge of Crime in a Free Society* and its related Task Force Reports, down to the recent work of Carey and Cicourel and that of Martin-Fitzpatrick-Gould.[4]

These scholars have concentrated on major social injustices of the juvenile court. In essence, the argument is that youths appearing before the court have been deprived by the court of their basic rights. Moreover, certain specific youths have been even more mishandled by the court because of their racial and other group identifications and their lack of established political influence. Thus, some youngsters are picked up, taken into custody, shunted off to the precinct and court hearings for acts which others commit without police and court interference. This is questionable

---

[3]Donald Clemmer, *The Prison Community*. New York: Holt, Rinehart, Winston, 1940; Gresham Sykes, *The Society of Captives*. Princeton, N.J.: Princeton University Press, 1958; Richard A. Cloward et al., *Theoretical Studies in the Social Organization of the Prison*. New York: Social Science Research Council, 1960; Donald R. Cressey (ed.), *The Prison: Studies in Institutional Organization and Change*. New York: Holt, Rinehart and Winston, 1961; Erving Goffman, *Asylums*. Garden City, N.Y.: Doubleday Anchor Books, 1961; Howard Polsky, *Cottage Six*. New York: Russell Sage, 1962; Rose Giallombardo, *Society of Women*. New York: John Wiley & Sons, 1966.

[4]Paul W. Tappan, *Juvenile Delinquency*. New York: McGraw-Hill, 1949; Erving Goffman, *Stigma: Notes on the Management of Spoiled Identity*. Englewood Cliffs, N.J.: Prentice-Hall, 1963; David Matza, *Delinquency and Drift*. New York: John Wiley & Sons, 1964; Stanton Wheeler and Leonard S. Cottrell, Jr., *Juvenile Delinquency: Its Prevention and Control*. New York: Russell Sage, 1966, pp. 22–28; *The Challenge of Crime in a Free Society*. Washington, D.C.: Government Printing Office, February 1967; Robert D. Vinter, "The Juvenile Court as an Institution," Edwin M. Lemert, "The Juvenile Court—Quest and Realities," and Virginia M. Burns and Leonard W. Stern, "The Prevention of Juvenile Delinquency," in *Task Force Report: Juvenile Delinquency and Youth Crime*. Washington, D.C.: Government Printing Office, 1967; James Carey et al., *The Handling of Juveniles from Offense to Disposition*, Vols. *1–3*. Washington, D.C.: U.S. Department of Health, Education, and Welfare, Office of Juvenile Delinquency and Youth Development, 1967; Aaron Cicourel, *The Social Organization of Juvenile Justice*. New York: John Wiley & Sons, 1968; Stanton Wheeler (ed.), *Controlling Delinquents*. New York: John Wiley & Sons, 1968; Martin, Fitzpatrick, and Gould, *op. cit*. On the court, see also: *The Future of the Juvenile Court*. Washington, D.C.: Joint Commission on Correctional Manpower and Training Consultants, Paper, June 1968.

in itself, but becomes all the more disconcerting when the effects of this process on those who are caught up in the net are realized. The court "labels" or stigmatizes its charges with the official status of "delinquent," and sometimes also the medical status of being "mentally disturbed." If it is difficult to live down one "tag," it is all the more difficult to live down two. Some youths may, in fact, begin to *live up to both,* in a self-fulfilling sort of way, by playing the role of "sick delinquent," as imposed on them by the court.

In effect, the juvenile justice labeling process works to single out adolescents from groups culturally alien to those in power. Those singled out, because of their powerlessness, are ill-equipped to stop the process or to intervene in it effectively to prevent themselves from having various and sundry tags imposed upon them by police, judges, probation officers, psychiatrists, and others who are employed as agents of the juvenile justice system. The child whose deportment is deemed "inappropriate" by the police will often be detained, as will the one who is "insolent," whereas the child who is "polite, cooperative, or obsequious" is less likely to be referred to court.

Often the judgments made by the police are chauvinistic, ethnocentric, and of limited validity. Using standards peculiar to their age-set, ethnoracial group, and social class, they inadvertently work toward the spiraling condemnation of adolescents, the poor, and the nonwhite segments of the society. The people whom the police process and move along to court are aware of the inequities of the system and of the ways in which police practices work to the disadvantage of the powerless.

When the case actually reaches court after police referral, it is heard by a juvenile court judge without a jury. Juvenile judges, who usually enjoy relatively low prestige as compared with most other judges, are often second- and third-generation, white ethnics, whose judicial position, often appointive, reflects patronage—the rewards of a political machine. Their social and cultural characteristics, combined usually with scanty social or behavioral science training, leave them oftentimes identified with the established middle class, and this makes it difficult for them to be objective when it comes to judging the behavior of lower class children.

The juvenile court process usually calls for a probation investigation to be made so that a judge may more properly dispose of a case. The social relationship between the juvenile and his probation officer usually seems to be characterized by the same sort of cultural and power conflicts as those found in juvenile-police and juvenile-judge relationships. However, a new dimension compounds the problem of the powerless at this stage of the juvenile justice system. Probation officers, to the extent that they are at all scientifically oriented, tend to perceive their clients and their behavior from a psychologically oriented casework point of view, instead of from a social-cultural-political framework. This casework orientation is evident in the courses probation officers take in graduate schools of social work, in the professional literature they read, in their in-service training manuals, in the case histories they prepare, and in their work style and role. The result of this orientation, which characterizes trained and untrained probation officers, and many old guard psychiatrists as well, is that they tend strongly to interpret and put down culturally different behavior, particularly when it violates middle class standards, as arising out of the psychological aberrations of the isolated individuals standing before them.

Under such conditions the delinquent finds himself doubly labeled. To authorities he is not only legally deviant, but he also now appears to be psychologically ill, which in point of fact may or may not be true. The powerlessness of youth, the blacks, the poor, and other minorities leaves them totally unable to cope with this double stigma, either immediately in the judicial process, or later in life as it follows them in their chosen careers or imposed noncareers. The latter often are a consequence of commitment to a training school and later to a reformatory or prison where the clash between the powerless and the agents of the powerful in the legal processes is much more sustained and intensified.

This, then, is the juvenile justice system as it appears through the eyes of many of its critics. Issues of power and of powerlessness are brought to attention in various parts of the criticism. And a strain of social conflict runs throughout the observations made. What seems to be the relationship between the three—i.e., the juvenile justice system, power, and the strains of social conflict?

JUVENILE JUSTICE, POWER, AND SOCIAL CONFLICT

Today the "in" word, as well as the "in" line of analysis, is *power*. Academicians, politicians, black and white militants, and the man in the street talk about power as it relates to a variety of groups, especially students and blacks. In other words, discussions of relations between dominant and minority groups, whether ethnic-, race-, age-, or class-based, are now cast in terms of power plays. Unfortunately the very newness in this use of the concept, and the varied backgrounds of those employing it, make precise definition very difficult. Moreover, within the same field or academic discipline there is often disagreement as to its usage. For example, there are those political scientists who speak of power as something attributable to a small, crystallized, stable group, also known as an elite. There are others, however, who speak of power as a phenomenon relevant to the workings of a large, disparate, ever-changing collectivity known as the plurality. Unhappily neither conceptualization is well-founded in empirical research, and neither is very useful at this particular moment in history for an understanding of delinquent behavior.

The first conceptualization of power which became popular in the study of delinquency was that which might be termed a psycho-social definition. In it, power was seen as a somewhat vague ability which, when lacking in certain individuals, induces within them a poor self-image, a deep and lasting self-hatred, an apathy, and a barrage of other psychopathological consequences. The roots of the problem of powerlessness were clearly seen as social and were also seen as peculiar to certain groups, notably Negroes. The consequences of such powerlessness, however, were viewed in highly individualistic ways—that is, in the poor self-images and delinquency of individual Negro youths. This kind of orientation to powerlessness and its relation to delinquency was popular in some social science circles in the early 1960's. It was best stated in the demonstration project proposal for HARYOU in New York City, and takes its lead from the writings of the psychologist, Kenneth B. Clark.[5]

A second definition of power in the delinquency field emerged at a later date. As it has eventually developed, this view might be termed the structural conceptualization of power. It is based on an analysis of large-scale social conflict as the basis of much delinquent behavior. In this view, power relates to the ability of an interest group to be self-determining, to be closely involved with the larger social system, and to be manipulative of it by means of an institutional nexus which enables the group to protect its own interests and to get what it wants. While in many ways this concept is as poorly defined as the psycho-social, this use of the concept has the advantage of shifting attention from the individual and his malfunctioning psyche to an interest group, its web of affiliations, and its needs. No longer is the focus sharply on *anomic* individuals. Now it is on alienated, insulated, isolated, and politically deprived groups. No longer are the powerless, including many delinquents, seen as psychologically "deprived" because of socially-induced strain, in the classic Mertonian sense. Rather, the powerless are perceived as members of sociopolitically disadvantaged groups who lack commitment to the larger society's values, conformity to its norms, responsibility in its roles, and/or control of its facilities. Advocates of Black Power and Student Power reflect this type of social group and define themselves in ways which explicitly acknowledge the absence of commitment to the established social system that for them has proven meaningless, irrelevant, and often repressive.

While the explicit acknowledgment of power in the professional delinquency literature is a recent, scattered phenomenon, it was recognized in implicit ways some decades ago. Thus, for example, the essential re-

---

[5]*Youth in the Ghetto.* New York: Haryou, Inc., 1962; and Kenneth B. Clark, *Dark Ghetto.* New York: Harper and Row, 1965.

lationship of cultural difference to crime was established in 1938 by Thorsten Sellin in his classic, *Culture Conflict and Crime*.[6] Some of the underlying political ramifications of such differences, which were not developed by Sellin, were outlined most effectively the same year by Frank Tannenbaum in his discussion of the community dimensions of organized crime.[7] However, it is in the extensive publications of the Chicago School that the essential political dimensions of delinquency among the urban poor are most explicitly set forth. The work of Thrasher, Sutherland, and Alinsky, particularly as it related to the slums of Chicago, is replete with material linking traditional gang delinquency to the shutting out of gang members from legitimate political (power) channels and their efforts to find for themselves alternative—if illegitimate—structures that would provide them with access to power. For example, in Frederick M. Thrasher's *The Gang*,[8] and in William F. Whyte's *Street Corner Society*,[9] the chapters dedicated to the interdependence of the boss, the political machine, and the street gang amply document the relationship between slum delinquency, the social structure, and the influence of urban politics.

Thus, power has long been recognized as a useful line of analysis in describing delinquency. Yet, the concept has not often been expressed in the more recent delinquency literature. The reason would seem to lie in the nature of the major theoretical orientation which gained prominence in American thought about crime and delinquency during and after World War II, a period not known for its liberalism, and in the personal backgrounds of the scholars who contributed to such work. Crime and delinquency discussions were primarily oriented toward an *order model* of society during that period and even later. Those advocating a *conflict model* had trouble being heard. This same trend is evidenced in sociology proper by the relative popularity of writings by Merton and Parsons as opposed to those by Simmel, Coser, or Dahrendorf.[10] It has been argued that American sociology's overwhelming preference for the order model stems from the socialization process to which most pre-World War II American sociologists were exposed, a process rooted in smalltown, Midwestern, ministerial views geared to stability, homogeneity, and a conservative, static perspective on society. This world outlook permeated not only the writings of sociologists about deviant behavior, of which delinquency is only one manifestation, but also their work in other areas of inquiry as well.

---

[6]Thorsten Sellin, *Culture Conflict and Crime*. New York: Social Science Research Council, 1938.
[7]Frank Tannenbaum, *Crime and the Community*. New York: Columbia University Press, 1938.
[8]Frederick M. Thrasher, *The Gang*. Chicago: University of Chicago Press, 1927.
[9]William F. Whyte, *Street Corner Society* (rev. ed.). Chicago: University of Chicago Press, 1955.
[10]Consider the widespread use of such works as Robert K. Merton, *Social Theory and Social Structure* (rev. and enl. ed.). Glencoe, Ill.: The Free Press, 1957; or Talcott Parsons, *The Social System*. New York: The Free Press, 1951; in graduate courses, journal articles and standard texts as compared with such books as Georg Simmel, *Conflict*. New York: The Free Press, 1955; Lewis Coser, *The Functions of Social Conflict*. New York: The Free Press, 1956; and Ralf Dahrendorf, *Class and Class Conflict in Industrial Society*. Stanford: Stanford University Press, 1959.

Order theories of society are mainly concerned with the social forces which allow societies or communities to endure according to a given form. The adherents of this perspective have developed a core theoretical model which attempts to explain the conservation of existing social structures and institutions. The order line of analysis focuses on a single unit, whether it is a group, a community, or a total society, and seeks to explain how that unit remains integrated or lasting.

Conflict theories of society are mainly concerned with the social forces which produce social change through social strain, disruption, and eventual reintegration. The adherents of this perspective have developed a theoretical model which attempts to explain the emergence of structural change within social units, whether small groups or total societies. This line of analysis focuses upon the presence of social conflict as interaction between two or more normative structures and the emergence of change in their relationship as a consequence and outgrowth of their interaction.

According to the order model, disruptive forces in the dominant community's sphere of influence are defined as deviant or dysfunctional, as tensions or strains existing within a single normative order and social system. Behavior that challenges the power of the dominant community to maintain what it has established as its boundaries is defined as anti-social or anomic. Such deviancy is perceived to violate a single normative structure, assumed to be based on universal consensus. The possibility or need for recognizing alternative, competing normative structures is thus avoided.

Without further elaboration it seems obvious that most of the efforts of the professionals of the juvenile justice system to make sense out of delinquency and to do something about it are based on an *order* view of social deviancy. In fact, perhaps the outstanding characteristic of the juvenile justice system is that it is constructed on order model lines, reinforced by the ideology, theory, and treatment ideals of the mental hygiene movement, with scarcely a thought given to the consequences of the political imbalances which may flow from such arrangements.

Once such imbalances have been set up in the juvenile justice system, how might they be removed or at least reduced? An approach to this question may be facilitated by a brief discussion of social institutions, some dimensions of their power aspects, and the relationship of these to delinquency.

INSTITUTIONAL POWER AND
ITS RELATIONSHIP TO DELINQUENCY

The key to political power is, of course, the vote. The vote is a minimal requirement in a democratic society for a political voice, persuasion, or influence. One step higher than the vote is the ability to use it in an organized manner, a bloc, to insure that people who reflect a group's interests are elected to district, municipal, State, and eventually Federal positions. This means the ability of a group to so affect the political decisionmaking process, that it can influence the local boss, city hall, the State capitol, and Washington. At quite another level, political power means the ability not simply to see to it that those in office hear the voice of the group, but also for the group to be in a position to put its own members in office. Lest anyone deny the efficacy of this tactic, let him examine the history, patterns, and consequences of the political power exercised by either the Irish or the Italians in the United States, especially as these compare with the lack of influence apparent, for example, in the traditional Negro or Spanish-speaking community. In turning out the vote, significant aspects often overlooked in discussions of political power are its leadership and organizational elements, whether they are a part of one of the major parties or of an independent group which both parties court with patronage, plums, or favorable laws and law enforcement.

Political power relates not only to voting and officeholding. It also relates to the ability of a group to affect official decisionmaking in allied areas, for example, within the police department and the courts. Both, obviously, are of considerable significance in any discussion of delinquency in public policy terms. The power of a group determines its ability to keep its people out of trouble with the law, even in instances where they have actually violated it. The powerful enjoy a series of formal and informal liaisons or links into the political system, ranging from the ability to put in "the fix," to finding a friend in court, to getting its own members on the bench. Such groups are able to influence political and related structures because of their own numerical and organizational strength, brought to bear directly through political mechanisms and indirectly through a nexus of institutions created by them which afford them contact with the system. This nexus of institutions makes the group a force with which the larger society must reckon, an element in a winning coalition or a favored community with the power to swing an election or a referendum. The nexus implies organization not only in the political arena, but also in all other aspects of social life. It is dependent upon the group's consciousness of kind or identity and its recognition that, acting as an entity, it can affect the world around it. This identity is necessary, but not sufficient, for later successful political organization.

Aside from the straight political power of the vote, especially when used on a bloc basis by well-organized interest groups, other areas of institutional power which are particularly significant for delinquency are those of education, economics, and welfare. When an interest group's capacities to influence are high in any one of these three areas, these capacities tend to be high in all of the areas. When a group's general capacities to influence are high, the official delinquency rates of its children and youth tend to be low. Other institutions, of course, could easily be added to the list—for example, organized religion and the mass media.

Such capacities to influence across a broad spectrum of a community's social institutions seem to approximate closely what has been called a community's competence to take care of itself, to look after the needs of its adults, as well as those of its children and youth. Communities so characterized seldom have large numbers of children and youth in trouble with the police, courts, and other parts of the juvenile justice system. Of course, some of their young people may be "wild" or "out of hand," but comparatively few of them become cases in the juvenile justice system. Given the characteristics of that system and the many negative consequences of being under its care, who would argue that cases should not be diverted out of the system wherever possible. In fact, diversion of cases out of the official system is rapidly emerging as a national priority. And that is precisely what competent communities have long been doing. They have been diverting their troublemaking youths out of care by official agencies and into alternative channels. Plainly, they reduce official delinquency by the simple method of meeting the problem by unofficial means. Employment of this method is made possible, however, by the highly developed "institutionalized power" characteristic of such competent communities. This power may be defined as collective, as distinct from personal or individual power. It is also sustained, organized, recognized, and utilized power, which is wielded by an interest group—in this instance, a local community committed to the care and protection of its children and youth. It seems fair to conclude that in such communities there is little imbalance between the power of the juvenile justice system and that of local parents and their children. Or to put the matter somewhat differently: in such communities the police, courts, and other law enforcement agencies on the local level are very conscious of, and responsive to, the opinions and wishes of local citizens regarding how the law is enforced, especially with respect to local juveniles.

It should be made clear that competent communities do not usually organize themselves in the first instance in order to offset any imbalance of power their citizens may experience with respect to the local juvenile justice system. Sometimes, for example, a well-organized suburban community may follow a particular course of action for this purpose, such as developing its own local police department, instead of continuing to contract for police service with a more politically remote, and socially less responsive, sheriff's department. In such cases, the local department may be developed not because patrol by the sheriff's men was inefficient, but rather because, according to local opinion, the patrol was too efficient and too many local youths were being brought to court, instead of being dealt with by more informal means.

What actually seems to happen with regard to local community competence and its relationship to the practices of the local juvenile justice system is that local competence seems to have emerged on a broad front across many or all of the communities' institutions. Such competence did not begin, nor certainly did it end with the juvenile justice system. Rather, starting with a firm base in some other institution, such as an organized church, as was the case with many European immigrants, or with a firm middle class occupational base, as in the case of many contemporary suburban communities, a community's capacities to build, mold, influence, and use the totality of local institutions followed suit. In the process, the agencies of the juvenile justice system got involved, along with the local schools, elected officials, banks, labor unions, and real estate interests.

But the interesting empirical fact seems to be that when a community lacks such competence with respect to its other institutions, it also lacks it with respect to the local juvenile justice system. The clearest present instance of this seems to be found in the case of metropolitan ghettos. Here locally controlled institutionalized power seems to be in especially short supply. As a reflection of this, here also the imbalance of power between various, large-scale institutions such as the schools, welfare, and the juvenile justice system, on the one hand, and local citizens, on the other, seems to be most acute.

These, then, seem to be some of the relationships between institutional power and delinquency as it is dealt with by local agencies of the juvenile justice system. The key to reducing any imbalance of power between a juvenile justice system and the individuals with which it deals seems to lie in increasing the institutionalized power of those who are dealt with by the system—in a phrase, to establish between the two camps a better system of "checks and balances." The remaining sections of this paper will explore some of the premises upon which such a public policy might be based, and some of the methods by which it might be implemented.

TOWARD A BETTER SYSTEM OF "CHECKS AND BALANCES"

The problem to be addressed is how to reduce the imbalance of power between the juvenile justice system and those with whom it deals. Two important facts about the clientele of this system need to be made explicit. First, in most communities, official delinquency tends to be impacted in limited geographic sections. It is not uniformly distributed across the geographic face of the community. Such ecological concentration seems to reflect simply the geographic distribution of minority groups, the white poor, and other powerless groups whose children make up most of those handled by the juvenile justice system.

Second, most of the official delinquency and youth crime cases dealt with by the police, courts, and corrections involve relatively minor law violations, essentially unthreatening to the common interests.

These facts make the development of locally based agencies whose function would be to divert cases out of the juvenile justice system both logical and practical devices. Perhaps the best known mechanism being offered at present along these lines is what are now called Youth Services Bureaus. As recommended by the President's Commission on Law Enforcement and Administration of Justice, these would be local, community-based, youth serving agencies situated *outside* of the juvenile justice system. The police, juvenile courts, parents, schools, and others would refer adolescents, delinquent *and* nondelinquent, who are in need of special attention to such bureaus. Properly staffed and managed, such bureaus could be used to divert cases out of the juvenile justice system, thus avoiding many of the negative consequences which face individuals who in fact remain under the care of the system.

The Commission raised the idea of such bureaus and cited their diversionary functions explicitly, but unfortunately left most of the difficult questions about such bureaus unanswered.

Key among these questions is a clarification of the concept of "local, community-based" bureaus. Are they to be decentralized offices of State, county, or municipal agencies, physically located in high delinquency areas similar to the way in which police precincts or fire houses are now decentralized? Are they to be publicly run, decentralized agencies operated under policies set by local indigenous boards? Are they to be entirely privately operated agencies? Whether publicly or privately operated, what groups or organizations are to operate them in the different jurisdictions? In the President's Commission recommendation, the only thing that is clear is that such bureaus are *not* to be run by the juvenile justice system itself, thus permitting diversion of cases to take place.

A strong case can be made for situating Youth Services Bureaus in the private sector, instead of any place in the public sector. In the private sector they would be operated to the maximum extent possible by the representatives of the groups whose children are being cared for by the juvenile justice system. Such an arrangement would serve to meet the goal that cases should be diverted out of the system wherever possible. It could also begin to address the imbalance of power between the juvenile justice system and those who receive its care. Supported by tax dollars and administered by private organizations responsive to the needs of indigenous populations, such bureaus could accomplish goals which would not even be approached by bureaus run by some division of government. Martin, Fitzpatrick, and Gould put the matter in these terms:

> . . . Such service delivery systems could themselves become increasingly important bases of institutionalized power for presently disadvantaged groups, which could use these service structures and the taxes which would support them to help create their own welfare enterprises. Following an argument advanced by Frances Piven and Richard Cloward, private agencies of this order would be as much political as social welfare institutions, inasmuch as they would serve as organizational vehicles for the expression of the group's viewpoints on social welfare policy and also as the means for other forms of political association and influence. Once developed, the strength of these new welfare organizations, working in combination with similar local and communitywide enterprises in education, health, religion, and other fields, could be used by the disadvantaged to improve their own general bargaining position vis-a-vis other, more established, interest groups. It is the enhancement of this bargaining position and the consequent enrichment and emphatic modification of institutions and practices that offer the key to social change in the ghetto. The accomplishment of this kind of change is the goal of those who would take a structural approach to delinquency and related social problems. This general course of action has been followed in the past, and remains the case today, in New York, for example, with the Catholics, Jews, and also, of course, with the white Protestants. The political advantages to be gained by today's disadvantaged groups through the development of their own, privately controlled, tax-supported welfare delivery systems cannot be matched by launching new programs and continuing old programs for the disadvantaged through long-established agencies, either public or private, particularly where the recipients of service exercise little or no voice in policy. Put bluntly, the issue is one of control and influence: Who is going to run what for whom? And consequently, who is going to profit politically, psychologically, economically, and in many other ways from the enterprise?[11]

Another question arises with respect to the size and scope of Youth Services Bureaus' activities in program terms. Should they act simply as referral agencies, standing between the juvenile justice system and a variety of other public and private service agencies in the broader community? Or should they be large-scale super agencies which offer almost all imaginable forms of educational, vocational, psychiatric, medical, recreational, and welfare services to their clients. It is doubtful that such comprehensive programs can or should be launched in the name of Youth Services Bureaus. The strain of securing the multiple funding base neces-

---

[11]Martin, Fitzpatrick, and Gould, *op. cit.*, pp. 185–186.

sary for undertaking such services alone is sufficient to deter such effort. Yet more than a simple and traditional "paper" referral function seems necessary. The clientele to be dealt with does not respond favorably to such exercises. At a minimum, some sort of sustained, supportive type of referral program seems most desirable. And in all likelihood, some minimal type of educational and/or vocational program would seem necessary for any bureau that intends to engage effectively cases diverted out of the juvenile justice system. Probably each bureau would have to develop its own answer to the issue of the boundaries of its program, but a restricted program sharply focused on the needs of cases diverted out of the juvenile justice system, or likely to be taken up by it, seems most acceptable. A small, precisely directed program may, as it gains in competence, gradually expand to embrace other activities.

A third question relates to the coordinating role of local Youth Services Bureaus. Should they simply strive to coordinate the various activities of other large-scale public and private agencies which relate to local youth populations? Thus, in a given neighborhood with high delinquency rates, should such bureaus, with modest staffs of three or four and with modest budgets of $25,000 to $50,000, seek to coordinate the activities of the police, education, welfare, courts, corrections, and other multimillion dollar enterprises in such areas? Considerable experience with such efforts has not proved satisfactory. The weak cannot direct the strong in this field or in others. Some coordination may occur as budget lines become available to a local bureau and as those lines can be used to purchase services and to secure other commitments from larger agencies serving a local area. But without the money to make the bargain stick, coordination of the large by the small has not worked well. Even with funds available, large agencies are not necessarily responsive, since they usually have much to do on their own.

Perhaps the most compelling argument against a Youth Services Bureau trying to play simply a modest coordinating role in a high delinquency area is that such a function contributes very little to the development of the bureau as a local welfare agency which can serve as an important organizational base for the nurturing of local power. If the large service budgets and staff are to remain under the control of outside and essentially unresponsive agencies, the agreement by a local indigenous group to engage only in coordinating activities is not much of a step toward greater local power and autonomy. The psychic rewards may be great for the coordinating staff as it learns to role play with the managers of the large power systems servicing the area, but little concrete bargaining strength has been delivered to the local community in the process.

Any number of other questions remain to be explored about the way in which the Youth Services Bureau might best serve to reduce the imbalance of power between the juvenile justice system and those who receive its care. For example, what provision should such bureaus make for the development of legal service components as part of their on-going programs? Should such legal services focus upon all areas of decisionmaking in the system, including those decisions made by the juvenile correctional apparatus after cases which have not been successfully diverted have been committed to institutions or placed on probation? Obviously it is difficult to answer such questions except in the most general terms. Nevertheless, if the design of Youth Services Bureaus is aimed at establishing a better system of checks and balances in juvenile justice, then good legal representation for youths at all points of official decisionmaking seems essential.

The idea that such bureaus are necessary devices for reducing the present imbalance of power characteristic of the juvenile justice system would have to achieve widespread acceptance. In various States where Youth Services Bureaus are being started, it does not appear that many of them are following a design and a strategy similar to the one outlined here. In fact, the whole idea that there is a lack of fairness and justice in the juvenile justice system, and that this arises from a political imbalance inherent in the system, seems to have received very little discussion at the level of state planning.

This state of affairs most sharply points up the needs of local indigenous groups which might be in the market to run their own Youth Services Bureaus. Perhaps their primary need is for the articulation of this issue by spokesmen from the professions, the universities, the foundations, and government itself, who are sensitive to the political dimensions of what is involved in delinquency prevention. In the simplest of terms, even the allocation of sufficient funds for the development of large numbers of Youth Services Bureaus of the type being discussed represents a political decision of considerable magnitude in any given State. Delinquency prevention as an area for grant funding is poorly defined and conceptualized as an area of program activity. This has traditionally been the case in the delinquency field as the more concrete and visible activities of the police, courts, and corrections have dominated program ideas and budget categories. And this seems to be the way it is going today with the new State planning efforts. Prevention is badly in need of a competitive product which it can "sell" as effectively, for example, as the police are able to sell their constituencies on their programs.

Once funds do become available in the states for Youth Services Bureaus, of the type being discussed here, then particular local groups seeking such funds would probably have to enter into some sort of coalition with organizations such as universities or foundations in order to compete successfully for the money.

But viable coalitions are not composed of strong partners allied with weak partners, in this case strong outside parties allied with relatively weak indigenous local groups. Viable coalitions, according to Carmichael and Hamilton, require four preconditions:

> (a) the recognition by the parties involved of their respective self-interests; (b) the mutual belief that each party stands to benefit in terms of that self-interest from joining with the other or others; (c) the acceptance of the fact that each party has its own independent base of power and does not depend for ultimate decisionmaking on a force outside itself; and (d) the realization that the coalition deals with specific and identifiable—as opposed to general and vague—goals.[12]

Of the four preconditions, the third—each party having its own independent power base—perhaps offers the greatest difficulty in terms of the present discussion. The other preconditions can perhaps be realized if the third is assured. Without each party's having its own power base, the whole notion of a coalition becomes absurd.

In summation, Youth Services Bureaus mounted in the private sector by viable coalitions of local indigenous groups and outside allies seem to have considerable potential for reducing some of the imbalance characteristic of the juvenile justice system. Whether such bureaus do in fact come into existence will depend upon the *political support* such an approach to delinquency prevention receives in the various states and in the nation at large.

---

[12]Stokely Carmichael and Charles V. Hamilton, *Black Power: The Politics of Liberation in America.* New York: Vintage Books, 1967. pp. 79–80.

INDEX

Christian Science Monitor, 345
Cicourel, A., 50, 51, 347
Civil War, 158
Clark, A., 119n
Clark, J., 116n
Clark, K. B., 350
Clausen, J., 69n
Clausewitz, K., 339
Cleaver, E., 156, 157, 316
Clemmer, D., 347
Clinard, M., 50n
Cloward, R., 44, 50, 131, 347, 357
Cohen, A., 66, 67, 68, 150
Cohen, P., 2
Colajanni, N., 192, 199n
Cole, S., 50
Collective behavior, 64–65
Collector pirates, 301–02
College youth, 164
Columbia Records, 299, 302, 303, 305, 306
Come Out, 182, 183
Comfort, A., 91n
Communication media, 288–89
Communes, 168, 193
Communist movements, 122, 321
Compadre, 194
Conflict
  causes, 74
  definition, 121–22
  with deviance, 127–29
  functional, 121
  as group phenomenon, 25–28
  inequality, 4
  interests, 74
  introduced, 2
  nonrealistic, 121
  realistic, 121
  termination of, 336–44
  values, 74
Conflict theory, 352
  crime, 30–31, 89–107

Conflict theory—*cont.*
  and deviance, 13–14
  functions, 109–10
  groups, 78–80
  image of man, 12
  modes of analysis, 12–13
  Negroes, 21–23
  process, 78
  social problems, 13–14
  values in, 12
Congress, 299
  reaction to ecology problems, 278
Conscientious objectors, 82
Conspiracy in restraint of trade, 211
Contraculture, 61–72, 148, 149
  class and occupation, 69–71
  delinquent, 66–68
  and subculture, 63–65
Contro-squadre, 198
Cook County Juvenile Court, 81
Cook, T., 11n
Cooley, C. H., 58
Cooperative-cultures, 147–48
Copyright Office, 301
Copyright
  register of, 300
  statute, 299
Cosca, 194
Cosche, 199
Coser, L., 121, 322, 336–44, 351
Cottrell, L., 347
Counterculture, 303, 312, 318
  ideology of, 303–04
  pirates, 303–06
  See also Contra-culture
Counterfeited records, 300
Counter-ideology, 62
Cranston, A., 273, 286
Cray, E., 140n
Creem, 304
Creeping event, 286–87
Cressey, D., 37–47, 73, 347

Goffman, E., 24, 28, 112n, 319, 347
Gold, R., 250n
Golding, W., 325
Goldman, N., 116n
GOO (Get Oil Out), 272
 tactics, 273–74
Goodman, P., 11
Gordon, M., 18
Gould, R. E., 345, 357
Gouldner, A., 220
Gover, R., 6
Government agencies, 274
Grand Funk Railroad, 305
Grant Park, 171
Great White Wonder, 303, 304
Greenwich Village, 140
Gross, N., 60n
Group conflict, 25
"Group grope," 329
Growing Up Absurd, 11n
Guardini, 198
Guevara, Che, 231
Guevara, E., 231n
Gusfield, J., 64n, 121, 122, 229, 245, 248

Haight-Ashbury, 165
Hall, J., 100n, 256
Halleck, S., 323
Hamilton, C., 360
Hammond, P., 111n
Hard determinism
 defined, 1
 shortcoming, 1–2
Hardin, C., 111n
Harris, M., 59n, 314
Harris poll, 33
Harrison Act, 249
Hart, H., 99n
Hartley, F., 276n, 283, 290
Harvard, 157
Harwood, E., 227n
HARYOU, 350

"Hashbury, The," 322
Hassler, A., 83
Haurek, 324
Havighurst, R., 65
Hayes, C., 222n
Hell's Angels, 140, 141
Henderson, A., 98n
Heyns, R. W., 314
Hickel, W., 274, 275, 280
Hilberg, R., 311, 316
Hip culture, 161
"Hipbos," 313
Hippie Movement, 148, 161–170, 310–14
 culture, 162, 163, 319–20
 images, 322
Hills, S., 75
Hoa Hao, 229
Hobsbawm, E., 123, 168, 224, 227
Hoffman, A., 170, 315, 321
Hollingshead, A., 69n
Hook, S., 19
Homosexuals, 29, 33, 174–90
Hopper, R., 144n
Horowitz, I. L., 110n, 123, 125–45
Horton, J., 2, 6–24
Hot Jazz Club of America, The, 302
Howard, J., 227n
Humphrey, H., 168
Huxley, J., 112n
Hyneman, C., 111n

Ideology, 234
 nationalist, 221–23
Image of Man and Society, 12
"Immigrant problem," 39
Independent Cultures, 148
Industrial Workers of the World (IWW), 122
Inequality, source of conflict, 4
Infrastructure, 230
Inkeles, A., 67n
Institute for Sex Research, 179

Instrumental rationalism, 2
Internal divisions, 203
"Iron law of oligarchy," 136, 289

Jackson, G., 230
Jaco, E., 10
James, H., 345
Jazz musicians, 70–71
Jazz-Time, 302
Jeffery, C., 114n
Johnson, C., 240
Jencks, C., 325
Jolly Roger, 302
Johnson, C., 63
Johnson, L. B., 328
Johnston, B., 305
Jones, T., 303
Joplin, J., 303
Juvenile courts, criticisms, 346–48
Juvenile delinquency, 333
Juvenile vote, 352–353

Kadish, S., 235
Kaplan, A., 110n
Kardiner, A., 59n
Keefe, J., 278
Kefauver's Crime Enquiry, 193n
Kelly, R. J., 123, 220–237
Keniston, K., 164
Kennedy, J. F., 140
Kennedy, T., 294
Key, V. O., Jr., 111n
Kifner, J., 318
Killian, L., 65n
Kilson, M., 234
King, M. L., 8, 176, 232
Kinsey, A., 179
Kirchheimer, O., 91n, 114n
Kitsuse, J., 50, 51, 67n
Klapp, O., 232
Kluckholn, C., 59
Kobrin, S., 67n
Kohn, H., 221n
Kohn, M., 69n

Komarovsky, M., 57n
Korn, R., 74
Kornbluth, J., 165
Kristol, I., 148n
Kroeber, A., 58
Ku Klux Klan, 291
Kuh, R., 94n

La Fave, W., 333
Labeling theory, 50–53
  juveniles, 348
  process, 2
Labes, M., 134n
Lacey, F., 267n
Lait, J., 85n
Lang, G., 141
Lang, K., 141
Langner, T., 59n
Lanternari, V., 225, 227
Lasswell, H., 62n, 110n
Latham, E., 111n
Latifundium, 194
law, 75, 246
  political product, 75
Law enforcement, corruption,
  214–16
Leary, M., 157n
Leary, T., 166, 316
Left, 140
Lefton, M., 50n
Legal agents, 116
Legality of norms, 96–100
Legal policies, 115
Lemert, E., 50, 127, 130
Leningrad, 180
Lentz, W., 119n
Lestingi, F., 194n
Lewis, H., 59n
Lewis, O., 85n
Lewisburg, 83
Liberalism, 14
  assumptions, 15–16
  pluralism, 16–17

Liberty Party, 204
Librarian of Congress, 300
LiCausi, G., 203
Liddell-Hart, B. H., 343
Lieberson, S., 133n
Liebow, E., 153n
Liebowitz, M., 125–45
Leighton, J., 37n
Leisure, 293
  cults, 160
  subculture, 149
Life, 322
Lincoln Park, 171
Lindesmith, A., 101n
Linton, R., 58
Lipset, S. M., 129n, 333
Livermore, Jr., N. B., 278
LIVEr Than You'll Ever Be, 304
Locker, M., 224n
Lofland, J., 25–36
Lombard, 192
London Records, 304
Long, D., 334
Lorber, J., 118n
Lord of the Flies, 325
Lorenzoni, G., 201n
Los Angeles Free Press, 305
Love generation, 167
Lower East Side, 312
LSD, 33, 167, 169, 170
Lubell, S., 129n
Luckmann, T., 113n
Luddites, 168
Lumpenproletariat, 3
Lysgaard, S., 69n

Maccoby, E., 69n
Mack, R., 57n
MacIver, R., 112
MacNamara, D., 235n
Maddox, L., 168
Mafia, 43, 124, 191, 224
  defined, 192–94

Mafia—*cont.*
  economics of, 207–19
  fight with fascists, 204–05
  internal divisions, 203–04
  Sicilian, 191–94
  as social movement, 191–206
Mair, L., 223n
Malcolm X, 132, 140
manifest interests, 240, 307
Mannheim, K., 20, 123, 239
Mao Tse Tung, 180
Marcus, G., 304
Marihuana, 169
  users, 139
Mark, M., 112n
Martin, J., 332, 333, 345–60
Martindale, D., 6
Marx, K., 2, 3, 8, 9, 56, 135, 178, 239, 240
  revolution, 3
Mason, W., 60n
Mattachine Society, 174, 177, 185
Matza, D., 1, 68, 347, 50n
Maxwell, G., 203n
May Day, 199
McArthur, C., 69n
McCaghy, C., 50n, 241, 242, 297–305
"McCarthy Era," 130
McCarthy, R., 245n
McConnell, G., 111n
McCord, W., 68, 226
McCorkle, L. W., 74
McEachern, A., 60n
McElrath, E., 45, 47
McIntyre, J., 119n
McKay, H., 81
McKinney, J., 154n
McLane, J., 229n
McPherson, J., 155
McReynolds, D., 186
Mead, W., 284
Mental health, defined, 10

New York Supreme Court, 299
New York Times, The, 313, 322, 323
Nicastro, S., 196n
Niederhoffer, A., 90
Nisbet, R., 96n, 108n
Nixon, R., 272, 276
NLF, 230
Nomad, M., 229n
Nonconformity, 53–56, 233, 234
  defined, 53
Normative conflict, 39, 43–47
  defined, 43–44
Norms, 44, 96–100
  delinquent, 44
North, W. J., 283n
Norton gang, 149, 153
Novak, R., 139n

Oakland Seven, 316
O'Brien, C., 278
Ohlin, L., 44, 50, 90n
Oil spillage, 271–72, 275–78
Old Believers, 229
Old Left, 135
Old Right, 137
Omerta, 192
One Hundred Dollar Misunderstanding, The, 6
Order theory, 8–9, 352
  and deviance, 13–14
  image of man, 12
  modes of analysis, 12–13
  and social problems, 374
  values, 12
  vocabulary, 9
Order theory, and Negro, 21–23
Organized crime, 207–19
  law enforcement, 214–15
  services, 212
Orleans, P., 229n
Oswald, L. H., 232
"Other Culture, The," 322
"Other-Worldly Churches," 226

Ottenger, R. D., 272
Over-socialized man, 15
Owens, B., 303

Packer, H., 331
Page, C., 227n
Palermo Procurator's Report, The, 193
Papachristou et al. v. *City of Jacksonville, Florida,* 241
Paradox Industries, Inc., 299
Paraintellectuals, 234
Parallel hierarchy, 230
Parallel system, 199
Park, R., 77n
Parsons, T., 9, 10, 65, 66, 112, 122, 351
Paxton, T., 329
Pearson, D., 288
Peasants' Revolt, 261
Peking, 180
Perrow, C., 111n
Perversion, 187
Pilgrim State Hospital, 323
Piliavin, I., 117n
Pitre, G., 196n
Piven, F., 357
Plato, 176
pluralism, 16–17, 30
Podhoretz, N., 17, 18
Police
  brutality, 165
  conflicting roles, 332
  corruption, 212
  persecution, 312–30
  selective enforcement, 333
Political crimes, 230–33, 235–36
Political criminal characteristics, 233–35
Political extremist, 132–45
Political hippies, 168
Political marginality, 129–32
Politicization, 227–30

Santa Barbara, Channel, 241
County Board of Supervisors, 280
Santa Barbara News-Press, 272
Santana, 305
Sapir, E., 58
Sarbin, T., 60n
Sargent, S., 57n
Sartre, J. P., 16, 18
Savio, M., 136
Sayad, A., 221n
Scharr, J., 220n
Schattschneider, E., 144n, 285
Schatzman, L., 142n
Scheff, T., 96n
Scheler, M., 147
Schelling, T., 123, 207–19, 338
Schermerhorn, R., 112n
Schilling, W., 111n
Schneider, L., 69n
Schuessler, K., 101n
Schur, E., 32, 51n
Schutz, A., 113n
Schwendinger, H., 153n
Scientific analysis, modes of, 12–13
Scientific neutrality, 287–88
Seale, B., 156
Second Great Children's Crusade, 171
Seldon, M., 221n
Sellin, T., 4, 37, 38, 45, 47, 351
Selznick, P., 37
Serend, E., 192
Sexual psychopath laws, 246
Shafer, B., 222n
Shaw, C., 42, 81
Sherif, M., 77n
Shibutani, T., 112n
Shils, E., 59n
Short, J., 67
Sibley, M., 82n
Sicilian Mafia, 123
Silver, A., 34
Silvers, R., 162n
Sirhan, S., 232

Simmel, G., 77n, 337, 338, 351
Simpson, G., 77n
Sinclair, J., 304
"Situated actions," 7
Skid Row, 267
Skipper, J., 50n
Skolnick, J., 116n, 171
Sloan Instruments Corporation, 290
Small, A., 78n
Smith, B., 59n
Snyder, G., 111n
Social action, 111–13
Social banditry, 224
Social control, 310–12
Social disorganization, 42
Social movement, 124, 164, 224–27, 247–49
Social reality, 113–20
Social Science Research Council, 37
Societal reactions approach, 50
Society, organic view, 2
Sociological perspective, 7
Sociologists
valuative errors, 24
view of deviance, 25
Solanas, D., 280
Solari, A., 134n
Somerton, W., 283
Sorokin, P., 44n
Spanish-American War, 339
Speier, H., 336
Spence, L., 136
Squadra, 199
Standard Oil
of California, 285
of New Jersey, 284
Standley, E., 286n
Stanford, 157
Stark, R., 334
Statics, 9
Stedtman, M., 111n
Steffens, L., 85n
Stephenson, R., 69, 70n
Stern, L., 347n